D1613347

Egalitarian Strangeness
On Class Disturbance and Levelling in Modern and Contemporary French Narrative

Contemporary French and Francophone Cultures, 75

Contemporary French and Francophone Cultures

Series Editor

CHARLES FORSDICK
University of Liverpool

Editorial Board

TOM CONLEY
Harvard University

JACQUELINE DUTTON
University of Melbourne

LYNN A. HIGGINS
Dartmouth College

MIREILLE ROSELLO
University of Amsterdam

DEREK SCHILLING
Johns Hopkins University

This series aims to provide a forum for new research on modern and contemporary French and francophone cultures and writing. The books published in *Contemporary French and Francophone Cultures* reflect a wide variety of critical practices and theoretical approaches, in harmony with the intellectual, cultural and social developments which have taken place over the past few decades. All manifestations of contemporary French and francophone culture and expression are considered, including literature, cinema, popular culture, theory. The volumes in the series will participate in the wider debate on key aspects of contemporary culture.

Recent titles in the series:

EDWARD J. HUGHES

Egalitarian Strangeness

On Class Disturbance and Levelling
in Modern and Contemporary
French Narrative

LIVERPOOL UNIVERSITY PRESS

First published 2021 by
Liverpool University Press
4 Cambridge Street
Liverpool
L69 7ZU

Copyright © 2021 Edward J. Hughes

The right of Edward J. Hughes to be identified as the author of this book
has been asserted by him in accordance with the Copyright, Designs and
Patents Act 1988.

All rights reserved. No part of this book may be reproduced, stored in a
retrieval system, or transmitted, in any form or by any means, electronic,
mechanical, photocopying, recording, or otherwise, without the prior written
permission of the publisher.

British Library Cataloguing-in-Publication data
A British Library CIP record is available

ISBN 978-1-80034-842-4

Typeset by Carnegie Book Production, Lancaster
Printed and bound by CPI Group (UK) Ltd, Croydon CR0 4YY

L'inégalité [...] est une passion primitive; ou, plus exactement, elle n'a pas d'autre cause que l'égalité. La passion inégalitaire est le vertige de l'égalité, la paresse devant la tâche infinie qu'elle exige, la peur devant ce qu'un être raisonnable se doit à lui-même.

[Inequality (...) is a primitive passion. Or, more exactly, it has no other cause than equality. Inegalitarian passion is equality's vertigo, laziness in face of the infinite task equality demands, fear in face of what a reasonable being owes to himself.]

Jacques Rancière, *Le Maître ignorant*, p. 134;
The Ignorant Schoolmaster, p. 80

I simply know next to nothing about my work in this way, as little as a plumber of the history of hydraulics.

Samuel Beckett, letter of 11 April 1972,
The Letters of Samuel Beckett, IV, 291

Contents

Figures

Acknowledgements

This book has taken me a number of years to write and along the way I have accumulated many debts which it is my great pleasure to acknowledge. Back in 2013, John D. Lyons kindly invited me to give a lecture at the University of Virginia and also liaised with Andrea Goulet at the University of Pennsylvania and André Benhaïm at Princeton University to allow me also to present to their respective French departments (my choice of subject was the work of Jacques Rancière). I am most grateful to them for their warm and generous welcomes and for the stimulating discussions I enjoyed in their universities.

Thanks are also due to Richard Hibbitt and Jim House for their invitation to speak at the Research Seminar of the Department of French at Leeds University in March 2017, and to Ève Morisi and Andrew Counter for inviting me to speak at the Maison Française d'Oxford in January 2018 as part of Oxford University's Modern French Seminar. A paper on Gauny delivered at the annual conference of the Society for French Studies at University College Cork in July 2018 forms the basis of Chapter 4 and I thank my co-panellists on that occasion, Neil Kenny and Ann Lewis.

I have greatly benefitted from exchanges with friends and fellow academics whose levels of expertise in areas covered by the book are often much higher than my own. Thus, warm thanks go to Peter Hallward for immensely helpful conversations about the content and scope of the present book; to James Williams for discussions around politics and aesthetics; to Jussi Palmusaari, Oliver Davis, Patrick Bray, and Siavash Bakhtiar for their willingness to discuss their own work on Rancière as well as the current project; to Judith Still and Shirley Jordan for their insights into Marie Ndiaye; to Eric Robertson for his guidance on Fernand Léger and other subjects; to Nathalie Mauriac-Dyer for generous help with Proust's manuscripts; and to Patrick O'Donovan for his wise advice on the project.

Many other colleagues, friends, and family members have also helped me, among them: Kirsteen Anderson, Patrick Crowley, Alison Finch, Cynthia Gamble, Rüdiger Görner, Francine Goujon, Julia Hartley, Jeremy Hicks, Eamonn Hughes, Lena Hughes, Nikolaj Lübecker, Jo Malt, Richard Mason, Will McMorran, Paul Murray, Émilie Oléron Evans, Leonard Olschner, Gerald Prince, Xelo Sanmateu, Libby Saxton, Andreas Schönle, Galin Tihanov, and Kiera Vaclavik.

Working with colleagues in the School of Languages, Linguistics and Film at Queen Mary University of London during the years of writing this book has been a pleasure.

An adapted version of the article 'Pierre Michon, "Small Lives", and the Terrain of Art', *Romance Studies*, 29.2 (2011), 67–79, is used in Chapter 7 with the permission of the publisher, Taylor & Francis. I am grateful to the trustees of Columbia University for kind permission to include as part of Chapter 8 an adapted and abridged version of an article on Proust published in the journal *Romanic Review*, vol. 105.3/4 (2014), and to Liverpool University Press for permission to include, as Chapter 10 of the present volume, a revised version of the chapter on Didier Eribon which appeared in Patrick Crowley and Shirley Jordan (eds), *What Forms Can Do: The Work of Form in 20th- and 21st-century French Literature and Thought* (Liverpool University Press, 2020). I also extend thanks to Raphaëlle Drouin, Laura Feliu Lloberas, Charles Gil, and Sandrine Sigiscar for their kind assistance with illustrations for the book.

Working with Liverpool University Press has been a wholly rewarding experience. Charles Forsdick as Series Editor of the Contemporary French and Francophone Cultures collection has been an always attentive, generous, and engaging interlocutor, as has Chloe Johnson as Commissioning Editor. I am most grateful to Siân Jenkins, Rachel Chamberlain, and the copy-editor of the book, Alwyn Harrison, at Carnegie Book Production. The anonymous readers who reviewed the book proposal and manuscript provided exceptionally helpful and insightful feedback. I have learnt much from their recommendations and am hugely in their debt. Needless to say, shortcomings in the present book are of my own making.

At a personal level, warm thanks go to my family, and especially to Kathleen, for their unfailing encouragement.

Introduction

By Way of Rancière

[L]a volonté raisonnable [...] de faire éprouver aux
autres ce en quoi on est semblable à eux

[the reasonable will to (...) make others feel the ways
in which we are similar to them]

Rancière[1]

In an article first published in 1923, the painter Fernand Léger set out
his views on the experience of modernity in an industrial age and on
the impact of such an age on aesthetics. Plastic beauty, he insists, is
independent from 'des valeurs sentimentales, descriptives et imitatives'
['sentimental, descriptive, and imitative values'].[2] Léger complains about
preconceived ideas surrounding the *objet d'art* that are every bit as
restrictive as the hierarchical classification of groups of people. In his
words, there is no hierarchical catalogue of the beautiful: 'Le Beau est
partout, dans l'ordre de vos casseroles, sur le mur blanc de votre cuisine'
['Beauty is everywhere, in your set of saucepans, on the white wall of
your kitchen'].[3] Impatient with the overlapping of artistic and commercial
criteria in the evaluation of decorative objects, Léger leans towards the
mass-produced and is drawn to objects in plain wood and metal. He

---

1   Jacques Rancière, *Le Maître ignorant. Cinq leçons sur l'émancipation
intellectuelle* (Paris: Arthème Fayard, 1987), p.120; *The Ignorant Schoolmaster:
Five Lessons in Intellectual Emancipation*, trans. and ed. Kristin Ross (Stanford:
Stanford University Press, 1991), p. 71; translation slightly modified.
2   Fernand Léger, 'L'Esthétique de la machine, l'objet fabriqué, l'artisan et
l'artiste', in Léger, *Fonctions de la peinture*, ed. Sylvie Forestier (Paris: Gallimard,
2009), p. 87.
3   Léger, *Fonctions de la peinture*, p. 88.

concludes his manifesto-style document by recounting how, some years earlier, his work had featured at the Salon de l'Automne exhibition in Paris. A partition, he notes, separated the arrangement of canvasses on that occasion from an adjoining exhibition to which Léger was drawn because of the sounds of hammering and the singing of workers involved in its installation, the Salon de l'Aviation. A mutual curiosity then sees Léger visit and admire the geometric, vibrantly coloured metallic structures in the aircraft exhibition, while the mechanics in turn go round to the other side of the partition to view the traditionally framed canvasses.

One image in particular stayed with Léger, that of a teenage worker contemplating one of the paintings on view. Red-haired, standing in his brightly coloured work overalls, one of his hands stained with Prussian blue paint, the young worker steals the show in Léger's eyes:

> le gamin éblouissant qui avait l'air d'être enfanté par une machine agricole, c'était le symbole de l'exposition d'à côté, de la vie de demain, quand le Préjugé sera détruit.[4]

> [the symbol of the adjacent exhibition and of the life of tomorrow, when Prejudice will be destroyed, was the dazzling kid who looked as though he had been born of an agricultural machine.]

The human figure thus becomes a product of industrial modernity. As one critic notes, Léger dreams of 'an ideal city' in which colour acquires a social function.[5] If Pierre Bourdieu writes of the 'icy solemnity of the great museums' and sees in this an expression of the 'sacred character, separate and separating, of high culture', Léger's account of the exhibition space allows him to draw into contiguity areas of human activity deemed antithetical by such culture.[6] He relishes the symmetry and levelling that sees aircraft workers and artist-painter making discoveries on either side of the partition.

The reciprocal curiosity also throws light on a social-class border which in his own work Léger sought to eradicate. He writes of how his experience of the First World War brought him into contact with working-class men, allowing him to 'découvrir le Peuple et de me renouveler entièrement' ['discover the People and renew myself

---

4   Léger, *Fonctions de la peinture*, p. 102.
5   Editorial note by Forestier, *Fonctions de la peinture*, p. 86.
6   Pierre Bourdieu, *Distinction: A Social Critique of the Judgement of Taste*, trans. Richard Nice (London: Routledge, 1984), p. 34.

entirely'].[7] The reality of workers' lack of exposure to art concerned him. In notes for a lecture entitled 'Peinture murale et peinture de chevalet' ['Mural Painting and Easel Painting'] and delivered in 1950, he would complain of the time constriction present in working-class life: 'Le peuple retenu, accroupi à son travail toute la journée sans loisirs, échappe entièrement à notre époque bourgeoise, c'est le drame actuel' ['the people, held back, condemned to work all day long and denied leisure, is entirely lost from view in our bourgeois era – that's the drama of today'].[8]

Léger's story of the partition captures literally and figuratively a tradition of schism at the levels of taste and social class. It is true that when he writes of a future time when 'Prejudice will be destroyed', he is championing the triumph of the geometric over the sentimental within an art historical context. He thus privileges plasticity, his aim being to see the objective take precedence over the subjective. In his preface to the catalogue for his 1952 exhibition 'Comment je conçois la figure' ['How I View the Human Figure'], he stresses the notion of the plasticity of form that came with abstract art.[9] Yet the encounter between the teenager in blue-and-orange overalls and the painter derives much of its potency from a social context that is intensely situated. This meeting around a partition provides an emblem for the present study, which explores intersections around class boundaries. More precisely, the present book asks how the aesthetic construct that is literature might draw into contiguity antagonistic social identities in such a way as to lead to the attenuation or interrogation of such antagonisms. Or to frame this somewhat differently, how might literary texts and other forms of prose narrative imagine worlds in which class borders might be weakened or occluded?

The case of writers drawing specifically on manual culture in order to describe their own endeavours provides an instructive angle on this question. In his correspondence, Samuel Beckett reflected sometimes grimly on the work that went into writing and composition. He describes his experience of such work as arduous: 'What hellish labour the "sedentary trade", the coal face nothing to it!', he wrote in 1974. Eight years earlier, he had observed: 'Work hard labour & not much comfort [...]. Hate the

---

7 Léger, in a lecture entitled 'L'art et le peuple' ['Art and the People'], published in 1946; Léger, *Fonctions de la peinture*, p. 247.

8 Léger, *Fonctions de la peinture*, p. 279.

9 Léger, *Fonctions de la peinture*, pp. 285–86.

thought and sight of it but must keep it going'. One of Beckett's editors wonders if these references might be whimsical in nature, before noting an assertion, made in good faith, it seems, elsewhere in the correspondence, that hard work seemed 'the best of the bad lot'.[10]

How are we to read the grudging acceptance of a work ethic and the apparently serious comparison between the efforts of the would-be writer-labourer and a manual work conventionally deemed less valuable in bourgeois culture? The linkage between the arduous, uninviting task facing the writer and the work of the miner instantly rids literary composition of glamour, unless, that is, it acquires a circuitous prestige by virtue of its association with a demanding physical work linked to productive necessity. In this latter sense, Beckett's comparison could be seen as a recycling of both the energy and the exhaustion associated with physical labour and as directing it to the activity W. B. Yeats called the 'sedentary trade', and all of this the better to evoke the writer's sacrifices.

Roland Barthes recalls an earlier historical context, around 1850 in France, when, with doubts being raised about the use-value of literature, a class of writers defended the practice as a 'responsible' one by insisting that writing had value, a *valeur-travail*, to the extent that it constituted work. 'L'écriture sera sauvée', Barthes writes of this moment of cultural transition, 'non pas en vertu de sa destination, mais grâce au travail qu'elle aura coûté [...]. Cette valeur-travail remplace un peu la valeur-génie' ['Writing will be saved, not by virtue of its destination but because of the work that has gone into it (...). This work-value replaces somewhat the stress on genius-value'].[11] The image of Flaubert grinding out his sentences in Croisset helps secure 'redemption' ['le rachat'] for writers in general, Barthes argues.[12] And to illustrate his notion of style as artisanship, he provides other examples of writers' industry – Gautier's compositional craft, Valéry's disciplined writing at dawn, and Gide standing at his desk as though at a workbench.[13]

---

10   The material here is drawn from Dan Gunn's editorial introduction to *The Letters of Samuel Beckett,* vol. 4: *1966–1989,* ed. George Craig, Martha Dow Fehsenfeld, Dan Gunn, and Lois More Overbeck (Cambridge: Cambridge University Press, 2016), p. cvi.

11   Roland Barthes, *Le Degré zéro de l'écriture,* in *Œuvres complètes,* I, *Livres, textes, entretiens, 1942–1961,* ed. Éric Marty (Paris: Seuil, 2002), p. 209. Barthes's comments come in a brief section of argument entitled 'L'Artisanat du style' ['The Artisanship of Style'].

12   Barthes, *Le Degré zéro de l'écriture,* p. 211.

13   Barthes, *Le Degré zéro de l'écriture,* p. 209.

For the contemporary thinker Jacques Rancière, the schismatic division of work into the intellectual and the manual is a central preoccupation. Not unlike Barthes in his reflection on literature as work in mid-nineteenth-century France, Rancière dwells on how the hand/mind division is itself historically situated. In *Le Maître ignorant*, published in 1987, he calls into question the hierarchization of knowledge and the logic of elitism. Oliver Davis notes how Rancière identifies as a central reference point the 'social privilege of intellect first articulated by Plato'.[14] Rancière highlights the section in *Republic* where the artisan is described as being required to attend to his role, without laying any claim to intellectual life. In Rancière's unvarnished synopsis of Plato's argument, the injunction runs thus:

> Ne fais rien d'autre que *ta propre affaire*, laquelle n'est pas de penser quoi que ce soit mais simplement de *faire* cette chose qui épuise la définition de ton être; si tu es cordonnier, des chaussures et des enfants qui en feront autant.

> [Don't do anything other than *your own affair*, which is not in any way *thinking*, but simply *making* that thing that exhausts the definition of your being; if you are a shoemaker, make shoes – and make children who will do the same.][15]

As Kristin Ross puts it, 'the last resource of philosophy is to eternalize the division of labor that grants it its place'.[16] Taking issue with this traditional apportionment, Rancière proposes instead an equalization between the pen and the workbench tool.

The inspiration for *Le Maître ignorant* was the nineteenth-century archive of an emancipatory movement in which Joseph Jacotot, the exponent of a philosophy of radical equality, played a prominent role. A French university teacher and member of parliament, Jacotot had left France in 1818 to take up a post at the University of Leuven in the Low Countries, the Bourbon Restoration having forced him into exile. As Rancière explains, he was a figure who had already lived an eventful life, having taught rhetoric in Dijon, served in the army of the Republic in 1792, and then worked as a high-ranking official in the Ministry of War under the Convention.

---

14 Oliver Davis, *Jacques Rancière* (Cambridge: Polity, 2010), p. 1.
15 Rancière, *Le Maître ignorant*, p. 59; *The Ignorant Schoolmaster*, pp. 33–34.
16 See the translator's Introduction to *The Ignorant Schoolmaster*, p. xviii.

The move to the Low Countries was to bring unanticipated fame. Rancière enthusiastically narrates how, with no Flemish, Jacotot was teaching students many of whom did not speak French. Using an interpreter, he asked his students to study a recently published bilingual edition of Fénelon's *Télémaque*. The students were to learn the French text using the Flemish translation to assist them and Jacotot asked them to practise regular exercises in repetition to assist them in their acquisition of French. What surprised him was that when he had his pupils write about *Télémaque* in French, these autonomous learners often performed very well. The experience was to feed into the movement that became known as 'l'Enseignment universel' ['Universal Teaching']. Mindful of the learning outcomes at Leuven, two followers of Jacotot's method would later ask rhetorically: were humans therefore potentially able to do and understand what other humans had done and understood before them?[17]

Rancière channels the emancipatory energy in the 'méthode de l'égalité' ['equality method'] and indeed frequently ventriloquizes Jacotot's style in *Le Maître ignorant*.[18] In a section of the work entitled 'La Communauté des égaux' ['The Community of Equals'], he firms up the equalization between artists and manual workers, between the will of the former to work with words ['manier les mots'] and of the worker to work with tools ['manier ses outils'].[19] He adds that in the act of speaking, 'l'homme ne transmet pas son savoir, il poétise, il traduit et convie les autres à faire de même. Il communique en *artisan*: en manieur de mots comme d'outils' ['man doesn't transmit his knowledge, he makes poetry; he translates and invites others to do the same. He communicates as an *artisan*; as a person who handles words like tools'].[20]

One can link this back to Léger's consideration of the artisan and the artist. There, we find him enthusing about the shop employee absorbed in the task of window dressing, Léger seeing in this painstaking and yet intrinsically ephemeral production an intense concentration that may exceed that of renowned painters:

---

17 Félix and Victor Ratier, 'Enseignement universel. Emancipation intellectuelle', *Journal de philosophie panécastique*, 1838, p. 155; quoted in *Le Maître ignorant*, p. 9 n. 1; *The Ignorant Schoolmaster*, p. 2.

18 For a reflection on the presence of free indirect style in Rancière's reconstruction of Jacotot's argument, see James Swenson, '*Style indirect libre*', in *Jacques Rancière: History, Politics, Aesthetics*, ed. Gabriel Rockhill and Philip Watts (Durham, NC and London: Duke University Press, 2009), pp. 258–72.

19 *Le Maître ignorant*, p. 121; *The Ignorant Schoolmaster*, p. 71.

20 *Le Maître ignorant*, p. 110; *The Ignorant Schoolmaster*, p. 65.

chez ces artisans, il y a un concept d'art incontestable, lié étroitement au but commercial, un fait plastique d'un ordre nouveau et équivalent des manifestations artistiques existantes quelles qu'elles soient.[21]

[for these artisans, a concept of art is unquestionably at work, tightly linked to commercial ends, a plasticity of a new order and equivalent to existing artistic manifestations of every kind.]

The blurring of the separation between the artisanal and the aesthetic is again critical.

In a related way, Davis observes that Rancière's work provides 'an egalitarian incitement' to think freely about political, aesthetic, and intellectual questions, his corpus being seen in terms of its 'exemplary singularity' and as an invitation to autonomous exploration.[22] Significantly, Rancière does not propose a reversal of the precedence of the intellectual over the manual. It's not a question, he argues, of deciding who built the walls of Thebes (the reference is to the brothers Zethus and Amphion, the legend suggesting how Amphion's playing on his lyre caused the stones to move into position in the construction of the ancient city). Nor is Rancière insisting on a people-versus-elite opposition. He explains the Greek etymology of the label 'Panecastic' which Jacotot gave to the movement he led, the name signalling that the *whole* of human intelligence is looked for in '*each* intellectual manifes-tation' ['*chaque* manifestation intellectuelle'].[23]

Rancière thus proposes an egalitarian view of 'l'art humain' ['human art'] and a recognition of the workings of the intellect in a broad spectrum of human endeavour. In that context, he rejects the view advanced by the influential nineteenth-century critic Jean-Louis-Eugène Lerminier that *le peuple* lacks intellectual capacity. In one of his early works, *La Nuit des prolétaires*, Rancière notes a December 1841 article in *La Revue des Deux Mondes* in which Lerminier writes in patronizing terms of factory workers going home to rest after their day of manual work, Providence ensuring that their toil ends there.[24] The thrust of Lerminier's argument is that the

---

21   Léger, *Fonctions de la peinture*, p. 94.

22   Davis, *Jacques Rancière*, pp. 160–61.

23   *Le Maître ignorant*, p. 68; *The Ignorant Schoolmaster*, p. 39; emphasis original.

24   Rancière, *La Nuit des prolétaires. Archives du rêve ouvrier* (Paris: Arthème Fayard/Pluriel, 2012 [1981]), p. 28; *Proletarian Nights: The Workers' Dream in Nineteenth-Century France*, trans. John Drury, intro. Donald Reid (London: Verso, 2012), p. 16.

two elements that make up his article title, 'De la littérature des ouvriers' ['On Workers' Literature'], are mutually incompatible.[25] As Christopher Prendergast observes, the article was 'a complacent injunction issued to the worker to remain in his properly appointed place'.[26]

For members of the 'Enseignement universel' movement, 'les savoirs de la main' ['manual knowledge'] and 'la rhétorique des élites' ['the rhetoric of the elite'] were not to be read as opposites, a stance which allows Rancière to reject Lerminier's thinking in trenchant terms:

> Demeure abruti celui qui oppose l'œuvre de la main ouvrière et du peuple nourricier aux nuages de la rhétorique. La fabrication des nuages est une œuvre de l'art humain qui demande autant – ni plus ni moins – de travail, d'attention intellectuelle, que la fabrication des chaussures et des serrures.

> [He who makes a distinction between the manual work of the worker or the common man and clouds of rhetoric remains stultified. The fabrication of clouds is a human work of art that demands as much – neither more nor less – labor and intellectual attention as the fabrication of shoes or locks.][27]

Rancière invites his reader, then, to accept an equivalence that encompasses material and mental, the hard graft of worker and writer alike. Seen in this light, Beckett's complaint of exhaustion could be read as corroborating the equivalence. Underscoring the idea of *œuvre* (from the Latin *opera*, meaning 'works'), Rancière argues capaciously – and again in a conscious imitation of Jacotot – that 'chaque citoyen est aussi un homme qui fait *œuvre*, de la plume, du burin ou de tout autre outil' ['each citizen is also a man who makes a *work*, with the pen, with the burin, or with any other tool'].[28] As if to echo this language of levelling, the philanthropic figure Charles Myriel in Hugo's *Les Misérables* describes his own work in similar terms:

> Tantôt il bêchait dans son jardin, tantôt il lisait et il écrivait. Il n'avait qu'un mot pour ces deux sortes de travail; il appelait cela *jardiner*. 'L'esprit est un jardin', disait-il.[29]

25 See C. Prendergast, *The Classic: Sainte-Beuve and the Nineteenth-Century Culture Wars* (Oxford: Oxford University Press, 2007), p. 221.
26 Prendergast, *The Classic*, p. 224.
27 *Le Maître ignorant*, pp. 63–64; *The Ignorant Schoolmaster*, pp. 36–37.
28 *Le Maître ignorant*, p. 179; emphasis in the original; *The Ignorant Schoolmaster*, p. 108; translation modified.
29 Victor Hugo, *Les Misérables*, 2 vols (Paris: Garnier-Flammarion, 1967), I, 42.

[Sometimes he would dig in his garden, sometimes he would read and write. He used the same word for these two kinds of work; *gardening* was how he referred to them. 'The mind is a garden', he would say.]

Yet Rancière's nineteenth-century archival sources include figures such as the tailor Constant Hilbey, who is sceptical about any suggestion that a worker can find the time to both labour and write poetry. Hugo may indeed be the self-styled 'ouvrier de la pensée' ['worker of thought'] but the apportionment of roles, Rancière notes, ensures the maintenance of 'la hiérarchie des penseurs et des ouvriers' ['the hierarchy of thinkers and workers'].[30]

Equalization forms one of the central planks in Rancière's work. Central to his and Jacotot's argument is that the linking of pen and engraving tool entails not only a valorization of manual labour but also a defence of writing. Lerminier may be stupid (an *abruti*, to use Jacotot's terminology) because of his social paternalism but his endeavour is no less valuable than that of manual workers:

> Et nous serions abrutis à notre tour si nous ne reconnaissions pas dans ses dissertations le même art, la même intelligence, le même travail que ceux qui transforment le bois, la pierre ou le cuir.

> [And we ourselves would be stultified if we didn't recognize in his theses the same art, the same intelligence, the same labor as those acts that transform wood, stone, or leather.][31]

In place, then, of a schismatic view of the scholarly and the everyday world of repetitive production, Rancière, in a continuing echo of the message of the 'Enseignement universel' movement, cautions against reciprocal forms of stultification or *abrutissement*. He spells out the transactional nature of the exchange, stressing that it is only when we appreciate the *labour* undertaken by Lerminier that we can understand the *intelligence* that goes into the artisan's endeavour.[32] By attributing labour to the prominent intellectual and commentator, and mental judgement to the socially less visible manual worker, Rancière endorses the steer provided by his nineteenth-century predecessors. In the process, the striking use of symmetry and binary formulations forms the scaffolding for his advocacy of radical equality.

---

30 *La Nuit des prolétaires*, p. 26; *Proletarian Nights*, pp. 13–14.
31 *Le Maître ignorant*, p. 64; *The Ignorant Schoolmaster*, p. 37.
32 *Le Maître ignorant*, p. 64; *The Ignorant Schoolmaster*, p. 37.

Rancière was likewise drawn to Jacotot's promotion of autonomous learning and to the counter-intuitive view that the master may be ignorant and yet still facilitate the learning of a pupil. In adopting this stance, he was reacting, as Kristin Ross explains, against the position taken by Louis Althusser, his teacher at the École Normale Supérieure in the early 1960s. Althusser's Marxist view of knowledge was unequivocally hierarchical. Writing in 1964, he described the function of teaching as being 'to transmit a determinate knowledge to subjects who do not possess this knowledge. The teaching situation thus rests on the absolute condition of *an inequality between a knowledge and a nonknowledge*'.[33]

Rancière's career saw him turn away from Althusserian Marxism in the years after May 1968. The verve with which he engages with the nineteenth-century emancipatory movement and workers' archives of the period is indicative of that new direction. Ross extends her contextualization of Rancière's work, explaining that he was also reacting against the tendency in the social sciences of the day to see in proletarian culture an ordinariness that was repetitive and socially contained. She cites the assertion of Michel de Certeau, for example, that working-class bodies 'follow the thick and thin of an urban text they write without being able to read'.[34] Ross's point is that, in their engagement with questions to do with popular culture, the approaches of thinkers such as de Certeau and Bourdieu may superficially resemble the argument advanced in *Le Maître ignorant*, but that in reality, concepts such as Bourdieu's *habitus* or de Certeau's stress on working-class unknowingness point to a consensual reading of identitarian fixity, something Rancière rejects. Instead we find in his work what Ross calls 'a fluid and unscheduled nonsystem of significant misrecognitions'.[35]

A series of interviews published in 2012 under the title *La Méthode de l'égalité* ['The Method of Equality'] confirms the pivotal place of radical equality in Rancière's work. Here again, the 'unscheduled', improvisatory dimension in his self-positioning is visible. Importantly, he stresses that he is not working towards an identitarian literature

33   Quoted by Ross in her introduction to *The Ignorant Schoolmaster*, p. xvi; emphasis original.

34   K. Ross, 'Historicizing Untimeliness', in *Jacques Rancière: History, Politics, Aesthetics*, ed. Rockhill and Watts, pp. 15–29 (p. 19). Ross is quoting from de Certeau's *The Practice of Everyday Life*, trans. Steven Rendall (Berkeley: University of California Press, 1984), p. 93.

35   Ross, 'Historicizing Untimeliness', p. 21.

and indeed that his aim is to propose a critique of identitarianism. In *La Nuit des prolétaires*, he tracks examples of nineteenth-century workers pursuing an 'errance individuelle' ['individual wandering'] that draws them out of the ambit of proletarian solidarity.[36] What unites humans, he argues pointedly, is their capacity for distance as they gravitate towards 'nonaggregation'.[37] Uneasy about strongly consensual, blanket categories such as working-class culture or bourgeois literature, Rancière argues in the 2012 publication that it is cultural intersections that intrigue him:

> ce n'est pas l'idéologie ouvrière contre l'idéologie bourgeoise, la culture populaire contre la culture savante, mais que tous les phénomènes importants comme déflagrateurs de conflit idéologique et social sont des événements qui se passent à la frontière, des phénomènes de barrières qu'on voit et qu'on transgresse, de passages d'un côté à un autre.

> [it's not about working-class ideology versus bourgeois ideology, popular culture versus educated culture, but that all the important, explosive, phenomena in ideological and social conflicts are events that happen at the dividing line; they are phenomena that have to do with barriers that one sees and transgresses, crossings over from one side to another.][38]

As if to echo Léger's anecdote about the exhibition hall, these frontier spaces and the notion of cultural trespass provide focal points for much of Rancière's analysis. He insists that his own working practice as a thinker and cultural analyst has not been to denounce the positions of others but rather to attempt to enter into 'la teneur d'une expérience, dans la manière dont un certain type de perception se conceptualise' ['the tenor of an experience (...) the way in which a certain kind of perception is conceptualized'].[39] Noting objections sometimes raised against his promotion of emancipation, he concedes that the effect of his work may be to unsettle, but expresses the hope that his methods may encourage others to rethink their own work.[40]

---

36 *La Nuit des prolétaires*, p. 10.
37 *Le Maître ignorant*, p. 99; *The Ignorant Schoolmaster*, p. 58.
38 Rancière, *La Méthode de l'égalité. Entretiens avec Laurent Jeanpierre et Dork Zabunyan* (Paris: Bayard, 2012), p. 51; *The Method of Equality: Interviews with Laurent Jeanpierre and Dork Zabunyan*, trans. Julie Rose (Cambridge: Polity, 2016), pp. 24–25 (translation modified).
39 *La Méthode de l'égalité*, p. 157; *The Method of Equality*, p. 87.
40 *La Méthode de l'égalité*, pp. 157–58; *The Method of Equality*, p. 87. Christopher Watkin argues that Rancière's account of equality, with its reliance on the notion of

The 'Egalitarian Strangeness' formulation in the present book's title reflects a direct borrowing from Rancière. At a particular juncture in his analysis of Roberto Rossellini's film *Europa 51*, he considers instances of disturbance in the regime of social inequality. He observes how the director, while agnostic in his outlook, embodies a cultural Christianity which identifies with what Rancière calls 'an equality of respect' ['l'égalité de considération'].[41] In a further reflection of that outlook, the film's bourgeois protagonist Irene, distraught at the death of her young son, literally traverses Rome, travelling to the end of the tramline where she encounters the working class [*le peuple*]. In her act of visiting those who are marginal, Rancière identifies the performance of what he terms a modest labour of attention.[42]

The same essay establishes a homology between the protagonist's act of visual attention and the eye of the camera, this allowing Rancière to propose as equivalents the morality of the story and, as he puts it, the morality of the lens:

> Cette pratique esthétique et éthique de l'égalité, cette pratique de *l'étrangeté égalitaire* met en péril tout ce qui est inscrit aux répertoires du social et du politique, tout ce qui représente la société.

human capacity, fails to accommodate 'society's most vulnerable', Watkin preferring the perspectives on equality to be found in Jean-Luc Nancy's notion of sense as explored in, for example, *Être singulier pluriel*. See Watkin, 'Thinking Equality Today: Badiou, Rancière, Nancy', *French Studies*, 67.4 (October 2013), 522–34 (pp. 522, 526–27). An alternative perspective on Rancière and the situation of the vulnerable is found in the analysis of Oliver Davis, who reflects on how, on the question of political subjectivation, Rancière emphasizes that 'being *together*' is conditioned by 'the extent that we are *in between*'. Rancière illustrates this tension with reference to the solidarity of his generation with the victims of the massacre of Algerians in Paris in October 1961. While the identification with the victims is seen as an impossible one, in that the person uttering it cannot embody it in the way the marginalized victims do, 'we could act as political subjects', Rancière explains, 'in the interval or the gap between two identities', the first identity being that of those denied voice, the second, that of the perpetrators of the massacre. Davis is quoting from Rancière's 'Politics, Identification, and Subjectivization', *October*, 61 (Summer 1992), 58–64 (pp. 61–62); see Davis, *Jacques Rancière*, pp. 87–88.

41   Rancière, *Courts voyages au pays du peuple* (Paris: Seuil, 1990), p. 158; *Short Voyages to the Land of the People*, trans. James B. Swenson (Stanford: Stanford University Press, 2003), p. 123.

42   *Courts voyages au pays du peuple*, p. 159; *Short Voyages to the Land of the People*, p. 123.

[This aesthetic and ethical practice of equality, this practice of *egalitarian strangeness* puts into peril everything that is inscribed in the repertories of society and politics, everything that represents society.][43]

Rancière thus homes in on that which unsettles a familiar order: with society only capable of representing itself under the sign of inequality, he adds, art becomes an intervention which disturbs that convention.

This drawing into suggestive alignment of ethical and aesthetic practice has a bearing on the works considered here. While many of them create disturbance, this is not to be confused with the forms of anti-democratic subversion and transgression to be found in authors such as Georges Bataille or the Marquis de Sade, for example. The radicality within the present corpus derives, rather, from the manner in which a number of the authors considered expose or unwrite antagonistic social relations which have congealed into a state of settled ordinariness. Narratives may acquire emancipatory capacity in that, through the medium of language, they make available to their readers modes of attention that resist the naturalization of inequality. By virtue of what it includes and shows and the manner of such showing (in other words, in its channelling through language), modern literature can become a forum for transformative encounter.

Claude Simon does not seem to be seeking to disturb socially when he comments laconically that writing involves the placing of words on a page – it is a following of 'le cheminement même de l'écriture' ['the very course taken by writing'].[44] Yet his novel *L'Acacia* (1989), with its foregrounding of the themes of war and social-class provenance, goes well beyond formalism by also inviting an ethical response.[45] What relationship obtains, then, between the words in circulation in Simon's narrative and the terrain of the social and the political? What hold

---

43 *Courts voyages au pays du peuple*, pp. 158–59 (emphasis added); *Short Voyages to the Land of the People*, p. 123. Swenson uses, entirely appropriately, the formulation 'egalitarian foreignness', which I have modified for the purposes of my overall argument.

44 Claude Simon in conversation with Viviane Forrester. See http://next. liberation.fr/livres/2013/10/11/l-album-de-l-ecrivain-claude-simon_938468 [accessed 10 March 2020].

45 Claude Simon, *L'Acacia* (Paris: Minuit, 2003 [1989]); *The Acacia*, trans. Richard Howard (New York: Pantheon Books, 1991). References to the French text are hereinafter cited as A, with an accompanying page reference; the English translation is indicated as AA.

does the theme of societal fracture have in an author whose work was, notably in the 1970s, heavily linked in with the project of the French new novel and the object of narrowly formalist criticism.[46]

The disarming flatness of Simon's remark about word assembly connects with Rancière's analysis of literature's growing democratization in the modern era. By the nineteenth century, Rancière argues, literature has become 'ce nouveau régime de l'art d'écrire où l'écrivain est n'importe qui et le lecteur n'importe qui' ['this new regime of the art of writing in which the writer is anyone at all and the reader anyone at all'].[47] As he points out, Voltaire, already alert to the emergence of this democratization, regretted the fact that his theatre failed to attract the socially influential figures who made up Corneille's audiences.[48] Simon's self-positioning as someone who works with words confirms the trend away from literature as a vehicle for the powerful. Yet while not an exponent of the engaged literature favoured by the generation of his immediate predecessors, writers such as Sartre and Nizan, he is acutely aware of political power. In *L'Acacia* he depicts it as functioning specifically as spectacle. The apportionment of affluence and leisure is similarly worked through the theme of social performance in the novel, as will be explored in Chapter 1.

Politics for Rancière involves a performance of power, as Peter Hallward explains. It is the process that 'founds the power to govern other people on nothing other than "the absence of any foundation"'.[49] Rancière's contention is that the fact that power must always seek to legitimize itself is proof – banal proof, he insists – of 'une égalité irréductible' ['the irreducibility of equality'].[50] Hallward expresses the reservation that Rancière's egalitarianism may be 'merely transgressive' and thus risk entailing resignation and inaction in respect of the prospect

46   For an exploration of the history and limits of the formalist approach to Simon's work, see Jean H. Duffy and Alastair Duncan, eds, *Claude Simon: A Retrospective* (Liverpool: Liverpool University Press, 2002), pp. 2–8.

47   Rancière, *Politique de la littérature* (Paris: Galilée, 2007), p. 21; *The Politics of Literature*, trans. Julie Rose (Cambridge: Polity, 2011), p. 12.

48   *Politique de la littérature*, pp. 20–21; *The Politics of Literature*, p. 12.

49   P. Hallward, 'Staging Equality: Rancière's Theatrocracy and the Limits of Anarchic Equality', in *Jacques Rancière: History, Politics, Aesthetics*, ed. Rockhill and Watts, pp. 140–57 (p. 146). Hallward is quoting from Rancière's *La Haine de la démocratie* (Paris: La Fabrique, 2005), p. 56.

50   Rancière, *La Haine de la démocratie*, p. 55; *Hatred of Democracy*, trans. Steve Corcoran (London: Verso, 2014), p. 48.

of radical social change.[51] By being less concerned with questions of social organization and mobilization, Rancière's theory may see us 'do little more than "play at" politics or equality'.[52] Hallward further cautions that Rancière's conception of equality is reliant on elements such as improvisation, disruption, and a claiming of visibility, such that its effects are 'unabashedly sporadic and intermittent'.[53] Yet the emancipatory potential in Rancière's interrogation of social apportionment is not to be discounted. Indeed, one of the crucial dimensions of his account of social emancipation is that, to borrow Hallward's formulation, 'the luxuries of unprofitable time, of "idle" contemplation, of individual or idiosyncratic taste', once these are more widely experienced, radically alter the distribution of social functions.[54]

Howard Caygill's study of resistance, while not written with Rancière specifically in mind, assesses the 'reciprocals' that are domination and defiance and argues that resistance endlessly requires a 'fresh posture with respect to a strengthened counter-resistance'.[55] Far from proposing a programmatic form of social transformation, Rancière's statements of resistance to the repertoires of power carry an at times avowedly utopian strain. In the introduction to his modestly titled collection of essays *Courts voyages au pays du peuple*, he disarms his readers by telling them how not, and who is not, to read them. The book is not for those who would see foreigners as naive, not for those for whom voyages merely serve to educate the young, and not for those who see reality as providing the necessary corrective to airy, chimerical thinking. Rancière rejects this bolstering of social consensus by endorsing 'le mirage ou la folie utopique' ['the mirage or utopian madness'] which is not held within 'les procédures par lesquelles les savoirs positifs et les politiques raisonnables construisent la réalité' ['the procedures that positive knowledge and reasonable politics use to construct reality'].[56] On the specific question of the criteria which historically influenced canon-formation in literature, Rancière argues in *Les Bords de la fiction*,

---

51 Hallward, 'Staging Equality', p. 153.
52 Hallward, 'Staging Equality', p. 157.
53 Hallward, 'Staging Equality', p. 152.
54 Hallward, 'Staging Equality', p. 145.
55 Howard Caygill, *On Resistance: A Philosophy of Defiance* (London: Bloomsbury, 2013), p. 208.
56 *Courts voyages au pays du peuple*, p. 11; *Short Voyages to the Land of the People*, p. 4.

drawing on Aristotle's *Poetics*, that those traditionally excluded from 'la rationalité fictionnelle classique' ['classical fictional rationality'] – those, he notes, whose daily pattern of living involves producing things, producing children, following orders, and providing services – inhabit a world in which the contingent and the particular dominate. He adds that the rationality at work in fiction in its classical form is based on assumptions about knowledge and ignorance: it privileges the influential ('les hommes actifs' ['active men']), their conspicuous presence in this fictional world being at the expense of 'la masse des êtres et des situations' ['the mass of beings and situations'].[57]

*   *   *

While the exclusion from, or the laying claim to, certain cultural objects or practices forms a leitmotif in this book, the authors explored do not form a tidy, familiar line-up based on literary movement or genre. Chapter 4, for example, explores the writings of Louis Gabriel Gauny, an obscure figure whose work Rancière retrieves from a nineteenth-century workers' archive. Other chapters consider Pierre Michon's celebration of socially anonymous lives in rural France (Chapter 7) and Didier Eribon's retracing of a life itinerary that sees him abandon, and then reclaim, his proletarian origins (Chapter 10). While these texts engage with working-class culture, their authors' concerns with questions of narrative poetics and cultural politics mean that the works do not fall into the category of popular or proletarian literature. The same holds true for François Bon's *Daewoo*, a work which maps the effects of deindustrialization in modern-day Lorraine on a group of women factory workers whose skills are deemed redundant. Chapter 9 explores how, centrally for Bon's project, the workers' engagement in aesthetic production sees them create restorative play from their experience of marginalization. The factory as a site of cultural disturbance also features in Chapter 6, which considers Simone Weil's journal of life on a production line in the mid-1930s and the experience of what she calls 'l'excès insensé de la spécialisation' ['the demented and excessive presence of specialization'].[58] Weil's insistence

57 Rancière, *Les Bords de la fiction* (Paris: Seuil, 2017), p. 10; *The Edges of Fiction*, trans. Steve Corcoran (Cambridge: Polity, 2020), p. 4.
58 Simone Weil, *La Condition ouvrière*, ed. Robert Chenavier (Paris: Gallimard, 2002 [1951]), p. 449.

on the evil of compartmentalization and mechanization is comple-
mented by Paul Nizan's depiction of the emergence of the technological
landscape of the Third Republic and his interwar novel *Antoine Bloyé*
provides the point of focus in Chapter 5.

With the refrain of class also being accessed through the thematics
of making (both material and mental), the links across to poeticity
form another strand. Chapter 2 proposes an in-tandem reading of texts
by Charles Péguy and Thierry Beinstingel, authors writing a century
apart and yet linked through a shared attentiveness to the aggregation
of manual making and social identity. Chapter 3 extends consideration
of the theme of knowledge experienced through hand and body by
exploring Marie Ndiaye's contemporary novel *La Cheffe, roman d'une
cuisinière*. I will attempt to show that, to a degree, the work functions
within a similar set of social coordinates to those found in Péguy: the
linkage between probity and work, intense class affiliation, and the
isolatory impact of obsessive endeavour. Certainly, the range of what is
shown and said in the three texts is again illustrative of the workings of
the democratic encounter that is modern narrative.

Two writers seen as canonical figures in modern French literature
are also drawn into the exploration of egalitarian strangeness: Claude
Simon, already mentioned, and Marcel Proust. Jacotot's homology that
links the handling of word and of matter has a bearing on *L'Acacia*. The
orientation of argument in Chapter 8, where *À la recherche du temps
perdu* is explored, takes in sections of the novel where the narrator's
focus precisely on the handler of words – a figure present across the
social classes in the novel – carries a democratizing potential.

In attempting to map intersections which form around questions
to do with aesthetics, class habitus, and other social coordinates, the
present book consciously eschews any chronological ordering of the
individual chapters. In addition, the material considered cuts across
a range of genres: the novel, the essay, autobiographical writing,
sociological reflection. The intention is not to generate a gratuitous
sense of randomness or dispersal but rather to reflect on the enduring
regime of inequality and also to gauge a range of responses to the
schismatic depiction of the order of productive necessity and aesthetics,
the material and the mental.

In recording his considerable indebtedness to Schiller and Kant,
Rancière describes the crucial role of play [*le jeu*] in bringing into being
a category of *expérience sensible* or experience of the sensible that is free
from hierarchical distribution and that 'renvoie à une capacité d'humanité,

à un horizon d'humanité qui n'est plus divisé' ['refers to a capacity of humanity, a perspective of humanity that's no longer divided'].[59] For Rancière, aesthetic experience has the capacity to suspend the workings of hierarchy and to counter notions of social mastery. Seen as 'a veritable *thinker of dissensus*', he frequently uses that term, 'dissensus', which can be linked to the notion of disturbance in the title of the present study.[60] In an autobiographical aside, he draws together seminal moments in his itinerary as reader and thinker: the chance discovery of Schiller's *On the Aesthetic Education of Man* and hence of the category of play in German Romanticism as just mentioned; the archive where he uncovered Gauny's account of a deep consciousness of aesthetic experience; his reading of Baudelaire's text on Pierre Dupont in which workers are seen to enjoy parks and palaces.[61] The dissensual emerges precisely from the access to beauty which those from the wrong side of the barrier, to use Rancière's image, come to have. With hierarchy suspended, the dissensual becomes a derivative of the notion of an aesthetic community.[62]

In a similar way, the scenario of communicative emancipation that Rancière constructs shows him rejecting a logic of social segregation:

> Et l'émancipation de l'artisan est d'abord la ressaisie de cette histoire, la conscience que son activité matérielle est de la nature du discours. Il communique en *poète*: en être qui croit sa pensée communicable, son émotion partageable.

> [And the artisan's emancipation is first the regaining of that story, the consciousness that one's material activity is of the nature of discourse. He communicates as a *poet*: as a being who believes his thought communicable, his emotions sharable.][63]

This has a bearing on the understanding of articulateness and communication. Rancière references the case of a mother anxious about her

59   *La Méthode de l'égalité*, p. 138; *The Method of Equality*, p. 76.
60   See the Introduction by Rockhill and Watts to their edited volume *Jacques Rancière: History, Politics, Aesthetics*, pp. 1–12 (p. 2); emphasis in the original.
61   *La Méthode de l'égalité*, p. 138; *The Method of Equality*, p. 76. In Baudelaire's tribute to Pierre Dupont, he commends the songwriter for having broken down the 'fortress' which had excluded popular poetry and for channelling 'l'amour de la vertu et de l'humanité' ['the love of virtue and humanity']. See Baudelaire, 'Pierre Dupont', in *Œuvres complètes* (Lausanne: La Guilde du Livre, 1967), pp. 685–95 (pp. 693–94).
62   *La Méthode de l'égalité*, p. 138; *The Method of Equality*, p. 76.
63   *Le Maître ignorant*, pp. 110–11; *The Ignorant Schoolmaster*, p. 65; emphasis original.

soldier son and draws on Jacotot's valorization of the parent's work as she attempts to articulate her feelings: 'toute cette *improvisation* en bref n'est-elle pas le plus éloquent des poèmes?' ['all that *improvisation* in short – is this not the most eloquent of poems?'].[64] The stress on solidarity and equality provides an illustration of what Davide Panagia notes to be the link in Rancière between 'sentimental dispositions' and their 'political corollaries'.[65]

The category of those who handle words thus comes to be democratized. François Bon, some of whose work is explored in Chapter 9, cites an enthusiastic observation made by Proust in relation to Flaubert's method of textual composition: 'Mais comme nous les aimons, ces lourds matériaux que la phrase de Flaubert soulève et laisse retomber avec le bruit intermittent d'un excavateur' ['But how we love the heavy materials that Flaubert's sentence gathers up and then drops down with the intermittent thud of an excavator'].[66] Energized by this image, Bon notes how a school edition of *L'Education sentimentale* inaccurately suggests that Proust's observation on Flaubert's style amounted to a dismissal of a seemingly unpromising, mechanical method of composition. The full text of the essay 'A propos du "style" de Flaubert' (1920) ['On Flaubert's "Style"'] shows, in fact, Proust's admiration for his predecessor. Yet the assumption in the annotated school manual – namely that a properly aesthetic appreciation of prose would necessarily exclude the mechanical-sounding notion of words as building material – returns us to the question of the status of literary language.

Rancière addresses this at length in *Politique de la littérature*, commenting specifically on the case of Flaubert. As he reminds his reader, what exercised many of the novelist's politically conservative contemporaries was that his habit of treating on equal terms 'high' and 'low' subjects, narration and description, humans and things, spelt a dangerous democratization. Hence Barbey d'Aurevilly's negative depiction of Flaubert pushing his sentences before him like a navvy with a wheelbarrow full of paving stones.[67] For Rancière, this laying down of words epitomizes an egalitarian activity. And unlike critics in

---

64 *Le Maître ignorant*, p. 115; *The Ignorant Schoolmaster*, p. 68; emphasis original.

65 Davide Panagia, *Rancière's Sentiments* (Durham, NC and London: Duke University Press, 2018), p. 2.

66 François Bon, *Proust est une fiction* (Paris: Seuil, 2013), p. 38.

67 *Politique de la littérature*, pp. 16–17; *The Politics of Literature*, p. 8.

Sartre's time, for whom the reputation Flaubert acquired for seeing style as an absolute signals aristocratic separateness, Rancière presents the insistence on art for art's sake as being consistent with

> la destruction de la vieille supériorité de l'action sur la vie, avec la promotion sociale et politique des êtres quelconques, des êtres voués à la répétition et à la reproduction de la vie nue.
>
> [the destruction of the old superiority of action over life and with the social and political promotion of ordinary human beings, beings dedicated to the repetition and reproduction of unadorned life.][68]

Interpreted in this light, art for art's sake becomes, critically, the terrain of the democratic. Moreover, in Rancière's stance as explained by Hallward, the aesthetic regime of art 'embraces the endless confusion of art and non-art' and 'genuine art is what indistinguishes, in newly creative ways [...] art and the other of art'.[69]

Rancière harnesses the energy of such indistinction and rejects any simple schematization that would see writing equate to political content. Rather, he proposes three strands of equality within the terrain of literature. One of these (influenced by the work of Gilles Deleuze) sees literature opening out 'l'égalité moléculaire des micro-événements' ['the molecular equality of micro-events'].[70] Deleuze, we note, rejects the view that writing imposes form on lived experience and instead characterizes it as a becoming, as a fleeing rather than a possession. Writing entails what he terms a zone of indifferentiation and he argues that

> la langue se doit d'atteindre à des détours [...] moléculaires [...]. Il n'y a pas de ligne droite, ni dans les choses ni dans le langage. La syntaxe est l'ensemble des détours nécessaires chaque fois créés pour révéler la vie dans les choses.
>
> [Language must devote itself to reaching these (...) molecular detours (...). There are no straight lines, neither in things nor in language. Syntax is the set of necessary detours that are created in each case to reveal the life in things.][71]

68   *Politique de la littérature*, p. 19; *The Politics of Literature*, p. 11.
69   See Peter Hallward's Introduction to an interview conducted with Rancière, in 'Politics and Aesthetics: An Interview', trans. Forbes Morlock, *Angelaki: Journal of the Theoretical Humanities*, 8.2 (August 2003), 191–211 (p. 193).
70   *Politique de la littérature*, p. 35; *The Politics of Literature*, p. 25.
71   Gilles Deleuze, *Critique et clinique* (Paris: Minuit, 1993), p. 12; *Essays*

Concurrent with this borrowed notion of the molecular as liberational are the two other strands of equality that Rancière maps out: firstly, the availability of words and sentences to convey any life and to make that available to any reader; and secondly, the democracy, as he puts it, of 'des choses muettes' ['mute things'], words on the page being more elegant, he asserts, than both a prince in a tragedy and an orator of the people. The tensions created by and within these three strands, what Rancière calls 'the clash of these politics' ['le heurt de ces politiques'], are central to the understanding of literature.[72]

Critical and Clinical, trans. Daniel W. Smith and Michael A. Greco (London: Verso, 1998), p. 2.

72 *Politique de la littérature*, pp. 11, 35–36; *The Politics of Literature*, pp. 3, 26.

PART I

The Refrain of Class

CHAPTER ONE

Events and Sensibility in Claude Simon's *L'Acacia*

Je localiserai donc la politique de la fiction non du côté de ce qu'elle représente, mais du côté de ce qu'elle opère: des situations qu'elle construit, des populations qu'elle convoque, des relations d'inclusion ou d'exclusion qu'elle institue, des frontières qu'elle trace ou efface entre la perception et l'action, entre les états de choses et les mouvements de la pensée.

[I will therefore localize the politics of fiction not in terms of what it represents but in terms of what it operates: the situations that it constructs, the populations that it convokes, the relations of inclusion or of exclusion that it institutes, the borders that it traces or effaces between perception and action, between the states of things and the movements of thought.]

Rancière[1]

'The contingent fact of the division between rich and poor', to borrow Rancière's uncomplicated formulation, forms an important narrative strand in Claude Simon's novel *L'Acacia* (1989).[2] Describing a family whose class composition is atypical, Simon tells the story of the protagonist's parents: a bourgeois mother from south-west France and

---

1 Jacques Rancière, *Le Fil perdu. Essais sur la fiction moderne* (Paris: La Fabrique, 2014), pp. 12–13; *The Lost Thread: The Democracy of Modern Fiction*, trans. Steven Corcoran (London: Bloomsbury, 2017), p. xxxiii.

2 Jacques Rancière, *On the Shores of Politics*, trans. Liz Heron (London: Verso, 2007), p. 26. The French original reads: 'le fait contingent du partage des riches et des pauvres'; *Aux bords du politique* (Paris: Gallimard, 2004), p. 59.

a peasant father from near the Swiss border who, through military promotion, marries into the middle class. The groom's family observe that 'Elle n'est pas de notre milieu!' ['She is not from our circle!'], while on the bride's side, they reflect that 'Il n'est pas de notre monde' (A, 265) ['He is not from our world' (AA, 205)]. A series of negatives thus ushers in misalliance, with responses from both sides of the impending marriage creating an effect of 'affrontement symétrique' (A, 267) ['symmetrical confrontation' (AA, 207)]. The stress on a distribution of class spaces and identities, of social prominence and relegation, corroborates Rancière's key notion of *le partage du sensible* or the distribution of the sensible, a system of sense perception 'qui donne à voir en même temps l'existence d'un commun et les découpages qui y définissent les places et les parts respectives' ['that simultaneously discloses the existence of something in common and the delimitations that define the respective parts and positions within it'].[3] The marriage in *L'Acacia* encapsulates the notion of a *common* around which are worked apportionment and distribution.

Intersecting with the scaffolding provided by class schism in the novel is a second framing, that of global conflict. With his father killed in action in the First World War, the protagonist will in turn experience defeat in a cavalry regiment in northern France in late spring 1940. Yet in these parallel sets of adversarial relations – the muted workings of class war and war between nations – the portrayal of rivals in *L'Acacia* sees them drawn productively into strange forms of contiguity (families pulled out of class segregation and forced to accept transient forms of interaction and cohabitation, enemies in armed confrontation, the respective roles of civilians and soldiers). Contiguity often mutates into a levelling and an equalization. The body of a fallen soldier is presented as a dead weight no different from that of a dead horse or a sack of grain; nature is indifferent to human suffering just as war combatants, in turn, fail to see nature around them; and the living conditions in a brothel, a place which the traumatized protagonist comes to see as a sanctuary, recall the cramped spaces of military shelters near the front line. The effect created of indistinction and equalization extends to Simon's use of narrative poetics in that, in what Rancière presents as the democracy

3   See Jacques Rancière, *Le Partage du sensible. Esthétique et politique* (Paris: La Fabrique, 2000), p. 12; *The Politics of Aesthetics: The Distribution of the Sensible*, trans. and ed. Gabriel Rockhill (London: Bloomsbury, 2013 [2004]), p. 7. See also *Politique de la littérature*, p. 12; *The Politics of Literature*, p. 4.

of literature, as we saw above in the Introduction, words and sentences serve to capture any life and make it available to any reader. Simon's textual practice exemplifies what Rancière presents as the democratic practice that is the writing of prose, 'la coulée infinie de l'encre sur l'aplat des pages' ['the infinite flow of ink over the surface of the page'].[4]

*   *   *

Hierarchy forms a conspicuous theme from the opening pages of *L'Acacia*, where in 1919 a group of three women and a boy go in search of the burial place of their relative in the battlefields of northern France. In the narrator's description of the interactions between the protagonist's aunts and mother (the two siblings of the dead soldier and his widow), sisters-in-law are depicted as being equal in their grief but social unequals. Simon is careful to record two poverties that bind together the travelling women, the one economic, the other, the 'poverty of disaster' (AA, 4) ['celle du malheur' (A, 12)]. Status provides the template for understanding their interaction:

> Comme si elles lui [à elle] avaient tenu lieu de servantes ou, au mieux, de dames de compagnie, embrassant pourtant chacune d'elles quand elles se retrouvaient le matin ou se séparaient le soir, leur parlant avec cette douceur et cette patience légèrement contrariée, comme on le fait avec des personnes de condition inférieure, des parents pauvres, des vieillards ou des enfants, quoiqu'elles fussent visiblement plus âgées qu'elle, différant d'elle non seulement par leurs visages carrés, leurs mains carrées aussi – et même crevassées – mais encore par leurs vêtements qui, quoique aussi de couleur sombre, n'avaient ni cette théâtrale et ténébreuse uniformité, ni l'aspect de robes ou de manteaux coupés sur mesure par une couturière, mais taillés d'après un patron sur une table recouverte de toile cirée, faufilés et essayés sur elles-mêmes, et enfin tant bien que mal bâtis, trop étroits ou trop grands, ornés de cols ou de parements de fourrures usagées. (A, 15–16)

> [As if they had been her servants or, at best, ladies-in-waiting, though kissing each of them when they met in the morning or separated in the

4 Jacques Rancière, *La Parole muette. Essai sur les contradictions de la littérature* (Paris: Arthème Fayard/Pluriel, 2010 [1998]), p. 172; *Mute Speech: Literature, Critical Theory, and Politics*, trans. James Swenson, intro. Gabriel Rockhill (New York: Columbia University Press, 2011), p. 172.

evening, speaking to them with that gentleness and that slightly vexed patience, as to persons of an inferior rank, poor relatives, old people, or children, though they were obviously older than she, differing not only by their square faces, their square – and creased – hands, but even by their garments which, though also dark, did not have that showy and somber uniformity, nor the look of coats or dresses cut to order by a seamstress, but sewn together from a pattern on an oilcloth-covered table, basted and tried on themselves, and finally stitched up once and for all, too tight or too loose, embellished with collars or scraps of worn fur. (AA, 7)]

Simon tracks rank and subordination functioning at multiple levels: superiorities based on class, on physical looks, on material possessions; hierarchies deriving from the bodily marks that come with different occupations or that are reflected in contrasts of dress (the bespoke and the mass-produced, the coordinated and the random, the eye-catching – 'cette théâtrale [...] uniformité' – and the drab); and rank by age, here overridden by social standing. The bourgeois widow's choice of dress (which is all the more arresting in what had been the killing fields of northern France) has 'quelque chose d'ostentatoire, de théâtral' (A, 13) ['something showy, stagey' (AA, 5)]. From the beginning of *L'Acacia*, then, Simon consciously constructs a *mise en scène* of distribution and separation, the theatricality of power becoming a point of reference in the novel. Europe on the eve of war in 1914 is evoked as

> ce crépuscule d'un monde qui allait mourir en même temps que des millions de jeunes gens enterrés sous la boue et où se mêlaient les paradoxales et caricaturales images figées ou sautillantes de parades militaires, de jupes entravées, d'hommes d'Etat en calèches, de chapeaux fleuris, de casques à plumes, de french cancan, de princes en goguette et de comiques troupiers. (A, 123–24)

> [that twilight of a world which was going to die along with millions of young men buried under the mud and in which mingled the paradoxical and caricatural images, frozen or jerky, of military parades, of hobble skirts, of statesmen in barouches, of flowered hats, of plumed helmets, of French cancans, of intoxicated princes and comical old troopers. (AA, 93)]

State power and the pursuit of pleasure are tied to stagecraft and performance that are channelled through the new media of the day. (Excluded from the image-making yet graphically portrayed in Simon's narrative are the corpses of the war dead which are materially absorbed by the earth.)

Parade and spectatorship similarly pave the way for the peasant-
turned-captain to marry a wealthy bourgeois bride, his military dress
providing the necessary social guise or cover. But in the antagonistic
closeness framing this atypical marriage, the gap between distinction
and the plebeian persists. In their communication with locals in the
aftermath of war, the widow delegates to her sisters-in-law the task
of making enquiries as they search for the burial place of their dead
relative:

> En fait, elle ne formulait pas elle-même les questions, usant des deux
> femmes mal habillées comme des sortes d'interprètes, comme si elle-même
> n'avait pas parlé la même langue ou comme si quelque rite lui interdisait
> de s'adresser directement à des inconnus, se tournant vers ses deux
> compagnes, leur dictant la question qu'elles devaient poser, attendant
> qu'elles la répètent, écoutant les explications, le gras visage bourbonien
> toujours impassible derrière la trame du crêpe, les yeux seuls [...]
> brillant dans l'ombre du voile avec une espèce d'ardeur desséchée, d'éclat
> charbonneux, de fièvre. (A, 16).

> [Even so, she would not ask the questions herself, using the two ill-dressed
> women as interpreters, as if she herself had not spoken the same language
> or as if some ceremony forbade her to speak to strangers directly, turning
> to her two companions, telling them the question they were to ask,
> waiting while they repeated it, listening to the explanations, the full
> Bourbonian face impassive still behind the crape veil, only the eyes (...)
> gleaming in the shadow of the veil with a sort of wasted ardour, a charred
> luster, a fever. (AA, 7)]

Reinforcing the notion of power as theatrical narrative, Simon identifies
delegation as the preferred mode of communication of a widow whose
assumptions about inequality are ostentatiously signalled in the epithet
'Bourbonian'. The scene plays with audibility and visibility, thus again
enacting a *partage du sensible* and the apportionment of roles deriving
from it. The tension Rancière points to in the term *partage* (it signals
both a sharing and a dividing) has a bearing on the dynamic at work
within Simon's group of three itinerant women.[5] With certain social
transactions devolved to inferiors, the bourgeois widow's veil in *L'Acacia*
not only signals mourning but also reinforces exclusivity. As such, it is a
screen erected against the plebeian. Yet behind the aura of imperiousness
lies an expression of need:

---

5   See *Le Partage du sensible*, pp. 12–13; *The Politics of Aesthetics*, p. 7.

'Demandez-leur s'ils savent où …', puis déjà debout […] disant: 'Allons', disant: 'Demandez-leur si c'est loin. Demandez-leur si on peut trouver une voiture. Demandez-leur s'ils connaissent quelqu'un qui a une auto ou une carriole. Nous laisserons nos bagages ici. Dites-leur …'. (A, 18)

['Ask them if they know where …', then, already standing […] saying: 'Let's go now', saying: 'Ask them if it's far. Ask them if we can find a car. Ask them if they know someone who has a car or a wagon. We'll leave our things here. Tell them …'. (AA, 8–9)]

While the insistent use of the imperative form confirms that it is the subordinate who deputizes, the act of delegation in no way mitigates the urgency of the bourgeois widow's enquiry.

Within her own family, marriage to a soldier of peasant origins is viewed warily: he has entered their 'forteresse', their 'citadelle', and when they bid him farewell as he goes off to war in 1914,

elles avaient vu partir pour ne jamais revenir l'homme qui était entré dans la famille pour ainsi dire par effraction, par ravissement si l'on peut dire encore, appeler ainsi, dans les deux sens du terme, ce qui, en somme, avait été une sorte de rapt, un enlèvement. (A, 203)

[they had witnessed (…) the definitive departure of the man who had entered the family so to speak by breaking and entering, by ravishing if such might be called, in both senses of the word, what had been a sort of rape, an abduction. (AA, 156–57)]

Metalanguage here draws attention to property and abduction, and underscores the schismatic view of class provenance.

Bourgeois Catholicism further underpins conservatism in the novel, so that when the search party of three women find themselves in a convent, it is the widow who speaks:

Le jour où elles couchèrent dans le couvent (ou l'institution pour jeunes filles), la veuve parla longtemps le soir, […] avec les religieuses qui les hébergeaient, ses compagnes restant silencieuses sur leurs chaises, raides, leurs mains crevassées jointes au creux de leurs cuisses, leurs deux visages d'hommes dépourvus d'expression, écoutant, sans plus. (A, 21)

[The night they slept in the convent (or the institution for young girls), the widow talked a long time (…) with the nuns who had taken them in, her companions remaining silent on their chairs, stiff, their wrinkled hands folded in their laps, their two mannish faces expressionless, listening, nothing more. (AA, 11)]

Alongside the loquacious widow, her anti-clerical in-laws sit passively, their bodies serving as a further reminder of social fracture – in Simon's depiction, they are masculinized by hard physical toil. This imbrication of class and gender merits comment in that it suggests an historically formed view of femininity as reflecting cultural practices predicated on a separation from the world of labour. By virtue of their association with physical work, the soldier's sisters fall outside an inferred, culturally dominant, perception of femininity as a middle-class attribute. Their acquisition of masculine traits thus spells not emancipation but class confinement and exclusion from power.

Beyond the novel's opening pages, subsequent sections of *L'Acacia* return to this coupling of labour and identity. In Chapter III, the narrator notes in the sisters an 'austérité [...] fortifiée par cette orgueilleuse soif de justice, de décence et de dignité, cet esprit d'intraitable insoumission' (A, 64) ['austerity (...) enforced by that proud thirst for justice, for decency and dignity, that spirit of intractable insubordination' (A, 44)]. In recording their trenchant rejection of anything suggesting decadence, the narrator reconstructs the aunts' moralized perspective on the world. Had they lived at the time of the Reformation, he surmises, they would surely have been followers of Calvin. But whereas, for them, manual endeavour is synonymous with moral probity, the world view of his mother's family radically repositions virtue. She is described as having a laziness inherited from her ancestors, 'comme non pas un privilège mais en quelque sorte une vertu familiale, une obligation constituant la marque distinctive de sa caste et de son milieu social' (A, 114) ['as not a privilege but somehow a family virtue, an obligation constituting the distinctive sign of her caste and of her social milieu' (AA, 85)]. In a family that consumes without producing, the avoidance of labour sees the soldier-protagonist's mother dabble in reading, guitar playing, and photography. Simon underscores the extent to which the bride of the soldier from the Saint-Cyr military academy is removed from the reality of productive necessity: 'Il semblait qu'elle ignorât même qu'elle avait un corps et à quoi celui-ci pouvait servir' (A, 111) ['Apparently she was utterly unconscious that she possessed a body and what such a thing might be used for' (AA, 82)]. She is described as floating in a foetal state (A, 141; AA, 107), out of reach of the contingent world when with her husband during his colonial service in the Tropics.

The peasant women's absorption in labour, made manifest specifically through their masculinization, is illustrated in the image of the sister who returns to work on the family farm after the death of her father. She is described as being 'chaussée de lourds brodequins d'homme, son visage un peu carré se changeant peu à peu en un visage d'homme' (A, 66–67) ['wearing heavy men's boots, her squarish face gradually changing into a man's face' (AA, 46)]. Alongside this visual scrutiny of changing physiques sit other portraits of bodies at work. The bourgeois home of the bride-to-be of the First World War captain is a site of proletarian activity:

> de même que les autres fournisseurs et tapissiers, les couturières venaient à la maison, proposaient des modèles, offraient à feuilleter de lourdes liasses d'échantillons, revenaient et s'agenouillaient, leurs bouches hérissées d'épingles, pour les essayages, apportant et remportant robes et manteaux dans des carrés de serge noire noués aux quatre coins. (A, 110)

> [like the caterers and upholsterers, the dressmakers came to the house, showed their wares and models, offered to leaf through the heavy bundles of samples, returned and knelt, their mouths bristling with pins, for the fittings, bringing and carrying away dresses and coats in squares of black serge knotted at the four corners. (AA, 81–82)]

The stress on fabrics and furnishings, on moving, lifting, pinning up, and kneeling, maps onto a wider concern in the novel with artefacts and with bodies in movement. Labour appears to enter the home from without, the relationship to objects serving as an interpretative grid for an understanding of different classes.[6] Reflecting on labour in modern times, Hannah Arendt looks back to the ancient world in which the institution of slavery was an 'attempt to exclude labor from the conditions of man's life'. Hence Aristotle's insistence in the *Politics* that the slave lacks, in Arendt's words, 'the faculty to deliberate and decide (*to bouleutikon*) and to foresee and to choose (*proairesis*)'.[7] Arendt also makes the link between the role of women and that of slaves in Ancient Greece, in that their labours (in the case of women, ensuring the survival of the species) were hidden away 'because their life was "laborious", devoted to bodily functions'.[8] Arendt writes

6 For a Marxist exploration of how human relations are worked via the 'intermediary of objects', see Robert Linhart, *L'Établi* (Paris: Minuit, 1981 [1978]), with its account of the author's experience of working on a factory production line in France in the late 1960s.

7 Hannah Arendt, *The Human Condition*, intro. Margaret Canovan (Chicago and London: University of Chicago Press, 1998 [1958]), p. 84.

8 Arendt, *The Human Condition*, p. 72.

of the concealment of labour at the start of the modern age and of labourers 'segregated from the community'.[9] While the upper middle-class household in early twentieth-century provincial France in *L'Acacia* reflects a different historical moment, a principle of segregation persists in the matrix constructed in the novel around gender, labour, and class. The description of the dressmaker generates a conspicuous contrast between consumer and producer: 'la couturière [...] tournait autour d'elle à genoux comme une sorte de naine, d'amputée, parlant toujours à travers les épingles serrées entre ses lèvres' (A, 116–17) ['the dressmaker (...) circled her on her knees like a sort of amputee or dwarf, murmuring through the pins clenched between her lips' (AA, 87)]. Miniaturization underscores the subordination of the manual worker who, working with and through her body, occupies the role of *animal laborans*. Speech is here articulated literally through one of the tools of the dressmaker's labour.

At the same time, the dressmaker's improvisation, physical effort, and dexterity are set against the dependence and inactivity of the one who delegates. Indeed, in the case of the character whom fate destines to become a war widow, her inactivity presages a disturbing bodily metamorphosis. The narrator ominously depicts this person of leisure in animalistic terms, her slowness to marry being likened to an obscure premonition about what marriage and the war might hold for her:

> Elle n'était pas pressée. Comme si, à la façon de ces génisses préservées des taureaux, ignorantes même de leur existence et amoureusement engraissées pour quelque sacrifice [...], elle se savait destinée à quelque chose d'à la fois magnifique, rapide et atroce qui viendrait en son temps. (A, 113)

> [She was in no hurry. As if, like those heifers kept from the bulls, actually unaware of their existence and lovingly fattened for some sacrifice (...), she knew herself destined for something at once magnificent, swift, and cruel which would come in its time. (AA, 84)]

As with Simon's characterization of bodies that are transformed through labour, a proleptic grief is presented as moulding (and animalizing) the human frame.

Flaubert's contemporaries reacted against his equalization of 'high' and 'low' subjects, seeing in it a dangerous democratism, as we noted

---

9 Arendt, *The Human Condition*, pp. 72–73.

earlier.[10] In *L'Acacia*, the conflation of human and non-human features is a recurring motif, with biomorphic form sometimes used to give urgency to questions of social inequality. Thus, a group of very thin Africans on a pre-1914 colonial postcard are described as standing 'à mi-chemin entre le végétal et l'humain' (A, 130) ['halfway between the human and the vegetal' (AA, 98–99)]. Similarly, the gap between civilian life and the intense experience of war is marked biomorphically, with soldiers described as being 'à mi-chemin entre l'homme [...] et ces bêtes à carapace' (A, 192) ['halfway between man (...) and those spiny shellfish' (AA, 148)]. In another speculative analogy, such is the synergy between a cavalryman and his mount that he appears to belong to 'une espèce, une race spéciale, à mi-chemin entre le cheval et l'homme' (A, 221) ['a species, a special race, halfway between horse and man' (AA, 169)]. In noting this thread of hybridity and a remodelling of the human form, we can appreciate the relevance of the biographical fact that, before becoming a writer, Simon tried his hand at painting and was heavily influenced by Cubism and Surrealism.[11]

The move away from anthropocentrism marks a departure from traditional mimesis, as does Simon's eschewal of sequential chronology. With chapters arranged in non-chronological order yet signalling, in the form of minimalist titles, landmark years in the family history, Simon constructs a narrative in which the energies associated with the memories of war and of social segregation and privilege freely circulate. In the penultimate chapter (XI, '1910 – 1914 – 1940 ...'), the story of the 1914 wedding of the *rentière* and the soldier-meritocrat is focalized through the perspective of the groom's peasant sisters. Their malaise is exacerbated by the style of dress expected of them and in their reluctant attendance at a cathedral mass. Again, it is at the level of embodied experience that the narrator conveys their investment in the education of a younger sibling whom they are distressed to see marrying into a bourgeois Catholic milieu:

> Les deux sœurs, les deux femmes [...] avaient en quelque sorte servi de
> mère à ce frère de plusieurs années leur cadet, non pas l'allaitant de leurs

---

10   Rancière, *Politique de la littérature*, pp. 16–17; *The Politics of Literature*, p. 8; see Introduction, p. 19.

11   On leaving school, the young Simon dedicated himself to painting. See Mireille Calle-Gruber, *Claude Simon. Une vie à écrire* (Paris: Seuil, 2011), pp. 73–74. Calle-Gruber cites a 1967 interview in which, asked if his ambition had always been to be a writer, Simon replied that he had originally wanted to be a painter or a jockey.

seins qu'aucun homme n'avait jamais touchés mais le nourrissant pour ainsi dire de leur propre chair (ou plutôt du refus aux désirs de leur propre chair) à mesure que celle-ci se desséchait dans cette virginité non pas stérile mais sacrifiée ou plutôt conservée en offrande à cette incestueuse et austère passion. (A, 303)

[The two sisters, the two women (…) had somehow served as a mother to this brother several years their junior, not nursing him with their breasts which no man had ever touched but so to speak nursing him on their own flesh (or rather on the refusal of the desires of their own flesh) as that flesh withered into a virginity not sterile but sacrificed or rather preserved as an offering to that incestuous and austere passion. (AA, 233)]

Simon's dense prose points to a conflicted emotional economy in which the sisterly, the maternal, and a repressed eroticism are imbricated. For the would-be devotees of Calvin, the body is spent in a constricting absorption in material necessity, with the instinct of sibling duty acquiring both an ascetic and an erotic charge. Sibling sacrifice also sees them working mule-like in the fields on Sundays on their return from the remote primary schools where they teach (A, 65; AA, 45). That life and work might be coextensive is confirmed by the decision of one of the sisters to return to labouring on the family farm: 'l'aînée se résigna à réintégrer la condition dont le père avait voulu les sortir à jamais' (A, 66) ['the older sister resigned herself to returning to the condition from which the father had sought to release them forever' (AA, 46)]. In the process, manual work acquires a biological inflection, the linkage recalling Arendt's account of labour as 'the activity which corresponds to the biological process of the human body, whose spontaneous growth, metabolism, and eventual decay are bound to the vital necessities produced and fed into the life process by labor'.[12]

With the narrative in *L'Acacia* straddling the decades of the Third Republic, visualization of the past serves as a key medium of retrieval. In the parental wedding photographs, the discomfort of the groom's sisters derives from a misalignment between bodily frame and the requirements of a bourgeois dress code that would mask their social origins:

elles […] sont toujours là, entourées de palmiers nains, d'aspidistras, de la forêt des plantes en pot, suppliciées, raidies, assises sur les chaises dorées, revêtues comme par moquerie de leurs robes aux épaisses broderies […], leurs visages sans sourires écrasés sous leurs lourds chignons, embarrassées

---

12   Arendt, *The Human Condition*, p. 7.

de leurs mains d'hommes, dans ces corsages baleinés, ces jupes aux pesants tissus qui les revêtent comme des carapaces, des élytres ou des armures. (A, 306–07)

[they (…) are still there, surrounded by dwarf palms, by aspidistras, by the forest of potted plants, tormented, rigid, sitting on the gilt chairs, dressed as though derisively in their heavily embroidered gowns (…), their unsmiling faces crushed under their heavy chignons, embarrassed by their mannish hands, encased in those whaleboned blouses, those skirts of heavy fabrics which swathed them like carapaces, like elytra, like armor. (AA, 236–37)]

The baroque description shows bourgeois opulence working as phantasmagoria. The staging of prestige again sees power orchestrated visually through the sepia-toned photograph, just as, elsewhere in the novel, it is a literal dressing up that signals the hold of militarism, with senior officers wearing 'des uniformes de théâtre' (A, 58). With power play inseparable from its visualization, the peasant sisters, by contrast, stand as figures alienated from their dress and bodies and from the stagecraft underpinning bourgeois celebration. In that sense, they lack what Rancière sees as the emancipatory move he found in workers' archives, namely 'a will to enter the political realm of appearance, the affirmation of a capacity for appearance'.[13]

The cross-class marriage likewise entails exposure to forms of language and material culture that are unfamiliar to the bride. When she and her mother travel to meet the peasant family of her future husband, it is he who carries their luggage at the station and whom the driver addresses using the familiar *tutoiement*. The intrusion of a particular sociolect and of the physical effort which another class routinely delegates to a subordinate serve as shibboleths. With the soldier in the role of intermediary shuttling between different worlds, his future mother-in-law looks on his sisters with consternation. Not unlike the figure of the *animal laborans* in Aristotle's *Politics*, the sisters are seen as

des femmes, des gens qui devaient probablement lui apparaître non seulement au-dessous de ce qu'elle avait toujours considéré (avait été

---

13   Rancière, 'Politics and Aesthetics: An Interview', by Peter Hallward; quoted in Hallward, 'Staging Equality', p. 147. While in Simon, authority parades as spectacle, Hallward notes, importantly, that in Rancière's characterization of 'the police', power moves to deny spectacle to political subjects. Hallward is quoting from *Aux bords du politique*, p. 242.

habituée à considérer) comme le niveau séparant deux classes sociales, mais encore deux espèces différentes d'humanité. (A, 127)

[women, people who must probably seem to her not only beneath what she had always considered (had been in the habit of considering) the level separating two social classes, but even two different species of humanity. (AA, 96)][14]

Talk of a species boundary extends to the evocation of the captain's colonial service, where his wife, in a letter home to her mother, writes of the indigenous population: 'on se demande si ce sont des créatures humaines comme nous' (A, 130) ['you wonder if these are human beings like ourselves' (AA, 98)].

The encounters between in-laws in *L'Acacia* are both scenes of rupture and of paradoxical encounter. Unfolding in a form of border country, they exist as moments of transversality, to use Rancière's formulation, in which 'les territoires se perdent' ['the different jurisdictions disappear'].[15] The parallel voyages across classes undertaken by bride and groom in *L'Acacia* show the class certainties inherent in bourgeois Catholicism and in a peasant lifestyle reaffirmed but also relativized and unsettled.

The axis formed by the two world wars significantly amplifies the documentary function of the novel. Here again, class markers come sharply into focus through reference to the body and language. Many of the soldiers in 1914 are described as being illiterate peasants who speak dialect and have only a rudimentary understanding of French (A, 52; AA, 34). Likewise, body shape and physiognomy are stressed, the narrator focussing on musculature and the shapes of soldiers' heads. In his depiction of combatants in the Second World War, he similarly stresses

leur violence naturelle d'anciens valets de ferme, de laboureurs ou de manœuvres (mêmes visages rougeauds et ronds, mêmes muscles saillants des mâchoires mastiquant, mêmes mains aux ongles carrés, même façon de maintenir du pouce les morceaux de fromage sur les lames de couteau en les portant à leurs bouches) comme domestiquée. (A, 191)

[the violence natural to former farmhands, plowmen, or laborers (same round, reddish faces, same protruding muscles of chewing jaws, same

14   As we have noted, Arendt discusses the views of Aristotle on labour, slavery, and the material necessities of life; see Arendt, *The Human Condition*, pp. 83–84.
15   *La Méthode de l'égalité*, p. 64; *The Method of Equality*, p. 32.

square-nailed hands, same way of holding the pieces of cheese on the
blade of the knife with one thumb as they raised them to their mouths)
somehow domesticated. (AA, 147)]

Simon captures telescopically a global conflict which draws on the
energies of a class shaped by manual labour performed in an adversarial
social order that is intensely local. The anaphoric use of *même* ['same']
shows anatomical description sealing a class homogenization. The
narration has a visual, sculptural quality, the emphasis on the bodily and
the sensory further connecting with the arrangement of social power in
the world Simon is evoking.

As if to illustrate what Rancière calls 'la distribution des humains en
fonction de la possession ou de l'absence du temps' ['the distribution of
human beings in terms of having or lacking time'], Simon's narrative
draws out the intense corralling that comes with war.[16] Cavalrymen are
described as being angry against a world which pushes them towards
'quelque inéluctable destin de bestiaux' (A, 229) ['some ineluctable fate
of cattle' (AA, 176)]. Indeed, the narrator evokes the precariousness of
the cavalry regiment (Simon himself served in one in 1940), likening it
to the goat which serves as bait to draw the wolf, in other words the
German army, out of the woods.

The visual attention paid to somatic detail underscores the theme of
bodily vulnerability in *L'Acacia* and throws into relief the exemption
of some from the material relations of production. On the eve of the
Second World War, the cavalryman who, as a young war orphan in 1919,
had accompanied his mother and aunts as they searched for their dead
relative, now enjoys family wealth:

> tout ce qu'il avait à faire était d'apposer sa signature au bas de petits
> rectangles de papier portant avec la date la somme à payer et ressortir
> d'une banque ou de quelque agence avec en poche la sueur monnayée
> des hommes et des chevaux qui arpentaient pour lui des hectares de
> vignes dont il ne connaissait même pas l'emplacement exact, seulement
> approximatif. (A, 162)

> [all he had to do was to scrawl his signature at the bottom of little
> rectangles of paper bearing along with the date the amount to be paid and
> walk out of the bank or the agency with, in his pocket, the coined sweat
> of the men and horses that worked for him on acres of vines of which he
> knew only the approximate whereabouts. (AA, 123)]

16   *La Méthode de l'égalité* p. 124; *The Method of Equality*, p. 67.

Reflecting on conventions underpinning monetary transaction, Aristotle saw in the use of coinage an 'artificial trumpery having no root in nature'.[17] Noting the etymological link in Greek between *nomisma* [coinage] and *nomos*, meaning convention, we see that Simon is articulating a protest against the convention that normalizes the disjunction between a wealth accessed through an act of inscription on paper and the physical labour which produces such wealth.[18] The experience of the *rentier*'s father who, a generation earlier, had toiled in remote postings in what is presented as a form of ascesis highlights the divide. Thus, it is physical labour that enables the father to purchase a diamond ring – 'le caillou magique' (A, 211) ['the magic pebble' (AA, 163)] – for his future bride. Here, too, the disconnection between a symbol of monetary value and the labour underpinning it, between commodity consumption and the spending of the body, confirms the sense of arbitrary apportionment.[19] Simon works redistributively by evoking 'the coined sweat' of both horses and humans, thereby not only rendering labour visible but also fostering a non-anthropocentric sensibility. Indeed, in his evocations of France's defeat in 1940, both in *L'Acacia* and elsewhere (notably in *La Route des Flandres*), the plight of non-human animals is central to the portrayal of disaster.

These forms of equalization signal protest functioning at the level of representation in respect of a number of excluded groups in *L'Acacia*: the mule-like peasant women who are the protagonist's siblings (A, 71; AA, 50); other humans and animals who toil on the land; 'tous les trains de la vieille Europe emplis de chairs juvéniles' (A, 172) ['all the trains of old Europe filled with young flesh' (AA, 132)] in the run-up to war in 1939; agricultural labourers heading off to war, the chin straps on their helmets likened to muzzles (A, 192; AA, 148); horses whose carcasses sink into the mud of the battlefield (A, 236; AA, 182); the mule-like prostitutes to whom a traumatized protagonist turns on his escape from a prisoner-of-war camp (A, 350; AA, 272). The constricted space

17   Aristotle, *The Politics*, trans. T. A. Sinclair, rev. ed. Trevor J. Saunders (London: Penguin, 1992), p. 83.

18   The information on etymology is here taken from the editorial note provided in Aristotle, *Politics*, p. 83 n. 6.

19   Hannah Freed-Thall reflects on a 'collective investment of belief' in certain forms of rock in her discussion of Proust's treatment of the Lemoine Affair, which involved a story of fake diamonds; see *Spoiled Distinctions: Aesthetics and the Ordinary in French Modernism* (Oxford: Oxford University Press, 2015), p. 28.

of the brothel, as was noted above, reminds him of the cramped living quarters on the battlefield. It is also in the brothel that he hears the use of familiar, diminutive forms of speech ['le diminutif de vocabulaire' (A, 366)], which for fourteen months had been a feature of his interaction with fellow soldiers and, later, prisoners of war. These echoes not only remind the reader of the interactions negotiated around social frontiers in *L'Acacia*, but also show an author mindful of the instrumentalization of bodies and the distribution of spaces exacted by war and exploitative labour.

*   *   *

While Simon stresses the linkage of work to productive necessity and foregrounds the place of cultural objects and identities, the poetic function of language in the novel rivals the prevalence of these themes. To put this in somewhat different terms, the narrative takes the reader to the frontier between what Rancière terms 'les états de choses et les mouvements de la pensée' ['the states of things and the movements of thought'].[20] Simon himself reflects explicitly on questions to do with compositional method and narrative poetics. His narrator describes sounds of explosions in war as coming out of 'un autre monde, anachronique pour ainsi dire' (A, 95) ['another world, anachronistic as it were' (A, 70)], while for those participating in it, the everyday is 'scandaleux et insupportable' (A, 358) ['scandalous and unendurable' (AA, 278)]. The post-event narration risks contributing to that scandal, being more betrayal than portrayal of the experience of *la débâcle* in that it constructs

> au lieu de l'informe, de l'invertébré, une relation d'événements telle qu'un esprit normal [...] pouvait la constituer après coup, à froid, conformément à un usage établi de sons et de signes convenus, c'est-à-dire suscitant des images à peu près nettes, ordonnées, distinctes les unes des autres, tandis qu'à la vérité cela n'avait ni formes définies, ni noms, ni adjectifs, ni sujets, ni compléments, ni ponctuation (en tout cas pas de points), ni exacte temporalité, ni sens, ni consistance sinon celle, visqueuse, trouble, molle, indécise, de ce qui lui parvenait à travers cette cloche de verre plus ou moins transparente sous laquelle il se trouvait enfermé. (A, 280)

20   The epigraph to the present chapter provides a fuller quotation from Rancière's *Le Fil perdu*.

[instead of something shapeless, invertebrate, a relation of events that
a normal mind (...) might constitute after the fact, according to an
established usage of sights and sounds accepted and agreed upon, that
is, giving rise to more or less clear and orderly images, distinct from
each other, while in truth this had neither definite shapes nor names nor
adjectives nor subjects nor complements nor punctuation (in any case no
periods), nor exact temporality, nor meaning, nor consistency if not that
– viscous, murky, soft, indeterminate – of what reached him, through
that more or less transparent glass bell under which he was imprisoned.
(AA, 216)]

In the inability of scriptural and other conventions to convey the
experience of lived trauma, Simon signals a perceptual misalignment.
The narrator identifies the challenge he faces at the level of poiesis:
'essayer avec des mots de faire exister l'indicible' (A, 340) ['trying with
words to make the unspeakable exist' (AA, 263)]. This notational
deficiency shapes the novelist's aesthetic endeavour, with the dazed
perceptions of the protagonist-combatant translating into a particular
form of narration. To frame this in terms of Rancière's reflection
on the politics of literature considered earlier, narrative poetics in
L'Acacia delivers its own politics in respect of the social referent.
Rancière writes, paraphrasing Deleuze, that equality in the novel is
not the equality of democratic subjects but rather 'l'égalité moléculaire
des micro-événements' ['the molecular equality of micro-events'].[21]
Simon's *informe*, the shapeless, can be linked to this stress on the
molecular.

Visual stills, mediated verbally, are pivotal in the representation of
perception in *L'Acacia*. Jean Duffy likens Simon's method to that of
Cézanne, observing that the use of the present participle allows the
novelist to cut 'gesture loose from its [beginning] and its [end], from
its motivation and its outcome'.[22] A description of cavalrymen caught
unawares by an enemy plane passing overhead takes on an ekphrastic
character:

figés soudain, s'immobilisant, la boîte de conserve tenue d'une main, le
couteau à mi-chemin des lèvres, cessant de mastiquer au milieu d'une
bouchée, assourdis, et restant encore ainsi, pareils à des statues de sel [...]

21   *Politique de la littérature*, p. 35; *The Politics of Literature*, p. 25. See the
closing section of the Introduction, above (pp. 20–21).
22   Jean H. Duffy, *Reading Between the Lines: Claude Simon and the Visual
Arts* (Liverpool: Liverpool University Press, 1998), p. 224.

glacés [...], comme pétrifiés, tandis que le bruit démentiel des moteurs diminuait, s'éteignait, aussi vite qu'il avait fondu sur eux. (A, 32–33)

[suddenly frozen, immobilized, the opened can held in one hand, the knife halfway to the lips, no longer chewing what was in their mouths, deafened, and immobilized right there, like statues of salt (...) paralyzed (...) as though petrified, while the maddening noise of the engine diminished, faded away, as quickly as it had burst over them. (AA, 19)]

In a movement of suspension, the visual and the textual hold the moment of danger and simultaneously work to circumvent it. Within the sensorium that is constructed, the visual and the auditory stand in a relationship of rivalry: accompanying the aural assault announced by aerial danger is the recording of the visual instant by a subject who is described, as the preceding quotation shows, as being held under a glass bell. The scene captures in emblematic form what Rancière refers to as 'events of sensibility that challenge causal hierarchies'.[23] War as a violent pursuit of ends forms one such causal hierarchy, whereas the event of sensibility that is memory's freeze-frame stands as a refusal of such ends and the means that serve them. Protesting against those who hold 'un droit absolu de vie et de mort' (A, 45) ['an absolute power of life and death' (AA, 30)], the narrator lays bare the mystique surrounding the powerful:

Pas un homme: une entité, un symbole, l'incarnation enfin visible [...], la délégation matérialisée de cette toute-puissance occulte et sans visage dans laquelle ils [les soldats] englobaient pêle-mêle généraux, politiciens, éditorialistes et tout ce qui touchait de près ou de loin à ce pandémonium. (A, 36)

[Not a man: an entity, a symbol, the at-last visible incarnation (...), the materialized delegation of that occult and faceless omnipotence in which (the soldiers) included, pell-mell, generals, politicians, journalists, and whoever else was in any way related to that pandemonium. (AA, 22)]

With ideological domination acquiring a life-denying force, the narrator's imagination draws on the resources of biomorphic form in an attempt to counter social coercion. Imagining a mythical creature formed of the fusion, in 'une matière semblable à du métal' (A, 31) ['some metallic

---

23   Jacques Rancière, 'On Aisthesis: An Interview, Jacques Rancière and Oliver Davis', trans. Steven Corcoran, in Oliver Davis (ed.), *Rancière Now: Current Perspectives on Jacques Rancière* (Cambridge: Polity, 2013), pp. 202–18 (p. 213).

substance' (AA, 18)], of cavalryman and horse, the narrator links this metonymically to the iron used to shoe the regiment's horses. The hybrid form signals a new kinesis, its aim being not to walk on the earth but to move above it:

> la frappant ou plutôt l'effleurant à peine de ses fins sabots graissés, et pas tellement pour y prendre appui que pour la faire allègrement retentir comme une sonore coupole de bronze sous les chocs légers et scandés. (A, 31)

> [barely striking (the ground) or brushing it with its delicate oiled hooves, and not so much to gain support from it as to make it echo gaily like a ringing bronze dome under the light and rhythmic blows. (AA, 18)]

In imagination's event, to use Rancière's term, the generation of cadence and euphony functions redemptively, the sensorial composition serving to occlude war's utilitarian ends. In the fraying of the link to representationality, it approximates to the 'poétique antireprésentative' that is central to Rancière's work on art.[24]

More broadly, as a project of writing, *L'Acacia* articulates a longing to suspend the hold that events have on the protagonist. He wearily sees history as a rotting corpse but also, warily, as an all-devouring force whose battlefields absorb dead horses and cavalrymen (A, 236; AA, 182). In 1914, as the protagonist's parents cross the ocean back to Europe, his mother is photographed on board ship,

> souriante, comme si le photographe avait saisi ce fugace instant d'immobilité, d'équilibre, où parvenue à l'apogée de sa trajectoire et avant d'être de nouveau happée par les lois de la gravitation la trapéziste se trouve en quelque sorte dans un état d'apesanteur, libérée des contraintes de la matière, pouvant croire le temps d'un éblouissement qu'elle ne retombera jamais, qu'elle restera ainsi à jamais suspendue dans l'aveuglante lumière des projecteurs au-dessus du vide, du noir. (A, 141)

> [smiling, as if the photographer had seized the fugitive instant of immobility, of equilibrium, in which having reached the apogee of her trajectory and before being once again subject to the laws of gravitation the trapeze artist finds herself in a sort of weightless state, liberated from the constraints of matter, able to believe for a second that she will never fall, that she will remain thus forever suspended in the blinding glare of the spotlights above the void, the abyss. (AA, 108)]

24 *La Parole muette*, p. 56; *Mute Speech*, p. 74.

With the photograph predating the return to France and the captain's death in battle, it captures a world before calamity. Like Genet's tightrope walker for whom entry into the 'dramaturgy' of the circus brings 'la solitude mortelle' ['mortal solitude'], the focus on kinesis in the trapeze act in Simon serves as both trailer and counterpoint to impending disaster.[25] Simon's prose tracks the instant of freezing and of apparent suspension in which the pull of matter seems momentarily nullified, allowing the acrobat to hang. It is as though the literary imagination, shaped by what subsequent events were to bring, effects a creative act of resistance. In this conjuncture, weightlessness acts as a force directed against the gravitational pull of war. In a similar retreat from what is material, the reflections of soldiers in troop-carrier windows are recorded as 'les doubles immatériels et immobiles des occupants assis ou couchés sur les banquettes' (A, 158) ['the immaterial and motionless doubles of the passengers sitting or lying on the benches' (AA, 120)].

The improbable prolongation of sound is another event of sensibility used by Simon to counter social mimesis. Hence the atmospheric reconstruction of the day in 1914 when news of the death of a soldier in battle is frantically relayed by his widow to her elderly relatives bathing on the coast in south-west France. While the sound of her voice on that occasion is dispersed, 'se perdant dans le fracas des rouleaux, les cascades de l'écume, l'immensité' (A, 205) ['lost in the racket of the waves, the cascades of foam, the immensity' (AA, 158)], it is as though sixty-eight years later, the cries continue to resonate on the beach. The work of orchestration in the narrator's synaesthetic reconstruction of calamitous news as it breaks on the beach pits the human voice against the expanse of land and sea. Protest is thus again articulated through aisthesis, in the etymological sense of feeling or perception.[26]

These tense moments of verbal choreography punctuate *L'Acacia*. They function almost as sound pieces, as though illustrating what

25 Jean Genet, *Le Funambule*, in *Œuvres complètes*, 5 vols (Paris: Gallimard, 1979), V, 15.
26 Rancière foregrounds the etymological link between aisthesis and sensory experience in *Aisthesis. Scènes du régime esthétique de l'art* (Paris: Galilée, 2011); *Aisthesis: Scenes from the Aesthetic Regime of Art,* trans. Zakir Paul (London: Verso, 2013). We can thus note, for example, that when conveying the idea of 'humans alone [having] *perception* of good and evil', Aristotle uses aisthesis in the original Greek. See *Politics*, p. 60 and the accompanying editorial note 19.

Rancière describes as the 'paradigme esthétique [qui] se construit contre l'ordre représentatif' ['aesthetic paradigm (...) constructed against the representative order'], as a rejection of plot seen as a series of actions.[27] Another conspicuous manifestation of this occurs as the narrator reconstructs the audibility of hooves as the protagonist's cavalry regiment moves out onto an asphalt road in northern France in 1940:

à peine avaient-ils commencé à s'ébranler que le brigadier entendit le bruit: immémorial, comme parvenant des profondeurs de l'Histoire, menu pour commencer, insidieux, comme un léger grignotement de rat, un grésillement qui, tout d'abord, lorsque les premiers chevaux (ceux de la tête de la colonne) s'engagèrent sur la route asphaltée, s'ajoutait simplement à celui de la pluie, puis allant croissant, s'amplifiant à mesure que les uns après les autres les cavaliers qui le précédaient s'engageaient à leur tour sur la route, puis tout près, puis il put entendre les quatre fers de sa propre monture martelant maintenant l'asphalte sous lui, le bruit, le crépitement qu'il pouvait à présent décomposer en une quantité de chocs proches ou lointains, non seulement devant lui mais tout autour de lui, continuant à s'enfler, à croître, de sorte qu'à la fin il se trouva complètement noyé, précédé et suivi par cette *alarmante et tranquille* rumeur faite de centaines de sabots chaussés de centaines de fers s'élevant et s'abaissant, frappant le sol en un dur et multiple crépitement, continu, qui semblait emplir la nuit tout entière, s'étaler, formidable, *désastreux et statique*. (A, 234–35; emphasis added)

[no sooner had they begun to move than the corporal heard the sound: immemorial, as though rising out of the depths of History, faint to begin with, insidious, like a faint nibbling of rats, a pattering which, at first, when the first horses (those at the head of the column) turned onto the paved road, was simply added to that of the rain, then growing louder, amplified as one after the other the cavalrymen ahead of him took the paved road in their turn, then very close by, then he could hear the four shoes of his own horse pounding the asphalt beneath him, the sound, the pattering which he could now decompose into a quantity of near or remote shocks, not only ahead of him but all around him, continuing to swell, to grow, so that at the end he found himself completely drowned, preceded and followed by that *alarming and tranquil* murmur, consisting of hundreds of hooves to which were nailed hundreds of iron shoes, rising and falling, striking the ground in a continuous hard and multiple pattering which seemed to fill the whole night, to spread everywhere, formidable, *disastrous, and static*. (AA, 181)]

---

27 *Aisthesis*, p. 15; *Aisthesis: Scenes from the Aesthetic Regime of Art*, p. xiv.

In the invitation simultaneously to read, hear, and visualize, Simon opens up an intersensorial space. In the darkness of the night, hearing dominates the sensory apparatus. The verbal composition approximates at one level to a musical score in its multiple annotations; at another, it seeks to replicate the effect of aural crescendo, the orchestration culminating in the generation of a sound which announces both imminent disaster and the idea of conflict as something immemorial. The retinal privilege associated with the written text is here challenged by the invitation to 'read with one's ears'.[28] In its performative dimension, the text allows the reader to see wartime experience and the associated traumatic memory reconstructed through, but also reconfigured as, word, sound, and image. Simon's manoeuvre thus acquires a dissenting function in respect of the referential world and illustrates Rancière's point that literariness undoes 'the relationships between the order of words and the order of bodies that determine the place of each'.[29]

The stress on audibility in Simon's reconstruction of the nocturnal cavalry scene throws into relief the visual medium of silent words on the page. In his introduction to *Courts voyages au pays du peuple*, Rancière refers to writers 'assemblant les mots qui marquent la recherche du lieu et la scansion de son absence' ['putting together the words that mark the quest for a place and the scansion of its absence'].[30] Arrangement and scansion are central to Simon's word sequence. He effects closure through reference to a perception of sonorous intensity which, on achieving full amplification, culminates in stasis. In casting the sound of cavalry as both 'alarmante et tranquille', and again as 'désastreux et statique', he acknowledges war's calamity while at the same time attempting a striking neutralization of that conflict, and seeking indifference to it, through immobility.

Reading the scenario of stasis through the lens constructed by Rancière in *Aisthesis*, it is immobility that signals an aesthetic moment. Rancière reflects on literature and the visual arts in the period between the eighteenth

28 Material drawn from Sarah Kay, 'How Opera Taught Me to Read', plenary lecture delivered to the Annual Conference of the Society for French Studies, Cork, July 2018.

29 Rancière, *Disagreement: Politics and Philosophy*, p. 37; quoted in Jussi Palmusaari, 'For Revolt: Breaks from Time and Uses of Spatiality in the Work of Jacques Rancière' (unpublished PhD thesis, Kingston University, London, 2017), p. 101.

30 *Courts voyages au pays du peuple*, p. 12; *Short Voyages to the Land of the People*, p. 5.

and twentieth centuries, seeing as foundational the role of the art historian Johann Winckelmann. He hails the eighteenth-century pioneer as opening

> cet âge où les artistes s'emploieront à déchaîner les puissances sensibles cachées dans l'inexpressivité, l'indifférence ou l'immobilité, à composer les mouvements contrariés du corps dansant mais aussi bien de la phrase, du plan ou de la touche colorée *qui arrêtent l'histoire en la racontant, suspendent le sens en le faisant passer ou dérobent la figure même qu'ils désignent.*

> [that age during which artists were busy unleashing the sensible potential hidden in inexpressiveness, indifference or immobility, composing the conflicting movements of the dancing body, but also of the sentence, the surface, or the coloured touch *that arrest the story while telling it, that suspend meaning while transmitting it or avoid the very figure they designate.*][31]

Although the immediate context to which Rancière is applying Winckelmann is early twentieth-century dance, he opens this out to include other aesthetic forms, referring to a plurality of compositions of movement. Simon's rendering of the nocturnal wartime scene provides an important instantiation of such compositional plurality in that he works with movement that is simultaneously textual, bodily, and auditory – the word chain depicting animal bodies and recording the percussive ringing of hooves on tarmac. The same extract from *L'Acacia* tells the story and suspends it, transmits history and freezes it. The revisitation of such scenes and their conversion into sound pieces and stills is consistent with the novel's eschewal of chronological sequence.

In military terms, the French use of cavalry in 1940 marked a leftover from another era, Simon referring to the regiment's 'anachroniques montures' (A, 234) ['anachronistic steeds' (AA, 180)] and to how it served as bait for the German wolf. His narration of the cavalry march echoes an earlier, memorable scene in twentieth-century French literature where we again find the technique of a story/history that is both told and frozen. In *À la recherche du temps perdu*, Proust's narrator celebrates the cavalry parade as it passes noisily through the streets of Combray. Unlike the Simon text, the event of heightened perception here takes place in peacetime, although the housekeeper Françoise links the young soldiers as they pass to the bloody conflict which, in her eyes, invariably awaits

---

31 *Aisthesis*, p. 28, emphasis added; *Aisthesis: Scenes from the Aesthetic Regime of Art*, p. 9 (translation modified).

them. Yet common to both textual moments is the effect of suspension of the kind Rancière identifies as a function of the aesthetic moment. In *À la recherche,* the movement of suspension acquires a primarily visual framing (in contrast with the stress on auditory intensity in the scene from *L'Acacia*). In Proust's street scene, the spectators who remain behind after the cavalry parade are described as forming

> un liséré capricieux et sombre comme celui des algues et des coquilles dont une forte marée laisse le crêpe et la broderie au rivage, après qu'elle s'est éloignée.

> [a border as dark and irregular as the border of sea-weed and shells whose crêpe and embroidery are left on the shore by a strong tide after it recedes.][32]

The metaphor of traces left by an earlier flow or agitation thus serves to close the run of prose that is the paragraph. Proust's reference to fabric and embroidery reminds us how, elsewhere in his novel, the narrator explicitly favours the link between sewing and textual assemblage when he likens his work to that of Françoise. As if to illustrate Rancière's point about aisthesis entailing 'une surface de conversion d'un corps dans un autre' ['a surface for converting one body into another'], the use of mutation and conversion in the street scene in Combray shows the vestiges of tidal movement – the crêpe and the embroidery – approximating to the scriptural traces left by the writer's composition.[33] A new order of words, to draw again on Rancière's formulation, unsettles the order of bodies.[34]

In a 1973 interview with Viviane Forrester referred to above, Simon, asked why he wrote, reflected that it was 'pour faire' ['to make'].[35] Just

32   M. Proust, *À la recherche du temps perdu*, 4 vols (Paris: Gallimard, 1987–1989), I, 89. Subsequent references to the novel are made using the abbreviation RTP. The English translation used is *In Search of Lost Time*, ed. Christopher Prendergast, 6 vols (London: Penguin, 2003); hereinafter cited as ISLT. The translation is here taken from *The Way by Swann's*, trans. Lydia Davis, ISLT, I, 91.

33   See *Aisthesis*, p. 28; *Aisthesis: Scenes from the Aesthetic Regime of Art*, p. 9. Adam Watt refers to the 'sensuality of texture and surface' in relation to the beginning and the closure of the passage in question; see *Reading in Proust's 'À la recherche': 'le délire de la lecture'* (Oxford: Clarendon Press, 2009), p. 43.

34   For my earlier discussion of the street scene in Combray, see Hughes, *Proust, Class, and Nation* (Oxford: Oxford University Press, 2011), pp. 79–84.

35   http://next.liberation.fr/livres/2013/10/11/l-album-de-l-ecrivain-claude-simon_938468. See above, Introduction, p. 13.

as someone else might build a bridge or a house or perform a surgical operation, he chooses to write in order to 'faire un objet écrit' ['make a written object']. The thing made should be free-standing, he added, like a table with its four legs. As the broader context of the interview makes clear, Simon's analogy is devoid of irony, ostentation, or undue modesty.

As *L'Acacia* moves towards its conclusion, the reader sees Simon's protagonist recalling wartime imprisonment. In exchange for cigarettes from his jailers, he had produced erotic sketches done in pencil. He likens drawing to other manual activities such as the pruning of plants and plastering. These images of equivalence which ground the order of art in making and materiality feed through into the denouement. In his family library, the protagonist reads books that show marginal annotations in ink; he acquires and reads the whole of Balzac's *La Comédie humaine*; he frequents a local painter who invariably draws the same orchard scene; and he resumes reading newspapers with their accounts of the continuing war. The focus on ink, text, paint, and canvas serves as prelude to the final image of the protagonist sitting in front of a blank page one spring evening and preparing to create a written object. At the window, he sees the branches of an acacia, 'avec leurs feuilles semblables à des plumes palpitant faiblement sur le fond de ténèbres' (A, 371) ['their leaves like feathers faintly palpitating against the darkness' (AA, 289)]. With the protagonist embarking on textual construction, the artisanal character of the writer's endeavour is thus transparently signalled in the conflation of paper and wood facilitated by the term 'feuille' (paper/leaf). The whole tree shakes and its leaves become agitated, 'après quoi tout s'apaisait et elles reprenaient leur immobilité' (A, 371) ['after which everything subsided and they became motionless again' (AA, 289)]. With a generation of stillness bringing about narrative closure, Simon takes the reader back to the link between the immobile and the aesthetic. War's calamity and social fracture are thus channelled through an individual sensibility which engages with the event (France's colonial legacy, global war, class segregation) while also constructing an event of sensibility. In an interview published in 2013, Rancière reflects on aesthetics in these terms: 'One builds, all in all, a system of conditions of possibility, a system which can be shown to render thinkable the singular mutations that gather in the existence of a sphere of experience called art or of a mode of subjectivation called sentiment or aesthetic judgement'.[36]

---

36 Rancière makes the comments in Jean-Luc Nancy and Jacques Rancière, 'Rancière and Metaphysics (Continued) – A Dialogue', trans. Steven Corcoran,

In the turn to paper and writing, Simon effects an act of disidentification to the extent that, by occupying a space of mutation, he attends to the referent and yet works to undo its hold.[37]

in Oliver Davis (ed.), *Rancière Now: Current Perspectives on Jacques Rancière* (Cambridge: Polity, 2013), pp. 187–201 (p. 191).

37   Kristin Ross refers to the breaking of allegiance to the State and its political system as 'a severing of identification'. She makes the comment in relation to the killing of protestors in Paris in October 1961, with Rancière's reflection on those events forming part of her analysis. See K. Ross, *May '68 and Its Afterlives* (Chicago and London: University of Chicago Press, 2002), p. 57. For earlier discussion of Rancière's perspective on October 1961 as set out in his 'Politics, Identification, and Subjectivization', see the Introduction, p. 12 n. 40.

CHAPTER TWO

'Les Savoirs de la main'

Dramas of Manual Knowledge
in Péguy and Beinstingel

[L]'honneur du foyer et l'honneur de l'atelier était le même honneur. C'était l'honneur du même lieu. C'était l'honneur du même feu.

[The honour of the home and the honour of the atelier were the same honour. It was the honour of the same place. It was the honour of the same fire.]

Péguy[1]

'Dragging texts from one time period into another, […] launching the provocative force of these past texts into the present' is how Rancière characterizes a method of juxtaposition which he frequently practises. It is a move that sees him sidestep historicism.[2] The current chapter attempts an alignment of texts, one an essay by Charles Péguy from the early twentieth century in which he protests against a new era of industrial mechanization in France, the other a short novel by Thierry Beinstingel published a century later in an age of post-industrial cultural change. Both works can be described as articulating a quarrel

---

1   Charles Péguy, *L'Argent*, in *Œuvres en prose complètes* (Paris: Gallimard (Bibliothèque de la Pléiade), 1992), III, 792. Subsequent citations of the text are made using the abbreviation Arg, with an accompanying page number.

2   'Understanding Modernism, Reconfiguring Disciplinarity: Interview with Jacques Rancière on May 11, 2015', in Patrick M. Bray (ed.), *Understanding Rancière, Understanding Modernism* (New York and London: Bloomsbury Academic, 2017), pp. 263–89 (p. 281); cited by Caitlyn Doyle in her review of the volume in *H-France Review,* 18.218 (November 2018).

between old and new social practices. In particular, the hold of new orthodoxies is contested in each case by an anti-modern orientation that is channelled specifically through an interrogation of the status of manually performed labour.

Few tributes in French literature to the world of artisanal craft are more passionate and urgent than the one to be found in Péguy's essay *L'Argent* (1913). Voicing nostalgia for an age that predates industrial mass production, the work glorifies an older order in which, Péguy asserts, workers pursued their tasks as a form of honour:

> Il fallait qu'un bâton de chaise fût bien fait. C'était entendu. C'était un primat. Il ne fallait pas qu'il fût bien fait pour le salaire [...]. Il ne fallait pas qu'il fût bien fait pour le patron ni pour les connaisseurs ni pour les clients du patron. (Arg, 791)

> [A chair rung had to be well made. That was the understanding. That was the rule. It didn't have to be well made for reasons to do with pay (...). It didn't have to be well made for the employer or the connoisseur or the employer's clients.]

In pages reminiscent of the nineteenth-century historian Michelet, whose writing he championed, Péguy insists that the artisan's attitude towards work and skill is shaped by a millennial tradition, 'montée du plus profond de la race, une histoire, un absolu, un honneur voulait que ce bâton de chaise fût bien fait' (Arg, 792) ['going far back in the history of the race, an absolute, an honour required that the chair rung be well made']. The meticulous pursuit of craft applies as much to what is out of view as to what is displayed, so that, in the case of France's cathedrals, their hidden parts, Péguy observes, are no less perfect than those that are plainly visible. He casts his mother as a counter-cultural figure, misaligned with a modernity that has seen the rise of the syndicalist organization of labour. As if to reverse Marx's exhortation to have the present dominate the past, Péguy dissents unambiguously from contemporaneous culture.[3] Yet Péguy's desire to look back is not to be explained by the bourgeois hold on accumulated economic capital. Recalling his mother's work as an upholsterer, he reminisces: 'J'ai vu toute mon enfance rempailler des chaises exactement du même esprit et

---

3   In the well-known line from *The Communist Manifesto*, the past's domination of the present in bourgeois society is reversed in communist society; see Karl Marx and Friedrich Engels, *The Communist Manifesto*, trans. Samuel Moore, intro. A. J. P. Taylor (London: Penguin, 1985), pp. 97–98.

du même cœur, et de la même main, que ce même peuple avait taillé ses cathédrales' (Arg, 790) ['Throughout my childhood I saw chairs being reseated with the same mind and heart and hand with which this same people had built its cathedrals']. The prominence of anaphora gives an insistent tone to an idealized, conservative language of filial piety. It also marks a wider tribute to earlier generations defined by their work:

> Comment travaillait ce peuple [...] qui tout entier aimait le travail tout entier, qui était laborieux et encore plus travailleur, qui se délectait à travailler, qui travaillait tout entier ensemble, bourgeoisie et peuple, dans la joie et dans la santé; qui avait un véritable culte du travail; un culte, une religion du travail bien fait.[4]

> [How this people worked, a people that in its entirety loved everything to do with work, a people that was hard-working and profoundly industrious, which delighted in working, which worked wholly together, bourgeoisie and people, in joy and health; which practised a veritable cult of work; a cult, a religion of work well done.]

The hypnotic lexical repetition marks an obsessive, often ponderous style of composition aimed at showcasing labour as a socially constitutive force. It is as though Péguy stages on the written page a ceremony in language, a compositional event, this in commemorative tribute to a past labour that is itself endowed with a ceremonial aura. The tension that underlies Péguy's nostalgic stance may be read as a continuation of what Rancière refers to as 'the Platonic paradigm of the democratic dissolution of the social body' which haunted the nineteenth century and the period's 'obsession with the lost social bond'.[5]

Shunning progressive politics, Péguy distances himself from organized labour's pursuit of freedom from capitalist exploitation in early twentieth-century France. Those who make workerist demands in the modern world of labour are drawn into such action, he complains, by 'l'événement de l'histoire économique' (Arg, 791) ['the event of economic history']. Refusing the nexus that links money capital and the commodification of labour power, Péguy suggests that the mere fact of pursuing pay demands shows workers foregoing autonomy by serving, and being beholden to, someone else. He explains further his critique of bourgeois capitalism, arguing that it has converted labour into a commodity value.

---

4 Péguy, *Notre jeunesse*, in *Œuvres en prose complètes*, III, 8.

5 'The Janus-Face of Politicized Art: Jacques Rancière in Interview with Gabriel Rockhill', in Rancière, *The Politics of Aesthetics*, pp. 45–61 (p. 53).

In a form of contagion, the worker adopts a similar outlook, with strikes becoming, he writes disparagingly, like speculative activity on the stock market (Arg, 795).

Péguy's encomium to craft is ideologically driven by his refusal of modernity and what he calls a bourgeois age. He depicts the period when he was growing up (he was born in 1873, in the early years of the Third Republic) as being continuous with the preceding centuries of the Christian era, the proposed link being to an unbroken sense of commitment to work. He presents in quasi-religious terms his predecessors' acceptance of their position in that world order: 'C'était, *dans une cité laborieuse*, se mettre tranquillement à la place de travail qui vous attendait' (Arg, 791; emphasis added) ['It involved quietly occupying the place of work that awaited you *in a city centred on labour*']. He complains that, in the age in which he writes, workers have adopted the bourgeois way of making demands, whereas in his youth, 'ce bel honneur de métier' ['the beautiful honour of a trade'] meant that the worker asked nothing of others but rather pursued his labour: 'Ces ouvriers ne servaient pas. [...]. Ils avaient un honneur, absolu, comme c'est le propre d'un honneur' (Arg, 791) ['These workers did not serve. (...) Their sense of honour was absolute, as honour should be']. The objects of such labour similarly acquire a sacred value: 'Nous avons connu cette piété de l'*ouvrage bien faite* poussée, maintenue jusqu'à ses plus extrêmes exigences' (Arg, 790) ['We have known the piety that goes with a job well done, taken to its most demanding level'].[6] Savouring the proletarian habit of using *ouvrage* as a feminine noun, Péguy adds that the spirit of that earlier age means that the free-thinkers of old were closer to Christianity than a devout person of his own day. He asks how it is that with the modern Zeitgeist, a people – 'le plus laborieux de la terre, et peut-être [le] seul peuple laborieux de la terre' (Arg, 790–91) ['the most hard-working on the earth and perhaps the only hard-working people on the earth'] – has lost its respect for patient artisanship. Antoine Compagnon notes the 'apocalyptic resonances' to be found in the style of an author who wrote as though possessed.[7]

---

6   Emphasis in the original. Robert Burac points out that, in the reference to 'l'ouvrage bien faite', Péguy is reproducing a formulation used in a letter he received from Pierre Milly in which Milly savours the workers' use of 'ouvrage' as a feminine noun; see editorial note, Péguy, *Œuvres en prose complètes*, III, 1683–84.

7   Antoine Compagnon, *Les Antimodernes. De Joseph de Maistre à Roland Barthes* (Paris: Gallimard, 2005), p. 228.

Another assessment of Péguy's place in French history records how the various traditions he celebrated – 'the Catholic, the Socialist [...], the Republican, the Jewish' – placed him 'at the confluence of many different Frances'.[8] A disillusioned Péguy heralds the artisans within the *petite bourgeoisie* of his day as the upholders of an ancient tradition of commitment to craft, whereas workers in the new age are trying to ape the ways of the established middle class.

The immediate context in which Péguy wrote *L'Argent* helps explain the work's polemical tone. While drafting what was to have been an introduction to a study by Théophile Naudy on how a system of primary education might best function, he uncovered the identity of a hostile reviewer of his *Œuvres choisies* back in July 1911, Charles-Victor Langlois, a Sorbonne professor. The discovery saw Péguy change direction, writing the combative text *L'Argent* which carried the full Langlois review (Arg, 829–31) and appeared in mid-February 1913 (Naudy's work appeared a fortnight later, in early March). Privately, Péguy confided to a friend the intense emotion and isolation he was feeling while drafting *L'Argent*: 'Je travaille presque désespérément' ['I am working in a state of virtual despair'].[9]

Linguistic composition thus becomes the tense and yet compensatory terrain on which Péguy articulates his despairing defence of a particular class consciousness. As if both to strengthen and mirror the conservative social model he is promoting, his eccentric textuality shows a conscious crafting of lexical retentiveness and narrowing. The recurrence of terms such as *honneur*, *tradition*, and *laborieux* in *L'Argent* is indicative of this contained range, the repetition and concatenation infusing the concepts with an incantatory power. Péguy likewise exploits the work-as-prayer motif ['travailler c'est prier' (Arg, 792)] in relation to peasant endeavour: 'Travailler était leur joie même, et la racine profonde de leur être' (Arg, 790) ['working was their very joy and the root of their being']. Referencing with nostalgia the vanished practice of workers singing in the *atelier* (and regretting his own failure to be part of that tradition), he further underlines collective identity by evoking Hugo's commemoration

8   Julian Jackson, *France: The Dark Years, 1940–1944* (Oxford: Oxford University Press, 2001), p. 6.

9   Péguy's letter of 4 January 1913 was to Simone Casimir-Perier. My argument draws substantially on Burac's evocation of the emotionally difficult backdrop to Péguy's writing of *L'Argent* in late 1912 and January–February 1913; see the editorial presentation of the text, Péguy, *Œuvres en prose complètes*, III, 1681–83.

of soldiers in Year II of the Revolution defending the nation against foreign invaders: '*Ils allaient, ils chantaient*' (Arg, 790) ['*They sang as they went*'].[10] A democracy of expression releases the expressivity of the socially subjugated, while Péguy's compositional style demonstrates how his combative rejection of modernity is inseparable from a making-in-language or poiesis. In this way, his wordcraft and the work of the tool-handling artisan come to be isomorphic.

The presence in *L'Argent* of rhetorical features such as chiasmus and anaphora draws attention in a strikingly visual way to words and their sequencing on the page. While Péguy is clearly not in retreat from social meaning, his writing generates an autonomous rhythm, thereby highlighting the tension between cultural and class fidelities, on the one hand, and the assembling of linguistic signs on the other.[11] When, in a restless, irritable complaint directed against parliamentarians among others, he refers scathingly to 'ces doigts d'orateurs, ces mains qui ne savent pas manier l'outil' (Arg, 797) ['those orators' fingers, those hands that are incapable of handling a tool'], Péguy's remark remains a conflicted one, coming from a writer who is himself an intensely engaged handler of language.

The responses of two of Péguy's contemporaries specifically to his style are relevant here. Langlois's review refers condescendingly to the use of litanies, to symptoms of echolalia in the writing, and also to a pride mixed with envy in Péguy, 'ce qui est très "peuple" aussi' (Arg, 829) ['which is also very "plebeian"'], Langlois concludes. A wounded Péguy upbraids him for denigrating – from a position of considerable economic advantage – his class background.

The second response is that of Proust who, writing in *La Revue de Paris* in November 1920, observes that Péguy could be reproached in his lifetime for trying ten different ways to say something that could

<hr/>

10   Péguy is quoting from Hugo, *Les Châtiments*, II, vii, 'A l'obéissance passive', verse 11. See Burac's editorial note, Péguy, *Œuvres en prose complètes*, III, 1683. On the subject of nineteenth-century literary tributes to proletarian song, it is worth noting Baudelaire's remark that reading the work of Pierre Dupont carries echoes for him of Proudhon's *Avertissement aux propriétaires* ['Warning to Proprietors'], with its injunction to workers to sing as they went off to work; see Baudelaire, 'Pierre Dupont', p. 693.

11   For Rancière, the politics of literature excludes any simple 'schéma [...] d'adéquation entre une forme d'écriture et un contenu politique' ['scheme of appropriateness between a form of writing and a political content']; see *Politique de la littérature*, p. 35; *The Politics of Literature*, p. 26.

only be said in one.[12] Yet he was quick to add that Péguy's 'glorious' death in the early months of the First World War entirely erased these compositional defects. The latter remark, which is clearly to be read in terms of the immediate post-war context in which Proust is writing, nevertheless produces a collision between what is desirable in narrative poetics and the requirements of social decorum in relation to the war dead.[13]

Confronted by modernity, Péguy's preferred vantage point in *L'Argent* is to dwell nostalgically on an everyday and a mode of self-conception that have disappeared:

> Tout était un rythme et un rite et une cérémonie depuis le petit lever. Tout était un événement; sacré. [...] Tout était une élévation, intérieure, et une prière, toute la journée, le sommeil et la veille, le travail et le peu de repos, le lit et la table, la soupe et le bœuf, la maison et le jardin, la porte et la rue, la cour et le pas de porte, et les assiettes sur la table. (Arg, 792)

> [From early in the day, everything was a rhythm and a rite and a ceremony. Everything was an event; sacred. (...) An inner elevation, and a prayer, throughout the day, both when sleeping and awake, work and the little bit of rest, the soup and the beef, the house and the garden, the door and the street, the yard and the threshold, and the plates on the table.]

Péguy chides the moderns who would see progress for the worker as translating into a reduction in labour. What, for those coming after, is a victory would seem a defeat to their predecessors, he laments. Indeed the older generation saw work as an achievement comparable to military triumph and as bringing with it the same honour as that enjoyed by the Imperial Guard (Arg, 793). In a similar vein, he sees as entirely compatible the French Republican ideals and the Christian principles which jointly featured in his upbringing in the 1870s.

In a continuation of his aggressively anti-modern stance, Péguy praises a culture of frugality and happiness, and pours scorn on what he terms the arithmetic of the sociologist (Arg, 794). The traditional workers

---

12   Marcel Proust, *Contre Sainte-Beuve* précédé de *Pastiches et mélanges* et suivi de *Essais et articles* (Paris: Gallimard (Bibliothèque de la Pléiade), 1971), p. 616.

13   Péguy was killed at the Battle of the Marne on 5 September 1914. Proust's text, entitled 'Pour un ami (remarques sur le style)', *La Revue de Paris*, 15 November 1920, later formed the preface to Paul Morand's *Tendres Stocks*, which appeared in 1921. See the relevant editorial notes of Pierre Clarac and Yves Sandre in Proust, *Contre Sainte-Beuve*, pp. 950, 955.

whom he champions would wish to work more than is the custom in modern places of work, he goes on, pointing to 'la main qui démange, qui a envie de travailler. Le bras qui s'embête, de ne rien faire' (Arg, 794) ['the hand that itches to be working, the arm that is bored with doing nothing']. In his provocative, emotional account of modernity, socialism stands as a bourgeois doctrine that dictates the underuse of the capacity to work, with capitalism adding to this atrophy. He uses the metaphor of the bourgeoisie infecting the workers, the result being that the 'vertus ouvrières' ['working-class virtues'] now migrate to the *petite bourgeoisie* whose industry Péguy commends (Arg, 794).

Pathos pervades Péguy's encomium to manual labour. He writes of work entailing 'un respect de l'outil, et de la main, ce suprême outil' (Arg, 793) ['a respect for the tool and for the hand, that supreme tool']. In the millennial scale that he proposes, reaching back to France's medieval cathedrals, to damage one's tools would have seemed, he asserts, like cutting off one's hand, as a conscript in the modern age might mutilate himself to avoid going to war (Arg, 793). In a short essay entitled 'Notes on Gesture', Giorgio Agamben writes of the cultural significance present in a loss of ease of gesture in the late nineteenth century, observing: 'An era that has lost its gestures is, for that very reason, obsessed with them; for people who are bereft of all that is natural to them, every gesture becomes a fate'.[14] Péguy underscores the notion of painful destiny in *L'Argent* when he casts as existential drama the decline in physical capacity in the elderly: '– *Je perds ma main à travailler*, disaient les vieux. Et c'était la fin des fins' (Arg, 793) ['*I'm losing the power of my hands from work*, the old people would say. And it was the end of everything']. Simon's observation in *L'Acacia* on the transformation of peasant bodies shaped by physical labour conveys a keen visual attentiveness but also detachment on the part of the narrator. In Péguy, by contrast, the sentimental celebration of artisanal work feeds ultimately into a eulogy for the manual and *le peuple*.

---

14   Giorgio Agamben, 'Notes on Gesture', in *Infancy and History: On the Destruction of Experience*, trans. Liz Heron (London: Verso, 2007), pp. 147–56 (p. 151). For a close reading of Agamben's reflections on gesture, see Patrick ffrench, 'Proust and the Analysis of Gesture', in Nathalie Aubert (ed.), *Proust and the Visual* (Cardiff: University of Wales Press, 2013), pp. 47–67.

*   *   *

We find a pointer to Péguy's decline in popularity in the later part of
the twentieth century in a passing reference made in Annie Ernaux's
Les Armoires vides (1974). Like many of her subsequent works, this
early text focusses on class betrayal, depicting a young protagonist
who claims to be liberated from her working-class background through
the reading of Sartre, Beauvoir, Kafka, and Camus. Literature would
thus become a crucial vehicle of protest and self-retrieval in a world of
antagonistic cultures: 'la vérité, elle était écrite noir sur blanc, dans les
livres' ['truth was to be found written in black and white in books'].[15]
In contrast with the ringing endorsement of literary moderns, the words
of the young protagonist's parents are presented as the morality of the
petty bourgeois shopkeeper, 'des vieilles conneries séchées' ['dried up old
crap']. Péguy is bundled in with the insult: 'C'est tout sec maintenant,
tout essoré la littérature, ces palabres à s'avaler, sur Péguy, l'amour
du peuple ...' ['the whole palaver about literature, Péguy, the love of
the people, it's all wrung out and dry now ...'].[16] Ernaux's impatient
protagonist thus dismisses any sentimental endorsement of her social
origins. Yet the narrator distances herself from the adolescent's view
that literature offers a route to liberty and that the contingent world
is merely 'un arrangement dû au hasard' ['an arrangement based on
chance'].[17] This rejection of class origins is later complicated when,
in edgy conversation with a young middle-class male, the protagonist
becomes troubled by the thought that her frantic embrace of literary
modernity might in fact be 'un symptôme de pauvreté' (AV, 169–70) ['a
symptom of poverty']. Ernaux is clearly not attempting to rehabilitate
Péguy, yet her ambiguous, glancing reference to him in *Les Armoires
vides* prompts us to reflect on how the work of this anti-modern, to use
Compagnon's term, might lend itself to connection with contemporary
literature's account of working-class culture. Péguy's lament stands as
an attempt to reverse what, in another context, is referred to as 'the
enormous condescension of posterity'.[18]

15   Annie Ernaux, *Les Armoires vides* (Paris: Gallimard, 1974), p. 156.
16   Ernaux, *Les Armoires vides*, p. 156.
17   Ernaux, *Les Armoires vides*, p. 156.
18   See E. P. Thompson, *The Making of the English Working Class* (London:
Penguin, 1968 [1963]), p. 12. Thompson argues that his method has been to include
in his history those movements and practices that came to disappear. Indeed, he

The theme of the artisan's loss of manual power decried by Péguy finds a restatement in Thierry Beinstingel's narrative of modern-day workplaces in the novel *Retour aux mots sauvages* (2010). Focussing particularly on call centres, the book opens with a throwback to a contemporary of Péguy. Specifically, the celebration of the switchboard operators in Proust's *Le Côté de Guermantes* provides the novel's epigraph. But whereas the scene in Proust offers a playfully exaggerated power reversal in which the women on the switchboard move from being servants of the mysterious new medium to becoming 'les Demoiselles du téléphone' ['the Young Ladies of the telephone'] who rule over their clients, *Retour aux mots sauvages* reflects soberly on the intense alienation that comes with twentieth-first-century call centre work and exposure to the wider world of 'cette boulimie commerciale' ['this commercial bulimia'].[19]

As if to illustrate Péguy's view that the hand at work is the greatest tool of all, the male protagonist in Beinstingel's novel faces existential angst having had to give up manually productive labour. A redundant electrician, the fifty-year-old now works in telesales under an assumed name (as required by his employer). 'Éric' is baffled by computer screens and by the scripted messages that employees are required to recite:

> ces séries de dialogues improbables et normés, soumis à l'aléatoire d'un logiciel qui décide pour vous des mots à dire. Est ainsi tronquée la perception d'une vraie vie. (RMS, 92)
>
> [these series of improbable, normed dialogues, submitted to the random promptings of a software that tells you what you are to say. In this way the perception of a real life is cut out.]

Nostalgia for his past is captured metonymically in recurring references to his now pale, shrunken hands, the muscle loss resulting from his being desk-bound and handling nothing heavier than a plastic mouse. 'Éric' cannot control the fear of seeing 'chacune de ses mains se changer en chou-fleur inutile' (RMS, 53) ['his two hands turning into useless cauliflowers'] and he frets about how quickly the know-how of the fingers is lost (RMS, 172). Unconvinced by a workplace trainer who sets out a grand narrative of human progress that runs from the reign of the

---

points to a double exclusion: 'and, if they were casualties of history, they remain, condemned in their own lives, as casualties' (p. 13).

19   Thierry Beinstingel, *Retour aux mots sauvages* (Paris: Arthème Fayard, 2010), p. 146; hereinafter cited as RMS.

foot (with the culture of hunting and agriculture) through to that of the hand (in a Taylorist age of manufacturing) and finally to the 'règne du cerveau' (RMS, 116) ['reign of the brain'], the protagonist struggles to make the transition. But whereas the pursuit of profit is characterized as totalitarian and alienating (RMS, 157), taking his car to be repaired brings him into restorative contact with the mechanical world. 'Ici, c'est la dictature de la matière' ['here, it's the dictatorship of matter'], the narrator comments wryly, conscious of a genealogy of occupations and the cultural disruption caused by a modern-day economy in which, Beinstingel reflects, commercial relations of the kind signalled by the call centre form a 'false democracy' (RMS, 177). Significantly, a vocabulary which harks back to an earlier age marks a form of material turn, much to the consolation of the protagonist:

> existence tangible, palpable, concrète, physique, matérielle, authentique, véritable, sûre, sincère, loyale, fidèle, convenable, apparente et manifeste. *Dire tous ces adjectifs fait du bien.* (RMS, 92–93; emphasis added)

> [an existence that is tangible, palpable, concrete, physical, material, authentic, true, sure, sincere, loyal, faithful, appropriate, apparent, and evident. *Pronouncing all those adjectives does one good.*]

Working back from a contemporary order, Beinstingel, not unlike Péguy, thus attempts a merger of the material, the manual, and the verbal. Enumeration and vocabulary-assembly are liberational for both authors, opening up channels of resistance to unpalatable modernity – industrial-scale manufacturing in *L'Argent*, or the new form of mass labour that is the call centre in *Retour aux mots sauvages*. Beinstingel succeeds in endowing the novel with emancipatory potential by having call centre spiel and literary narration stand as rival forms of verbal communication. In its resourcefulness, literature's language mocks, and counters, the programmed recitation of call centre repetitiveness. Parallel to this, the return to connection with the wider contingent world (childcare, shopping lists, dustbins) will counter 'un travail affranchi des limites du corps' (RMS, 29) ['a work that operates free from the limits of the body']. With the motor mechanic advocating work as the antidote to self-questioning, the prescription, together with the uncompromising image of the mechanic painted by the narrator, stresses an engagement with materiality: 'n'a-t-il pas raison, le mécanicien, poings sur les hanches, fondu dans le décor de son atelier?' (RMS, 178) ['the mechanic is right, is he not, standing with hands on hips, blending in with the decor of his workshop?']. No less reassuring than the muscular, oil-covered hands is the mechanic's linguistic performativity as he itemizes different aspects in the process of combustion:

> Les mots *taux de compression, bougie de préchauffage, injection, suralimentation* résonnent dans l'espace de l'atelier, s'accrochent aux poutres métalliques, finissent de remplir un espace concret, entièrement voué à la mécanique, quelque chose de rassurant, de logique et de concret. (RMS, 176–77)

> ['The words *compression ratio, glow plug, injection, turbocharging* ring out around the space of the workshop, cling to the metal beams, completely fill the concrete space which is given over entirely to mechanics. It's something reassuring, logical, and concrete.]

The acoustic and material properties acquired by words contrast with the protagonist's brittle self-conception, 'Éric' seeing himself as comprising merely a few living cells in an organization which overwhelms the individual. In an echo of the iconography of Mai 68, he reflects nostalgically on a previous self-image: 'Autrefois, il se serait représenté comme une main, un ensemble de tendons, un avant-bras noueux, quelque chose d'utile' (RMS, 191) ['In the past, he would have represented himself as a hand, a set of tendons, a gnarled forearm, as something useful']. Applying Patrick ffrench's gloss on Agamben's 'Notes on Gesture', experience here shows its gestural character and acquires a transhistorical slant.[20]

Other motifs around the image of the hand at work are woven into the narrative of *Retour aux mots sauvages*. From a set of press cuttings, the protagonist compiles a list of tragedies befalling the socially forgotten 'gens de peu'. Cases of suicides, premature deaths involving homeless people, and those suffering from paralysis: 'Miracle et persistance de l'écriture' (RMS, 215) ['The miracle and persistence of writing'] is how the narrator assesses the protagonist's endeavour, which is later referred to as his meagre tribute to the affected families. That these families are unaware of the former manual worker's studious, textual commemoration heightens the pathos, as does the material fragility of the handwritten document: 'L'encre noire de la feuille affichée finira par pâlir' (RMS, 228) ['The black ink on the sheet posted on the wall will end up fading']. The choice of medium recalls both Simon's wish to 'faire un objet écrit' ['make a written object'] and the moment late in *L'Acacia* when the protagonist settles down in front of the page to begin

---

20   ffrench, 'Proust and the Analysis of Gesture', p. 60.

Fig. 1: Fernand Léger, 'Le Profil à la corde: étude pour *Les Constructeurs*'
['Man in Profile with Rope: Study for *The Constructors*'].
National Galleries of Scotland. © ADAGP, Paris and DACS, London 2020.

In Léger's ink and black-chalk drawing, produced in 1950 or 1951, the fingers of the worker's hands and the strands of the rope are connected isomorphically. While we need to acknowledge the specificities of the different media involved, Beinstingel's nostalgic evocation of the hand at work and of the affirmation that comes with materiality may be compared with Léger's alignment. Péguy's insistence in *L'Argent* on the linkage between tool and hand likewise finds an echo here.

the work of inscription.[21] In both novels, written composition can thus signal a meditative seriousness. Yet Beinstingel contrasts his protagonist's dutiful written log of tragic cases with the lurid coverage provided in the popular press, the latter's 'quincaillerie de phrases et de photographies' (RMS, 130) ['cheap display of sentences and photographs'] serving the commercial exploitation of human misery. Beinstingel reinforces the image of individuals' isolation by casting the computer screen as an emblem of loss of community, the surface onto which personal grief is reflected: 'la tragédie s'éparpille dans les pixels' (RMS, 131) ['tragedy is scattered across the pixels'].

The term *sauvage* as defined by *Le Petit Robert* signifies that which has not been modified by the actions of men (the term can also mean 'fleeing human relations' and 'preferring a life of seclusion'). In the case of Beinstingel's novel, the first of these meanings captures the sense in which the protagonist comes finally to experience emancipation from society's nefarious influence. Roland, a call centre colleague of the protagonist, having received abuse from a client, protests that the social corralling that militates against individual expression in the workplace is embraced by everyone in what he refers to as 'notre folie grégaire' ['our collective folly' (RMS, 185)]. Beinstingel's novel thus shows literature functioning as an invitation to transformative encounter through the ethical dimension that it generates.

Tightly worked into *Retour aux mots sauvages* is the theme of labour's location switching literally from hand to mouth. As another employee, Robert, comments, mindful of the challenge facing former manual workers, 'ce métier est le combat de la bouche contre la main' (RMS, 52) ['this job involves the mouth's combat against the hand']. And in an eccentric defence of the new *métier*, he insists that one must be wary of silence and keep exercising one's jaws: 'ne jamais laisser ses mâchoires au repos' (RMS, 52). The socio-economic conjuncture which sees the call centre become the new factory again throws into relief the nostalgia for manual labour. Beinstingel's perspective takes us close to the terrain mapped by Rancière in *Le Maître ignorant*, where the cultural fracture between 'material' and 'mental', 'hand' and 'head', forms a key narrative driver. Indeed, Jacotot's dictum, which we considered in the Introduction, that 'each citizen is also a man who makes a *work*', has a bearing on *Retour aux mots sauvages*. There, the protagonist desires to initiate dialogue between a person

---

21   See the closing argument of Chapter 1, pp. 49–50.

who literally talks for a living and someone else whose livelihood depends on the performance of manual work. As if to echo the notions of mutuality and of a non-hierarchical acquisition of knowledge that we find in *Le Maître ignorant*, Beinstingel's protagonist imagines a day of encounter when commuter traffic is halted and motorists get out of their vehicles and converse: 'Tout stopper? [...] Echanger les métiers. Tout s'apprend' (RMS, 54) ['Bring everything to a standstill? Have people swap jobs. Everything can be learnt']. This reluctance to reproduce social apportionment can be taken alongside the argument of an exponent of transformative cognitive practice for whom imagination can act counterfactually by proposing an 'integration of possibility with the given'.[22] In *Retour aux mots sauvages*, where those who govern are intent on erasing the memory of utopian aspiration that came specifically with Mai 68, the narrator records the juxtaposition between a contemporary, consumerist individualism and an earlier, collectivist egalitarianism (RMS, 146).

Late in Beinstingel's text, the protagonist's awareness that his hands have little use – 'La bouche qui devait prendre le relais des mains, devenir experte' (RMS, 221) ['The mouth that had to become expert and take over from the hands'] – causes him anguish and insomnia. Yet this is offset by the story of the paralysed man whom the protagonist befriends, in contravention of company regulations stipulating that contact with customers be restricted to the formulaic, phone-based conversations which Beinstingel reproduces in sometimes tragicomic vein in the novel. The paralysed man uses a mouth-held sensor to enter on a computer screen a message of greeting for the protagonist. In this unlikely encounter, the world of alienated work throws up redemptive human contact. In a further demonstration of affective engagement, the paralytic's family present the call centre employee with a silver tray which they have had engraved with the name 'Éric' back in their native Algeria. The gesture obliges the protagonist to accept that, while his workplace pseudonym alienates him, it has, ironically, become a channel for human affirmation and exchange.

Beinstingel paints a wide canvas of social fracture. One of the protagonist's fellow workers mourns both his parents and his loss of manual skill (RMS, 216); a virtual world spells social atomization and loneliness; and workplace suicides are on the increase. In a manner that

---

22   See Jennifer Anna Gosetti-Ferencei, *The Life of Imagination: Revealing and Making the World* (New York: Columbia University Press, 2018), p. 5.

illustrates Rancière's reflections on the division of the sensible, the novel invokes sensory amputation to capture the protagonist's realization that his new job entails a physiological mutation:

> Pour ici, c'est uniquement l'audible, l'amputation du reste, la douleur du membre fantôme, la question récurrente: combien de temps ça va prendre pour que la main prenne la consistance de la bouche? (RMS, 31)

> [Here, the audible trumps everything: the rest is cut away, leaving phantom limb pain and the recurrent question: How long will it take for the hand to acquire the consistency of the mouth?]

The lament accompanying the atrophy of parts of the body reminds us of the fraught moment of loss confronting the elderly in Péguy's narrative: '– *Je perds ma main à travailler*' (Arg, 793) [*'I'm losing the power of my hands from work'*]. For both writers, the preservation of manual power in the lives they portray is pivotal to self-identity and has an anachronistic dimension. In both cases, forms of modernity are contested in moves to restore an earlier 'sensible fabric – a given order of relations between meanings and the visible'.[23]

In Beinstingel's novel, work's assault on sentience constitutes the source of alienation. The image of a diminution of the senses serves as corollary to a world grounded in the inegalitarian. Yet *Retour aux mots sauvages* is also a narrative of escape from an order of containment. The protagonist's colleague Maryse may insist on hierarchy in the workplace – 'On ne mélange pas les torchons et les serviettes' (RMS, 187) ['you have to separate the sheep from the goats'] – while he himself harbours a fear of losing manual dexterity and vigour. Yet his cataloguing of tragedies involving ordinary lives stands as an act both of witness and affirmation; his friendship with the paralysed customer brings relationality and actual, bodily presence (instead of conversation through a headset); and in taking up running, the sensory-motor experience this involves gives an enhanced experience of embodied existence. His hands may have lost their vigour but in the act of movement, he imagines he might regain the status of 'l'homme sauvage' ['man in a state of nature'], placing one foot in front of the other (RMS, 117). In that sense, Beinstingel's novel becomes an exemplary tale with therapeutic benefit, outstripping call centre protocols and productivity registers.

---

23   The formulation is used by Rancière in 'The Janus-Face of Politicized Art', p. 60.

*   *   *

While Beinstingel's narrator notes the then-current media focus on the question of national identity, he speculates that what citizens need is 'la possibilité de se sentir ainsi réuni avec soi-même, dans son propre corps' (RMS, 209) ['the possibility of feeling reunited with oneself in one's own body']. The closing chapter of the work provides an eloquent rebuttal of any suggestion that such a life is to be lived under the shadow of what Rancière, referencing Plato, calls 'la fable de son infériorité', the fable of the dispossessed worker's inferiority.[24] Taking part in a local run, Beinstingel's protagonist sees the event as a physical challenge yet also comes to live it as an experience that is both collective and singular. With the intensity of effort required releasing a sense of perspective, the call centre prattle gives way to a restorative connection with those unable to run, who urge him on: 'Cours pour moi!' (RMS, 231) ['Run for me!']. Some participants go faster than others, yet the overtaking or being overtaken is incidental for the protagonist in Beinstingel's closing section of narrative. The focus falls, rather, on how an act of whole-body participation, so to speak, undoes the entrapment of someone whose earlier, narrow goal had been to convert a competence of the hand into a competence of the mouth. That narrowness of perspective is magnified by the anxious concern about 'sa place à gagner dans le vaste monde' (RMS, 232) ['the position to be secured in the vast world']. While the 'mots sauvages', the wild or savage words of the book's title, make 'brutal' appearances at those moments in the text that carry news of suicide (RMS, 86, 123), the final use of the formulation signals affirmation: 'Le monde? Faire avec [...] s'abandonner aux mots sauvages' (RMS, 233) ['The world? Live with it (...) give oneself over to the wild words']. With its rejection of 'tout ce qu'on nous apprend' (RMS, 232) ['everything society teaches us'], the catharsis experienced by the protagonist sees a radical redistribution of perception.

24 Jacques Rancière, *Le Philosophe et ses pauvres* (Paris: Flammarion, 2007 [1983]), p. iv.

*   *   *

The 'practice of language' foregrounded in *Retour aux mots sauvages* and Péguy's *L'Argent* emerges in contrasting ways across the two texts.[25] In Beinstingel's novel, it functions at a diegetic level, the linguistic performance of the call centre employee literally acting in the service of economic power. The subordination of the protagonist's voice to capital follows the decline, in a post-industrial age, of the physical, manual work which had served earlier forms of economic control. For 'Éric', who had himself performed such work, the atrophy of manual capacity arising from his redundancy as an electrician alarms him and he longs for reconnection with tangible, hand-generated productivity. Yet, significantly, his reconnection with the material world also works in part through a practice of language. His reinsertion in material culture (the visit to the garage, decorating the home of the disabled client and so on) brings with it the reassurance of a lexical accumulation. Certain vocabularies thus become emancipatory in their impact. In a similar way, he commits to creating and preserving written traces of diminished lives, the protagonist's tribute capturing what Beinstingel calls, as we have noted, the 'miracle and persistance of writing' (RMS, 215).

In the case of Péguy, linguistic performance is integral to his strained defence of a bygone social order which for him holds the allure of a mystical age. Deleuze's comments on that performance draw out the particular manipulation of the signifier in Péguy: he sees him using

> [des] substantifs dont chacun va définir une zone de variation jusqu'au voisinage d'un autre substantif qui détermine une autre zone [...]. Les reprises de Péguy donnent aux mots une épaisseur verticale qui leur fait perpétuellement recommencer l''irrecommençable'.

> [substantives, each of which defines a zone of variation until it reaches the neighborhood of another substantive, which determines another zone (...). Péguy's repetitions give words a vertical thickness and make them perpetually recommence the 'unrecommenceable'.][26]

---

25   In his consideration of the linkage between the arts and capitalism in the late eighteenth and early nineteenth centuries, Franco Moretti explores the question of 'instrumental reason as *a practice of language*'. See Moretti, *The Bourgeois: Between History and Literature* (London: Verso, 2013), p. 39 (emphasis in the original).

26   Deleuze, *Critique et clinique*, p. 140; *Essays Critical and Clinical*, p. 111.

With work acquiring the character of sacred ministry in *L'Argent*, Péguy's endorsement of the artisanal is channelled through a language marked by repetition, tautology, and redundancy. A practice of linguistic retentiveness thus creates the 'thickness' that Deleuze identifies and becomes the vehicle of fidelity. Celebrating the contribution of a family to the life of the French Republic (the family in question, the Milliets, had offered their archive to the *Cahiers de la Quinzaine*), Péguy writes a defence of Republican ordinariness in *Notre jeunesse*. He refers to the 'inguérissable modestie' ['incurable modesty'] of the Milliets even as they make available this vital resource to the *Cahiers*.[27]

Discarding the narrative of the socially dominant, which he casts as 'une histoire endimanchée' ['history in its Sunday best'], he appeals instead to what is presented as a real that is grounded in the everyday:

> Ce que nous voulons voir et avoir [...], c'est l'histoire de tous les jours de la semaine, c'est un peuple dans la texture, dans la tissure, dans le tissu de sa quotidienne existence [...] dans le labeur du pain de chaque jour, *panem quotidianum*, c'est une race dans son réel, dans son épanoui-ssement profond.[28]

> [What we want to see and have (...) is the history of all the days of the week, is a people in its texture, in the weave and thread of its everyday existence (...) in the work that is the daily bread, *panem quotidianum*, it is a race in its real, in its deep blossoming.]

Péguy adds that in acquiring the Milliet papers, the *Cahiers de la Quinzaine* will have access to 'la pâte même dont le pain était fait' ['the very dough from which the bread was made'].[29] As though ushering in a community through the medium of language, he uses alliteration (*texture/tissure/tissu*, and again *pâte/pain*) to signal a grouping which, by virtue of its being discarded by modernity, he deems exemplary in the history of social modesty. If, in another context, Franco Moretti identifies 'prose, as the style of the useful', Péguy's incantatory prose serves in the sanctification of artisanal labour.[30]

27 Péguy, *Notre jeunesse*, p. 5.
28 Péguy, *Notre jeunesse*, p. 7.
29 Péguy, *Notre jeunesse*, p. 24.
30 Moretti uses the formulation in his textual analysis of Defoe's *Robinson Crusoe* which he feeds into an examination of the emergence of bourgeois 'mentality'; see *The Bourgeois*, p. 39. Moretti identifies Defoe's prose as his 'contri-bution' to the formation of that mindset.

Fig. 2: Charles Péguy in 1913 in the shop of the journal which he edited,
Les Cahiers de la Quinzaine, 8 rue de la Sorbonne, Paris.
© Le Centre Péguy, Orléans. Photograph by Dornac.
The aura of symbiosis between the material presence of the journal volumes
and the writer is striking.

Relevant to the works of both Péguy and Beinstingel is Claude
Simon's observation that Proust works and 'produces' in the only
material available to him, namely language.[31] Péguy clings to the idea of
writing as work. A long-serving editor of the *Cahiers de la Quinzaine*,
he refers to the beauty of typography which holds a compensatory value
in an age when the political parties of the Republic (at war over the
Dreyfus Affair) have degraded what he calls Republican mystique: 'la
typographie [...] est un des plus beaux art et métier' ['typography is one
of the most beautiful arts and crafts'], he asserts.[32] Dismissing Langlois's
hostile review of his work (mentioned above), he describes the Sorbonne
academic as having lived an unproductive life:

31   See Simon, *Quatre conférences*, ed. Patrick Longuet (Paris: Minuit, 2012),
p. 25.
32   Péguy, *Notre jeunesse*, p. 156.

c'est dans la production qu'il y a le plus de travail, c'est dans l'œuvre qu'il y a le plus de labeur et il y a plus de travail dans un conte de Tharaud et dans quatre vers de Porché que dans toute une vie d'érudition. (Arg, 833)

[it is in production that there is the most work, it is in the *œuvre* that there is the greatest toil, and there is more work in a tale by Tharaud or four lines of verse by Porché than in a lifetime of erudition.][33]

With word-handling serving as shield in the defence of labour, Péguy attempts a binding together of work and literary word. His practice, like that of Beinstingel, recalls the homology in Jacotot which draws together the manual worker's handling of tools and the writer's manipulation of words.[34]

33   Langlois's hostile review of Péguy's *Œuvres choisies, 1900–1910* (Paris: Grasset, 1911) was published in the *Revue critique des livres nouveaux*, 15 July 1911.
34   *Le Maître ignorant*, p. 121; *The Ignorant Schoolmaster*, p. 71.

CHAPTER THREE

A Solitary Emancipation

Ndiaye's *La Cheffe, roman d'une cuisinière*

[C]ette combinaison de fougue, d'aveuglement et de sens obsédant de ses responsabilités, a fait de la Cheffe ce qu'elle est devenue, une grande artiste.

[that combination of nerve, heedlessness and a consuming sense of her responsibilities (...) made the Cheffe what she became, a great artist.]

Ndiaye[1]

'Et l'atelier était un oratoire' (Arg, 792) ['And the atelier was an oratory']. The intense probity which Péguy associates with the workplace, which he here elevates to the status of devotional site, finds a perhaps unlikely contemporary echo in Marie Ndiaye's *La Cheffe, roman d'une cuisinière* (2016). Ndiaye's narrator describes the eponymous heroine, a future award-winning chef, as being involved in a vital ministry ['ce ministère crucial' (CRC, 64)]. As with Péguy, the hymn to labour in Ndiaye, far from being oriented towards an emancipatory view of class struggle, acquires an obsessive, near-delirious character. In her novel, work is associated with ceremonial and nostalgia. For Péguy, the artisanal serves as guarantor of what is a miraculous and, significantly, bygone social cohesion:

Tous les honneurs convergeaient en cet honneur. Une décence, et une finesse de langage. Un respect du foyer. Un sens du respect, de tous

---

1 Marie Ndiaye, *La Cheffe, roman d'une cuisinière* (Paris: Gallimard, 2016), p. 193 (subsequently abbreviated to CRC); *The Cheffe: A Cook's Novel*, trans. Jordan Stump (London: MacLehose Press, 2019), p. 191; hereinafter cited as TC.

les respects, de l'être même du respect. *Une cérémonie pour ainsi dire
constante.* (Arg, 792; emphasis added)

[Every honour converged in that honour. A decency and a fineness of
language. A respect for the home. A sense of respect, of every respect,
of the very being of respect. *A ceremony that was, as it were, constant.*]

In the narrative of fidelity to a lost artisanal age in *L'Argent*, incantatory
linguistic performance is a conspicuous feature.

In the case of *La Cheffe*, class and the practice of language again
intersect but to different effect. In a fluent, confident prose narrative,
oral inhibition forms, paradoxically, a recurring thematic feature.
The eponymous heroine displays a reticence about language and more
precisely about the patter associated with bourgeois ritual around
culinary pleasure. Cutting an enigmatic figure who shuns public visibility,
she is seen by some as lacking in intelligence. La Cheffe delights in this
error which shields her from the intrusion of others. When pressed on
the secret of her culinary success, she replies: 'il suffit d'être organisé'
(CRC, 10) ['you just have to be organised' (TC, 2)]. The use of litotes
marks a broader social situation, preserving a mode of speech and a class
provenance that signal a rejection of middle-class leisure: 'Nulle part elle
n'appréciait ni ne respectait l'emphase, le grand genre' (CRC, 11) ['She
had no taste for preciousness or grandiloquence, no respect for them'
(TC, 3; translation modified)]. The milieu of material poverty la Cheffe
grew up in spells exclusion and, with it, it would seem, inarticulacy.

Yet if the avoidance of *le grand genre* appears to define the personality
of la Cheffe, the reality of her lived experience is more complex.
Achieving remarkable success in her work, she strives ambitiously to
awaken culinary sensations in her clients while nevertheless shunning the
linguistic commentary that traditionally accompanies it. Her dismissal
of what is presented as a class-specific discursive practice is clear: 'tout ce
cinéma comme elle disait' (CRC, 193) ['fancy talk, as she called it' (TC,
191)]. She brands elaborate linguistic ritual as exhibitionistic, her own
desire being to achieve anonymity, indeed unrecognizability. Tensions
that are both linguistic and social are explored within the text. One
reviewer refers to the virtuosic character of *La Cheffe* and sees the novel
drawing stylistically on the classics of French literature to capture the
life of a cook.[2] But any sense of mismatch between subject and genre,

---

2   See Nelly Kaprièlian, '*La Cheffe, roman d'une cuisinière* de Marie Ndiaye:
une vie mystique', *Les Inrockuptibles*, 27 September 2016.

utilitarian industriousness and linguistic ornamentation, diminishes when one remembers Rancière's reflection (informed by Jacotot) on the arbitrary separation between the manual and the verbal: 'Demeure abruti celui qui oppose l'œuvre de la main ouvrière et du peuple nourricier aux nuages de la rhétorique' ['He who makes a distinction between the manual work of the worker or the common man and clouds of rhetoric remains stultified'].[3]

Ndiaye's novel tracks the young cook's flight from linguistic expressivity or, more accurately, her search for a language that signals a fidelity to proletarian origins. Her mode of dress, uniform-like and impersonal, reflects a conscious will to imitate the ways of her native village, Sainte-Bazeille, with the same paper dress pattern serving for both summer and winter clothes. As with the paternal aunts in Simon's *L'Acacia*, the dressmaking template references a wider social framing in which subordinate lives are contained: 'la coupe comme les tissus [...] ne voulaient rien dire, aspiraient à ne rien dire' (CRC, 100) ['the cut and the fabric (...) weren't trying to say anything, they were trying to say nothing' (TC, 95]. La Cheffe's body covering, so to speak, would thus be an attempt to retreat from social meaning and intercourse – we read of 'ce dépouillement volontairement dénué de signification' (CRC, 101) ['that plainness deliberately stripped of meaning' (TC, 96–97)]. Yet if such a withdrawal is at one level a refusal of consumerist modernity, it also, and necessarily, signifies, in that it marks allegiance to a relationality grounded in family life back in her village.

The sense of a cramped, local fidelity is captured by the narrator when he runs into la Cheffe on her way to a family wedding. Her style of dress on that occasion causes her intense anxiety. Wearing clothes of a type expected of her for the celebration, she stands uneasily in the shiny satin dress that serves as a marker of class-bound conventions of fashion. These seemingly different styles – la Cheffe's working clothes and the choice of outfit for a family wedding – share nevertheless the characteristics of a uniform and point to a constricting social-class formation.

The narrator dwells in a fetishistic manner on the contrast between la Cheffe's body – wiry, desexualized, unfeminine – and the clothes that cover it. He confesses to feeling physical attraction for her as she stands self-consciously and yet compliantly in the mode of dress that society apportions. In an ethnographic-style observation, he likens

---

3 *Le Maître ignorant*, p. 64; *The Ignorant Schoolmaster*, p. 37. For earlier discussion of Jacotot's assertion, see above, Introduction, pp. 8–9.

her physique to that of his own mother – in both cases, the shaping of working-class bodies by daily physical effort sees them fail to align with the commodity-driven world of fashion.

Ndiaye's narrator urges the implied bourgeois reader to work, as it were, in order to understand working-class ways. As a confidant of la Cheffe and one-time employee in the restaurant she owned, he challenges the reader's negative assumptions about the conditions of material poverty in which she has grown up: 'C'est à nous de nous efforcer de l'atteindre là', he insists, 'dans ce bonheur qui a été le sien au début, qu'il nous est si difficile d'imaginer' (CRC, 20) ['It's our job to work at reaching her there, in her early happiness we find so hard to imagine' (TC, 12)]. Literary reading, then, would become a space in which social understanding is reviewed and adjusted. A further attempt to activate reader empathy comes with the invitation to understand the experience of la Cheffe as a child, often not at school but rather working in the fields alongside her parents and feeling the 'plaisir de se sentir utile, et par là vivante' (CRC, 28) ['pleasure of feeling useful, and so of feeling alive' (TC, 21)]. The early, happy exposure to productive necessity cuts against the bourgeois assumption that the childhood in question marks a world of archaism and social injustice (CRC, 19; TC, 11). In a rejection of specifically French Republican doxa, the parents of la Cheffe actively shape her outlook, teaching their children to refute the view of poverty as conveyed by the 'sens commun représenté à Sainte-Bazeille par les voisins et les instituteurs' (CRC, 25) ['common sense (...) embodied in Sainte-Bazeille by their neighbours and teachers' (TC, 18)]. Later in life, she will wonder how it was that, deprived of all that makes others happy, her family experienced such 'joie de vivre' and 'unbearable integrity' ['cette insoutenable intégrité' (CRC, 33–34)]. The rejection of a society's 'common sense' extends to a striking image of the parents 'en retrait de l'école comme de toute institution [...] inaltérablement rétifs [...] comme deux petits ânes repliés sur leur mystérieux quant-à-soi' (CRC, 29) ['bucking the school as they bucked all institutions (...) immovable and obdurate (...) like two little donkeys wrapped up in their own mysterious world' (TC, 22)]. The patronizing analogy sees the narrator celebrate the excentric, asocial position occupied by the family. The appeal in *La Cheffe* to what is posited as the natural intelligence and absence of self-consciousness of the parents acquires further resonance when set against the place accorded to the school in Republican ideology. Péguy was an eloquent advocate of that ideology, hailing secondary education as 'la citadelle, le réduit de la culture en France' ['the citadel, culture's enclave in France'].[4] Yet he dismissed the 1881 legislation which saw schooling made compulsory in France as the work of intellectuals who were removed from the people. 'Le peuple, avant la culture, [...] le peuple sait d'instinct et d'épreuve' ['The people, before culture, (...) the people knows from instinct and experience'], he protested.[5] Far from articulating any socially progressive, collective aspiration, *La Cheffe* depicts a heroine who actively embraces austerity, her cooking conveying 'sa frugalité presque fanatique' (CRC, 93) ['almost fanatical plainness' (TC, 87)].

The description in *La Cheffe* of the protagonist's counter-cultural asceticism and of the social atomization this brings is thrown into relief at numerous points in the novel. In a series of italicized textual interludes, the narrator, now living in retirement in Lloret de Mar, records the humdrum routine of shared eating and drinking within a French expatriate community. The predictability of collective leisure points up the intensity of la Cheffe's commitment to her craft and the extent of her marginality. Frugality for her entails a denial of exuberance and of bodily excess. She abhors close physical contact with her first employers, seeking to avoid seeing 'leur langue, leurs lèvres, leur échauffement après le repas' (CRC, 42) ['their tongues, their lips, their post-meal glow' (TC, 35)]; and the severity of her hairstyle – her aim is to 'faire oublier qu'elle avait une chevelure' (CRC, 267) ['make others forget she had hair at all' (TC, 267)] – likewise signals a radical self-effacement in the wish to suppress bodily allure. Yet the protagonist implicitly practises an act of self-perpetuation through her work, which she sees as having a therapeutic potential for its recipients: 'elle voulait que le mangeur entre dans un état de contemplation sereine et modeste' (CRC, 43) ['she wanted the eater to fall into a state of quiet, modest contemplation' (TC, 36)].

With the narrator asserting that his own moral compass has been altered through contact with la Cheffe, he speculates that his project as the teller of her life story might be hagiographic in character. While he abandons that perspective, fearing la Cheffe's disapproval, her work in the kitchen is presented nevertheless as an atypical endeavour. Ritual is intrinsic to her work. Her conviction on first entering the kitchen in the summer home of a bourgeois couple in the Landes region is that 'on pose

---

4 Péguy, *Notre jeunesse*, p. 34.

5 Péguy, *Personnalités* (1902), in *Œuvres en prose complètes*, I, 909–10; quoted and discussed in Compagnon, *Les Antimodernes*, p. 226.

sur la cuisine des mains autorisées, délicates, légères et conscientes de ce qu'elles font' (CRC, 56) ['cuisine is a thing on which only authorised hands are to be laid, respectful, delicate, mindful of what they're doing' (TC, 49; translation modified)]. In the heat of the kitchen, the adolescent likewise experiences 'la grâce joyeuse de la créativité [qui] absorbait tout' (CRC, 69) ['the joyful grace of creation (that) absorbed it all' (TC, 63)]. The conspicuously priestly tones are reinforced in the image of la Cheffe metaphorically holding aloft 'la flamme de sa mission' (CRC, 95) ['the flame of her mission' (TC, 90)]. As if to echo the work-as-prayer motif in Péguy, Ndiaye proposes a no less elevated conception of artisanship but with socially isolating consequences.

La Cheffe's conception of work is linked variously to the obsessional, the puritanical, and the ethical – she is 'une illuminée paisible, une fanatique réservée (CRC, 95) ['a quiet visionary, a sober fanatic' (TC, 90)]. With her kitchen experiments extending into the night in the business premises she later acquires, she is described as being 'toute seule et souveraine dans le silence compact de la nuit' (CRC, 69) ['all alone and all-powerful in the thick silence of the night' (TC, 63)]. She acquires a particular kind of self-knowledge: 'elle fit connaissance avec son propre corps' (CRC, 77) ['she discovered her own body' (TC, 72)]. A liberating autonomy is energetically worked through an amplified sense of corporeal movement, la Cheffe drawing on 'sa propre harmonie, […] son adaptation équilibrée, heureuse et belle à tout endroit où elle devait cuisiner' (CRC, 90) ['her own inner harmony, unruffled and adaptable, happy and beautiful wherever she was cooking' (TC, 84)]. Kinaesthetic movement thus becomes her expressive medium, her investment in bodily expression being what in another context is evoked as a 'strategic embrace of materiality'.[6] With poor literacy and seldom using recipe books, Ndiaye's protagonist uses her prodigious memory to compensate. In her culinary creations, she is ambitious in what appears to be an ethical way, as illustrated by her goal to 'invent[er] la probité et le respect de soi dans le dessert' (CRC, 99) ['bring integrity and self-respect to dessert' (TC, 95)]. La Cheffe attains a state of self-belonging which is lived significantly through the sensible, to use Rancière's vocabulary: through artisanal endeavour, bodily movement, and a tactile response to materiality. 'Another kind of knowledge' is

---

6   For discussion of materiality and manual technique in works by eighteenth-century French artists, see Ewa Lajer-Burcharth, *The Painter's Touch: Boucher, Chardin, Fragonard* (Princeton: Princeton University Press, 2018), p. 3.

thus in play, to borrow from Zeynep Çelik Alexander, who reflects on how the link between two meanings of 'taste' has been erased, 'the exalted faculty for aesthetic discrimination that so many philosophers had theorized and its more corporal twin that had been historically depreciated'.[7] Yet Ndiaye's protagonist rejects any suggestion that her achievements in the kitchen might equate to high culture. As if to endorse the continuum between material production and aesthetics on which Jacotot insists, the narrator surmises that in her work she performs what in other circumstances might have been the work of a painter or writer. Her dismissive response – 'elle se méfiait des grands mots' (CRC, 193) ['she didn't like fancy talk' (TC, 191)] – reinforces a censorious, self-deprecating language that enshrines a conservative order, in which the apportionment of roles in relation to ornamentation and social usefulness is rigidly policed. She does not see herself as having a special talent, counterarguing that she has 'seulement la chance d'être organisée, travailleuse, intuitive et d'héberger en soi, sans garantie que ce fût pour toujours, le petit génie de son métier' (CRC, 193) ['only the good luck to be organised, hard-working, intuitive, and to house within her, with no guarantee it would last, the little spirit of her craft' (TC, 191)].

While achievement is grounded in a narrow work ethic, the complicating motif of the near-fanatical, the 'presque fanatique' (CRC, 93), however, shows intense elan. The prevailing societal constraint la Cheffe wrestles with is thus refracted in the description of her almost vehement engagement in her work. Expressivity remains at its freest for her when it is manual, kinetic, and non-verbal: in these guises it opens up a utopian space that allows temporary secession from a social order grounded in oppositionality (bourgeois leisure versus alienated work, art versus labour, the refined versus the vulgar). The strand of escapist fantasy is perhaps also signalled in the *roman d'une cuisinière* of the title, the *roman* label retaining something of the marvellous adventure with which early uses of the term were historically associated.[8]

Yet the mood elsewhere in the novel is one of a fall from grace, as the hold of conflicted social relations and contingency reasserts itself.

7 Zeynep Çelik Alexander, *Kinaesthetic Knowing: Aesthetics, Epistemology, Modern Design* (Chicago and London: Chicago University Press, 2017), pp. 8, 27.
8 The twelfth-century use of the term *roman* denoted a story involving fabulous adventures. See *Le Grand Robert de la langue française* (Paris: Dictionnaires-Le Robert, 2001).

Ndiaye's protagonist is intensely conscious, for example, of the material conditions underpinning culinary production:

> un écœurement, une immense lassitude pouvaient vous donner envie de fuir les lieux, disait la Cheffe, et de ne plus jamais vous sentir uni à la chair morte, aux odeurs lourdes, aux entrailles et à la graisse, aux tourments divers et monotones, à l'inévitable saleté, et aux souffrances de ceux, bêtes et hommes, qui préludaient à l'arrivée sur la table de la cuisine des denrées taciturnes, obtuses, hurlements des bêtes, fatigue des hommes, vous aviez envie de vous sauver au plus loin quand cette misère répétitive vous sautait au visage, que la froide exaltation créatrice ne vous protégeait pas. (CRC, 85)

> [an enormous weariness and nausea might make you wish you could just run away, the Cheffe said, and never again feel yourself bound up with that dead, stinking flesh, the entrails, the fat, the tedious labours, the inevitable filth, and the pain of all those, human and animal, by way of whom an ineloquent, mindless food made its way from kitchen to table, the animals' shrieks, the humans' exhaustion, you wanted to run away as far as you could when that monotonous misery hit you full force, when the cool ecstasy of creation wasn't protecting you. (LC, 79–80)]

In registering the accumulation of miseries (both animal and human animal) that come with proximity to productive necessity, Ndiaye implicitly references class-specific notions of distinction associated with gastronomic pleasure, which here collide with the often violent contingent reality of food sourcing and production.

The ambition of Ndiaye's protagonist, as noted earlier, is to have her commitment to artisanship acquire a moral dimension. The kinaesthetics associated with her work in the kitchen functions both as an ethics of self-giving and as a communion with materiality. Yet the novel checks any automatic correlation between probity and manual skill. Employed for a time in a Bordeaux restaurant, la Cheffe works with a chef whose misogyny does not preclude great culinary dexterity: 'Comment était-ce possible, se demandait la Cheffe [...], que la vilaine âme de Millard ne fût pas un obstacle au labeur consciencieux de ses mains [...]?' (CRC, 180) ['How could it be, the Cheffe wondered (...), that Millard's ugly soul never got in the way of his hands' diligent labours (...)?' (TC, 178)]. The coexistence of malignity and diligent craft challenges the puritanical, isolationist work ethic that shapes la Cheffe (and challenges, too, we might note in passing, the assumptions underpinning Péguy's eulogy to artisanship in *L'Argent*). By conjoining industriousness and spitefulness in the figure of Millard, Ndiaye provides a foil for the probity and asceticism embodied by the eponymous heroine.⁹ Elsewhere in *La Cheffe*, however, the pursuit of work continues to hold therapeutic value as when the narrator, recovering from drug abuse, is re-employed by la Cheffe, for whom work's discipline is 'l'unique remède auquel elle accordait foi' (CRC, 269) ['the only remedy she had any faith in' (TC, 269)].

That la Cheffe is an unworldly protagonist is further reflected in her uneasy relationship with the logic and practice of capitalist profit. The modest pricing structure in her restaurant scrupulously accords value to labour, so that wine is sold at virtually cost price, her reasoning being that she has contributed nothing to its production. Compliments from the Mayor of Bordeaux unsettle her: 'Comment [...] rester juste, implacable, distante et honnête [...]?' (CRC, 226) ['How (...) to remain decent, detached, rigorous and honest (...)?' (TC, 224)], she wonders. Likewise, the award of a Michelin star distresses her, the refrain of shame ('la honte') confirming how class allegiance exerts a visceral hold on la Cheffe.¹⁰ The prospect of ceremonial elevation conferred on her by bourgeois clients is seen as disquieting. In a more matter-of-fact vein, she notes how, with her client base becoming more middle-class, such customers colonize willy-nilly the space of the restaurant:

> la clientèle aisée, avertie finissait par chasser, sans le vouloir ni s'en douter, celle qui ne lui ressemblait pas, par la seule force d'inertie de son autorité, de son bon droit, de tout ce qui émanait d'elle de sélectif et de clos. (CRC, 224–25)

> [the chic, well-heeled crowd was driving away everyone who wasn't like them, not that they wanted that or dreamt it was happening, but simply by the inertial force of their authority, of their innate right, of everything that was exclusive and closed about them. (TC, 223)]

In what serves as an illustration of Rancière's notion of an apportionment of the sensible, Ndiaye draws attention to cultures of entitlement and the often unspoken grammar underpinning them.

9   Shirley Jordan explores the presence in Ndiaye's work of modes of behaviour that 'transgress hospitality's most basic requirements'; see Jordan, *Marie Ndiaye: Inhospitable Fictions* (Cambridge: Legenda, 2017), p. 117.
10   CRC, 225 (TC, 224) and following pages. See Chapter 10, p. 262, for consideration of the theme of social shame in the work of Eribon. See also the brief discussion of Ernaux's reflections on the psychology of class migration, pp. 59, 116.

Yet while it maps the coordinates of social power and in crucial ways depicts characters who are squarely situated within them, Ndiaye's novel also imagines spaces beyond class antagonism. La Cheffe looks back on her experience as a sixteen-year-old, cooking in the middle-class household in the Landes, as a state of grace (CRC, 225; TC, 223). Significantly, the trio she forms that summer with her would-be employers appears to inhabit a space of mutual fulfilment, in a temporary occlusion of the class dialectic.

For the adolescent, the scene of autonomy and emancipatory possibility clashes with her experience within her own family. When she proposes to her parents dishes of the kind she prepares for her employers, they view her efforts as excessive and are disconcerted by 'l'élégante excentricité de ce qui entrait chez eux' ['the elegant eccentricity now coming into their house']. From their standpoint of obdurate frugality, such effort is 'gaspillé, extravagant' (CRC, 132) ['wasted, extravagant' (LC, 129)]. The novel thus dramatizes the stand-off between a social conservatism shaped by the demands of productive necessity and open-ended exploration, the parental reticence corroborating a view found in sociology regarding working-class hostility towards formal experimentation.[11] In their anxious response to their daughter's evolution, the narrowly utilitarian butts up against what is deemed redundant ornamentation.

Ndiaye underscores the cook's ambivalence towards her social origins:

elle a toujours pensé que sa réussite et son ambition l'avaient entraînée bien loin des rivages purs qu'habitaient ses parents, elle en a toujours éprouvé de la peine et une intense mélancolie. (CRC, 34)

[she'd always think her success and ambition had dragged her far, far away from the pure shores her parents lived on, and at that she felt a loss and a deep sadness. (TC, 27)]

The constriction of outlook deriving from familial piety and the obsessive pursuit of culinary success thus collide. The melancholia induced in la Cheffe by the weakening of her class links adds to the broader social disjunction present in the novel. Yet the teenager's will to connect with an older generation finds a compensatory outlet in contact with her employers, for whom she comes to act in a therapeutic role. Their interaction sees the marginal figure of the teenager redeem the guilt associated with the couple's gluttony, so that, as they shed self-loating, la Cheffe becomes 'le parfait véhicule entre les Clapeau et la splendeur' (CRC, 145) ['the perfect

---

11   See Bourdieu, *Distinction*, p. 32.

intermediary between the Clapeaus and magnificence' (TC, 142)]. The embedded routine of service provided by a subordinate thus acquires a particular form in *La Cheffe* in that the Clapeaus' neediness and dependence are remedied by the young cook serving in an educative role. Taken together, the contrasting responses of parents and employers to la Cheffe's artisanship neatly frame a spectrum running from proletarian inhibition and containment to practices of bourgeois consumption.

In place of the class resentment that assumes caricatural form in the relationship between the Clapeaus and their previous cook, la Cheffe's resolve appears utopian in its motivation. It is as though, through gastronomy, a new space beyond social determinism might emerge. The narrator makes this explicit, la Cheffe's intense aspiration in the home of her middle-class employers being to 'cuisiner dans un [...] oubli des contingences de leurs situations respectives' (CRC, 58) ['cook with (...) little regard for the contingencies of their respective situations' (TC, 52)]. While the unvarnished reality of rich and poor is acknowledged, the young cook looks to transcend alienation and conflicted class relations. Bourdieu defines class habitus as entailing 'the practice-unifying and practice-generating principle [...] the internalized form of class condition and of the conditionings it entails'.[12] The fairy-tale euphoria of scenes in the middle-class home in *La Cheffe* suspends this, albeit briefly however in that the couple, who, as class practice dictates, delegate tasks associated with everyday material need, come to experience the exclusion such delegation entails. The Clapeaus' failure to be part of what is presented as the miracle of the kitchen throws into relief the perspective of la Cheffe, who sees her work transcending class difference. Thus, she displays 'une volonté si acharnée d'œuvrer vers une perfection qui outrepasserait leurs goûts fortuits à tous, les leurs comme les siens' (CRC, 58) ['a will so bent on creating a perfection far beyond the chance likes and dislikes of all concerned, them and her alike' (TC, 52)]. Ndiaye disturbs class conditioning by exposing the randomness present in the social apportionment of taste and roles.

The teenage girl's intervention is presented, then, as restorative in its ambition, as a dream that would allow both her and her employers to step out of the alienated world of master-servant relations. In this new configuration, the compliant Clapeaus are entranced by la Cheffe's work and presence while she exults in her autonomy. Whereas the peasant sisters in Simon's *L'Acacia* adhere tightly to class habitus, the young

12 Bourdieu, *Distinction*, p. 101.

protagonist in *La Cheffe* abandons such compliance, it would seem, becoming 'heureuse pour des raisons qui ne tenaient qu'à elle-même [...] à sa confiance en ses capacités' (CRC, 76) ['happy for reasons that came only from herself, (...) her faith in her abilities' (TC, 70)]. That her will to be self-sufficient is disidentificatory in its social impact shows an absence of any conception of collective emancipation in *La Cheffe*. Indeed, in featuring an individual's temporary liberation, the novel comes increasingly to restore a residual, socially oppressive backdrop. The absence of any sustained emancipatory directedness working at a collective level in Ndiaye's novel reminds us, then, of Hallward's caution that sporadic expressions of equality risk being restricted to what Schiller calls the 'unsubstantial kingdom of the imagination'.[13]

In its description of the first meal prepared for the Clapeaus by the sixteen-year-old girl, the novel identifies the power dialectic at work. The teenager is presented as being confused about the twin forms of control she exerts: firstly, her 'humiliation' of the chicken, which is served in the form of a 'cromesquis' and involves what Judith Still calls 'a costly work of artifice (costing money, time, and a life)'; and secondly, the hold ('l'emprise') which the girl believes she has over her bourgeois employers (CRC, 120; TC, 115).[14] Readers of Proust will hear an echo in Ndiaye of the kitchen scenes in *Combray* where questions of domination and subordination are similarly threaded into the narrative. Providing a baroque inventory of foodstuffs and of culinary implements and receptacles, Proust's narrator describes ironically how, in the literal heat of the kitchen, the family cook Françoise commands the forces of nature (coal, steam, fire). The scullery scene in which she is seen viciously killing the chicken furthers the sense of a will to dominate. Yet, as the dishes she prepares reflect, Françoise is not excluded from the practice of virtue in the eyes of the boy Marcel. While these twin dimensions

---

13   Hallward, 'Staging Equality', p. 155. See above, Introduction, pp. 14–15.

14   Still reflects on the grotesque presentation which sees the cooked meat, eggs, and the other ingredients that make up the *cromesquis* being worked back into a simulacrum of the shape of the chicken that has been killed. She contrasts this with the closing scene of *La Cheffe*, where the protagonist invites the narrator to a virtual meal which consists of spectacle, in that they look on as chickens walk about freely in a garden where vegetables grow. See Judith Still, 'Disorderly Eating in Marie NDiaye's "La Gourmandise", *or* The solitary pleasure of a *Mère de famille*', in Shirley Jordan and Judith Still (eds), *Disorderly Eating in Contemporary Women's Writing*, special issue of *Journal of Romance Studies*, 20.2 (June 2020), 365–89 (pp. 368–69).

allow the narrator neatly to cast Françoise's performances as latter-day avatars of Giotto's 'Vices' and 'Virtues', they also allow him to frame in often ludic terms the themes of compliant service and violent authority.[15] Like la Cheffe, Françoise is the channel for the pleasure of her middle-class employers. For both protagonists, any disturbance to a pattern of residual subordination (as when a superior needs what an inferior provides) remains restricted to the delegated area that involves attending to the material necessities of everyday life.

In *À la recherche*, which will be the focus of Chapter 8, the language of social dialectic is regularly invoked in parodic form. Nor is parody absent in relation to questions of status and social value in *La Cheffe*. When Ndiaye's protagonist serves up food in the casserole dish in which she has cooked it, the scene is ludically construed as a frontal assault on bourgeois good taste: 'la puissance de la cocotte (autoritairement décrétée par la cocotte même) les intimideraient en les prenant par surprise' (CRC, 116) ['the power of the casserole (regally decreed by the casserole itself) would intimidate (the Clapeaus), having caught them off guard' (TC, 111)]. The self-worth of the casserole dish is also affirmed in a mimicking of revolutionary fervour: 'la cocotte ouvrière [...] dans sa féroce dignité, n'était pas honorée de contenir et de présenter la soupe raffinée' (CRC, 117) ['the proletarian casserole (...), in its stern dignity, was not honoured to be containing and presenting that refined soup' (TC, 112)]. The mocking characterization of a kitchen utensil as exercising powerful agency implicitly places limits on what are the intermittent elements of serious social critique in the narrative. In a similar way, the image of ominous power being exerted by the pine trees outside the kitchen window points to magic and melodrama in the account of the summer months of cohabitation in the Landes home, as does the nervous glance from Mme Clapeau that suggests la Cheffe is a witch casting her spell ['une jeteuse de sorts' (CRC, 119)].[16]

A different tone marks those sections of the novel which foreground the protagonist's euphoria. There, autonomy is lived in an intensely corporeal way, as we have seen, with the sixteen-year-old in the dark kitchen of the bourgeois home described as living '[une] vocation comprise et reconnue par chaque partie du corps' (CRC, 76) ['a calling recognised and understood by every part of her body' (TC, 71)]. Her

---

15   See Proust, RTP, I, 119–20; ISLT, I, 122–23.
16   A novel in which Ndiaye places centre stage the dimension of sorcery and magic is *La Sorcière* (Paris: Minuit, 1996).

nimble hands and feet work as though independently from her: 'les mains expertes de la Cheffe menaient leur vie propre en toute discrétion' (CRC, 77) ['the Cheffe's expert hands discreetly led their own life' (TC, 71)]. The experience assumes a mystical character, with both la Cheffe and the consumers of her dishes experiencing a form of blissful madness. Rancière's reflection on modes of liberation working at the level of the sensible has a bearing on Ndiaye's text. He insists that

> avec [...] la promotion de l'art des artisans au grand art et la prétention nouvelle de mettre de l'art dans le décor de toute vie, c'est tout un découpage ordonné de l'expérience sensible qui chavire.

> [with (...) the elevation of artisans' art to the status of great art, and the new claim to bring art into the décor of each and every life, an entire well-ordered distribution of sensory experience is overturned.][17]

Yet the destabilizing effect Rancière identifies assumes a particular character in *La Cheffe*. For while the book's heroine may be seen as partaking in a redistribution of the sensible, her obsession with cooking ultimately becomes a form of derangement to rival the addiction afflicting her employers:

> Mais qu'ils aient augmenté par leur passion de la nourriture l'amplitude réduite de leur existence, qu'ils aient permis à une telle folie de structurer chaque moment de leurs journées, elle le comprenait, le respectait, sentant déjà en elle le germe d'une folie très semblable, plus souhaitable simplement parce qu'elle saurait en faire l'instrument de sa renommée, qu'elle se laisserait entraîner mais jamais dominer par cela, en tout cas jusque dans ses ultimes années d'exercice où cette folie l'a peut-être engloutie en effet. (CRC, 80)

> [But the fact that they'd expanded the shrunken dimensions of their lives with a passion for food, that they'd allowed that mania to structure every moment of their days, she could understand that, respect it, already feeling in herself the stirrings of a very similar mania, more enviable only because she would make it her way to fame, because she would let it carry her but never overpower her, until her last years, at least, when that mania might indeed have finally submerged her. (LC, 74–75)]

As if to signal the impossibility of imagining social relations other than those predicated on rank, the interaction between employers and

---

17 *Le Partage du sensible*, p. 21; *The Politics of Aesthetics*, p. 12 (translation modified).

employee acquires a manic dimension. The narrator explains how la Cheffe admits that

> ils s'étaient retrouvés pris tous les trois [...] dans un tourbillon d'exaltation qui les [...] épuisa[it] sans qu'ils s'en rendent compte, et la conscience des devoirs inouïs de sa fonction vis-à-vis d'eux comme la conscience qu'avaient les Clapeau de la vénération qu'ils lui devaient auraient fini par les anéantir [...] s'ils étaient demeurés dans cette violente, cette fanatique solitude à trois. (CRC, 125–26)

> [all three of them were caught up (...) in an ecstatic whirlwind that (...) exhaust(ed) them without their even noticing it, and the awareness of the incredible responsibilities of her work, like the Clapeaus' awareness of the reverence they owed her, would (...) eventually have destroyed them (...) if they'd remained in that violent, fanatical solitude à trois. (TC, 121–22)]

The theme of ethical probity evoked elsewhere in the novel to convey la Cheffe's working practice here risks mutating into an alienating relationality and social isolation.

*   *   *

Like Ndiaye's fiction more broadly, *La Cheffe* thus draws on the energies of obsessiveness working both creatively and destructively. As Judith Still explains, gluttony and radical abstemiousness, for example, form a leitmotif in the novelist's work.[18] An illustration of this is the perilous loss of measure present in the short story 'Le Jour du président', where the anorexia afflicting the first-person narrator (the young student Olga) signals an expression of radical social withdrawal. Yet she plans an improbable intervention, her aim being to address directly the president of the Republic on the occasion of his visit to Le Havre. Ndiaye uses the compressed medium of the short story to accentuate the drama, the closing scene showing the weak teenager falling over, with the president, his face mask-like, leaning down towards her in a moment of disturbing apotheosis. 'Le Jour du président' provides a demonstration in miniature of 'practice-unifying' social dispositions, to use Bourdieu's terminology, and the denouement, with the asymmetry of power relations it generates, evokes what amounts to a parody of encounter between two citizens of the Republic. Additional tensions are at work in this brief text: ability

18   See Still, 'Disorderly Eating', pp. 365–66.

versus disability, the role of gender in social hierarchy, bodily hexis and concern about appropriateness in the area of forms of spoken address – these all feed into the narrative in which the distribution of the sensible, to draw again on Rancière, sees 'la domination impose[r] l'évidence sensible de sa légitimité' ['domination imposing, at the level of the sensible, the evidence of its legitimacy'].[19] Judith Still reflects on how Olga acts out 'a protest and a lament, which relates to the exclusion, or over-forceful inclusion, in a community which feels hostile' to her. In the same context, Still observes that the category 'anorexia' is not specifically mentioned by Ndiaye. Signalling the risks present in reader diagnosis and being 'drawn into naming', she argues that the novelist shows an ability to work with 'the "both/and" rather than the authorial cut of conclusion'.[20]

Elsewhere in 'Le Jour du président', Ndiaye draws attention to shifts in dress sense that see young middle-class women wear painters' overalls. In a similar way, the fashionable shabbiness of two female students living in the same guest house as Olga has them wearing jackets like the one worn by a man who has fallen on hard times. The narrator reflects ironically on 'la vieille veste si démocratiquement identique' ['the old jacket, identical in a very democratic way'].[21] The illusion of equalization belies asymmetrical social distribution, as does the presidential visit where access to the guardian of Republican democracy is carefully screened.

Ndiaye's provocative coupling of celebrity and obscurity in 'Le Jour du président' may be mapped onto the coordinates present in *La Cheffe*. Described as being 'dans son genre [...] indélogeable' ['in her own way (...) impossible to dislodge'], the working-class mother of the anorexic student is an avatar of the young cook in her stubbornness and sense of honesty.[22] A strain of delirium is thus also present in 'Le Jour du président'.

To return to *La Cheffe*, the radical autonomy so keenly enjoyed by the heroine in earlier times is disrupted by her experience of parenthood. When, as a young mother, she relives memories of the Clapeaus' kitchen, her desire is to

> recouvrer les pensées qui faisaient se mouvoir les mains habiles, les mains industrieuses et justes et qui se rappelaient tout, elle voulait rentrer en

19   Rancière, *Aux bords du politique*, p. 17.
20   Still, 'Disorderly Eating', p. 367.
21   Ndiaye, 'Le Jour du président', in Didier Vergnaud (ed.), *La Double Entente du jeu* (L'Eté du livre en Gironde, 1997), pp. 29–46 (p. 44).
22   Ndiaye, 'Le Jour du président', p. 35.

possession de ce qui lui avait appartenu [...], l'immense et calme plaisir de ces gestes, l'intelligence des mains scrupuleuses, cette vision aimable et enviable d'elle-même en jeune femme capable de se suffire, ouvrière de sa joie, de sa tranquille fierté. (CRC, 151)

[recover the thoughts animating those skilled hands, those industrious, precise hands that had forgotten nothing, she wanted to retake possession of what was once hers (...) the immense, quiet pleasure of those motions, the intelligence of those careful hands, that delightful, enviable image of herself as a young woman who needed no-one but herself, a worker forging her own joy, her own tranquil pride. (TC, 148–49)]

Ndiaye provides an image of double autonomy in that, through memory, la Cheffe is freed in her person as are the intelligence and memory of her hands. The novelist thus evokes what one critic, describing a different context, refers to as 'the implications of the particular habits of hand and mind'.[23] It is as a self-managing subject that la Cheffe attends to her well-being, becoming, in Ndiaye's significant formulation, the maker of her joy ['ouvrière de sa joie']. In this affirmation of self-creation, a worker's productivity consists in generating her own fulfilment independently from any group endeavour or the workings of economic power.

If much of *La Cheffe* hinges on the obsessive and socially isolating hold of honest graft on its eponymous heroine, the scenes of late-night experimentation in the restaurant kitchen in Bordeaux where the narrator observes la Cheffe cast a different light on social disaggregation. As in Rancière's *La Nuit des prolétaires*, where nineteenth-century workers are presented as dreaming of escape from capitalist exploitation, as focussing on 'l'anti-marchandise' ['the anticommodity'], the nocturnal scenes in *La Cheffe*, prior to the physical decline of the protagonist, function as spaces beyond conflicted class relations in which an individual subjectivity lays claim to sovereignty.[24] In the narrator's eulogistic portrayal,

c'était [...] des matérialisations de rêves qui naissaient sous ses doigts durant ces nuits ondulantes, détachées de la nuit des autres aussi nettement qu'un monde parallèle de l'univers ordinaire. (CRC, 223)

[those were dreams taking shape in her hands in those undulating nights, as different from other people's nights as a parallel world from the everyday universe. (TC, 221)]

23 See Lajer-Burcharth, *The Painter's Touch*, p. 4.
24 *La Nuit des prolétaires*, p. 20; *Proletarian Nights*, p. 8.

In one very precise sense, the link being suggested between *La Nuit des prolétaires* and *La Cheffe, roman d'une cuisinière* is inexact: the cook's night-time experiments, to the extent that they feed into the development of new menus for her restaurant, clearly have an instrumental function, whereas Rancière's subjects are seeking to 'exorciser leur inexorable avenir de travailleurs utiles' ['exorcise their inexorable future as useful workers'].²⁵ Utilitarian constraint is what Rancière's figures of the night energetically shun. Yet in both Rancière and Ndiaye, voice is given to a longing to flee an 'ordinary world' bowed under the daily round of alienated social relations – what Rancière calls the 'jour le jour de la domination' ['daily round of domination'].²⁶ Night provides that emancipatory backdrop in both texts. The strong valorization of autonomy reminds us that, as contemporary authors, Rancière and Ndiaye, while belonging to different generations and clearly engaged in different projects, draw on the thread of *autogestion* running through the cultural change ushered in by 'les années 68' ['the '68 years'].²⁷

Ndiaye's *La Cheffe* depicts a work-obsessed heroine whose labour transcends, and yet also reconstructs, the strictures imposed by class habitus. The novel thus explores the tension between a fidelity to modest social beginnings that borders on derangement and la Cheffe's no less obsessive pursuit of the objects of her burning curiosity. In this latter area, she records a duty of memory to her initiation to cooking in the Landes household and to 'la dense quiétude qui avait enrobé, apaisé, dans la cuisine des Clapeau, la fébrilité propre au travail' (CRC, 152) ['the dense serenity that in the Clapeaus' kitchen enveloped and eased the fever that came with her work' (TC, 150)]. That the protagonist's emancipation is both isolatory and consigned to her past confirms the theme of radical singularity in *La Cheffe*. More broadly, the ephemeral nature of the cross-class healing illustrates the fitful presence in the novel of spaces that can function outside class alienation.

25   *La Nuit des prolétaires*, p. 20; *Proletarian Nights*, p. 8.
26   *La Nuit des prolétaires*, p. 22; *Proletarian Nights*, p. 10.
27   The term was popularized by Michelle Zancarini-Fournel. See Julian Jackson, 'Rethinking May 68', in Julian Jackson, Anna-Louise Milne, and James S. Williams (eds), *May 68: Rethinking France's Last Revolution* (London: Palgrave Macmillan, 2011), p. 5.

CHAPTER FOUR

The Worker-Philosopher

Gauny and Self-Belonging

Le métier [*Handwerk*], c'est l'affaire des mains. Et ces mains, à leur tour, n'appartiennent qu'à *un* homme, c'est-à-dire une âme unique et mortelle, qui avec sa voix et sans voix cherche un chemin.

[Craft has to do with the hands. And those hands in turn belong to a *single* person, in other words to a unique and mortal soul, which with its voice and without voice is seeking a way.]

Celan[1]

In a 2018 interview, Rancière reflected on how, in the post-1968 climate when his research trajectory was changing direction, the *voix d'en bas* or voices-from-below motif formed an important strand of social interrogation.[2] The texts by Ndiaye, Beinstingel, and the chronologically earlier figure of Péguy discussed in preceding chapters may be read through such an optic in that they foreground the theme of voices overlooked and lifestyles discarded. Rancière insists in the same interview that two 'excentric' thinkers played a 'vital' role in his personal development. Joseph Jacotot provides the inspiration for *Le Maître ignorant*, while the second inspirational figure, the nineteenth-century writer and social commentator Louis Gabriel Gauny, was

1   Paul Celan, letter of 18 May 1960 to Hans Bender, in Celan, *Le Méridien et autres proses* (Paris: Seuil, 2002), pp. 43–44. I am grateful to Leonard Olschner for drawing my attention to Celan's reflections on the hand.

2   Interview with Julien Le Gros, 'Jacques Rancière, "Le Philosophe plébéien"', *Le Dissident*, 2 April 2018. https://the-dissident.eu/jacques-ranciere-philosophe-plebeien/ [accessed 12 December 2018].

rescued from obscurity in 1983, when Rancière published a collection of his writings under the title *Le Philosophe plébéien.*[3]

The republication in 2017 of that earlier edition reflected the growing critical interest in Rancière's work in the intervening decades but it also confirms the foundational importance of his original work on the Gauny corpus in the municipal library in Saint-Denis. Rancière spent many years in the 1970s researching in workers' archives and he used the occasion of the new edition to question the underlying presupposition of those working on 'thought from below', namely that such thought would reveal proletarian compliance with socially attributed roles. According to such a view, workers suffer and yet they sing (we saw an echo of this in Péguy's portrayal of the nineteenth-century artisan in *L'Argent*). Crucially for Rancière, the unequal society is a fundamentally orderly one. He rehearses Plato's assertion that as part of the fabric of the ordered society, the 'worker-being' or *être-ouvrier* has no time to be involved in governance (PP, 10). Yet the contents of the Gauny archive taught Rancière quite the reverse: there, the worker writes of taking the time not accorded to him in order to pursue the emancipation that comes from the time to think. It is an emancipation that undoes the stereotypical view of adherence to an authentic popular culture. The result for the researcher, Rancière argues, is that the expected distribution of roles and voices is subverted, with 'amphibian' figures such as Gauny failing to adhere to class type: 'nous ne savons plus où ils sont et où nous sommes' (PP, 8) ['we no longer know where they are and where we researchers are'].[4]

Rancière provides a thumbnail sketch of Gauny, who was born in the then working-class Faubourg Saint-Marcel in Paris in 1806 and died in 1889 in the rue des Gobelins. He offers a pithy summing up of this obscure life: 'Quatre-vingt-trois ans pour se déplacer d'une centaine de mètres' (PP, 13) ['Eighty-three years to move about a hundred metres']. The image of geographical narrowness would seem to betoken a life of social containment yet the Gauny papers were to confound Rancière's expectations. Unlike a figure such as Agricol Perdiguier, the joiner-turned-parliamentarian who sang the praises of workers' brotherhoods,

---

3   Louis Gabriel Gauny, *Le Philosophe plébéien*, ed. Jacques Rancière (Paris: La Découverte/Presses Universitaires de Vincennes, 1983). A revised edition of the 1983 edition was published in 2017 (Paris: La Fabrique). References to the text are to the 2017 edition, cited with the abbreviation PP.

4   Rancière refers to 'a class of amphibian beings' ['une classe d'êtres amphibies'] in the preface to the 2007 Flammarion edition of *Le Philosophe et ses pauvres*, p. v.

Gauny emerges as an advocate not of collective aggregation but of social disassociation. Hence Rancière's surprise at finding in the municipal archive in Saint-Denis material ranging from metaphysical speculation to a budgetary methodology to plan for everyday needs, such a plan being aimed at reducing the claims made by productive necessity on an individual's life.

Literature, labour, living, ecology, and philosophy all feature in the Gauny papers. Rancière adduces a number of biographical details that signal his author's refusal to comply with the proletarian conformism that might have been expected of him. At the last minute, Gauny decides against visiting George Sand, the high-profile sponsor of worker-writers of her day; and in another mark of his failure to conform to type, an attempt to be admitted to the Club de l'Organisation des Travailleurs in 1848 came to nothing.

Unlike the fidelity to manual ways that so motivates Péguy in *L'Argent* and is also pivotal in Ndiaye's *La Cheffe* and Beinstingel's *Retour aux mots sauvages*, Gauny's perspective on the world of labour is an ambivalent one. A joiner by trade, he is reluctant to accept the view of the worker as someone restricted by 'disposition', by 'a *way of being, a habitual state* [...] a *predisposition*', to use Bourdieu's terms.[5] Campaigning against what he presents as the servitude constituted by organized labour in the France of his day, Gauny lays claim to philosophy and 'culture'. As a *philosophe plébéien* or worker-intellectual, he identifies and celebrates the power of thought to absorb him (PP, 56). Rancière, asked about the risk of paternalism in his use of the 'plebeian philosopher' designation, counterargues that, for him, the term 'plebeian' calls to mind the revolt of 494 BC on the Aventine Hill, when the plebeians argued that they, no less than the patricians, were beings of language. The arbitrary apportionment of word (*logos*) to the patricians and noise (*phonē*) to the plebeians is collapsed when Menenius Agrippa is obliged to speak to those who have withdrawn their labour. The fable which the representative of the patricians offers them is one of a hierarchical order (within the body public, they are the limbs in that they attend to material things, while the patricians form the stomach, without which the limbs, Menenius Agrippa insists, could not function). Yet the

---

5   Bourdieu, *Outline of a Theory of Practice*, trans. Richard Nice (Cambridge: Cambridge University Press, 1977), p. 214; emphasis in the original. Quoted in Karl Maton, 'Habitus', in Michael Grenfell (ed.), *Pierre Bourdieu, Key Concepts* (London: Routledge, 2014), pp. 48–64 (p. 50).

transmission of the fable is effected through language, thereby pointing to 'l'égalité présupposée d'un vouloir dire et d'un vouloir entendre' ['a presupposed equality between a wish to speak and a wish to hear'].[6]

The movement in France in the 1960s and beyond that saw contestation of the embedded tendency to separate out manual and intellectual endeavour has a bearing on Rancière's promotion of Gauny. A one-time member of the *gauchiste* movement La Gauche Prolétarienne ['The Proletarian Left'], Rancière is drawn to the interrogation of who the producers of culture are and to the questioning of conventional forms of apportionment that see workers excluded from philosophy. Davis explains how the interest in Gauny lies less, for Rancière, in the actual beliefs that mobilized the followers of the social theorist Henri de Saint-Simon (beliefs about which Gauny may have been somewhat ambivalent) and more in the way in which such a body of material impacted on 'the self-concept of workers' in Gauny's day.[7]

Rancière's edition of Gauny's writings covers a wide span of texts, from the 1830s, when he was involved with the Saint-Simonians, through to the late 1870s. Far from rejecting intellectual thought, Gauny insists on the right of the individual to such thought, irrespective of social position. In an autobiographical fragment entitled 'Le Belvédère', his reasons for choosing to be a joiner are explained: it is a *métier* that brings with it involvement in a number of 'arts mécaniques' ['mechanical arts'], it develops an appreciation of 'les différentes nuances des bois' (PP, 254) ['the different nuances of wood'], and importantly, it combines manual and intellectual skill in that it develops 'l'adresse de la main, la rectitude du coup d'œil et l'attention de la pensée' (PP, 41) ['manual dexterity, a good eye, and mental attention']. Gauny adds an overtly religious inflection to the range of attributes by referencing the figure of Christ the carpenter.

Writing in *La Ruche populaire* in April 1841, Gauny rejects two perspectives – firstly, the standpoint of those who consume and do not produce (and in this he echoes the Saint-Simonians' stress on citizenship and economic productivity); and secondly, the position of those who confine themselves to a materialist view of the world:

6   *Aux bords du politique*, p. 159; *On the Shores of Politics*, p. 82. See also *Le Maître ignorant*, pp. 162–64; *The Ignorant Schoolmaster*, pp. 96–98. Davis sets out the importance for Rancière of Pierre-Simon Ballanche's 1830 account of the Aventine Secession; see Davis, *Jacques Rancière*, pp. 81–83.

7   Davis, *Jacques Rancière*, p. 56.

Il faut apprendre, apprendre sans fin, toujours apprendre! – Afin que l'esclave puisse, avec vérité et conviction, prouver au maître ce qu'il y a de meurtrier pour l'individu et surtout pour l'espèce humaine, dans celui qui consomme sans produire en privant la masse de son intelligence, ou dans celui qui produit sans autre résultat que d'obtenir une pâture matérielle et toujours insuffisante à l'organisation d'un *être humain*. (PP, 51; emphasis in the original)

[One must learn, learn constantly, always be learning! – In order that the slave may, with truth and conviction, demonstrate to the master how fatal it is for the individual and especially for the human race when someone consumes without producing, thereby robbing the mass of its intelligence, or when someone produces with the sole outcome of securing a gain that is material and always insufficient to the development of a *human being.*]

In drawing attention to the question of what constitutes the human, Gauny introduces an ethics of living to which he returns at numerous points in his writing.

His focus on lives cramped by material necessity also prompts him to view critically the literary canon. Heroes of social isolation such as Senancour's Obermann and Chateaubriand's René, as well as the world evoked by Dante, are dismissed on the grounds that, in experiential terms, many of the figures from canonical literature never had to contend with the hell of

la douleur vulgaire [...] du plébéien en proie aux horribles séances de l'atelier; cette ressource pénitentiaire qui ronge l'esprit et le corps par l'ennui et par la folie de son long travail. Ah! vieux Dante, tu n'as point voyagé dans *l'Enfer réel*, dans *l'Enfer sans poésie*. (PP, 51–52)

[the commonplace suffering of the plebeian subjected to the horrible shifts in workshops, that penitentiary resource which eats away at mind and body in the tedium and madness of long hours of work. Ah! dear old Dante, you have not walked in the *real Hell*, in the *Hell without poetry.*]

Yet Gauny's objective is not to have the manual worker exclude himself from literature but rather to see him move towards it. If the worker is enmeshed in a 'structured and structuring structure' to use Bourdieu's chiastic formulation, in what Gauny presents as the 'activités contre-nature de notre civilisation' (PP, 53) ['activities in our civilization that go against nature'], Rancière's plebeian philosopher advocates a moving beyond the contingent fact of economic necessity: 'Cet ouvrier veut absolument du bonheur. Il se hâte de manger pour s'appartenir un peu et s'égarer vingt minutes au fond de cette vague espérance' (PP, 55)

['Such a worker has an absolute desire for happiness. He eats quickly in order to belong to himself a bit and to lose himself for twenty minutes in this vague hope'].[8] In a more expansive formulation of the same longing, Gauny, writing to Louis Ponty in September 1855, notes that despite the factory conditions endured by Ponty, each evening, on leaving the workplace, 'tu plonges dans les étendues de la réflexion' (PP, 243) ['you dive into the great expanse of reflection']. The image of a spatialized system of domination and social containment to be found in Bourdieu contrasts with 'de-assigning' in Rancière, whose aim in editing Gauny is to reveal his subject to be one of the 'historical and fictional characters that frustrate causal narratives'.[9]

Gauny manipulates words every bit as much as he handles tools, his writerly craft becoming a vehicle for emancipation. Evoking the case of railway workers who are dominated by the demands of work and thus obliged to curtail the urge to reflect on happiness and the infinite, he writes: 'il faut [...] qu'ils *m*âchent, et *m*ordent, et *m*acèrent, et *m*utilent leurs pensées' (PP, 79) ['they must chew and bite and macerate and mutilate their thoughts']. The alliteration in the French original draws attention to Gauny's compositional style and shows the conspicuous presence of poiesis (in a manner not dissimilar to the forms of lexical concatenation we see in Péguy). In the September 1855 letter to Louis Ponty just mentioned, Gauny stresses the importance of writing as a proactive step in their self-realization in order to wean them off their frenetic reading of others: 'écrivons-nous pour nous désabrutir [...] et tenir nos cœurs en flammes au frottement de nos pensées' (PP, 242) ['let's write to each other to shed our stultification (...) and keep our hearts inflamed in the rubbing together of our thoughts'].[10] As an expression of autonomy, this recognition of the need to come out from under reading, as it were, signals another turning away from roles that are socially apportioned.

Gauny's valorization of his situation as a joiner on piecework is consistent with his advocacy of self-belonging. He has no one standing

---

8   Quoted in Maton, 'Habitus', p. 50.

9   Marina van Zuylen, 'Dreaming Bourdieu Away: Rancière and the Reinvented Habitus', in Patrick M. Bray (ed.), *Understanding Rancière, Understanding Modernism* (New York and London: Bloomsbury Academic, 2017), pp. 199–218 (pp. 210–11).

10   Kristin Ross reflects on the challenge of translating the verb *abrutir*. See Rancière, *The Ignorant Schoolmaster*, p. 7, translator's footnote.

over him, and contrasts this with life in the *atelier*, which is seen as imprisonment: 'je travaille à mon heure! Ouvrier en bâtiment, je pose mon parquet à la toise!' (PP, 242) ['I set my own timetable! I'm a construction worker, I lay my wood floor using a height gauge!']. While not claiming to be immune from exploitation, he creates space for a whimsicality that has an emancipatory dimension, imagining that he might have been a blacksmith, the driver of a locomotive engine, a botanist, or a forestry worker. The worker-intellectual thus lays claim to the leisure of speculation and fantasy. As Rancière observes, Gauny proposes a 'counter-economy' that puts freedom before riches.[11]

Self-belonging is achieved both at a bodily level and through expressivity. Free from the surveillance regime of a workshop or factory, 'cet homme se tranquillise par la propriété de ses bras qu'il apprécie mieux que le journalier; car aucun regard du maître n'en précipite les mouvements' (PP, 62) ['this man is content to feel the ownership of his arms, which he appreciates more than the day labourer does; for no master's surveillance obliges those arms to move more quickly']. And while the risk facing the pieceworker is that in his social isolation he experiences the atrophy of language – 'la rouille du langage qui corrode l'expression' ['the rust of language that corrodes expression'] – he nevertheless develops in his solitude 'le tour et la couleur de la phrase intuitive de sa pensée' (PP, 62) ['the turn and colour of the phrase that intuitively conveys his thought']. The atypicality of his situation is also his liberty: 'Il s'élance à la piste du travail avec la conscience de sa liberté' (PP, 62) ['He eagerly embarks on his work, conscious of his freedom'].

A central lesson emerging for Rancière from his work on the Gauny archive is the fact that the worker-philosopher homes in on the question of time – 'le temps volé, le temps qui fragmente la vie' ['time that is stolen, time which fragments life'].[12] Access to perception, thought, and language is guarded by the barrier formed by the availability of time (PP, 10). The broader historical backdrop to Rancière's work on the Gauny archive again has a bearing. In France in the 1960s, several hundred *gauchiste* militants had taken up manual jobs in factories to experience at first hand the realities of time-driven production. One such activist, as is noted above, was Robert Linhart, whose work on

---

11 While the blurbs used on the back covers of the 1983 and 2017 editions of *Le Philosophe plébéien* differ, the term *contre-économie* features in both.

12 Le Gros, 'Jacques Rancière, "Le Philosophe plébéien"'.

a car production line forms the basis of the narrative in his *L'Établi*.[13] Linhart describes how a worker might, over the course of an hour or two, manage to improvise a couple of minutes' break by being fractionally ahead in the tasks assigned to him: 'voluptueux rentier qui regarde passer sa carrosserie déjà soudée, les mains dans les poches pendant que les autres travaillent' ['with his hands in his pockets while others are working, he looks on voluptuously like a person of private means, as his already welded bodywork passes along'].[14] While noting the mock grandeur in the depiction of the *rentier*, we see how the image of nonchalance and the associated act of surveying afforded by the freed-up minutes – 'fabuleux capital' ['fabulous capital'] – provides a link back to the Gauny archive. There, the discovery of autonomy allows the pieceworker to escape from 'la contrainte de l'exactitude aux heures' (PP, 63) ['the constraint of fixed hours'].

Indeed, the floor layer who goes in search of work becomes simultaneously an observer of the city. When it is necessary to walk a long distance to his work, Gauny sees this as favouring 'les grands plaisirs de la pensée' (PP, 243) ['the great pleasures of thought']. He invokes the figure of the philosopher-pedestrian – 'le piéton philosophe' (PP, 128) – who relishes being in the open air, temporarily liberated from the demands of material necessity. In this physically active, peripatetic state, Gauny as *flâneur* traverses the 'quartiers somptueux' ['the lavish *quartiers*'], bringing to his surroundings a keenness of vision which he likens to that of a bird of prey (PP, 63). As the worker walks, 'l'esprit se met en branle, il imagine, il médite, il scande quelques hémistiches en oubliant la traite, les bourrasques de l'air ou son fardeau' (PP, 243) ['his mind is exercised, he imagines, he ponders, he scans some hemistichs, and forgets the distance covered, the gusts of wind, and the burden of work']. Verbal poiesis thus supplants concern about economic dependence, the act of scansion displacing the measurement of time that governs an alienating labour. Drawing on Aristotle's *Politics*, Arendt reflects on how the institution of slavery in classical antiquity was an attempt 'to exclude labor from the conditions of man's life'.[15] For Gauny, by contrast, the world of labour and the notion of a fuller experience of the human are imbricated, with

---

13   See above, p. 32 n. 6. For consideration of the case of Maoist militants who 'established' themselves in factories (as *établis*) at that time, see Palmusaari, 'For Revolt', pp. 84–89.

14   Linhart, *L'Établi*, p. 12.

15   Arendt, *The Human Condition*, p. 84.

the philosopher-pedestrian enjoying the 'ravissantes nonchalances de la liberté' (PP, 63) ['delightful carefreeness of freedom'].

Gauny explains that, while less free than the pieceworker, those on ten-hour days in an *atelier* still experience intermittent disturbance in which the act of reflection reduces the worker's arms to inactivity: 'sa pensée [...] l'absorbe en paralysant ses bras; la méditation le subjugue' (PP, 56) ['his thought absorbs him, paralysing his arms; the act of meditation captivates him']. Suspending manual labour, the worker accesses, and is indeed held within, the space of thought. Crucially, Gauny does not propose a divorce between manual toil and contemplation. He chooses oxymoron to convey the reality of the worker's lived experience: the mortification that comes with hard physical labour is the prelude to a liberation of the soul. In that regard, he sees the worker unwittingly emulating the Fathers of the desert (elsewhere, he invokes with earnest enthusiasm the figure of John the Baptist and also the Greek philosopher Diogenes (PP, 151)). The worker's existence brings both restriction and independence: 'S'abandonnant aux richesses de sa liberté, les lieux du travail, le temps qu'il doit y passer ne l'assombrissent jamais!' (PP, 60) ['He abandons himself to all that his freedom offers, and the places where he works and the time he must spend there never fill him with gloom!']. Autonomy thus comes to be experienced by the worker who transcends the conventional separation of toil and philosophical reflection.

Commenting on Gauny's use of language, Rancière notes the slippage between the figurative and the literal. He observes how his style captures 'une pensée pour laquelle tout état des corps représente une certaine incarnation et toute pensée doit se manifester en modifications lisibles sur les corps' (PP, 275) ['a thought for which every bodily state represents a certain incarnation and every thought must become visible in changes that can be read on the body']. By taking thought back to notions of embodiedness and materiality, Rancière identifies a central dynamic in Gauny's work. Linguistic improvisation is part of this, with the joiner's formulation 'planer en idée' ['to glide or soar in thought'] capturing the moment of euphoria experienced in contemplation (the term *planer* means to soar but also to level or plane).

Plato's *Republic* provides a frequent reference point in Rancière's reflection on the distribution of the sensible as we have seen. The cover for the 1983 Gauny edition carries a reproduction of Raphael's *School of Athens* (1509–1510), with its depiction of Plato and Aristotle at the centre of the composition. In the *Republic*, Socrates disapproves of the practice of 'letting absolutely anyone, even when entirely unsuitable, come to rational argumentation'.[16] The assertion features in discussion of the education of philosopher kings and reinforces the hierarchy established when Plato comes up with the tale in which God, 'at the kneading phase', included different metals in the formation of the three social orders: gold for rulers, silver for auxiliaries (the militia), and iron and copper for farmers and other workers.[17] With the myth endorsing specialization, Plato debars the manual worker from the pursuit of philosophy, which is categorized as the preserve of a social elite: 'this specialization of function', Plato argues, 'will ensure that every person is not a plurality but a unity, and thus that the community as a whole develops as a unity, not a plurality'.[18]

Consistent with the logic of qualification and expertise, poets and painters are viewed negatively in the *Republic*. Socrates argues that a representer 'knows nothing of value about the things he represents; representation is a kind of game, and shouldn't be taken seriously'.[19] Thus, neither the painter nor his audience knows what shoemaking actually entails: 'They just base their conclusions on the colours and shapes they can see', Socrates complains.[20] When he asks Adeimantus if success is more likely to come from someone doing a variety of jobs or focussing on one, the reply given reinforces the logic of specialization.[21]

In the case of Gauny – manual worker, social commentator, and writer – the concept of friendship cuts against this distribution of functions and thus points to a reconciliation beyond differentiation. While in his editorial introduction Rancière reminds his reader of 'cette *philia* que présuppose la pratique de la philosophie' (PP, 15) ['the *philia* which the practice of philosophy presupposes'], Gauny describes himself handling the tools of his trade 'avec une sorte d'amitié' (PP, 60) ['with a kind of friendship']. These different objects of *philia* confirm the move beyond the apportionment of roles, as does Gauny's characterization of *l'indépendant*, the worker of independent outlook: 'jamais il n'était plus beau qu'au milieu de ses outils, tout éclatant d'idées' (PP, 169) ['never was he more attractive than when surrounded by his tools, his head

16   Plato, *Republic*, trans. Robin Waterfield (Oxford: Oxford University Press, 2008), p. 274.
17   Plato, *Republic*, pp. 118–19.
18   Plato, *Republic*, p. 127.
19   Plato, *Republic*, p. 354.
20   Plato, *Republic*, p. 352.
21   Plato, *Republic*, p. 60.

brimming with ideas']. What for Gauny is the felicitous co-presence of hand, mind, and tool finds an echo in *Le Maître ignorant* (published four years after the 1983 Gauny edition), where again the stress falls on a dynamic of declassification and reapportionment.

In advocating the pleasures of learning, the plebeian philosopher sees the practice as facilitating self-belonging. He predicts a social evolution in which, were the next generation to shed a servile response to work and appreciate the 'marvels' of human association, the human race could, like the Magi, follow a star, one that would gradually take them 'vers cet inconnu, ce bonheur dont le désir la tourmente mais dont l'essence est en elle!' (PP, 65) ['towards that unknown, that happiness the desire for which torments it and yet the essence of which lies within it!']. Gauny's argument is frequently couched in ascetic terms, as when he suggests that the notion of the worker looking beyond manual labour in order to be in touch with the soul carries echoes of the ancient prophets of the desert (PP, 61). In a preface entitled 'Aux prolétaires' ['To the Proletarians'], he appeals to the 'lointaines aspirations de notre âme vers l'infini' (PP, 32) ['deep longings of the soul for the infinite']. Elsewhere, he advocates flight from what he describes as 'notre siècle savant et pervers' (PP, 82) ['our learned and perverse century']. The stress on self-scrutiny did not go unnoticed in his day. Louis Ponty refers in a letter of 1855 to Gauny's Trappist rigidity and to 'ton esprit tout ascétique' (PP, 255–56) ['your intensely ascetic turn of mind'].

Reflecting on engulfment by life itself and on his desire to escape 'des extravagances et des crimes de ma race' (PP, 251) ['the extravagances and the crimes of my race'], Gauny promotes the concept of a quasi-religious community in his theory of a coenobitic economy: 'L'homme de notre régime, contemplateur, méditatif, passionné d'existence, rendant l'action forte par la pensée, et réciproquement, aime le grand air' (PP, 133) ['in our regime the human being is a figure of contemplation, meditative, passionate about existence, whose action is fortified by thought and vice versa, and who loves the outdoors']. The economy governing the coenobitic community will thus foster emancipatory discovery of the self. Thrift and asceticism are seen as the route to such liberation: 'Vivons de peu, c'est un grand moyen de défense' (PP, 125) ['Let us make do with little, it's a great way to protect oneself'], he urges.

How might Gauny's advocacy of abstinence be read when taken alongside the tense narratives by Simon, Péguy, and Ndiaye considered in earlier chapters? We find the motif of frugality as defence in Péguy's evocation of the artisan, in Ndiaye's description of la Cheffe as someone who clings to social anonymity, and in Simon's account of austerity and continence in the images of the protagonist's peasant sisters in *L'Acacia*. While they are all figures of intense, fervent restraint, each lays claim to an autonomy lived in contexts that are remote from centres of conspicuous social capital. In the process, Péguy contrasts the artisan's self-belonging with a contemporaneous order that is cast negatively as a space of progressive *embourgeoisement*; Ndiaye presents a character who excels in her craft while remaining wary of mercantilism and resisting society's moves to appropriate her success; and Simon records the 'esprit d'intraitable insoumission' (A, 64) ['spirit of intractable insubordination' (AA, 44)] of peasant women who affirm their self-worth in a refutation of material opulence. With behaviours in each of these cases shaped by the requirements of productive necessity, manual culture risks serving as a vector for social conservatism. Gauny is no less conservative to the extent that he does not set out a programme of collective social transformation. Yet he looks beyond class containment, aiming to appropriate an otherness, that of thought and 'idle' speculation, traditionally not apportioned to the proletarian.

Aristotle writes of masters employing overseers to manage their slaves, this to allow the masters better to 'devote themselves to statecraft or philosophy'.[22] The emancipation mapped out by Gauny, by contrast, is lived provisionally, to the extent that it is experienced, Rancière insists, within a range of constraints: 'le menuisier [Gauny] décrit les voies courbes mais irréversibles de la réappropriation de soi dans l'aliénation même du travail exploité' (PP, 25) ['the joiner Gauny describes the winding but irreversible route to a reappropriation of self in the very alienation caused by exploitative labour']. In other words, self-belonging is not to be achieved in the wake of liberation. In this regard, Rancière contrasts the revolutionary perspective on struggle to be found in Sartre with what he terms the surprising phenomenology of emancipation in Gauny's writing on the subject of piecework in 'Le Travail à la tâche' (PP, 25). Distancing himself from what he terms an explosive, apocalyptic event involving the masses, Rancière insists that Gauny realizes himself precisely within the space of exploitation.[23] Louis Ponty depicts himself

---

22   Aristotle, *Politics*, p. 75.

23   Rancière refers to the symbolic value of having his edition of Gauny appear in the same year as the first edition of his *Le Philosophe et ses pauvres* (1983). The latter work, with its rejection of 'the professionals of thought', was republished in 2007; see the blurb on the back cover of that edition.

in a similar light: 'Protestant comme toi de la loi de contrainte qui nous tord et lamine' (PP, 246) ['Like you, I'm a dissenter from the law of constraint which twists and obliterates us'].

One of Gauny's points of reference is La Boëtie's *La Servitude volontaire* ['Slaves by Choice'] (1578), where liberation and containment are shown to be held in a dialectical relationship. La Boëtie draws on cases in the animal kingdom of creatures either able or unable to tolerate the loss of their freedom. Those incapable of accepting any incursion on their liberty and choosing death as a consequence would be deemed aristocratic, La Boëtie remarks, were social rank to be a property of the animal world. Other animals 'resist capture with claws, horns, beaks, feet, declaring their attachment to what they are losing'.[24] A hunted elephant, in a desperate bid to retain its freedom, will smash its teeth and tusks against a tree, he reflects, thereby breaking off and sacrificing a part of itself, its ivory, to satisfy its attackers. Subjection and liberty are similarly co-present in Gauny, where the inquisitive manual worker, though held in a state of economic containment, is energized by intermittent experiences of emancipation. In the context of Rancière's own thought, provisionality and intermittence often mark the forms of emancipation he explores, one commentator writing of 'a disappointing modesty when it comes to actual practice' in relation to a process of change occurring over time.[25]

* * *

The concept of specialization and know-how which Plato presents as a principle of social organization in the *Republic* assumes a subversive form in Gauny. In a polemical reflection on questions to do with competences, he denounces those involved in the material construction of new prisons for the incarceration of fellow workers. Gauny decries the willingness of builders to carry out the wishes of legislators and their architects. He sees the design of cell-based prisons, 'prisons cellulaires', as providing 'le degré exact de la haine de l'homme contre l'homme, et de l'ignorance fratricide de ceux qui viennent en aide aux inventeurs de ces cauteleuses tortures' (PP, 86) ['the exact degree of

24 See Estienne de La Boëtie, *Slaves by Choice*, trans. Malcolm Smith (Egham: Runnymede Books, 1988), p. 46.
25 See Palmusaari, 'For Revolt'. The quotation is taken from Palmusaari's thesis abstract.

hatred of man for his fellow man, and the fratricidal ignorance of those who come to the aid of the inventors of these cunning tortures']. The couching of ethical concerns in a high linguistic register is again present in his condemnation of 'ces membres subalternes [qui] se prêtent dans leur hébétement liberticide aux lâches cruautés des inventeurs' (PP, 90) ['the subaltern members who, in their liberticidal stupor, give themselves over to the cowardly cruelties of the inventors']. But in exposing collusion with a culture of repression, Gauny injects a ludic dimension into his dissent, imagining a new social order in which it would be for the designers of such prisons themselves to undertake their physical construction. He envisages the catalogue of calamitous errors that would come with such a reversal of roles and the unstable buildings that would result:

> ils eussent modelé la plus incroyable Babel du monde: ruine difforme percée de cryptes de tortures s'écrasant dans leur amalgame [...]; abattoir construit si peu d'aplomb, que le peuple, en considérant ce Moloch nouveau, eût craint d'être enseveli sous sa chute. (PP, 92)

> [they would have fashioned the most incredible Babel in the world: a shapeless ruin full of torture crypts collapsing chaotically in on themselves (...); an abattoir built so out of plumb that when contemplating this new Moloch, the people would have feared being buried under it.]

In this lavish vision of dystopia, it is precisely in the removal of specialization and qualification (workers withhold their know-how) that a fratricidal social order is contested. The scenario of precarious construction illustrates what Rancière refers to as 'une extraordinaire dramaturgie de l'émancipation' ['an extraordinary dramaturgy of emancipation'] in Gauny's work, the joiner-philosopher arguing that the sight of such malfunction would give the people a sense of its 'résistance pacifique' (PP, 92) ['peaceful resistance'].[26]

In *La Mésentente*, Rancière constructs the thesis whereby social order is built on inequality, and the disruptive, disorderly force of equality is that which generates disturbance.[27] The scene of secession in Ancient

---

26   See back cover of *Le Philosophe plébéien* (2017 ed.). For Rancière's reflection on Gauny's scenario, see *La Nuit des prolétaires*, pp. 104–06; *Proletarian Nights*, pp. 95–97.

27   See Nick Hewlett's gloss on Rancière's thesis of disorderly equality: Hewlett, *Badiou, Balibar, Rancière: Re-thinking Emancipation* (London: Continuum, 2007), pp. 101–02. See also Hallward, 'Staging Equality', p. 141.

Rome, when the plebeians withdrew to the Aventine Hill, encapsulates this disturbance and forms a leitmotif in Rancière's work. He contrasts two perspectives on the event, that of the Roman historian Livy, with its apology for hierarchical order, and Ballanche's rewriting of the episode in 1830 in which Ballanche asks: Do the plebeians speak or not?[28] Rancière explains the grounds of the patricians' argument, namely that these beings without name lack a *logos*, the consequence being that the plebeians are denied an 'inscription symbolique dans la cité' ['symbolic enrollment in the city'].[29]

Rancière unsettles the Marxist view that workers' pride in their craft constitutes a progressive force, insisting that ordinary people are most disruptive when they seek to act like those from more privileged social groups. In a provocative image used to depict Gauny and his contemporaries, he works against the notion of a concerted, collective will by portraying them as a group of liberators who abandon social roles and 'toutes les adhérences, individuelles et collectives, de la vieille société' (PP, 28) ['all the allegiances, both individual and collective, of the old order']. In doing so, they form 'une armée d'apôtres déserteurs' (PP, 28) ['an army of deserter-apostles']. Rancière's provocation has been seen as problematic. Hewlett expresses reservations about a selective adoption of archive material rather than a more thorough engagement with wider historical exploration.[30] Similarly, Hallward is cautious about 'the presumptions of a disruptive equality' in Rancière, citing the latter's reflection that 'equality is the power of inconsistent, disintegrative and ever-replayed division'.[31] Stressing the conditions required to effect social transformation, Hallward draws out by way of contrast, with reference to the link in Rancière between the human capacity to think and 'the resources of displacement', the risk of 'everyone think[ing] through the freedom of their own self-disassociation'.[32]

28   See *La Mésentente. Politique et philosophie* (Paris: Galilée, 1995), pp. 45–50; *Disagreement: Politics and Philosophy*, trans. Julie Rose (Minneapolis: University of Minnesota Press, 1999), pp. 23–27. In *La Méthode de l'égalité*, pp. 124–25, *The Method of Equality*, p. 68, Rancière notes the historical moment that sees both the appearance of Ballanche's article in *La Revue de Paris* and popular protests calling for press freedom in Paris in 1830.

29   *La Mésentente*, p. 45; *Disagreement*, p. 23.

30   See Hewlett, *Badiou, Balibar, Rancière*, pp. 89–90.

31   Hallward, 'Staging Equality', pp. 140–41. Hallward is here quoting from Rancière, *On the Shores of Politics*, p. 33.

32   Hallward, 'Staging Equality', p. 141.

* * *

In an extended editorial commentary entitled 'Les Socrate de la plèbe' ['Plebeian Socrates Figures'], Rancière begins by identifying as a neglected area in the modern era the role of philosophy in workers' experience. He attributes this neglect to socialist voices of the nineteenth century promoting what they judged to be an appropriately materialist view of proletarian life (PP, 113). An additional factor for Rancière is the insistence in Marxism on class consciousness being freed from what are dismissed as petty bourgeois ideologies such as classical culture and metaphysical speculation. While acknowledging the importance of Fourier, Saint-Simon, and Proudhon for an understanding of radical thought in nineteenth-century France, Rancière characteristically gives visibility to less frequently referenced names in the field of 'savoirs et [...] pratiques dissidents' (PP, 115) ['dissident knowledges and practices']: the writer Ballanche, with his promotion of a doctrine of human progress; Gléizès campaigning against the killing of animals; the private lessons the grammarian Andrieux gave to the cabinetmaker Hamel and the tailor Hilbey in Le Havre; the former royalist who taught young Gauny botany; the practice of homeopathy; the call for temperance as a way of opening the gates of wisdom – 'l'eau est le breuvage des forts' (PP, 132) ['water is the drink of the strong']. The points of reference, then, in 'Les Socrate de la plèbe' are consistent with the radical equality with which Rancière's work is associated. *Le Maître ignorant* serves as a further plank in that extensive work on narratives of dissidence that immediately predate Marx's analysis of class struggle, as Hallward notes.[33]

Urging caution in how the narratives he uncovers in the Gauny archive might be categorized, Rancière argues that they point not to popular cultural practices (he is uneasy about the connotations of social containment in the label *populaire*) but rather to a parallel culture. He sees the opinions expressed by Gauny and others as working through channels other than the education system and mainstream culture, as deriving from often chance readings, as being alternative forms of culture or linked to the multiple forms of 'l'enseignement parallèle' (PP, 115) ['parallel education']. He further comments that Gauny's writing does not reflect popular usage but is, rather, a poetic language 'systématiquement forgée à des fins d'expressivité maximale' (PP, 274) ['systematically fashioned to deliver maximal expressivity'].

33 Hallward, 'Staging Equality', p. 140.

Gauny sees thought opening up a vision of futurity that is glimpsed obscurely when the body is at rest: 'il me semble que je cherche une amitié encore incréée, dans les déserts du futur' (PP, 252) ['It seems to me I am seeking a friendship that is yet to be created, in the deserts of the future']. The speculative tone as he struggles with the idea of thought being imprisoned in a body may be compared to the note of wonder struck by Rancière in the conclusion to his preface to 'Economie de la liberté', where he asks of the writer whose archive so stimulated him:

> Mais le menuisier s'illusionne-t-il vraiment dans la superbe peinture d'un baptiste 'devenu universel' et 'compris de tous', menant le peuple en marche vers la cité de Dieu? Sans doute en a-t-il conscience. Son rôle à lui, c'est de demeurer un de ces Socrate inconnus de la plèbe, un de ces indépendants dont il suit la trace et dont il nous dessine les portraits. (PP, 123–24)

> [But is the joiner really deluding himself in the superb depiction of a Baptist figure who emerges as 'universal' and 'understood by all', leading the people towards the City of God? No doubt he is conscious of this. His role is to remain one of those unknown Socrates of the people, one of those independents whose trace he follows and whose portraits he draws for us.]

The complicity with Gauny's visionary tone anticipates the ventriloquizing that will see Rancière's critical voice becoming at times indistinguishable from that of Jacotot in *Le Maître ignorant*.[34]

Wistfully evoking a scenario of miraculous deliverance, Rancière presents Gauny as an independent figure who for sixty years 's'est promené dans son rêve' (PP, 14) ['walked in his dream']. His response to the archive reflects an attitude of receptivity and speculative enthusiasm that seeks to harness the energy accruing from Gauny's imagining a new social order. In the worker-philosopher's own formulation, 'si la terre était une philadelphie, jardin de fraternité' (PP, 126–27) ['if the world were a philadelphia, a garden of fraternity'].

Rancière concludes the editorial piece on 'ces Socrate inconnus de la plèbe' by noting the differences between the revolutionary socialist Louis Blanqui's activism and the strains of monastic self-discipline in Gauny (PP, 124). It is telling that he refuses to choose between activism and asceticism. By including in his edition both Gauny's correspondence with

---

34 For discussion of this ventriloquizing effect, see James Swenson, '*Style indirect libre*'.

worker activists and his essays on the pursuit of individual autonomy, Rancière imagines the coming into being of

> un peuple en armes mais aussi en discussion permanente, comme si son pouvoir ne pouvait s'assurer qu'à s'identifier à ce dialogue ininterrompu qui caractérise pour Platon le loisir du philosophe. (PP, 124)

> [a people in arms but also in permanent discussion, as though its power could only be assured by being linked to the uninterrupted dialogue which, for Plato, is the hallmark of the philosopher's leisure.]

That social status should not be a determinant when it comes to access to the exercise of (radical) thought is key, then, to Gauny's message and to Rancière's endorsement of the *philosophe plébéien*. In underscoring the leisure that indeed facilitates the work of the philosopher, Rancière advocates an opening out of the space of autonomy and contemplation.

Analysing the evolution in style to be found in the Gauny archive, Rancière identifies a progression from the early work of the 1830s to the extension of vocabulary visible in the 1840s material. In his view, Gauny's language works beyond the articulation of a social consciousness: 'la cascade des images [...] s'ordonne en un jeu de significations dont la précision, à la seconde lecture, apparaît surprenante' (PP, 275) ['the cascade of images (...) is structured as a play of meanings, the exactness of which, on second reading, appears surprising']. Narrative poetics thus forms a no less important dimension of Gauny's work than his representation of the social referent. Histories of French literature, Rancière concludes, are no longer able to ignore voices such as Gauny's, 'cette parole grondante, cette écriture superbe' ['that booming message, that glorious writing'].[35] Yet Rancière's implied exhortation notwithstanding, literary-critical practice has not been quick to implement such a revision. While the present chapter is a modest attempt at the kind of rectification needed in this area of knowledge deficit, the Gauny corpus itself provides an important illustration of subjectivation as defined by Rancière: 'une désidentification, l'arrachement à la naturalité d'une place' ['a disidentification, removal from the naturalness of a place'].[36] Hence the pertinence of that archive in a present age of interrogation about privilege, labour, and social vision.

35   The formulation features on the back cover of the 1983 edition of *Le Philosophe plébéien*.
36   Rancière, *La Mésentente*, p. 60; *Disagreement*, p. 36.

PART II

Disturbance and *Dressage*

CHAPTER FIVE

Animal laborans

Missing Life in
Paul Nizan's *Antoine Bloyé*

Or as eye, hand, foot, and in general each of the parts
evidently has a function, may one lay it down that
man similarly has a function apart from all these?

Aristotle[1]

[A]bandonner cette existence qu'il menait, pour
devenir quelqu'un de nouveau, quelqu'un d'étranger,
qui serait vraiment lui-même.

[to quit the life he was leading and become someone
new, a foreign someone who would be more like his
real self]

Nizan[2]

In *The Man Without Content*, Giorgio Agamben addresses the question
of the progressively more invasive hold in modern times of the world of
work. He explains that in Ancient Greece, by contrast, work held less
privileged status in the understanding of active life. Agamben tracks the
new development through Locke (where work is linked to property),

---

1   Aristotle, *Nicomachean Ethics*, trans. David Ross, ed. Lesley Brown
(Oxford: Oxford University Press, 2009), p. 11.
2   Paul Nizan, *Antoine Bloyé* (Paris: Grasset, 2013 [1933]), p. 146; *Antoine
Bloyé*, trans. Edmund Stevens, intro. Richard Elman (New York and London:
Monthly Review Press, 1973), pp. 114–15. Subsequent citations of the French
original are indicated using the abbreviation AB, with the English translation cited
as AEB.

Adam Smith (where work is the generator of all wealth), and Marx who sees in work an expression of man's humanity. He concludes: 'This productive doing now everywhere determines the status of man on earth – man understood as the living being (*animal*) that works (*laborans*)'.[3]

Looking back to Aristotle allows Agamben nevertheless to see how man could indeed be defined as a workless being. He references lines from the *Nicomachean Ethics* in which Aristotle, having noted that the carpenter, the tanner, the flute player, the sculptor, and the artist all have their respective functions, asks what function, separate from these, man might have as man.

A striking portrait of *animal laborans* is to be found in Paul Nizan's *Antoine Bloyé* (1933). The novel's narrator explains how the eponymous protagonist has worked unreflectingly as a railway company employee:

> Pendant quatorze ou quinze ans, il n'y eut pas d'homme moins conscient de soi et de sa propre vie, moins averti du monde qu'Antoine Bloyé. [...] Il agissait, mais les ressorts de sa vie, les mobiles de son action n'étaient pas en lui. (AB, 144)

> [For a space of fourteen or fifteen years, there was no man less conscious of himself and of his own life, less informed on the world than Antoine Bloyé (...). He, Antoine, moved and acted, but the springs of his life, and the drive of his actions were not within himself. (AEB, 113)]

Worklessness is the state least applicable to a character who conceives of work as a truth 'que personne n'a pensé à mettre en question depuis que le monde tourne' (AB, 145) ['that no one under the sun had ever thought of questioning' (AEB, 114)]. Were one to apply the terms of reference found in the *Nicomachean Ethics*, Antoine Bloyé's actions are unleisurely and aimed at an end, whereas the happy man is drawn to 'the activity of reason, which is contemplative'. Aristotle thus advocates 'self-sufficiency, leisureliness, unweariedness (so far as this is possible for man)'.[4] With such a perspective unavailable to Nizan's protagonist, the narrator in *Antoine Bloyé* reflects diagnostically on the character's situation in terms not dissimilar to those found in Aristotle:

> Antoine n'avait pas de loisirs pour d'autres mouvements humains que les mouvements du travail. [...] Point d'occasion de penser à soi, de méditer, de se connaître, de connaître le monde. (AB, 144)

---

3   Giorgio Agamben, *The Man Without Content*, trans. Georgia Albert (Stanford: Stanford University Press, 1999), pp. 70–71.
4   Aristotle, *Nicomachean Ethics*, p. 195.

[Antoine had no time to go through human motions other than the motions of his work. (...) There was no opportunity to think about himself, to meditate, to know himself and know the world. (AEB, 113)]

Rancière, as we saw in the last chapter, headlines the moment when Gauny, laying a parquet floor, rests on his plane, the movement of his arms being interrupted as he takes in his surroundings. The act of contemplation signals a refusal of unreflecting immersion in manual labour; or, as Aristotle might present it, Gauny practises a looking beyond the function of the woodworker. Rancière reflects on what he terms the colourful etymology of the term *anthropos* found in Plato: man is the animal who examines *what he has seen*, 'anathrôn ha opôpé'.[5] Etymology and with it the memory of earlier forms of signifying here serve as correctives to the discourse of productive rational labour working in the service of capital. In the period of the *fin de siècle*, which forms part of the chronological range covered in *Antoine Bloyé*, the rise in mechanized transport networks is likened to 'une courbe de température: l'élan du capitalisme entraînait de gré et de force les machines et les hommes qui travaillaient pour lui' (AB, 129) ['a temperature curve. The momentum of capitalism drew along willy-nilly the men and machines that worked for it' (AEB, 100)]. Indeed the hold of ideology is explicitly and regularly signposted in Nizan's didactic text.

Early in the work, which is based on the life experience of Nizan's father, constraints associated with gender, class, the mechanization of culture, and technological progress are catalogued in quick succession. In the case of a family birth in a peasant milieu, the preferred option is to have a son; those who work the land feel drawn inexorably to the rapidly expanding railway companies in Second Empire France; and employees in the new companies must adapt to the demands that come with clockwork management and control. The drive to instrumentalize labour is unambiguous: 'l'industrie réclamait de nouveaux matériaux humains' (AB, 76) ['industry required new human material' (AEB, 57)]. The narrator's unvarnished reference to exchange relations in the world of labour links directly to the work's status as a *roman à thèse* published in a decade of intense ideological conflict. Then a member of the French Communist Party, Nizan sets out in often theorized terms a trenchant critique of capitalism in which the discourse of

5   Quoting from Plato's *Cratylus*, 399c, Rancière refers to 'une des étymologies de fantaisie du *Cratyle*' ['one of the fantastic etymologies of the *Cratylus*'], *Le Maître ignorant*, p. 62; *The Ignorant Schoolmaster*, p. 36.

nineteenth-century technological progress is contested. His protagonist is depicted as being held in a system of social control: 'Antoine était pris comme un insecte dans cette toile vibrante des voies ferrées, que surveillaient à distance des araignées calculatrices et abstraites' (AB, 131) ['Antoine was caught like an insect in this quivering web of railway lines, surveyed from a distance by calculating, abstract spiders' (AEB, 102)]. The arachnophobic analogy offers a lurid image of the ubiquitous reach of capitalist rationality.

Two narrative strands feed into *Antoine Bloyé*, with a trenchant critique of capitalism woven into a tale of ultimately unhappy migration across a social-class boundary. In an anticipation of the work's denouement, its opening chapter focusses on the death of the eponymous class migrant. This proleptic introduction signals a governing of the life that is to be told. In the extended analepsis that follows, Bloyé's life is presented as a linear progression leading ineluctably to disillusionment with the social advancement that comes with both career progression (from manual worker to manager) and marriage into the *petite bourgeoisie*. The latter development is likened to Ariadne's distress at the sight of Theseus disappearing over the sea off Naxos (AB, 124; AEB, 95). In the words of one critic, the work functions as a negative exemplary novel.[6]

Whereas Rancière's exploration of nineteenth-century workers' archives in *La Nuit des prolétaires* unearths narratives of emancipation in which individual subjects turn away from productive labour, the father of Nizan's eponymous protagonist lives a life of work-centred containment at the time of the Second Empire. The protagonist's own experience of work sees him similarly held within a set of exchange relations:

> ces milliers d'hommes vivant, peinant, mourant pour le service des Lignes, anonymes.
>   Antoine était un homme en série parmi eux. Il aimait les enchaînements de leurs travaux, il les comprenait, il était au centre de cette connaissance, prisonnier de tous ses rameaux. Comme beaucoup d'agents des Chemins de fer, il avait l'orgueil de son métier [...]. Il vivait entouré des symboles de sa tâche. (AB, 131)

> [thousands of men living, toiling, dying for the services of the line, nameless men.

6   Michael Scriven, *Paul Nizan: Communist Novelist* (Basingstoke: Macmillan, 1988), p. 118.

Antoine was one of them. He loved the concatenation of their jobs. He understood them. He was at the center of it all, a prisoner of the ramifications. Like many railway officials, he had his professional pride (…). He lived surrounded by the symbols of his calling. (AEB, 102)]

Nizan thus evokes a world of transaction in which individual autonomy is forfeited in exchange for insiderness, with surrender to an organization ostensibly buying dignity. The use of free indirect style relays Antoine Bloyé's perspective and the workings of consensus around issues of social prestige.

In the eyes of Nizan's narrator, the effect of *la massification* or collective depersonalization is clear. To apply Rancière's formulation in *Le Maître ignorant*, the protagonist undergoes a negative dynamic of social aggregation. Elsewhere, Rancière uses the term consensus to denote the intelligence that is at work in the governing of social relations in capitalist society.[7] The counterpoint to this – as championed in the writings of the 'L'Enseignement universel' movement celebrated in *Le Maître ignorant* – is not group formation but rather disaggregation. To cite one of Rancière's nineteenth-century sources: '*Donc c'est précisément parce que chaque homme est libre qu'une réunion d'hommes ne l'est pas*' ['*Therefore*, it is precisely because each man is free that a union of men is not'].[8] While Rancière has reservations about the assertion (as he readily concedes, it is a supposition, an adventure at the mental level on the part of its author), he nevertheless views sympathetically the argument that sees human beings linked precisely because of their individual separateness.[9]

The father of the newly born Antoine Bloyé has no access to such a perspective of openness. The reader learns that in 1864 he is working as a postman at Orléans railway station, socially passive and without illusions, knowing that he is

7 See Panagia, *Rancière's Sentiments*, p. 69. Citing Rancière's argument in *Disagreement*, Panagia writes: 'Marx's theory of exchange relations and the efficient fluidity of substitution that the equivalency affirms also marks the crux of Rancière's critique of consensus'. Panagia is drawing specifically on *Disagreement*, pp. 115–16.

8 Rancière is quoting from Jacotot, *Enseignement Universel. Mélanges posthumes* (Paris: H.-V. Jacotot, 1841), p. 116; cited in *Le Maître ignorant*, pp. 131–32; *The Ignorant Schoolmaster*, p. 78 (emphasis in the original).

9 On Rancière's notion of 'disincorporation' working against the production of 'des corps collectifs' ['collective bodies'], see *Le Partage du sensible*, p. 63; *The Politics of Aesthetics*, p. 35.

attaché à une certaine place dans le monde, une place décrétée pour la vie entière, une place qu'il mesure d'avance comme une chèvre attachée mesure l'aire ronde de sa corde, *et qui est voulue comme toutes les conditions du monde par le hasard, par les riches, par les gouvernants.* (AB, 45; emphasis added)

[anchored to a certain lot in the world, a lot ordained for the rest of his life, a lot which he surveys as a tethered goat measures the circumference of its rope, *a lot which, like every lot in life, was willed by chance, by riches, by the rulers.* (AEB, 33)]

Social mimesis in *Antoine Bloyé* thus channels an oppressive message of class constriction.

Fast-forwarding half a century from Nizan's novel of 1933, and more than a century on from this Second Empire vignette of social *dressage*, to use his term, we find a restatement of the apportionment-of-place motif in Annie Ernaux's *La Place*. There, too, the parent protagonists are assigned a tightly circumscribed position. Their role as *petits commerçants* may carry a measure of standing within the prevailing socio-economic order but the history of Ernaux's nineteenth-century forebears corroborates the backdrop mapped out in *Antoine Bloyé*. Moreover, Ernaux's choice of book title headlines the fact that the 'place' of the *petits commerçants* marks a precarious foothold that is resolutely defended. Lapsing back into the working class ['retomber ouvriers'] is the underlying fear that motivates the parents in *La Place*, where the shaping of ideological dispositions is no less transparently signposted than in *Antoine Bloyé*.[10] Ernaux cites the striking example of a school textbook, Augustine Fouillée's *Le Tour de la France par deux enfants* ['The Journey Around France by Two Children'] (1877), which conditions the outlook of deference visible in the narrator's father and in generations of schoolchildren in the Third Republic.[11]

In the wider context of his work, Rancière's social critique extends to a reflection on the link between politics and aesthetics and in particular to the question of how visibility is apportioned to certain cultural forms, as was noted earlier. Who determines that visibility is central to his exploration of the division and distribution of the sensible.[12] Nizan argues, we have seen, that social position is decreed by chance, wealth,

---

10 Annie Ernaux, *La Place* (Paris: Gallimard, 1984), p. 39.

11 Ernaux, *La Place*, p. 30.

12 See chapter 1 of *Le Partage du sensible*. See also Davis, *Jacques Rancière*, p. 91.

and those who govern. How cultural forms are customarily accorded prestige is implicit in the interrogation of the social in *Antoine Bloyé*, the novel effectively giving voice to a lament for the class and generation to which the protagonist's parents belong: 'cette vie qui avait toujours été si mince, si peu importante, *qui avait éveillé si peu d'échos, touché de ses ondes si peu d'êtres*' (AB, 257; emphasis added) ['lives that had always been so small, so unimportant, *that had set off so few echoes, that had touched so few beings with their ripples*' (AEB, 206)]. While the lament derives, then, from the inaudibility of undocumented lives, it is, crucially, in the democratic space of the literary text that such discarded lives are chronicled. As Rancière stresses in relation to the career and life of the historian Michelet, 'celui qui sort du peuple *en est sorti*. Il ne peut plus y retourner que par le détour du livre' ['He who comes *from* the people is no longer *of* the people. He can only return to the people by the detour of the book'].[13] Nizan's access to family origins is similarly accessed circuitously through literary production.

The gravitational pull of high culture feeds into the polemical dimension present in the texts of both Ernaux and Nizan. In *Le Partage du sensible*, Rancière comments:

Il est toujours une distribution polémique des manières d'être et des 'occupations' dans un espace des possibles. C'est à partir de là que l'on peut poser la question du rapport entre l''ordinarité' du travail et l''exceptionnalité' artistique.

[It is always a polemical distribution of modes of being and 'occupations' in a space of possibilities. It is from this perspective that it is possible to raise the question of the relationship between the 'ordinariness' of work and artistic 'exceptionality'.][14]

While Rancière is addressing the issue of the status accorded to works of art, his remarks have a wider applicability. Ernaux is indeed exercised by the perception of prestige and rank associated with a canonical literature that is seen as a cultural object intended for bourgeois consumption. Hence her aversion in *La Place* to using the medium of the novel as a vehicle for conveying her father's life.[15]

---

13 *Courts voyages au pays du peuple*, p. 97; *Short Voyages to the Land of the People*, p. 74. See Chapter 10, below, where a similar dynamic in the work of Eribon is explored.

14 *Le Partage du sensible*, pp. 66–67; *The Politics of Aesthetics*, p. 39.

15 See Ernaux, *La Place*, p. 23.

That high culture should serve as a conduit for social control is no less relevant to *Antoine Bloyé*. At a school prize-giving, the presenter of awards refers paternalistically to the young Antoine as the hope of 'nos populations laborieuses' (AB, 70) ['our industrious population' (AEB, 52)]. The triumph is hollow for a boy who remembers that his mother cannot write and can only read print and not handwriting. How, Antoine Bloyé asks, is he to reconcile the subject of his school learning (the names of heroines and heroes from Racine and Corneille) and the manual work of his mother who does other people's laundry. In Nizan's novel, the academic curriculum itself marks segregation. Thus, Antoine Bloyé will not study Latin or Greek: 'Les belles volutes des Arts libéraux ne sont pas réservées à leurs fronts. Arts des hommes libres? Les hommes libres sont ceux qui sont rentiers …' (AB, 58) ['The laurels of the liberal arts are not for their brows. Arts of free men? Free men are those who have incomes' (AEB, 43)]. Just as certain disciplines are ruled out for Antoine Bloyé, so, for Ernaux's father, a visit to the public library sees him steered towards a work by Maupassant, a writer deemed to be 'popular'. Ernaux is no less attuned, then, to the linking of literary and social selection, referenced by Nizan's narrator as the 'mots de passe et de ralliement' (AB, 58) ['stock of passwords and expressions' (AEB, 43)]. Both scenes illustrate what Michel Foucault, borrowing from an early seventeenth-century source, calls 'le bon dressement' ['good training'], a process that functions on the basis of a social economy that is 'calculée, mais permanente' ['calculated but permanent'].[16]

*   *   *

A crucial agent of class containment at the level of material culture in *Antoine Bloyé* is industrialization. The narrator reflects that inventors are often more influential than heads of state in driving social change. But if the railway revolution raises aspiration within certain classes, it spells disruptive transformation for many industrial workers. Antoine Bloyé's bedtime reading is a biography of George Stephenson, yet

---

16   Foucault's source is J. J. Walhausen, *L'Art militaire pour l'infanterie* (1615). See chapter 2 of Part III of his *Surveiller et punir. Naissance de la prison* (Paris: Gallimard, 1975), 'Les Moyens du bon dressement' ['The means of correct training'], pp. 172–96 (p. 172); *Discipline and Punish: The Birth of the Prison*, trans. Alan Sheridan (London: Penguin, 1991), pp. 170–94 (p. 170).

ironically exhaustion from his day's work means that he never gets beyond the book's opening pages (AB, 144; AEB, 113). The counterpoint to his enthusiasm for the narrative of technological change is the bodily exhaustion such change brings. Yet the relationship between man and machine is ambiguously handled in Nizan's novel. Learning to drive a fast train, the protagonist (in the period predating his taking charge of the Tours railway depot) experiences an initiation that seems emancipatory: 'Antoine avait l'orgueil de cette profession difficile et ces heures de course vers Bordeaux étaient les premières heures de sa vie' (AB, 108) ['Antoine was proud of his difficult profession, and the hours of his run to Bordeaux were the outstanding hours of his life' (AEB, 82)]. Notwithstanding the sense of exhilaration, the individual worker's subjectivity undergoes an experiential narrowing in what serves as a variant on Rancière's notion of the apportioning of the sensible:

> [Antoine] ne voyait pas défiler le paysage, il n'y a pas de paysage pour un mécanicien de rapide, il n'y a que des lignes étirées par la vitesse à droite et à gauche du train, les rivières les plus larges ne sont qu'un bruit de métal. Il n'y a que la voie, l'extrême tension des yeux, des oreilles, de l'esprit, *l'attention à la dictée sonore que fait entendre la machine*: tout peut arriver, la vaporisation peut manquer, une roue peut chauffer, une chape de bielle sauter, il y a ces hommes et ces femmes du train qui dorment, qui lisent, qui causent et qui n'aiment pas arriver en retard, leur vie est précieuse ... (AB, 108; emphasis added)

> [Antoine (...) does not see the passing countryside, there is no countryside for the engineer of an express. There are only lines, tautened by speed, to the right and left of the train. The broadest rivers are nothing but a clank of metal. There is only the track, the extreme tension of your eyes, ears, and mind, *listening to the deep metallic voice of the machine*. Anything can happen – the boiler go dry, a wheel overheat, a connecting rod jump. There are sleeping, reading, talking men and women on the train who do not like arriving late. Their lives are precious. (AEB, 82)]

The use of preterition captures the restricted sensorium that is a by-product of instrumentalization. In a reference to the overworked train crew, the narrator reports that 'tout le long de la ligne, les hommes renâclaient: "Ça n'est pas la vie", disaient-ils' (AB, 110) ['All along the line the men grumbled. "This isn't a life", they would say' (AEB, 83)]. Whereas rail passengers both enjoy and demand leisure and conviviality, alienated labour requires a hypertrophy of vigilance in relation to the mechanical and brings a denial of life itself.

The image of Antoine Bloyé obliged to follow the dictation of the machine, to use Nizan's pedagogical metaphor, echoes Schiller's account of an enforced adhesion to labour in his *On the Aesthetic Education of Man*: 'Eternally shackled to one small fragment of the whole', Schiller laments, 'man [...] simply became the impress of his occupation, his particular knowledge'. He likewise casts in haptic terms the imprisonment in mechanical work: 'In his ear the constant and monotonous noise of the wheel that he turned'.[17] The mode of containment again manifests itself at a sensorial level.

Yet whereas the human is curtailed, the machine in Nizan's novel assumes an anthropomorphic expansiveness: 'Toute machine est comme un être, elle a ses mœurs, ses facilités, ses résistances, et des caprices' (AB, 106) ['Every engine is like a living being; it has its habits, its faculties, its obstinate streak, and its whims' (AEB, 80)]. In its very materiality, the locomotive, as a metallic construction, embodies an enigmatic 'personnalité' (AB, 106; AEB, 80). In marked contrast, Nizan describes how the railway companies require of employees a uniformity of response to tasks – hence Antoine Bloyé's status as one in a series, *un homme en série*. In industrial-scale labour, capriciousness is unauthorized. To apply the concepts used by the philosopher of technology Bernard Stiegler, the repetitive manual and bodily performance of tasks sees workers' gestures undergo a process of *grammatization* that leads to a loss of individuation and ensures proletarianization.[18]

Nizan reconstructs for the reader the historical conjuncture of the 1880s in which Antoine Bloyé reaches early adulthood. In a period of rapid technological expansion, the protagonist undergoes training at one of the Ecoles Nationales d'arts et de métiers where the doxa of progress and a promise of escape from poverty initially energize him. The narrator reflects ironically on the quasi-military formation of 'des sous-officiers et des officiers subalternes pour les armées de la grande industrie française' (AB, 76) ['the petty officers for the armies of big

---

17   F. Schiller, *On the Aesthetic Education of Man*, trans. Keith Tribe, ed. Alexander Schmidt (London: Penguin, 2016), p. 19.

18   See B. Stiegler, 'Individuation et grammatisation: quand la technique fait sens', *Documentaliste-Sciences de l'Information*, 42.6 (2005), 354–60. Stiegler draws on Gilbert Simondon's view that the 'corps outillé', the body that is made into a tool, generates the process of proletarianization. See also Stiegler, *De la misère symbolique* (Paris: Flammarion, 2013), pp. 111–12.

French industry' (AEB, 56)].[19] With 'toute la France et toute la vie' (AB, 75) ['all France and all of life' (AEB, 56)] seeming to beckon to Antoine Bloyé, Nizan captures the scale of technological aspiration in the Third Republic and the hidden hand of the French bourgeoisie (AB, 76; AEB, 57).

In the description of Antoine's journey east to begin his apprenticeship in Angers, nostalgia for his native Brittany briefly stems the advance of new forms of mechanization. In the experience of seeing the Loire and the railway line running alongside it, the course of the river allows the young Antoine to look back to his childhood and think of long-established modes of work and travel. Standing on a bridge on his days off, 'il croyait entendre sous le bruit coulant du grand fleuve sableux les marteaux de Penhoët et les sirènes des grands navires qui lèvent l'ancre vers Santander' (AB, 75) ['he fancied he heard beneath the flowing murmur of the great sandy river the hammers of Penhoët and the sirens of the great ships weighing anchor for Santander' (AEB, 56)].

The nostalgia for a sensibility shaped by the rhythms of nature parallels the narrator's insistence that long before Antoine Bloyé's birth, high capital was planning his and others' futures. The reifying power of a new industrial age is not confined to the expansion of the railways: 'Mille grandes machineries dévorantes entraînent ainsi les hommes dans leur rotation: les banques, les mines, les grands magasins, les navires, les réseaux' (AB, 130) ['thousands of ravenous machines (…) thus involve men in their rotation: the banks, the mines, the big stores, the ships, the railways' (AEB, 102)]. The metaphor of power as a rotational force is recast by Nizan when he refers to the new era as a dance requiring rapid steps, one that leaves no time for individual self-examination. The protagonist's experience of twelve-hour days involving workshop training and classes feeds into that rapid dance. It is specifically contrasted with the cultivation of self-knowledge enjoyed by those pursuing 'les études ouvertes, libres et lentes des universités' (AB, 79) ['the open, free, and leisurely life of the universities' (AEB, 59)]. The alliterative pairing of 'libres et lentes' conveys a rhythm of unhurriedness and ease, and throws into relief the alienation that comes with industrial specialization. Nizan's own experience, it is worth recalling, as a student at the École Normale Supérieure in Paris in the 1920s meant initiation

---

19   Stiegler references Marx's analysis of discipline in the army and in workshops as noted by Foucault in his *Dits et écrits*, vol. II (Paris: Collection Quarto, Gallimard, 2001), p. 1006; see Stiegler, 'Individuation et grammatisation'.

into a culture radically different from the milieu in which Bloyé *père* had grown up. In the thinly veiled biography of his father provided in the novel, we read of 'un homme soumis à tous les commandements, qui dominait seulement une machine dont il connaissait les façons' (AB, 110) ['a man subject to every command, lord only of an engine whose habits he knew' (AEB, 84)].

The promise of liberation through the experience of the aesthetic held out by Schiller (and endorsed by Rancière) would seem, then, to elude Nizan's hero. As Davis explains, 'inherent in the art of the aesthetic regime, as Rancière understands it, is what he calls a political "promise" of equality'.[20] Yet Nizan's novel does not exclude such a promise, as the pleasures experienced by *homo faber* show. Later in the narration, when the earlier focus on the pressures that come with mechanical progress weakens, Antoine Bloyé reflects on workmanship: 'on a sa tâche devant les yeux, on la contemple, [...] on l'élève devant soi comme une œuvre. On ne craint personne' (AB, 217) ['You have your task before your eyes. You can look at it (...). You bring it into being before you, like a creation. You are not afraid of either man or nature' (AEB, 172)]. In the gradation from task to creation, the act of production and its contemplation come to signal an emancipatory gesturing towards the aesthetic regime. A task well executed becomes enhancing in experiential terms and also, significantly, displaces hierarchy and the intimidation that accompanies it. The reflection comes at a point in the narrative where Antoine Bloyé and a team of workers succeed in getting a derailed train back out of a river and onto the track: 'ils avaient vaincu la pesanteur, le courant, la masse du métal, la saison' (AB, 218) ['they had conquered the weight, the current, the mass of metal, the time of year' (AEB, 172)]. A heightened activation of the senses, of aisthesis, thus emerges in a complex work of technical recovery. In the process, praxis acquires an aesthetic dimension – the resistance of matter, the sensitivity to temperature, the sound and volume of water. The experiential fullness forms, to borrow Rancière's formulation, the 'tissu d'expérience sensible' ['sensible fabric of experience'].[21]

Identifying in the modern era a convergence between poiesis and praxis, Agamben comments on how this represents a move away from the original notion of poiesis – *poiein* meaning '"to pro-duce" in the

20   Davis, *Jacques Rancière*, p. 152.
21   *Aisthesis*, p. 10; *Aisthesis: Scenes from the Aesthetic Regime of Art*, p. x.

sense of bringing into being'.[22] In the scene of derailment in *Antoine Bloyé*, employees are not working *ex nihilo*. They engage, rather, in concrete, productive activity (they are in the order of praxis therefore) and yet the intense encounter with matter releases an enhanced aisthesis. While such scenes are the exception to the prevailing mood of alienation in the novel, the perspectives on the human which they make available reach beyond reification and instrumentalization.

As part of his reflection on Plato, Rancière reminds the reader of how the philosopher casts manual work as a force that confines the worker to the 'espace-temps privé de son occupation, son exclusion de la participation au commun' ['the private space-time of his occupation, his exclusion from participation in what is common to the community'].[23] Being denied access to the public forum entails specialism and confinement to a precise corner in the world of labour. In the same reflection, Rancière refers to Schiller's call for aesthetic education to function as the vehicle for social transformation. 'The state jealously guards a monopoly over its servants', Schiller writes, adding that it remains 'for ever alien to its citizens, finding no feeling for it'.[24] Nizan's portrait of a work-weary, unreflecting protagonist offers an arresting counterpoint to the emancipation Schiller advocates when he calls for aesthetic experience to reunify the human faculties.[25] In Nizan's declamatory formulation, 'L'homme ne sera-t-il donc toujours qu'un fragment d'homme, aliéné, mutilé, étranger à lui-même?' (AB, 144–45) ['Will man never be more than a fragment of a man, alienated, mutilated, a stranger to himself?' (AEB, 113].

The existential inflection in the evocation of human alienation is clear in the observation that 'cette force s'usait sur la meule d'un travail étranger [...] il ne la faisait pas servir à un développement humain' (AB, 145) ['his strength was being spent on the grindstone of alien work (...). He was not using it to further his own human development' (AEB, 114)]. An overtly pedagogical tone thus colours much of the novel. Denis Hollier argues that, as the work of a Marxist writer of the 1930s, *Antoine Bloyé* reflects 'a hatred for thought's quiescence, [... a] wish to tie intellectual activity to risk, to danger, to personal commitment'. Yet Hollier also points to the presence of these characteristics in what the

22 Agamben, *The Man Without Content*, p. 68.
23 *Le Partage du sensible*, p. 67; *The Politics of Aesthetics,* p. 40.
24 Schiller, *On the Aesthetic Education of Man*, p. 20.
25 See Schmidt's editorial comments on Schiller's advocacy of a reconciliation of sensuous nature and intellect; *On the Aesthetic Education of Man*, p. xxxi.

critic Arnaud Dandieu in 1932 referred to as 'the philosophy of anxiety' to be found in Heidegger.[26] Indeed Hollier draws out conscious echoes of the German philosopher's work in *Antoine Bloyé*.[27]

Nizan's novel offers a trenchant critique of social calls to embrace inequality. He references how the appeal of Guizot at the time of the July Monarchy resonates with a particular class fraction in the modern era: 'l'Enrichissez-vous du vieux ministre était comme le Sermon sur la Montagne de la jeune bourgeoisie aux dents longues' (AB, 62) ['the "get rich" of the old minister was the Sermon on the Mount of the young sharp-toothed bourgeoisie' (AEB, 45)]. Nizan's ironic tone pours scorn on the appeal to rapacious wealth accumulation.

In a less aggressive expression of ambition than that espoused by Guizot's followers, the prospect of marriage into the Guyader family sees the young Antoine Bloyé enjoying the leisure pursuits of a class wedded to the values of the Third Republic – the 1889 Exposition universelle, the advent of the phonograph, civic pride taken in displays to celebrate the centenary of 1789 (AB, 120; AEB, 92). Antoine Bloyé eagerly acquires a repertoire of new social attitudes, embracing the petit bourgeois ways of his spouse's milieu, including the prejudices of his father-in-law who complains of excessive social levelling and for whom 'les ouvriers sont des ouvriers' (AB, 116) ['workers are workers' (AEB, 89)]. The tautology signals not only class aggression but also a refusal to give visibility to industrial labour. Later, the working-class district in Tours which the novel's protagonist must pass through on his way home induces in him a reaction of phobia. While manual labour is commodified, its producers retain an inescapable visibility, such that Bloyé must perform an act of conscious exclusion by shunning their dwellings. With the material segregation in the city made clear (the bourgeois, the petits bourgeois, and manual workers each have their neighbourhood), Nizan describes provincial French towns circa 1910 in terms of their social division: 'toutes choses étaient établies, la société

26   Denis Hollier, '1931, June – Plenty of Nothing', in D. Hollier (ed.), *A New History of French Literature* (Cambridge, MA: Harvard University Press, 1994), pp. 894–900 (p. 895).

27   By way of illustration of a perspective that derives from Heidegger, Hollier cites the line in *Antoine Bloyé*: 'It takes a great deal of force and creation to escape from nothingness' (AEB, 228–29); see '1931, June – Plenty of Nothing', p. 897. The French original reads: 'Il faut beaucoup de force et de créations pour échapper au néant' (AB, 284).

comportait des étages' (AB, 190) ['all things were ordered; society had its levels' (AEB, 149)]. For the workers themselves, the contiguity of dwelling and workplace leaves them 'éternellement plongés dans les échos du travail' (AB, 187) ['constantly steeped in the echoes of work' (AEB, 147)]. The inference in Nizan that labour's audibility is socially contained helps account for Marx's endeavour, as explained by Davide Panagia, to 'render human labor perceptible as a social and political category, thereby making industrialized labor at once visible and sayable'.[28] The act of rendering visible is again present in the democratic space that is Nizan's novel.

Rancière's work on nineteenth-century theories of radical equality provides an instructive template for a contextualized reading of Nizan. Writing about the Panecastic movement with its call for 'l'Emancipation intellectuelle' in the 1830s and 1840s, he conveys the movement's understanding of the energy required to maintain social inequalities. Claims to superiority are invariably brittle, the movement argues, the paradox being, as Rancière relays it, that the wish of the would-be superior to compare himself with his inferior necessarily draws him back into an orbit of endless hierarchization. Hence the category of the 'superior inferiors' ['inférieurs supérieurs'].[29]

Rancière's sympathetic response to the advocates of the Panecastic movement often sees him transmitting their message through ventriloquy, as James Swenson has demonstrated.[30] Thus, the insistence on 'cette passion ou cette fiction de l'inégalité' ['this passion or fiction of inequality'] derives from his nineteenth-century sources.[31] The collective submission to the hold of inequality suggests an order based on a law of conflict and sustained by a misapplication of human intelligence:

> les individus, en se *reliant* les uns aux autres par la *comparaison*, reproduisent cette déraison, cet abrutissment que les institutions codifient [...] ce travail est un travail de deuil.

> [In *linking* one person or group to another by *comparison*, individuals continually reproduce this irrationality, this stultification that institutions codify (...) this work is a work of grief.][32]

28 Panagia, *Rancière's Sentiments*, p. 69.
29 *Le Maître ignorant*, pp. 144–45; *The Ignorant Schoolmaster*, p. 86.
30 See Swenson, '*Style indirect libre*'. For earlier references to this ventrilo-quizing mode in Rancière, see above, pp. 6, 107.
31 *Le Maître ignorant*, p. 135; *The Ignorant Schoolmaster*, p. 81.
32 *Le Maître ignorant*, p. 137; *The Ignorant Schoolmaster*, p. 82.

The proposition in *Le Maître ignorant* that an inegalitarian culture is one of mourning throws up a recurring metaphor, that of an oppressive law of social gravity ('la pesanteur'). The term conveys the will to inequality, such a will being seen as the exertion of a force that is societal. As the Panecastic message runs: 'Partout où des hommes s'agrègent les uns aux autres sur la base de leur supériorité, ils se livrent à la loi des masses matérielles' ['Wherever people join together on the basis of their superiority over others, they give themselves over to the law of material masses'].[33] The corollary to this is that the flight from social aggregation towards intellectual emancipation triggers 'cette puissance sans pesanteur' ['that power without gravity'].[34]

Antoine Bloyé charts its protagonist's eventual refusal of the aggregation that sees him admitted to the *petite bourgeoisie*. The failure of a workers' strike draws out his conflicted view of his social origins, triggering indeed a repressed desire for reconnection with proletarian culture: 'il y avait plus de vérité dans leur défaite que dans sa victoire de bourgeois' (AB, 213) ['there was more truth in their defeat than in his bourgeois victory' (AEB, 168)], he concedes. At the same time, Bloyé's resentment at having married into the lower middle class fails to mask the misogyny in his make-up. Indeed, his psychology reflects a strong undercurrent of predatory erotic fantasy, as illustrated in the ageing protagonist's mental projections about 'une sorte de vaste corps anonyme' (AB, 265) ['a sort of huge nameless body' (AEB, 213)] that is ubiquitous and alluring. While subsidiary to the politics of labour in the novel, sexual politics adds to the climate of alienation in the work.

The didacticism in the novel around the issue of class affiliation is reflected in the desire of the older Antoine Bloyé to retrieve an earlier social identity. As he oversees the work of others, he is described as experiencing the hollowness of his achievement, reaching a stage 'où l'on regarde travailler les mains des autres' (AB, 199) ['where he watched the hands of others work' (AEB, 157)]. Forgetting momentarily his supervisory role, he re-experiences the tactile sensation of using a workshop tool. The haptic moment is described as a shedding of social importance and an attempt to rediscover the manual reflexes that were once integral to his life. In the later part of the novel, the recurring formulation 'son importance' ['his status'] carries invariably negative

33   *Le Maître ignorant*, pp. 145–46; *The Ignorant Schoolmaster*, p. 87.
34   *Le Maître ignorant*, p. 179; *The Ignorant Schoolmaster*, p. 108.

connotations. The turning away from rank and position heralds an emptying out that is emancipatory and with it, importantly, a restoration of the manual.

A more momentous challenge to the hold of abstract capitalist rationality comes with the death of the protagonist's six-year-old daughter. The workplace, with its homosocial world of industrial labour and clockwork management, provides the disturbing backdrop to Antoine's mourning:

> il n'y avait pas d'autre hérésie que de se demander si le travail a un sens [...]. Il travailla, parce que la douleur et la mort sont des oisivetés, et que toute sa sagesse contenait simplement l'obéissance au travail. (AB, 163; emphasis added)

> [*There was no greater heresy than to ask if work had any sense* (...). He worked because sorrow and death are slothful and the whole of his wisdom consisted simply of obedience to work. (AEB, 128)]

The free indirect style shows Nizan's protagonist in the position of a compliant, specialized subject restricted to a tightly assigned role, not unlike that deriving from the apportionment prescribed by Plato in *Republic*. Or, to argue from another angle, Bloyé embodies what Rancière refers to as 'la mâle unilatéralité du travail industriel' ['the virile one-sidedness of industrial labor'] that exercised the Saint-Simonians in the 1830s.[35]

The rivalry between work ethic and the work of mourning points to a wider tension. The *animal laborans* motif, to return to Agamben's perspective, contrasts with the image of Antoine Bloyé and his wife in their grief: 'Ils recomposaient avec une patience d'animal inférieur leur vie mutilée' (AB, 166) ['with the patience of a lower animal, they reordered their life that had been mutilated' (AEB, 130)]. The flow of affectivity in the grieving parents prompts ontological speculation on the part of the narrator about the experience of loss: 'Peut-être la douleur est-elle le plus animal des sentiments humains' (AB, 166) ['Grief is, perhaps, the most animal-like of human feelings' (AEB, 130)]. The perspective that would restrict man's status to that of *animal laborans* is dislodged by what is presented as a deeper interrogation of what constitutes the human.

---

35   Rancière is quoting from a letter of 21 February 1833 by Émile Barrault to Prosper Enfantin. See *Courts voyages au pays du peuple*, p. 42; *Short Voyages to the Land of the People*, p. 31.

The hold of a work-centred view of life is further weakened when, back in his native Brittany on holiday, Bloyé experiences emancipation as a form of emptying:

> vacant, à la disposition de la nature, possesseur d'une liberté que ne menaçaient jamais la plénitude et la cordialité de la saison. C'était une trêve et une suspension. Toutes les chaînes de la vie industrielle, de la vie bourgeoise, toutes les chaînes de la vanité étaient brisées, les conflits suspendus ... (AB, 223–24)

> [vacant, at nature's disposal, endowed with liberty which was not gainsaid by the fullness and the friendliness of the season. It was a truce, an interim. All the fetters of industrial life, of bourgeois life, all the fetters of vanity were broken, all conflicts were suspended. (AEB, 177)]

Theorizing the protagonist's idyllic vision, Nizan has worklessness belatedly emerge as a force of restorative vacancy. Bloyé thus comes to contest the discourse of progress and modernity by learning to dissent from the view according to which, in Agamben's formulation, 'the philosophy of man's "doing" continues to be a philosophy of life'.[36]

The image of later-life experience breaking the cycle of social determinism mirrors the evocation, earlier in *Antoine Bloyé*, of childhood seen as a state untouched by that cycle. In his rural boyhood, the eponymous protagonist plays with local children from bourgeois families. The cohabitation is made possible, the narrator explains, by the distance both from the city, with its social segregation, and from adulthood, where the inegalitarian is entrenched. The young boy 'n'est pas humilié, il ne sait pas faire de comparaisons, il joue' (AB, 56) ['is not humiliated, he does not know how to draw comparisons. He plays' (AEB, 41)]. Preceding the advent of class-based schism, play thus forms a crucial vehicle for social interaction:

> *Tous les petits humains sont d'abord semblables*, avant de laisser s'évanouir cette égalité naïve dans la lumière impitoyable des rencontres et des dressages mal accordés aux fantaisies de l'enfance. Entre cinq et douze ans, tous les hommes sont faits pour s'entendre: des enfants échappés à l'espionnage des grandes personnes se rencontrent, les coups de foudre des camaraderies enfantines négligent toutes les barrières et jouent sans respect avec les idoles sinistres et les chaînes des familles. (AB, 57; emphasis added)

---

36   Agamben, *The Man Without Content*, p. 71.

[*All little human beings are alike*, before this naive equality withers in the pitiless light of incidents and teachings that ill accord with childhood fantasies. Between the ages of five and twelve all people understand each other. When children escape the supervision of grown-ups, childish comradeship neglects all barriers and they play unmindful of sinister idols and family ties. (AEB, 42)]

In a variation on Rousseau's maxim that 'Tout dégénère entre les mains de l'homme' ['Everything degenerates in the hands of men'], Nizan proposes childhood as an egalitarian space.[37] More specifically in relation to the broader configuration of the present study, he anticipates the central premise of Rancière's *Le Maître ignorant* by positing equality as pre-existing a move into the inegalitarian. Nizan's novel argues against hierarchy, then, in that it dramatizes the psychological undermining of a protagonist subjected to narrow social *dressage*.[38]

Jacotot and his contemporaries were forthright in questioning assumptions about hierarchy and Rancière draws on this, seeing the obdurate insistence on inequality as aberrant: 'Il n'y a d'insensés que ceux qui tiennent à l'inégalité et à la domination' ['There are no madmen except those who insist on inequality and domination'].[39] In *Antoine Bloyé*, a deranged alienation from self provides corroboration of Jacotot's social diagnosis. Late in the novel, the protagonist concludes that he has lived life as though headless, the searing image of the *décapité* or headless being (AB, 309; AEB, 248) capturing graphically the unexamined life. Early in the novel, workers are described as being strangled ['étranglés'] by work (AB, 46; AEB, 33). Had circumstances allowed him as a boy to be more receptive to the message contained in the book by Jules Simon that he won as a school prize, he would have known that man is free: 'L'homme [...] reconnaît toujours à lui-même le pouvoir de ne pas faire ce qu'il fait, de faire ce qu'il ne fait pas' (AB, 72) ['Man (...) is ever aware of his power not to do what he does do and to do what he does not do' (AEB, 54)], writes Simon. The formulation recalls Agamben's reflection on Aristotle's distinction between potentiality and actuality in Book Theta of *Metaphysics*: 'if potentiality is to have its own consistency', Agamben writes, 'and not always disappear immediately into actuality,

---

37   J.-J. Rousseau, *Émile, ou de l'éducation* (Paris: Garnier, 1957), p. 5.

38   Rousseau uses the verb *dresser* in the opening lines of *Émile* when he likens man's wish to dominate and shape other humans to breaking in a horse: *Émile, ou de l'éducation*, p. 5.

39   *Le Maître ignorant*, p. 123; *The Ignorant Schoolmaster*, p. 72.

it is necessary that potentiality be able *not* to pass over into actuality'.[40] In *Antoine Bloyé*, the schoolboy finds Simon's words 'trop célestes pour un fils d'ouvrier' (AB, 72) ['too exalted for a worker's son' (AEB, 54)]. The force of socio-economic constraint sees the young Bloyé ask rhetorically if his mother is free not to ache physically from her labours, or his father not to work nights. Yet the prescription in Jules Simon which perplexes the schoolboy has proleptic force, in that it connects with Nizan's didactic message, later in the novel, that humans fail to live their own lives: 'Imprudents humains, avec leurs vies composées d'autres vies, mourant d'autres morts que de leur propre mort ...' (AB, 258) ['Careless men, with their lives made up of other lives, dying deaths other than their own deaths' (AEB, 207; translation modified)]. If Gauny champions self-belonging as the previous chapter makes clear, in *Antoine Bloyé* Nizan shows life functioning as a drama of unlivability and as a contest between rival social visibilities.

40　Giorgio Agamben, *Homo Sacer: Sovereign Power and Bare Life*, trans. Daniel Heller-Roazen (Stanford: Stanford University Press, 1998), p. 45.

CHAPTER SIX

A Degrading Division
Hands and Minds in Simone Weil

manual: 'Of work, an action, a skill, etc.: of or relating to the hand or hands; done or performed with the hands; involving physical rather than mental exertion'.

Oxford English Dictionary

Travail manuel. Pourquoi n'y a-t-il jamais eu un mystique ouvrier ou paysan qui ait écrit sur l'usage du dégoût du travail? [...] Ce dégoût est le fardeau du temps. Se l'avouer sans y céder fait monter.

[Manual work. Why has there never been a mystic, either worker or peasant, to have written on the use to be made of disgust for work? (...) This disgust is the burden of time. To acknowledge it to oneself without giving in to it elevates the mind.]

Weil[1]

While Nizan's *Antoine Bloyé* is a fictional text with a biographical substratum, his contemporary Simone Weil chooses diary, essay, and personal correspondence to document her exploration of ideological

---

1   Simone Weil, *La Pesanteur et la Grâce*, intro. Gustave Thibon (Paris: Plon, 1948), p. 204; *Gravity and Grace*, rev. trans. Emma Crawford and Mario von der Ruhr (London and New York: Routledge, 2002 [1952]), p. 179; translation modified. The wording 'le fardeau du temps' recalls Baudelaire's formulation in the poem 'Enivrez-vous' ['Inebriate yourself'] in *Le Spleen de Paris*: 'l'horrible fardeau du Temps qui brise vos épaules' ['the horrible burden of Time which crushes your shoulders']; Baudelaire, *Œuvres complètes*, p. 332.

conflict in the interwar years in France. An important strand of her writing is its urgent interrogation of the world of manual work. As a middle-class intellectual desperate to escape the privilege which that condition represented, she went in search of what was for her the otherness of productive necessity, becoming a factory worker in the period between late 1934 and August of the following year. She charts that encounter in *La Condition ouvrière*, a book published posthumously in 1951 in the Espoir series which Albert Camus directed for the publishers Gallimard.

Weil was troubled in particular by a post-artisanal industrial culture in which machines appeared to think, with man reduced to the role of automaton: 'On dirait que la méthode a transféré son siège de l'esprit dans la matière' ['It's as though method no longer resides in the mind but in matter'], she asserted.[2] 'Journal d'usine', which records her personal experience of factory production lines, conveys in a detailed, notational style the reifying impact of factory life. She would later refer to her immersion within 'la masse anonyme' ['the anonymous mass'] of factory workers as an experience where the mark of slavery was placed on her, like the practice of branding on the forehead endured by the most lowly of slaves in Ancient Rome: 'le malheur des autres est entré dans ma chair et dans mon âme' ['the unhappiness of others entered my body and my soul'].[3]

Weil finds a dramatic iteration of the individual subject's confrontation with the contingent world in the story of Archimedes, killed, according to history, by a drunken soldier. She speculates that, had Archimedes been condemned to put his weight to turning a millstone under the punitive gaze of a slave driver, the renowned geometrician would have pushed in exactly the same way as someone of very limited intelligence.[4] Her point about human levelling is an egalitarian one and she cautions that 'dans la mesure où la pensée plane au-dessus de la mêlée sociale, elle peut juger, mais non pas transformer' (RCLOS, 108) ['to the extent that thought remains above the social melee, it can judge

---

2   Simone Weil, *Réflexions sur les causes de la liberté et de l'oppression sociale* (Paris: Gallimard, 1998 [1955]), p. 99. Subsequent citations of the text are indicated using the abbreviation RCLOS.

3   Simone Weil, *Attente de Dieu* ['Awaiting God'], preface J. M. Perrin (Paris: Fayard, 1966), p. 42.

4   Weil's formulation is 'l'homme le plus épais' (RCLOS, 108) ['the most obtuse of men'].

but not transform']. This expression of unease about the situation of the intellectual in an irreducibly material world connects with Weil's own work and life. She insists on the place of physical human presence in the world: 'Ce monde où nous sommes tombés existe réellement; nous sommes réellement chair' ['This world into which we have fallen really exists: we are indeed made of flesh and blood'].[5] The story of Archimedes distracted by intellectual endeavour and inattentive to the imminent threat posed by a conquering army provides corroboration of Weil's point about an embodied human condition. The scenario she constructs, in which the Greek mathematician is forced to undertake servile work, captures in graphic terms one of Weil's overriding concerns about her own day, namely the place of physical toil in a material world, what she calls 'une nécessité absolument inflexible' (RCLOS, 88) ['an absolutely inflexible necessity'].

The reference to Archimedes features in *Réflexions sur les causes de la liberté et de l'oppression* ['Reflections on the Causes of Liberty and Oppression']. Like *La Condition ouvrière*, this work was published posthumously, in 1955. Weil begins the essay with a critique of Marxism which is in part laudatory but more broadly disapproving. She commends Marx's analysis of capitalist oppression, although she fears that the impact of his account is to leave the reader doubting that such an impregnable system might ever be overturned. Yet Weil cites approvingly from the opening page of *The Eighteenth Brumaire of Louis Bonaparte* where Marx argues that 'les hommes font leur propre histoire, mais dans des conditions déterminées' (RCLOS, 23) ['Men make their own history, but (…) they make it in present circumstances, given and inherited'].[6] Stressing the bearing of material conditions on the human capacity for action, she commends Marx's theory of the mode of production as being indispensable for any serious social analysis and indeed for those who exercise governance. She objects nevertheless that his materialist method, which she describes as being 'vraiment précieuse' (RCLOS, 23) ['invaluable'], was never sufficiently utilized either by himself or his followers.

5   Weil, *La Condition ouvrière*, p. 348; subsequent references are indicated using the abbreviation CO, with an accompanying page reference.
6   The English translation is here taken from *The Eighteenth Brumaire of Louis Bonaparte*, trans. Terrell Carver, in Mark Cowling and James Martin (eds), *Marx's 'Eighteenth Brumaire': (Post)Modern Interpretations* (London and Sterling, Virginia: Pluto, 2002), p. 19.

The attention Weil pays to the division between manual and intellectual work and to the separate functions of those who direct and those called upon to execute connects with a central preoccupation of the present book (RCLOS, 17). Weil sees both bourgeois society and the workers' movement as reinforcing what elsewhere she refers to as 'l'excès insensé de la spécialisation' (CO, 449) ['the deranged excess of specialization']. She describes science as a monopoly from whose methods the unschooled or those deemed profane are excluded. She is likewise sceptical about a 'scientific socialism', arguing that intellectuals have the same privileges in the communist world as in bourgeois society. Her suspicion about a dogmatic Marxism may be read as anticipating Rancière's rejection of Althusser's view that knowledge was to be transmitted to subjects who were not in possession of it.[7] Indeed Rancière's wider complaint, derived from the Panecastic movement, that society can only represent itself under the sign of inequality, aligns, to a degree, with the perspective set out in *Réflexions sur les causes de la liberté et de l'oppression sociale*.[8]

Yet Weil does not advocate radical equality. In *L'Enracinement* ['The Need for Roots'], she stresses the importance of equality of opportunity but argues that proportion, as she terms it, serves social equilibrium by managing 'la combinaison de l'égalité et de l'inégalité' ['the combination of equality and inequality'].[9] She quickly adds nevertheless that the conditions for equality are enhanced when social roles are seen in terms not of rank but of otherness. Weil uses two brief textual sequences early in *L'Enracinement*, one on equality (Section V), the other on hierarchy (Section VI), to set out her lines of argument. Taking the examples of the miner and the minister, they are seen by Weil as pursuing 'simplement deux vocations différentes' ['simply two different vocations'], like those of a poet and a mathematician, Weil adding that the material hardship confronting the miner should be reflected in the honour shown to him.[10] Yet while the child of a minister becoming a

7   See above, Introduction, p. 10.

8   *Courts voyages au pays du peuple*, p. 159; *Short Voyages to the Land of the People*, p. 123.

9   Simone Weil, *L'Enracinement, ou Prélude à une déclaration des devoirs envers l'être humain* (Paris: Flammarion, 2014 [1949]), p. 91. The English translation, *The Need for Roots: Prelude to a Declaration of Duties towards Mankind*, trans. Arthur Wills (London and New York: Routledge and Kegan Paul, 1952), carried a preface by T. S. Eliot.

10   Weil, *L'Enracinement*, p. 92.

farm labourer should be no less possible than the child of a labourer becoming a minister, 'limitless' equality of this kind, Weil asserts, would give rise to a 'degree of fluidity' ['un degré de fluidité'] that would undo social life.[11] Hierarchy, she argues, has its place, although the veneration associated with it is not to be directed towards those in superior positions but rather towards a symbolic function that is above them and indeed above all humans. The bedrock of that function is 'les obligations de chaque homme envers ses semblables' ['the obligations of everyone to their fellow humans'].[12]

Weil offers a wary view of the collective organization of social and political life. She sees the capitalist system, with its orientation towards economic conquest, as being on course for total destruction (RCLOS, 136). At the same time, she likens the experience of the peasantry in the Soviet Union to the servile conditions facing factory workers. She dismisses a Soviet five-year plan as a veneration not of labourers but of the products of labour (RCLOS, 117). Rejecting the view that religion is the opium of the people, she counterargues that the belief in communist revolution is itself a drug ['un stupéfiant' (CO, 422)]. In place of what she terms 'le vertige collectif' ['collective vertigo'], Weil calls loftily for reconnection with 'le pacte originel de l'esprit avec l'univers' (RCLOS, 151) ['the mind's original pact with the universe'].

The stress on individual subjectivity and the turning away from strong forms of collective association become axiomatic in Weil's testimony. In this regard, the social disaggregation which Rancière identifies in his analysis of nineteenth-century proletarian figures also forms part of Weil's outlook. Writing at length in a private, confessional capacity to the Catholic priest Père J. M. Perrin in May 1942, she describes herself as being necessarily 'étrangère et en exil' ['a stranger and in exile'] in relation to all human groupings.[13] Yet in the same correspondence, she writes of her longing to immerse herself in the anonymity of 'la pâte de l'humanité commune' ['the common body of humanity'], 'disparaissant parmi eux, cela afin qu'ils se montrent tels qu'ils sont et sans se déguiser pour moi' ['disappearing among them, that they might reveal themselves as they are and without disguising themselves for me'].[14] An intense social curiosity and openness to others thus runs alongside an emptying

11   Weil, *L'Enracinement,* p. 91.
12   See Weil, *L'Enracinement,* section VI, 'La hiérachie', p. 93.
13   Weil, *Attente de Dieu,* p. 26.
14   Weil, *Attente de Dieu*, pp. 19–20.

of the self, constituting what Weil presents as an essential need and indeed a vocation.[15]

Marx's view that one of the evils of capitalism was its insistence on the division between physical and mental work finds an echo in Weil.[16] Jacques Cabaud observed that 'from the bottom of her heart', Weil was to argue for the abolition of this 'degrading division'.[17] Covering the period 1934–1935, her 'Journal d'usine' records the quantification of work done, the levels of pay received (and also lost because of reduced productivity in what was a system of piecework), and the oppressive hierarchical structures governing the workplace. As if to corroborate the theme in Rancière of the social apportionment of roles, she records how she witnessed on several occasions manual workers queueing in torrential rain outside a factory, waiting to be allowed in at their clocking-on time, whereas managers entered freely upon arrival. The conventions of social practice articulated around space and time underscore a routineness of inequality against which Weil reacted intensely. Rancière writes of a vertical hierarchy stretching from Antiquity to the nineteenth century which saw those paradoxically designated as 'hommes actifs ou hommes de loisir' ['active men or men of leisure'] positioned above 'ceux qu'on appelle hommes passifs ou mécaniques' ['those who are called passive or mechanical'].[18] The linguistic sleight of hand allows for an enduring screening off and devalorization of active manual labour.

As a production-line worker, Weil recorded her state of physical and mental exhaustion in existential terms, noting that for the eight hours and more of the working day spent on a machine, 'il faut [...] tuer son âme' (CO, 60) ['one has to kill one's soul'] in order to attend to what Rancière would later call 'le travail qui n'attend pas' ['work which will not wait'].[19] In his philosophical analysis of industrial technology, Stiegler, for whom the repetitive performance of tasks spells *grammatization*, as

15   Weil, *Attente de Dieu*, p. 19.

16   Marx and Engels argue that 'the production of ideas, of conceptions, of consciousness, is at first directly interwoven with the material activity and the material intercourse of men'. See Marx and Engels, *The German Ideology*, Part One, ed. C. J. Arthur (New York: International Publishers, 1970), chapter 1.

17   Quoted in Palle Yourgrau, *Simone Weil* (London: Reaktion, 2011), p. 38.

18   See Rancière's discussion of 'la justice du temps' ['the justice of time'] in *Les Temps modernes: Art, temps, politique* (Paris: La Fabrique, 2018), pp. 20–21.

19   *Les Temps modernes: Art, temps, politique*, p. 21.

was noted earlier, acknowledges the influence of Weil's factory journal on his work.[20]

Weil's lack of physical coordination when it came to using machinery also concerned her. In his biography of Weil, Palle Yourgrau notes that her hands were very small, weak, and clumsy.[21] Her advice to former pupil Simone Gibert in a letter of March 1935 was to exercise her muscles, her hands, and her eyes, since, in the absence of such a development, 'on se sent singulièrement incomplet' (CO, 72) ['one feels singularly incomplete']. Weil's response to the factory mishaps which befell her because of poor coordination was a studious one: '*Questions à me poser*: Part du "tour de main" dans le travail à la machine. Caractère plus ou moins conscient de ce tour de main' (CO, 188) ['*Questions to be asking myself*: the role of "manual dexterity" when working on a machine. More or less conscious nature of that dexterity']. In her *Réflexions sur les causes de la liberté et de l'oppression sociale*, she draws enthusiastically on Hegel's idea of the body 'rendu comme fluide par l'habitude' (RCLOS, 96) ['as though rendered fluid through habit'], this as part of her ongoing reflection on 'la pensée et l'action' (RCLOS, 88) ['thought and action'].

Weil puzzled over the respective demands made by manual and intellectual skill. In 'Journal d'usine' she records the career history of Robert Guihéneuf, a factory worker, engineer, and member of the Communist Party. In a letter in 1936, she asks him, given the breadth of his experience, to gauge the intellectual effort required of, respectively, a manual employee, a draughtsman, and an engineer. Writing in May 1935 to her former teacher, the philosopher Alain, she praises Guihéneuf for managing to combine the contrasting standpoints of the one who designs machines and the many who are forced to use them.[22] As a figure desperate to live the experience of manual toil in an unmediated way, her sense of quest in the experience of factory work could be read as illustrating Rancière's definition of subjectivation as 'the formation of a one that is not a self but is the relation of a self to an other'.[23] Weil

---

20   In a radio broadcast entitled 'Serions-nous en train de perdre la raison?' ['Could we be losing our reason?'], *Les Nuits de France-Culture*, 25 June 2016, Stiegler, in conversation with Etienne Klein, explores Weil's reflection that, where 'la technique' dominates, evil ensues.

21   Yourgrau, *Simone Weil*, p. 30.

22   See Chenavier's editorial note, CO, 494–95.

23   Rancière, 'Politics, Identification, and Subjectivization', p. 60.

was also curious to understand analytically the particular *savoir faire* that went with factory life. She reflected urgently on the exercise of the faculty of attention at a micro-temporal level. Her factory journal logs how the hours and indeed the quarter and half hours of the working day were experienced and how rates of production were calculated.

A keen reader of Conrad, Weil mulls over the novelist's reflection on how man and machine interact. In Conrad's experience, the mariner feels at one with his vessel, so that the orders he issues are given without hesitation. Weil concedes immediately that this is the perspective of someone used to instructing others, but she nevertheless concludes that Conrad's reflex 'suppose *un régime de l'attention* très différent et de la réflexion et du travail asservi' (CO, 187) ['is based on *a regime of attention* very different from both the work of reflection and servile work']. The experience of the navigator, attuned to the movement of the ship, thus contrasts with what for Weil are the very different figures of the labourer and the intellectual. In universities, she argues caustically, teachers are paid to think and analyse (or at least to appear to do so); in factories, it is as though workers are paid not to think (CO, 68). Vexed by the schismatic character of these relations, she writes that, as a factory hand, she experiences reification and that her fellow workers share that condition, often unbeknown to themselves. Weil speculates about the circumstances in which a harmonious union of worker, machine, and task might be achieved: 'Cette union est évidemment la condition d'un bonheur plein. Elle seule fait du travail un équivalent de l'art' (CO, 187) ['Such a union is clearly the condition of a full happiness. It alone makes of work an equivalent of art']. She found the polar opposite of such harmonization in the Carnaud factory in Boulogne-Billancourt, commenting: 'I never once saw a worker lift her eyes off her work'.[24] The regime of factory work thus sees the policing, and resulting atrophy, of perception.

Weil contrasts factory life with the world of agricultural labour. Unconvinced by a discourse of rational efficiency, she brands the timing of tasks in the factory as fanciful, a 'chronométrage fantaisiste' that leads to deep-seated individual humiliation (CO, 182). While the work of factory machines is predicated on an unrelenting principle of cadence (CO, 337), she suggests that a principle of rhythm marks the experience of the peasant labourer, allowing time to pause, however briefly.[25]

---

24 Quoted in Yourgrau, *Simone Weil*, p. 53.
25 See Alain Supiot, 'Simone Weil', *L'Obs*, 27 July 2017, 56–59 (p. 58).

Referencing the seventh day as a day of rest in the Creation myth, she describes the break from work as 'cet éclair de pensée, d'immobilité et d'équilibre' (CO, 337) ['that flash of thought, immobility, and equilibrium'] and argues that it is precisely this reflex that is aggressively denied to those working in a factory.[26] In contrast with the farm labourer (and excepting the case of the peasantry in the Soviet Union), the factory worker faces 'une précipitation misérable' (CO, 337) ['a miserable and violent haste'].

Underpinning Weil's writing on manual work is a longing to see consciousness form part of such labour. Camus, we have seen, would later champion her work, publishing it in the Espoir collection which he directed for Gallimard in the 1950s. In his essay on the Sisyphus myth, *Le Mythe de Sisyphe* (1942), he too identifies the redemptive moment of pause for Sisyphus, a prisoner of materialism who experiences consciousness of his situation in those breaks from labour when the stone that he is eternally condemned to push up the mountain rolls back down the incline.[27] The gesture of the labourer's pause from work in order to gaze is homed in on by Rancière in Gauny's description of the layer of parquet floors suspending the action of his plane and accessing the liberating space of visual curiosity.[28] For Rancière, Gauny 'offers the gaze of an aesthete on the décor of his servitude'.[29] It is as though Gauny is mindful, Rancière imagines, of Kant's observations in the *Critique of Judgement* on a universally available aesthetic pleasure. Davis makes the point that while Gauny's experience was doubtless not lived consciously in Kantian terms, this does not invalidate Rancière's claim that the category of the aesthetic has the capacity to be universally experienced.[30] The act of looking, then, undoes the hold of instrumentalization, this as much for Gauny as for Camus and Weil. In each of these cases of social disaggregation, the one who exerts the gaze stands outside the intense constraint generated variously by factory production, the requirements of piecework, or, in the case of Sisyphus, divine decree.

26   See Genesis 2:2–3.

27   See Albert Camus, *Le Mythe de Sisyphe*, in *Œuvres complètes*, 4 vols (Paris: Gallimard (Bibliothèque de la Pléiade), 2006–2008), I, 302.

28   See Chapter 4, above.

29   Jacques Rancière, *The Philosopher and His Poor*, trans. John Drury, Corinne Oster, and Andrew Parker, ed. Andrew Parker (Durham, NC: Duke University Press, 2003), p. 199; quoted in Davis, *Jacques Rancière*, p. 133.

30   Davis, *Jacques Rancière*, p. 133.

Fig. 3: Front cover of the first edition of Simone Weil's *La Condition ouvrière*
(Paris: Gallimard, 1951). The work appeared posthumously, featuring in the
Espoir collection directed by Albert Camus.
Reproduced by kind permission of Editions Gallimard, Paris.

In another context, Rancière, reflecting on the act of careful looking, refers to 'la modestie de ce travail du cerne' ['the modesty of this labor of attention'].[31] The observation comes in his essay on Rossellini's film *Europa 51* to which reference was made earlier.[32] There, the bourgeois protagonist Irene, played by Ingrid Bergman, works a shift in a paper

---

31 *Courts voyages au pays du peuple*, p. 159; *Short Voyages to the Land of the People*, p. 123.
32 See above, Introduction, pp. 12–13.

factory, standing in for a young mother who has a romantic rendezvous that day and yet who needs to hold on to her job. Rancière refers to Rossellini's scene as echoing specifically the experience of Weil, although as he points out, the decision of Rossellini's protagonist to go to the factory is not a conscious move 'pour aller au peuple' ['in order to go the people'].[33] Weil's move, by contrast, very consciously is. Yet in both cases, it is outsiders – Weil and Irene – who, through *looking*, offer a critique of the reifying regime that is factory life. For both Rossellini and Weil, Rancière argues, the resigned are those who no longer observe; they are those who live oppression as something 'native' in Rancière's terms, in that for them such experience 'fait sens et souffrance' ['is meaningful (...) and is painful'].[34] The assonance in the twinning of *sens* and *souffrance* intensifies the narrowing of perspective around the requirements of labour, with access to leisure categorically excluded.

Rancière's conflation of social 'sense' and suffering is again germane to how we might read Weil. He likens Irene's reaction of horror faced with factory life to the response of Gauny, for whom the experience of being in a railway workshop acts as an assault on 'les sens de l'observateur' ['the observer's senses'].[35] In Rancière's penetrating analysis of *Europa 51*, the factory stands as 'un système de défilement, de décharge incessante de *stimuli* où se perd, avec la capacité du regard, la puissance de la considération' ['a constant and unceasing procession of sensory shocks, in which, along with the ability to look, the possibility of thoughtfulness and respect is lost'].[36] He identifies two major agents or 'techniques of the social' in Rossellini's film. The first of these, *la décharge*, refers both to the sensory assault that comes with life in a factory and to the electro-convulsive therapy to which Irene, deemed a socially disruptive figure, is subjected in the asylum she is taken to. The second technique of the social, Rancière explains, is the repressive explicatory/interpretative regime that passes judgement on Irene's behaviour. The individual strands made up of factory,

---

33 *Courts voyages au pays du peuple*, p. 160; *Short Voyages to the Land of the People*, p. 124.

34 *Courts voyages au pays du peuple*, pp. 160–61; *Short Voyages to the Land of the People*, p. 125.

35 *Courts voyages au pays du peuple*, p. 161; *Short Voyages to the Land of the People*, p. 125. Rancière is quoting from Gauny (PP, 70).

36 *Courts voyages au pays du peuple*, p. 161; *Short Voyages to the Land of the People*, p. 125.

newspaper, and mental institution, then, all feed into a particular form of social rationality and constriction.[37]

Rancière's concept of a weapon-like discharge has relevance to Weil's 'Journal d'usine'. She singles out the impact of Taylorism with its stress on the speed with which factory tasks are completed and notes her personal experience of mental vacuity ['vide mental' (CO, 63)] and of violent headaches (CO, 143). Piecework in a hostile environment is lived as an assault. In her conclusion to 'Condition d'un travail non servile' ['The Condition of Non-Servile Work'] written in 1942, she brands Taylorized labour as being unlike any other. It is a work that cannot be redeemed and as such stands as an unforgivable sin, comparable to the crime against the Holy Spirit deemed unpardonable in the New Testament.[38] Taylorism, for Weil, involves 'le pire attentat [...] l'attentat contre l'attention des travailleurs. Il tue dans l'âme la faculté qui y constitue la racine même de toute vocation surnaturelle' (CO, 433) ['the worst assault, the assault on workers' attention. It kills in the soul the faculty which constitutes the very root of every supernatural calling'].

A radical, religious inflection thus marks Weil's protest against the instrumentalization of the manual worker. In *La Pesanteur et la Grâce*, she argues that no 'finalité terrestre' ['earthly goal'] stands in the way of workers reaching out to God. In their state of deprivation, no screen, she writes, need separate them from pure good ['le bien pur']. Juxtaposing the image of the worker as an animal turning in a cage and that of the celestial sphere in its rotation, Weil attempts to summon up a spectrum of experience that is potentially available to those subjected to manual toil: 'Extrême misère et extrême grandeur' ['Extreme misery and extreme grandeur'], she insists.[39] In a conscious rewriting of Pascal, she exhorts the manual worker to convert by embracing a glorious deliverance in the very experience of humiliation.[40] Or, to put this in the secular terms used by Camus, 'les vérités écrasantes périssent d'être reconnues' ['crushing truths perish through being recognized'].[41]

37   *Courts voyages au pays du peuple*, p. 162; *Short Voyages to the Land of the People*, p. 126.
38   See Luke 12:10, where the Evangelist writes that blasphemy against the Holy Spirit will not be forgiven.
39   Weil, *La Pesanteur et la Grâce*, p. 205; *Gravity and Grace*, p. 180.
40   Pascal argues that knowledge of one's misery is the way to human greatness: 'la grandeur de l'homme est grande en ce qu'il se connaît misérable'. See Pascal, *Pensées*, ed. Michel Le Guern (Paris: Gallimard, 2004), p. 106.
41   Camus, *Le Mythe de Sisyphe*, 303.

Fig. 4: Front page of the monthly trade journal *La Machine moderne* (February 1931).
© BnF.

The half-page advertisement vaunts the rational functionality of milling machines (*fraiseuses*) in the cutting of metal shapes. Weil's factory journal, in marked contrast, records the risk of physical injury for users of such equipment and she references the case of a woman whose hand was pierced through by a milling cutter (CO, 145). Weil worked on such a machine at the Renault factory in Boulogne-Billancourt for a number of weeks in June 1935 before being injured. Returning to work on 4 July, she records her relief at being given different work: 'Retourne pas à ma fraiseuse, grâce au ciel!' (CO, 150).

Abjection as a trigger for heightened consciousness is a question also addressed by Rancière in *La Nuit des prolétaires*. In his research on nineteenth-century workers' archives, he draws out how metaphysical questions held most relevance for those for whom the daily sustenance of the body required arduous toil:

> Qui mieux que ceux qui louent leur corps au jour le jour pourrait donner sens aux dissertations sur la distinction du corps et de l'âme, du temps et de l'éternité, sur l'origine de l'homme et sur sa destinée?

> [Who better to give meaning to dissertations on the distinction between body and soul, time and eternity, or on the origin of man and his destiny than those who hire out their bodies day after day?][42]

The workings of metaphysics thus become 'supreme luxury' and 'supreme necessity' for the labourer. Against this backdrop, one worker is urged by Gauny to immerse himself in texts such as Thomas à Kempis's *The Imitation of Christ* and George Sand's *Lélia*, these readings being intended to arouse passions which will allow the proletarian to 'se dresser contre ce qui s'apprête à le dévorer' ['rise up against that which is ready to devour him'].[43] Unlike Weil, Rancière brands religious belief as chimerical, defining it elsewhere as 'a repertory of phrases and histories' that can be 'divert[ed]'.[44] But in *Réflexions sur les causes de la liberté et de l'oppression sociale* as in the perspective of Gauny as relayed by Rancière, a radical otherness operating at the level of thought serves as a means of transcending '[le] seul instinct de subsistance' ['the mere instinct for survival and subsistence'].[45]

One of the epigraphs used in *Réflexions sur les causes de la liberté et de l'oppression sociale*, a quotation from Marcus Aurelius, chimes with Weil's stoic call for a redemptive view of the confrontation with matter: 'L'être doué de raison peut faire de tout obstacle une matière de son travail, et en tirer parti' (RCLOS, 7) ['the being who is endowed with reason can make of any obstacle the object of their endeavour and draw benefit from it']. (Spinoza's call to understand human affairs

42   *La Nuit des prolétaires*, p. 31; *Proletarian Nights*, p. 19.

43   *La Nuit des prolétaires*, p. 31; *Proletarian Nights*, p. 19. Rancière is quoting from Gauny's letter of 12 May 1842 to Louis Ponty.

44   Rancière in dialogue with Jean-Luc Nancy, 'Rancière and Metaphysics (Continued)', p. 195.

45   *La Nuit des prolétaires*, p. 32; *Proletarian Nights*, p. 20.

rather than react emotionally to them forms the second epigraph.)[46] In her May 1942 letter to Père Perrin which takes the form of a spiritual autobiography, Weil refers enthusiastically to the Stoic theme of *amor fati* ['love of fate'] in the writing of Marcus Aurelius.[47] Rancière, as has been noted, sees Gauny experiencing an aesthetic transcendence consistent with a Kantian perspective. Weil here nudges the oppressed worker towards a redemption grounded in religious austerity.

Less lofty expressions of compensatory experience also feature in Weil's factory narrative. Enthusing about a moment of comradeship shared in conversation with two men well used to the factory grind, she contrasts their outlook with the customary atmosphere of servitude in the workplace. One of the two men wishes he had the time and energy to paint, the other to pursue photography, while Weil tells them that her passion is reading. She notes elatedly:

> Camaraderie totale. Pour la 1re fois de ma vie, en somme. Aucune barrière, ni dans la différence des classes (puisqu'elle est supprimée), ni dans la différence des sexes. Miraculeux. (CO, 134)

> [Total camaraderie. For the first time in my life, in short. No barriers, neither in the difference between classes (since it is suppressed) nor in the difference between the sexes. Miraculous.]

With traditional modes of inequality dissolved, the effect is emancipatory.

Other markers of intense engagement with the lives of workers feature in Weil's journal. She makes a note for herself: 'Ne jamais oublier cette observation: j'ai toujours trouvé, chez ces êtres frustes, la générosité du cœur et l'aptitude aux idées générales en fonction directe l'une de l'autre' (CO, 171) ['Never forget this observation: I've always found in these uncultivated people a generosity of heart and an aptitude for general ideas, the one a direct function of the other']. Her refusal to accept a schismatic culture is strengthened by observations made about individual factory workers. She cites the example of Nénette, an efficient worker who partakes in the banter of factory life and also has 'un respect immense pour l'instruction' (CO, 185) ['an immense respect for education'].

---

46 The quotation from Spinoza's *A Political Treatise* reads: 'En ce qui concerne les choses humaines, ne pas rire, ne pas pleurer, ne pas s'indigner, mais comprendre' ['As far as human matters are concerned, do not laugh, do not cry, do not be indignant, but understand']; quoted at RCLOS, 7.

47 Weil, *Attente de Dieu*, p. 40.

The quest for dignity for 'la classe de ceux qui ne *comptent pas* – dans aucune situation – aux yeux de personne ...' (CO, 170) ['the class of those who *don't count* – in any situation – in the eyes of anyone'] was a powerful motivation for Weil. Her formulation appears to prefigure Rancière's view of the 'sans-part' ['those who have no part'], those excluded from visibility in what he terms a police order in which '*l'avoir part* du travailleur est strictement défini par la rémunération de son travail' ['the worker's *having a part* is strictly defined by the remuneration of his work'].[48] For Rancière, the political is to be defined tightly as countering this established order which allocates 'les modes du faire, les modes d'être et les modes du dire' ['ways of doing, ways of being, and ways of saying'] and which prevents the ways of the public space from impinging on the would-be private space of the workplace.[49]

Yet while an advocate for those who 'don't count', Weil was pessimistic about the prospect of radical change secured at a collective level, writing that a state of social subjugation would always obtain, notwithstanding the injunction in the last line of the first verse of 'L'Internationale' (CO, 170). The line in question – 'Nous ne sommes rien, soyons tout' ['We are nothing, let us be everything'] – forms a notably ambivalent point of reference in Rancière. While alluding to it at several points in *Les Bords de la fiction*, he distances himself there from the narrative of the masses entering triumphantly into History. Rather, in an extension of the movement of social disaggregation explored in *La Nuit des prolétaires*, Rancière cites modern literature as a locus of democratic revolution in which fiction incorporates 'un tissu temporel dont les rythmes ne sont plus définis par des buts projetés' ['a temporal fabric whose rhythms are no longer defined by projected goals']. It is in the turn to 'l'univers des micro-événements sensibles' ['the universe of sensible micro-events'], a turn not governed by hierarchy, that the revolution whereby those who were nothing become everything – 'ceux qui n'étaient rien deviennent tout' – occurs.[50] By way of illustration, he reflects enthusiastically on Auerbach's idea that there is at work in Virginia Woolf's *To the Lighthouse* an everyday marked by the insignificant and also on Auerbach's expansive view of a new form of common life.[51]

---

48   *La Mésentente*, pp. 52–53; *Disagreement*, pp. 29–30.
49   *La Mésentente*, p. 52; *Disagreement*, p. 29.
50   Rancière, *Les Bords de la fiction*, pp. 152–53; *The Edges of Fiction*, pp. 133–34.
51   Auerbach's comments, which come in the final chapter of his *Mimesis: The Representation of Reality in Western Literature*, are hailed by Rancière as a

While Rancière's gloss on Auerbach and Woolf is centred on literary narrative in a strong sense, Weil is clearly working with a different mode of writing. The resources of storytelling form a dimension of her testimony although her journal functions in a primarily documentary vein. Yet neither author's mode of intervention should be dismissed as amounting to political quietism. Rancière argues that in the process of subjectivation, the subject is drawn into an interstitial space: 'A subject is an outsider or, more, an *in-between*'.[52] In a similar way, Weil's trajectory provides an urgent, outsider's interrogation of the social order. Commenting on the intensification of goal-driven, industrial production for war in the 1930s, she proposes the interconnectedness of thought and action as a means to counter evil. Indeed, she defines liberty as entailing a link between thought and action (RCLOS, 88) and the least bad society as one in which 'le commun des hommes se trouve le plus souvent dans l'obligation de penser en agissant' ['ordinary mortals are generally speaking obliged to think when acting'].[53] The endorsement of Gauny by Rancière, to which we will return presently, throws up an analogous practice of applying thought to productive necessity. In a related way, Rancière sees fiction having shifted its centre of gravity away from the tradition of narrative plot, with human subjects released from 'l'inframonde du temps de la reproduction' ['the infraworld of reproductive time'].[54]

Weil's journal constructs its own form of contestation in respect of that infraworld. As Yourgrau observes, she clung to her belief in the mysticism of work.[55] In her article 'Condition d'un travail non servile' ['The Condition of a Non-Servile Work'] (1942), she advocates 'la plénitude de l'attention' ['the fullness of attention'], this being her definition of prayer itself (CO, 426). We considered in preceding chapters the motif of artisanal work as prayer in Ndiaye's *La Cheffe* and in Péguy's *L'Argent*. In Weil's case, factory work is servile in character – she describes herself as a beast of burden struggling to remember that she is a thinking being. (Parenthetically, we can note the contrast between the

---

'statement [that is] extraordinary' ['une extraordinaire affirmation']; see *Les Bords de la fiction*, p. 147; *The Edges of Fiction*, p. 128.

52   Rancière, 'Politics, Identification, and Subjectivization', p. 61.

53   Chenavier, quoting from *Réflexions sur les causes de la liberté et de l'oppression sociale*, pp. 116–17; see editorial Introduction, CO, 20.

54   Rancière, *Les Bords de la fiction*, p. 152; *The Edges of Fiction*, p. 134.

55   Yourgrau, *Simone Weil*, p. 37.

claim of industrialist André Citroën in October 1927 that workers were 'enchanted' with the new American methods of factory work, and the view of Georges Navel, who wrote of the Citroën factory at St Ouen: 'the huge drum-beat of the machines [...] speeded your movements [...]. When I left the factory, it followed me, it had entered into me. In my dreams I was a machine'.)[56] Weil protested that workers needed 'une lumière d'éternité' (CO, 423) ['a light of eternity'] in order to bear the monotony of labour; they needed poetry more than they needed bread, she argues in *La Pesanteur et la Grâce*.[57] In her factory journal some years earlier, she mapped out her view of what would constitute an ideal order. Firstly, the human subject would have authority over objects but not over other human subjects; and secondly, such an order would ensure that 'tout ce qui, dans le travail, ne constitue pas la traduction d'une pensée en acte soit confié à la chose' (CO, 204) ['everything which, in the world of work, does not constitute the translation of a thought into action be entrusted to the world of things'].

While the reification of human endeavour points to servitude, Weil argues paradoxically that it is in this nexus that workers may transcend their condition. Her contention is that in order to see God, the material that one works – 'les instruments, les gestes de leur travail' ['the instruments, the actions in one's work'] – must become 'miroirs de la lumière' (CO, 425) ['mirrors of light']. In a restatement of this, she argues that man's vocation is to 'atteindre la joie pure à travers la souffrance' (CO, 434) ['attain pure joy through suffering']. Consciousness of what elsewhere Weil calls the disgust induced by work thus becomes, to use her metaphor, the ladder that allows the worker to ascend. In the case of the peasant, the connectedness with the land means attending to 'cette vertu végétale qui est une parfaite image du Christ' (CO, 427) ['that vegetal virtue which is a perfect image of Christ']. The millennial perspective recalls Péguy's nostalgic characterization of what he terms work in the Christian era – 'le plus beau de tous les honneurs, le plus chrétien' (Arg,

56   The material is here drawn from Julian Jackson, *The Popular Front in France: Defending Democracy, 1934–38* (Cambridge: Cambridge University Press, 1988), p. 85.

57   Weil, *La Pesanteur et la Grâce*, p. 206; *Gravity and Grace*, p. 180. As Patrick Sherry explains, the stress on ethics in Weil (with the link between beauty and 'very grand concepts like goodness and truth') points away from contemporary aesthetic theory. See Sherry, 'Simone Weil on Beauty', in Richard H. Bell (ed.), *Simone Weil's Philosophy of Culture: Readings toward a Divine Humanity* (Cambridge: Cambridge University Press, 1993), pp. 260–76 (p. 268).

790) ['the most beautiful of all honours, the most Christian']. It is, he reflects irritably, an era forced to make way for the modern age.

In the vision of transcendence Weil proposes, labourers and intellectuals are drawn together 'sans aucune inégalité' (CO, 429) ['in a total absence of inequality']. While the carrying of weights and the use of levers signals the worker's subjection to 'la pesanteur des choses' (CO, 426) ['the gravitational force exerted by objects'], Weil's mystical view of work gestures towards a different kind of leverage. She asserts that those who toil can 'faire contrepoids à l'univers' (CO, 427) ['establish a counterweight to the world'] if they focus on the sky and use that perspective of immense distance as a multiplier to be applied to the weak force that is theirs. As a mathematician, Weil was familiar with the laws of mechanics, but she also experienced these in a very material way through factory labour. Yet they now informed her thoughts about the supernatural, so that the frail body of Christ, like that of the worker, when multiplied by the distance between heaven and earth, serves as counterbalance to the world. In Weil's transcendent, radically atypical vision, a process of leverage and magnification sees the situation of the manual worker redeemed.

Rancière writes of nineteenth-century figures temporarily escaping from the role of useful workers through their nocturnal pursuit of the non-utilitarian, of 'l'anti-marchandise' ['the anticommodity'], as we noted above.[58] In Weil's case, the form taken by release is a more tortured one. Work is not discarded but the debasement it brings provides a platform for a redemptive flight from self. In *La Pesanteur et la Grâce*, she writes aphoristically of manual work turning man into matter, just as Christ becomes the Eucharistic bread. Likening the world of work to death, she reflects: 'Il faut être tué, subir la pesanteur du monde' ['One has to be killed, one has to endure the weight of the world'].[59] Grace is to be found in a turning outwards and in deliverance from self.[60]

In her letter of March 1935 to Simone Gibert, Weil confides that despite the suffering which factory life brought her, she could not be happier (CO, 68). Advocating a non-servile conception of work, Weil urges, as she puts it, men and women of the people to bathe in 'une atmosphère de poésie surnaturelle' (CO, 429) ['an atmosphere

58 *La Nuit des prolétaires*, p. 20; *Proletarian Nights*, p. 8. See above, p. 89.
59 Weil, *La Pesanteur et la Grâce*, p. 207; *Gravity and Grace*, p. 181 (translation modified).
60 Weil, *La Pesanteur et la Grâce*, p. 3; *Gravity and Grace*, p. 3.

of supernatural poetry'], this in order to combat a climate in which unhealthy deference, disdain, and demagoguery reinforce the split between the manual and the intellectual. Differences in education, she further argues, produce disparities in terms of riches but, more fundamentally, they sow 'l'illusion de l'inégalité sociale' (CO, 431) ['the illusion of social inequality']. Something akin to Jacotot's view of inequality as a social construct is present here, yet the connection remains a partial one, Weil's reference to 'ceux dont la culture est nulle et l'intelligence faible' (CO, 423) ['people of limited intelligence and without culture'] running counter to the thesis of radical equality advanced by Jacotot. The thrust of Weil's argument is that manual workers and intellectuals achieve their point of unity in the 'plenitude of attention' that is the 'plenitude of prayer' (CO, 429–30).

The two epigraphs chosen by Weil for her 'Journal d'usine' capture the opposition between servile labour and autonomy. A quotation from the *Iliad* refers to the obligation to toil because of a harsh, externally imposed necessity. The other epigraph issues a call to consciousness: 'que pour chacun son propre travail soit un *objet de contemplation*' (CO, 81) ['May the individual experience of work be an *object of contemplation* for everyone']. In his editorial presentation of Gauny, Rancière reflects on how the experience of the manual worker has been a neglected area of philosophical enquiry. He attributes this deficit to two factors: firstly, the collectivizing logic present in the Marxist view of a class consciousness freed from would-be petty bourgeois ideologies; and secondly, socialism's questioning of the relevance of classical culture or metaphysical speculation to an understanding of popular culture. Gauny, we have seen, explores figures from antiquity (Diogenes and John the Baptist) whose positions are radically singular. His analysis, like Weil's, reveals an ascetic inflection, as when he argues that the worker's liberation from manual labour in order to be in touch with the soul carries echoes of the ancient prophets of the desert.[61] In another of Gauny's comparisons, workers are drawn, magnet-like, 'vers leur principe: le bonheur, l'infini!' ['towards their principle: happiness, the infinite!'].[62]

Returning to Rancière's analysis of Rossellini's *Europa 51* and in particular the film's denouement, we find Irene's decision to remain in the asylum providing a moment of paradoxical closure. Her final

61   Gauny, *Le Philosophe plébéien*, p. 61.
62   Gauny, *Le Philosophe plébéien*, p. 79.

gesture when, from behind the bars of her room, she discreetly waves down to the urban poor [*les gens du peuple*] who have come to visit her, is interpreted by Rancière as the conferral of a blessing and as a leave-taking, as 'le souvenir d'un égarement devenu acte de paix' ['the memory of a wandering astray that has become an act of peace'].[63] Rancière links this back to the statue of Marcus Aurelius beneath which Irene is seen deliberating earlier in the film. The stoic emperor whose work attracts Weil's attention thus also appears to inspire Irene's stoic resolve. Rancière sees Irene's gesture of peace as a way of rejecting the institutional pacification to which she has been subjected and as a form of self-retrieval through becoming a stranger to oneself.[64]

Weil's encounter with the dispossessed entails an analogous loss and regaining of self. She writes of how the sense of human dignity as defined by society has been broken in her case through her experience of factory work and that she must forge a new one, 'bien que l'épuisement éteigne la conscience de sa propre faculté de penser!' (CO, 170) ['although exhaustion may extinguish consciousness of one's own ability to think!']. Rancière sees in Irene's final act a moment that is 'atopique et scandaleux' ['scandalous, and atopian'].[65] In Weil's case, the paradox whereby the self that is broken on a factory production line becomes a site of resurrection is the source of the scandalous, in the etymological sense of a stumbling block or obstacle (in Greek, *skandalon*). The religious turn in Weil marks not only a refutation of Marxist materialism but also of capitalism's inversion of subject/object relations. What Rancière calls 'the weight of the social' becomes for Weil the terrain on which she seeks to attenuate the bleakness present in her social vision.[66] Just as *La Condition ouvrière* sets up a tension between reification and redemption, so in *Réflexions sur les causes de la liberté et de l'oppression sociale* the sequel to her analysis of oppression is a 'Tableau théorique d'une société libre' ['Theoretical Table of a Free Society']. In what she herself presents as a reverie, she writes effusively

63 *Courts voyages au pays du peuple*, p. 164; *Short Voyages to the Land of the People*, p. 127.

64 *Courts voyages au pays du peuple*, p. 164; *Short Voyages to the Land of the People*, p. 128.

65 *Courts voyages au pays du peuple*, p. 163; *Short Voyages to the Land of the People*, p. 127.

66 *Courts voyages au pays du peuple*, p. 164; *Short Voyages to the Land of the People*, p. 128.

of a return to medieval artisanship in a tone reminiscent of Péguy's *L'Argent*. She envisages the setting up of new popular *fêtes* to mark rites of passage, such as adolescents assuming autonomy for manual tasks within their communities. She refers in Romantic terms to the lone fisherman assailed by danger and fatigue. The ploughman, the blacksmith, and the mariner all work *comme il faut*, Weil relishing the ambiguity in the term (it has the sense of 'what necessity dictates' but can also mean adherence to the rules and customs of social behaviour). She continues to juxtapose artisanal work and the factory production line, contrasting the spectacle of a foreman standing over factory employees with a scene involving a small group of independent workers who together solve a problem: 'l'image d'une collectivité libre apparaît presque pure' (RCLOS, 113) ['the image of a free collectivity appears almost pure'], she enthuses.

Civilization in its most human form, Weil affirms, would be one in which manual work (though crucially not of a mechanical kind) would constitute the supreme value. Culture had been seen by some as an end in itself, she notes, or as a means of escape from real life. Yet in the would-be better order that she envisages, culture would act as a preparation for 'la vie réelle' ['real life']; it would

> armer l'homme pour qu'il puisse entretenir, avec cet univers qui est son partage et avec ses frères dont la condition est identique à la sienne, des rapports dignes de la grandeur humaine. (RCLOS, 119)

> [equip man so that he might maintain relations worthy of human greatness both with this universe which is his endowment and with his fellow humans whose condition is identical to his own.]

In an egalitarian civilization, Weil contends, art would see balance between mind and body, humankind and the universe, a balance 'qui ne peut exister en acte que dans les formes les plus nobles du travail physique' (RCLOS, 120) ['which can only exist in actuality in the most noble forms of physical work']. As an act of 'soumission consciente' (RCLOS, 122) ['conscious submission'] to necessity, work would thus come to form the centre of culture.

Consistent with this realignment, Weil sees as limited the capacity of the literary imagination to depict factory life. In late 1935, she read 'Montée des périls', volume nine of Jules Romains's novel *Les Hommes de bonne volonté* ['Men of Good Will'], after which she set about drafting a letter to its author on the subject of factory labour. While it probably remained unfinished, the letter eventually appeared in the journal *Economie et humanisme* in 1942.[67] Weil expresses the hope there that her direct experience of a factory will equip her to propose a critique of it. But she doubts that those condemned to factory labour for years are equipped to identify remedies. The worker's *malheur* or hardship, she remarks, militates against lucid reflection. *Malheur* is mute, she notes, drawing on a Greek proverb (CO, 341); and when the wretched [*les malheureux*] complain, they often fail to identify the deep causes of their misery. Weil's stance appears close, on this occasion, to the Althusserian position which Rancière came to reject, namely that workers languish in ignorance of their situation.[68]

* * *

In two contrasting scenarios of factory life, Weil juxtaposes harmonious and hostile work environments. In the first, workers are drawn positively into a collective life that is *unanime* ['unanimous'] in character (there is a nod here to the concept of *unanimisme* developed by Romains). The sounds of the workplace are intense but each has its meaning and the worker is conscious both of the *basso continuo* of the factory floor and the sound of the machine that she operates. The worker is not dwarfed but feels indispensable. At the level of what Rancière refers to as the *sensible* or the perceptible, 'les courroies de transmission [...] permettent de boire par les yeux cette unité de rythme que tout le corps ressent par les bruits et par la légère vibration de toutes choses' (CO, 329) ['the transmission belts (...) allow one to absorb through the eyes this unity of rhythm which the whole body can feel through the noises and the faint vibration emanating from everything']. The experience, far from being fractured, points to a sensory plenitude which sees the worker living intensely the contact with matter: 'tout concourt à la transmutation de l'homme en ouvrier' (CO, 329) ['everything works towards the transmutation of man into worker']. This first scenario in which man and matter are thrown into contact (Weil uses the term *heurt*, meaning 'collision') signals intense human engagement.

In the second evocation of factory life, man's subordination is total. In this state, the worker's situation is that of 'un étranger admis comme simple intermédiaire entre les machines et les pièces usinées' (CO 331)

67 See Chenavier's editorial note, CO, 327.
68 See Introduction, p. 10.

['an outsider admitted solely as intermediary between machines and manufactured goods']. It is a regime that forces body and thought to shrink and withdraw. Unlike the artisan who has some foreknowledge of what work in the short term will entail, production-line workers receive no explanation as to how their labour might be deployed. The factory is an anthropofugal space: 'Les choses jouent le rôle des hommes, les hommes jouent le rôle des choses; c'est la racine du mal' (CO, 336) ['Things assume the role of humans, humans the role of things; it is the root of evil']. Weil extends her trenchant critique of the corrosion of human relations, the individual worker becoming a figure of solitude, indifferent to the plight of fellow workers. Characterizing the levels of human misery experienced as 'la brutalité diffuse' (CO, 343) ['a diffuse brutality'], she reflects on the paradox whereby disassociation and intense individual isolation are at work in the most collective of spaces.

Weil identifies further paradoxes. Alienated when working in the factory, workers feel at home there when on strike, she observes. Occupation of the factory allows them to circulate freely within it and to invite people to see where it is that they work. She comments how this brings a transient joy and pride, in contrast with 'les douleurs permanentes de la pensée clouée' (CO, 343) ['the permanent sufferings when thought is utterly restricted'].[69] But the elevation of thought – 'posséder l'usine par la pensée' (CO, 343) ['to possess the factory through the act of thought'] – however much it is tied on this occasion to the exceptional circumstance of the strike, points to an educative dimension which Weil was keen to promote. In a variant of a letter of 3 March 1936 to Victor Bernard, she sets out her conception of an ideal society, one in which work, and more precisely physical work, would be the first means of education (CO, 448–50). She makes clear how such an ideal is an exact reversal of the Ancient Greek position which saw leisure as the necessary state in which learning was to be achieved (Weil reminds Bernard how slavery, to ensure the completion of material work, had formed the corollary to this).[70] In her diagnosis of the social conditions of her own day, she sees neither manual workers nor managers deriving educative benefit from their respective positions. Weil argues that intellectuals and

---

69   Jackson explores Weil's evocation of the celebratory atmosphere of the strikes of 1936; see *The Popular Front in France*, pp. 96–97.

70   Arendt quotes from Aristotle's *Politics* on the need to master necessity and on the role of slaves in this regard: 'without the necessaries life as well as good life is impossible': *The Human Condition*, p. 83 n. 9.

artists, unlike their Greek predecessors, derive little from their privileged position. They practise excessive specialization, have no contact with life, and infringe freedom of thought. In her *Réflexions sur les causes de la liberté et de l'oppression sociale*, she expresses reservations about what are seen in the modern age as the disinterested activities of sport, art, and thought, arguing that these may not allow one to experience what happens when one is directly 'aux prises avec le monde par un travail non machinal' (RCLOS, 118) ['grappling with the world through a non-mechanical form of work'].[71] Her caustic conclusion is that in the France of the 1930s, the cultures of work and leisure are mutually corrosive, this notwithstanding the impact of the Front Populaire and the radical change in public discourse about work which this heralded. Referring to the atmosphere following on from 1936 as a period of dream, Weil notes official pronouncements on the intention of the French state to rid 'la condition prolétarienne' of its social degradation (CO, 328). Yet she contends that the realities of factory life in the years prior to the Front's accession to power better reflect the actual condition of workers.

In a reinforcement of what Weil consciously presents as a reverie, she draws on literary figures who are concerned to engage with the world of work, notably Tolstoy but also Rousseau, Shelley, and Goethe. Stressing the place of work in Goethe's *Faust*, she depicts the hero fleeing from the search for abstract truth, shunning political and military position, and longing to be rid of his magical power. Faust comes to envisage a life lived with a free people in which he would experience 'un labeur physique pénible et dangereux, mais accompli au milieu d'une fraternelle coopération' (RCLOS, 123) ['a hard and dangerous physical labour but one accomplished amidst fraternal cooperation']. As Rancière writes on the subject of the uses of democracy, 'le postulat du sens commun est toujours transgressif' ['to postulate a world of shared meaning is always transgressive'].[72]

Weil does not lose sight of embodied reality and indeed places this at the heart of her ideal in *Réflexions sur les causes de la liberté et de l'oppression*. Yet the reverie she constructs eschews the contingent reality of mass labour, her narrative gravitating towards the artisanal and the particular. It ambitiously aspires to the development of forms of work requiring the application of the mind, this in an age of mechanical

---

71 Cited in Chenavier's editorial note, CO, 509.
72 *Aux bords du politique*, p. 92; *On the Shores of Politics*, p. 49.

production which sees manual labour become a byword for what is repetitive and brutalizing. Her use of a discourse of religious redemption likewise signals a turning away from social aggregation. Yet in its very consciously aspirational character (CO, 450), Weil's ideal nevertheless refutes a logic of specialization and narrowing and thus challenges the schismatic depiction of the manual and the intellectual.

CHAPTER SEVEN

Pierre Michon, 'Small Lives', and the Terrain of Art

[C]es témoins étaient d'humbles gens, de ceux qui font emploi du mot 'intelligence' pour rendre compte de ce qu'ils pensent n'avoir point.

[that testimony comes from humble folk, from those who use the word 'intelligence' to account for what they think themselves absolutely lacking.]

Michon[1]

Weil's perspective on the subject of human intelligence is more circumspect than that of Jacotot whose promotion of a philosophy of radical equality Rancière eagerly explores, as we have been seeing. As if to qualify Jacotot's claims, Weil posits a distinction between the intellectual faculty and the exercise of that faculty. In a philosophical fragment from the early 1930s, she accepts the existence of inequality at the level of intellectual capacity, but on the question of the application of intelligence, Weil insists on 'l'égalité dans l'exercice des facultés' ['equality in the exercise of the faculties'].[2] She argues moreover that an encounter between those who are free is necessarily one between equals: 'chacun a […] le pouvoir de diriger sa propre pensée' ['everyone has (…) the ability to direct their own thought'].[3] Weil was unequivocal in her

---

1 Pierre Michon, *Vies minuscules* (Paris: Gallimard, 1984), p. 78 (henceforth cited as VM); *Small Lives*, trans. Jody Gladding and Elizabeth Deshays (New York: Archipelago Books, 2008), p. 69. The English translation is henceforth cited as SL.

2 Simone Weil, *Premiers écrits philosophiques*, eds Gilbert Kahn and Rolf Kühn, in *Œuvres complètes*, 5 vols (Paris: Gallimard, 1988), I, 281.

3 Weil, *Premiers écrits philosophiques*, p. 283.

later assertion that equality is a 'vital need' of the human soul: 'le respect est dû à l'être humain comme tel et n'a pas de degrés' ['respect is due to the human person *per se* and allows no gradations'].[4]

These views on equality of capacity and the ethics of respect have a bearing on the text by Pierre Michon which provides the principal point of focus for the present chapter. In the eight life histories that make up his *Vies minuscules* ['Small Lives'] (1984), he describes the witnesses who inspire these short biographies as humble folk whose self-awareness is predicated on an internalized sense of their inferiority, as the epigraph to the present chapter suggests. Thus, whereas Weil sees 'accidental' inequalities arising from precise forms of social exposure, Michon's subjects interpret an asymmetrical distribution of social attributes as an expression of intrinsic human difference. *Vies minuscules* shows how apportionment and societal exclusion of the kind signalled by Rancière's notion of the distribution of the sensible are deeply embedded in the economically deprived rural area of La Creuse in central France where his subjects lived. Yet, as if to illustrate 'the *equality* of represented subjects [and] the indifference of style with regard to content' present in what Rancière calls the aesthetic regime of art, *Vies minuscules* uses a highly wrought prose to portray lives that are often marked by inarticulacy.[5] Ann Jefferson captures this tension, writing of how Michon generates 'rhetorical splendour' around the anonymous lives that are narrated.[6] The mapping of the banal and the everyday onto Michon's baroque linguistic matrix sees humdrum lives acquire the conspicuous status of the near-miraculous, a prose style laced with antithesis and hyperbole serving to channel this.

Michon reflects that it was not difficult to draw from the world he grew up in characters who had a 'calling to the legendary' ['une vocation au légendaire'].[7] Exploring how he links these lives to writing and art, the present chapter also examines, with reference to Michon's *Vie de Joseph*

4 Weil, *L'Enracinement*, p. 90. Weil stresses that concepts such as obedience, responsibility, freedom, equality, hierarchy, and honour all constitute 'vital needs of the human soul'.

5 The definition here is provided by Gabriel Rockhill. See his gloss on 'the aesthetic regime of art' in the 'Glossary of Technical Terms' appendix to Rancière, *The Politics of Aesthetics*, p. 84.

6 Ann Jefferson, *Biography and the Question of Literature in France* (Oxford: Oxford University Press, 2007), p. 346 n. 42.

7 Pierre Michon, *Le Roi vient quand il veut. Propos sur la littérature*, ed. Agnès Castiglione and Pierre-Marc de Biasi (Paris: Albin Michel, 2007), p. 37.

Roulin (1988) ['The Life of Joseph Roulin'], the interface between artistic creativity and what a narrow aestheticism deems to be more banal forms of labour. Arguing that 'every individual human passage on the earth' has something 'minimally sacred' about it, Michon posits as linked destinies the life of the social subordinate (who, when confronted with dominant cultural forms, is a figure who is, now uncomprehending, now seeing and visionary) and the position of the writer and the painter who are daunted both by their artistic practice and the enigmatic lives they seek to portray.[8] As one commentator notes, Michon's work reflects in an emblematic way the trend present in a number of narrative texts of the 1980s to generate, as a primary literary-political ambition, reflection on the redistribution of the sensible that has been a hallmark of Rancière's work.[9]

'The Dark Continent of Writing'

'Vie d'André Dufourneau' ['The Life of André Dufourneau'], the first of Michon's 'small lives', provides a biographical sketch of its eponymous hero, an orphan growing up in a peasant community and adopted by the narrator's family. In adult life, Dufourneau goes to Africa in search of his fortune, his parting words now embedded in the folk memory of his adoptive family: 'J'en reviendrai riche, ou y mourrai' (VM, 21) ['I will come back rich, or die there' (SL, 18)]. Struck by the clichéd expression of adventurism, the narrator observes that 'cette phrase pourtant bien indigne de mémoire' ['that phrase which is nevertheless quite unworthy of being remembered' (translation modified)] is exhumed a hundred times from the ruins of memory by his grandmother. For their author, the words seem noble and literary; for the narrator, they reflect the limitations of André Dufourneau's education. Yet the protagonist's stab at grandiloquence does not prevent his life from being 'une de ces destinées qui furent les sirènes de mon enfance et au chant desquelles pour finir je me livrai, pieds et poings liés, dès l'âge de raison' (VM, 22) ['one of those fates who were the sirens of my childhood, to whose song I would, in the end, surrender myself, wrists and ankles tied, right from

---

8   'ce qu'a de minimalement sacré tout passage individuel sur terre'; *Le Roi vient quand il veut*, p. 22.

9   See Alexandre Gefen, 'Politiques de Pierre Michon', in Pierre-Marc de Biasi, Agnès Castiglione, and Dominique Viart (eds), *Pierre Michon, la lettre et son ombre* (Paris: Gallimard, 2013), pp. 375–90 (p. 375).

the age of reason' (SL, 19)]. Enslaved to the task of retrieving that life, the narrator reflects on how the enormity of the risks involved in the project of writing only become visible with hindsight:

> je ne savais pas que l'écriture était un continent plus ténébreux, plus aguicheur et décevant que l'Afrique, l'écrivain une espèce plus avide de se perdre que l'explorateur; et, quoiqu'il explorât la mémoire et les biblio-thèques mémorieuses en lieu de dunes et forêts, qu'en revenir cousu de mots comme d'autres le sont d'or ou y mourir plus pauvre que devant – en mourir – était l'alternative offerte aussi au scribe. (VM, 22)

> [I did not know that writing was so dark a continent, more enticing and disappointing than Africa, the writer a species more bent on getting lost than the explorer; and, although that scribe may explore memory and memory's libraries instead of sand dunes and forests, may return flush with words instead of gold, or die there poorer than ever, 'to die of it' was the alternative offered to him as well. (SL, 19)]

The scribe, then, faces other risks than those awaiting Dufourneau, not an exotic, geographical terrain but the vastness of memory, of, in Michon's archaic formulation, 'les bibliothèques mémorieuses'.[10] Words and, by extension, books, are the writer's gold, and if the risky venture should fail, the scribe, like the colonial adventurer, is damned.

Michon thus twins a risk-filled pursuit of literariness and colonialist adventurism. Museum images of soldiers in the infantry heading off to the colonies are interspersed with literary figures in *Vie d'André Dufourneau*. We find an unattributed reference to Rimbaud, whose life is elsewhere enthusiastically evoked by Michon.[11] There is mention of Gide's *Paludes* and his colonial travels, as well as a direct evocation of Faulkner, whom Michon sees as exerting a paternal form of influence over him.[12] As Michon strains to imagine what Dufourneau might have experienced, the theme of risk in both colonial and literary adventure is reaffirmed. Thus, as Dufourneau journeys inland, travel and the book converge: 'La forêt [...] se referme comme un livre: le héros est livré à la chance, son biographe à la précarité des hypothèses' (VM, 24) ['the forest closes over like a book;

---

10   The term *mémorieuse* does not feature in *Le Grand Robert de la Langue française*. Jefferson notes that the last recorded use of *mémorieux* is to be found in the prose of George Sand; see *Biography and the Question of Literature in France*, p. 348.

11   See Pierre Michon, *Rimbaud le fils* (Paris: Gallimard, 1991).

12   See Patrick Crowley, *Pierre Michon: The Afterlife of Names* (Oxford: Peter Lang, 2007), p. 32.

the hero is delivered over to chance, his biographer to the precariousness of hypotheses' (SL, 21; translation modified)]. With the terrain of writing lacking firm reference points, the writer's inevitable recourse to conjecture gives Michon's lives a speculative, imaginary dimension.

The letters sent back by Dufourneau are part of the recognizable genre of colonialist impressionism (VM, 25; SL, 22). Had the narrator not been a baby when Dufourneau visited his parents in 1947, 'j'aurais pensé que "la sauvagerie l'avait caressé sur la tête", comme le plus brutal des coloniaux de Conrad' (VM, 26) ['I would have thought that "savagery had caressed his head", like the most brutal of Conrad's colonials' (SL, 23)]. The mention of Conrad connects with Michon's image of the dark continent of writing. Conrad's title, *Heart of Darkness*, itself works ambiguously. Though a story of conquest and travel to what nineteenth-century colonial narratives caricatured as the dark continent of Africa, the novel also uses the 'heart of darkness' motif to signal a crisis in the European mindset.[13] This ambiguity mutates in Michon's narrative, where the risks in colonialist undertakings give way to the dangers inherent in the domestic enterprise of biography. Writing, then, may be exposed as insufficient and as exposing the writer to a dangerous frontier territory.

Cliché about colonial Africa is worked into the muted drama of 'Vie d'André Dufourneau'. The narrator imagines the possible causes of Dufourneau's death before coming to 'l'hypothèse la plus romanesque – et, j'aimerais le croire, la plus probable – [qui] m'a été soufflée par ma grand-mère' (VM, 29) ['the most romantic – and, I would like to think, most likely – hypothesis (which) was whispered to me by my grandmother' (SL, 25)]. The latter's hypothesis is based on memory of Dufourneau's reference to an atmosphere of mutiny on the plantations:

et à cette date, en effet, les premières idéologies nationalistes indigènes devaient émouvoir ces hommes misérables, courbés sous le joug blanc vers un sol dont ils ne goûtaient pas les fruits. (VM, 29)

[and indeed, the first indigenous nationalistic ideologies must have been rousing those wretched men at that time, bent under the white yoke toward a soil whose fruits they did not taste. (SL, 25)]

13   For a discussion of the ways in which Conrad is read and interpreted in the postcolonial period, see Nicholas Harrison, *Postcolonial Criticism: History, Theory and the Work of Fiction* (Cambridge: Polity Press, 2003), especially chapter 2, pp. 22–61.

Another family member, Elise, assuming that Dufourneau has indeed been killed, visualizes his attackers in stereotypical, colonialist terms. As a child the narrator imbibed this point of view and he confesses to still doing so to an extent. Yet in a more analytical vein, he proposes the hypothesis that Dufourneau in Africa was most probably pitiless in his treatment of those whose experience of disadvantage and hardship approximated to his own as an orphan farmhand. Imagining Dufourneau meting out punishment to his workers, the narrator surmises that what was firstly a rejection of connection between African and European becomes a form of encounter but one destined to be lived through violence (VM, 30–31; SL, 26). Michon's reflection on his protagonist's sense of inferiority connects with critical accounts of the colonial mindset.[14] The workings of hierarchy extend to the narrator's reflection on power and language, in that the farmhand Dufourneau, having been 'repudiated' (SL, 17) ['répudié' (VM, 19)] by his French mother tongue, would use French as a symbol of domination in the colony. He would thus acquire 'le seul pouvoir qui vaille: celui qui noue toutes les voix quand s'élève la voix du Beau Parleur' (VM, 20) ['the only (power) that matters: the power that throttles all other voices when the Fine Speaker raises his own' (SL, 17)].

If the strands of Dufourneau's assumed violence are conceived of by the narrator as one victim's aggression against another, the suggestion is of an equalization of conditions in which violence is reciprocal. In this way, the drama of 'Vie d'André Dufourneau' pivots around hierarchy and equality. Thus, Dufourneau's bragging that he will either return wealthy or die in Africa stands as a form of wager which banks on hierarchy's continuing sway. But as the narrator reflects, the wealth-or-death enigma, 'cette alternative fanfaronne avait été réduite sur le livre des dieux à une seule proposition: il y était mort de la main même de ceux dont le travail l'enrichissait' (VM, 31) ['this boastful alternative had been reduced to a single proposition: he died at the very hands of those whose labor had made his fortune' (SL, 27)]. Hierarchy's boast is thus

---

14   In his depiction of colonial adversaries, Albert Memmi, to take a well-known example, stresses how the most willing colonizer is the one who finds compensation for his mediocrity in the colonial environment: 'C'est lui qui est le véritable partenaire du colonisé, car c'est lui qui a le plus besoin de compensation et de la vie coloniale' ['He is the real partner of the colonized, since it is he who has most need of compensation and of colonial life']; Memmi, *Portrait du colonisé* précédé de *Portrait du colonisateur* (Paris: Gallimard, 1985 [1957]), p. 75.

undone, the stress on the themes of mortality and memory's evanescence underscoring a logic of equalization.

In an affect-laden conclusion, the narrator commemorates André Dufourneau, who 'ne laissa de trace que dans la fiction qu'élabora une vieille paysanne disparue' (VM, 32) ['left no traces but in the fiction spun by an old peasant woman now dead' (SL, 27)]. An obscure woman's oral testimony, then, and its corollary, the narrator's own intervention, serve to arrest the onset of oblivion. In a crucial form of levelling, the written narrative is as tenuous as the memory of the now deceased grandmother. Indeed, Dufourneau's assumed failure has an inauspicious bearing on the narrator's own endeavour.

If the capacity of writing is problematized by this first life in *Vies minuscules*, literacy and literariness form a leitmotif in Michon's narration of socially obscure lives, his 'dark continent' analogy carrying broader implications. In one of a number of self-incriminating moments, the narrator recalls how, as a boy, he asked his mother when older members of his family might die. Her reply – that this would happen when he was at boarding school (VM, 94; SL, 82) – is meant to imply a distant future. Yet the narrator reflects that a thirst for knowledge and schooling (and writing itself, we might add) has implicitly brought death in its wake: 'mon appétit de savoir marcherait sur des cadavres: l'un n'allait pas sans les autres' (VM, 95) ['my appetite for knowledge would mean walking over corpses; I could not have one without the other' (SL, 83)]. Elsewhere, Michon describes his characters as having undergone confrontation with the language used in the composition of *Vies minuscules*:

> la belle langue [...] est d'une certaine manière ce qui les a tués, eux, dans leur vérité, dans leur vie. Ce sont des gens qui étaient démunis de langage et qui ont été tués par ce qui les re-tue une seconde fois ici.
>
> [ornate language (...) is what killed them in a certain way, in their truth, in their lives. They are people who were deprived of language and who were killed by what is killing them here a second time.][15]

In Michon's censorious self-scrutiny, the aggression visited on the inarticulate by the literary language he deploys demonstrates how the terrain of writing threatens both the writer and the human subjects who are its point of focus.

---

15   Arlette Farge, 'Pierre Michon, Arlette Farge: Entretien', *Les Cahiers de la Villa Gillet*, 3 (1995), 151–64 (p. 153); quoted in Crowley, *Pierre Michon*, p. 74.

In 'Vies des frères Bakroot' ['The Lives of the Bakroot Brothers'], the world of the *lycée* and formal learning is tightly linked to images of separation and death. More specifically, such a world pulls the young boy away from his mother. Through the lurid metaphors used of primordial danger, the acquisition of knowledge serves as adjunct to the 'dark continent of writing' motif: 'le Savoir, bête antique, inexistante et pourtant goulue, qui vous prive de votre mère et vous livre, à dix ans, à un simulacre du monde' (VM, 95) ['Knowledge, an ancient, imaginary, and nevertheless gluttonous beast, who deprives you of your mother and delivers you up, at ten years old, to some pretence of a world' (SL, 83)]. At the *lycée*, the autobiographical first-person narrator meets Roland Bakroot, the bookish pupil who lives on a poor farm and is described as being tied to the page in a form of sickly compulsion. As he reads, 'il [...] avait une moue dégoûtée, comme si un haut-le-cœur permanent et nécessaire le liait sans recours à la page qu'il haïssait peut-être, mais amoureusement décortiquait' (VM, 106) ['he wore a look of disgust, as if a permanent, necessary nausea bound him without recourse to the page that perhaps he hated but passionately scrutinized' (SL, 93)]. The image of the peasant boy at home up on the bleak plateau and steeped in the erudite documentarism of *Salammbô* strikes the narrator as being 'inexplicablement comique' (VM, 107) ['inexplicably comic' (SL, 94)], the clear suggestion being that the sumptuousness of Flaubert's Carthage-based narrative is out of place in La Creuse.

Published three years after *Vies minuscules*, *Le Maître ignorant* reflects precisely on the subject of cultural apportionment and can be read as providing a useful template for understanding the narrator's bemusement in 'Vies des frères Bakroot'. Rancière energetically poses questions about the distribution of social roles: 'L'inégalité n'est la conséquence de rien [...] ou, plus exactement, elle n'a pas d'autre cause que l'égalité. La passion inégalitaire est le vertige de l'égalité' ['Inequality is not the consequence of anything (...). Or, more exactly, it has no other cause than equality. Inegalitarian passion is equality's vertigo'].[16] The sense of the vertiginous triggered by the prospect of equality intersects with the comic disturbance in the Michon scene where the peasant boy reads *Salammbô*. It stands as a scene of egalitarian strangeness, the boy being no less absorbed than any other reader. Yet Michon points to psychologies shaped by deeply ingrained social conditioning. Thus, underlying Roland Bakroot's 'exégèse forcenée' ['frantic exegesis'] is

---

16   *Le Maître ignorant*, p. 134; *The Ignorant Schoolmaster*, p. 80.

'une foi amère en son indignité' (VM, 114) ['a bitter conviction of his unworthiness' (SL, 99)].

By heightening the juxtaposition of canonical literature and rural backwater, then, Michon illustrates the schismatic social conditions that Rancière refutes in his sympathetic account of Jacotot's method. For Michon, something predating literacy and the book persists in the primeval figure of Roland Bakroot. While the pupil uncomfortably sees his reading as imposture (VM, 114; SL, 100), the narrator endorses the adolescent's perspective, sensing in it 'épurée et écrite en lettres de noblesse, une constellation essentielle de la vie même, quand n'y suffisent plus les livres, de la passion même, enfouie, illettrée et très ancienne, de Roland Bakroot' (VM, 114) ['purified and written in letters of nobility (...) an essential constellation of the life itself, when books no longer sufficed, of the very passion, buried, ancient, and illiterate, of Roland Bakroot' (SL, 100)]. In a studied reversal of cultural value, Michon gives prestige to atavism and the unschooled, and has literature concede its insufficiency.

'The Weight of the Letter'

The image of the bookish Bakroot confirms one of the central tensions in *Vies minuscules*, the mediation of socially obscure lives through an intensely baroque literary composition. The movement between life and textuality is pivotal. Patrick Crowley persuasively draws out the dramatic charge of the confrontation with the book by citing Michon's reflection on his choice of Velázquez's *Saint Thomas the Apostle* for the cover of the Folio edition of *Vies minuscules*. The presence of materiality in the apostle's very pronounced holding of the book conveys, for Michon, an ambiguous gesture. He reflects that the book is both hindrance and source of salvation for the apostle: 'Entre l'obstacle vénéré du livre, le poids de la lettre et de la référence, et cette bouche ouverte et muette de paysan ivre, [...] là sont les *Vies minuscules*' ['*Vies minuscules* lies between the venerated obstacle that is the book, the weight of the letter and of textual reference, and the open, silent mouth of a drunken peasant'].[17]

17 Michon, in an interview with Thierry Bayle, 'Pierre Michon: un auteur majuscule', *Le Magazine littéraire*, 353 (April 1997), 97–103 (p. 98); quoted in Crowley, *Pierre Michon*, p. 77.

Fig. 5: Front cover of the Gallimard (Folio) edition of Pierre Michon's
Vies minuscules featuring part of Velázquez's *St Thomas the Apostle*.
Reproduced by kind permission of
(i) Orléans, Musée des Beaux-Arts © cliché Christophe Camus
(ii) Editions Gallimard, Paris.
Velázquez's depiction of the saint's manual purchase on the book suggests an allegiance
that is built around physicality in a biblical figure, 'Doubting Thomas', known for the
stress he places on embodied consciousness, as when he asks for physical, bodily proof that
the crucified Christ has risen from the dead. For Michon, the Velázquez portrait is 'the
very image of the voice that speaks in *Vies minuscules*'. See Crowley, *Pierre Michon*, p. 77.

'Le poids de la lettre' ['the weight of the letter'], an intense source of
pathos in Michon's reading of the Velázquez, is worked in a particular
direction in 'Vie du père Foucault' ['The Life of Old Foucault'], the story
of an elderly man befriended by the narrator in a hospital where they are
both patients. What draws him to Foucault, who has throat cancer, is the

ordinariness of this retired miller whose name nevertheless, as Michon's narrator notes, recalls the philosopher Michel Foucault and the Catholic missionary Charles de Foucauld (1858–1916).

The singularity of Michon's Foucault is that he refuses to leave the provincial hospital to undergo treatment in a specialist unit in the Paris area. Faced with the weight of medical opinion and the pressure to undergo treatment, Foucault offers his explanation in a manner that appears quasi-miraculous to the narrator:

> il leva les yeux sur son tourmenteur, sembla osciller sous le poids de son étonnement toujours recommencé et augmenté du faix de ce qu'il allait dire, et, avec le même mouvement de toutes les épaules qu'il avait peut-être pour se décharger d'un sac de farine, il dit d'un ton navré mais d'une voix si étrangement claire que toute la salle l'entendit: 'Je suis illettré'. (VM, 155)

> [he raised his eyes to his tormentor, seemed to waver under the weight of his astonishment, forever fresh and increased by the burden of what he was going to say, and, with the same shrug of both shoulders with which he might have lowered a sack of flour, apologetically, but in a voice so strangely clear that the whole ward heard it, he said, 'I am illiterate'. (SL, 134–35)]

The patient's utterance inverts a relationship of hierarchy and connects with what Rancière understands by the politics of literature, seen as a way of intervening in the division of the socially visible and the invisible, speech and noise.[18] The narrator's reaction to the scene is one of jubilant solidarity with someone who resists 'cet univers de savants et de discoureurs' (VM, 155) ['this world of the learned and the pontificators' (SL, 135)] and whose statement about being illiterate is baroquely acclaimed as both admission of ignorance and joyous musical expression:

> quelqu'un, comme moi peut-être, pensait quant à lui ne rien savoir, et voulait en mourir. La salle d'hôpital résonna de chants grégoriens.
> Les docteurs se débandèrent comme un vol de moineaux entrés par erreur ou bêtise sous les voûtes, et qu'eût dispersés la monodie; petit chantre du bas-côté, je n'osais lever les yeux sur le maître de chapelle inflexible, méconnaissant et méconnu, dont l'ignorance des neumes faisait le chant plus pur. (VM, 155–56)

> [someone, like me perhaps, thought that he knew nothing and wished to die. The hospital ward resounded with Gregorian chants.

---

18   See *Politique de la littérature*, p. 12; *The Politics of Literature*, p. 4.

> The doctors disbanded like a flight of sparrows that had gathered by mistake or stupidity under the arches, and that the monody now dispersed; little cantor in the aisle, I did not dare lift my eyes to the unbending choirmaster, unknowing and unacknowledged, whose ignorance of neumatic notation made the song more pure. (SL, 135)]

Old Foucault has thus become an orator with declarative power. His ignorance of the written signs used in plain chant is construed as rendering his song purer. The narrator links his identification with the illiterate patient to his own struggles as a writer overawed by others in the field:

> Moi aussi, j'avais hypostasié le savoir et la lettre en catégories mythologiques, dont j'étais exclu: j'étais l'analphabète esseulé au pied d'un Olympe où tous les autres, Grands Auteurs et Lecteurs difficiles, lisaient et forgeaient en se jouant d'inégalables pages. (VM, 157)

> [I too had hypostatized learning and letters into mythological categories, from which I was excluded; I was the forgotten illiterate at the foot of Olympus where all the others, the Great Authors and Difficult Readers, read and made child's play of incomparable pages. (SL, 136)]

The motif of the writer in the wilderness and the thematics of self-abasement are dramatically spliced with the greatness of Foucault, whose elevation in the eyes of the narrator is cast as a drama occasioned by the social prestige accorded to the written word: 'à l'absence de la lettre, il préférait la mort' (VM, 158) ['in the absence of the letter, he preferred death' (SL, 137)]. The topos of writing as menace is thus obliquely reworked in the collocation of the letter and the patient's demise.

As the ageing Foucault foregoes treatment in Paris, the capital is seen as

> cette ville où les murs mêmes étaient lettrés, historiques les ponts et incompréhensibles l'achalandage et l'enseigne des boutiques, cette capitale où les hôpitaux étaient des parlements, les médecins de plus savants aux yeux des savants d'ici [...]. Que serait-il entre leurs mains, lui qui ne savait pas lire le journal? (VM, 157)

> [that city where even the walls were lettered, the bridges historic, and the merchandise and signs in the shops incomprehensible(...). This capital where the hospitals were parliaments, the doctors the most learned in the eyes of the learned doctors here (...) What would he be in their hands, he who could not even read a newspaper? (SL, 136)]

With the imperium of the word serving to underscore the Paris/provinces divide, the narrative tone fluctuates emotionally between images of dejection and glorification in its portrait of the Père Foucault. The dying patient acquires the lure of an Old Master painting in the closing page of the chapter where he is likened to the 'vieilles épaves lettrées de Rembrandt' (VM, 159) ['Rembrandt's ruined old men of letters' (SL, 138)]. Yet in this august company, the written word is denigrated and Foucault's death becomes exemplary: 'nul dérisoire écrit, nulle pauvre demande griffonnée sur un papier n'aura corrompu sa parfaite contemplation' (VM,159) ['no pathetic writing, no poor claim scribbled down on paper would corrupt his perfect contemplation' (SL, 138)]. The lexis of idealization is insistently configured. And as the angels come to take him, his hand already begins to acquire the status of a precious relic: 'à jamais immobile, intacte d'œuvre, refermée sur le rien de la lente métamorphose où elle a aujourd'hui disparu, *cette main qui jamais ne traça une lettre*' (VM, 159; emphasis added) ['stilled forever, virginal, closed around the void of the slow metamorphosis into which it has now disappeared, *that hand, which never traced a letter*' (SL, 138)]. By facing death without recourse to the written word, Foucault is heralded as a figure of glorious transcendence, the self-effacement that marked his life appearing to extend into his death. A graphological void stands as the guarantee of Foucault's singular, near-saintly status. Yet what gives Michon's story both an ethical and an aesthetic charge is the paradoxical way in which text and image, intertextual allusion and painterly association, converge in the tribute to the eponymous hero, whose life eschews these media in significant ways.

Illiteracy is thus celebrated through the medium of an often sumptuous prose laced with allusions to European high culture. Much of *Vies minuscules* shows this imbrication of compositional intricacy and images of lifestyles dominated by banality and the repetitiveness of the ordinary. One of Michon's most influential source texts for the collection, though not specifically cited, is Michel Foucault's essay, 'La Vie des hommes infâmes' ['The Lives of Infamous Men'], written in 1978. In his analysis of public records of social marginals and their criminalization in seventeenth- and eighteenth-century France, Foucault identifies in the archives the linguistic hyperbole which contrasts with, and improbably crowns, 'la petitesse de l'affaire' ['the pettiness of the matter']: 'Les vies les plus pitoyables y sont décrites avec les imprécations ou l'emphase qui semblent convenir aux plus tragiques' ['The most pitiful lives are described there with the imprecations and grandiloquence normally applied to the most tragic'].[19] The gulf between signifier and signified prompts Foucault to reflect on 'ce théâtre si emphatique du quotidien' ['this intensely bombastic theatre of the everyday'].[20] The linguistic exuberance through which the everyday is channelled extends to Michon where, as Jefferson observes, the 'sumptuously literary [...] prose' reflects the baroque representation of peasant lives.[21]

Articulation

Michon attributes the extravagance of his style in part to Georges Bandy, a provincial priest whom the narrator had known when the latter was a boy. Later, as an in-patient in a psychiatric hospital, he glimpses Bandy as the latter pays a pastoral visit to one of the patients. Michon accentuates the opposition between linguistic sophistication and plainness in the range of contrasts around which Bandy's life story is worked. Tipped for rapid ecclesiastical promotion, the young bourgeois curate practises verbal seduction, and his performance of religious ceremonies entrances the narrator in his early years. Reflecting on the impact made by Bandy's first mass in the parish, 'j'y appris [...] que la Bible est écrite de mots et qu'un prêtre peut, mystérieusement, être enviable' (VM, 182) ['I learned (...) that the Bible is written in words and that a priest can, mysteriously, be enviable' (SL, 157)]. The narrator recalls his ecstatic reaction all those years ago:

> J'aurais voulu pleurer, et ne pus que m'extasier: car les mots soudain ruisselèrent, ardents contre les voûtes fraîches [...]; l'incompréhensible texte latin était d'une netteté bouleversante. (VM, 182)
>
> [I wanted to cry, and could only exalt; because the words suddenly streamed, passionate against the cool vaults (...); the incomprehensible Latin text took on overwhelming clarity. (SL, 157)]

For Michon, Bandy's high-flown sermons delivered to an uncomprehending peasant congregation are likened to 'un pauvre Mallarmé fascinant l'auditoire d'un meeting prolétarien' (VM, 188) ['a poor Mallarmé captivating the audience at a workers' meeting' (SL, 162).

19   Michel Foucault, 'La Vie des hommes infâmes', in *Dits et écrits, III (1976–1979)* (Paris: Gallimard, 1994), pp. 237–53 (p. 244).
20   Foucault, 'La Vie des hommes infâmes', p. 245.
21   Jefferson, *Biography and the Question of Literature in France*, p. 345.

Bandy's performances provide a trailer for the autobiographical narrator's intense linguistic journey (Michon recounts how his failed attempts to write had led to him being admitted to a psychiatric hospital). Now seen many years later in the hospital, the older Bandy is transformed. The tone of his sermon to the inmates intrigues the narrator: gone is the grandiloquence and the relish taken in biblical names. Now talking of birds, animals, and the cold weather, Bandy is likened to Francis of Assisi: 'parler pour les seuls oiseaux, les loups; car si *ces êtres sans langage* l'eussent compris, alors il en eût été sûr: c'eût été que la Grâce le touchait' (VM, 210; emphasis added) ['to speak only for the birds, the wolves; because if *those beings without language* had understood him, then he would have been sure that he had indeed been touched by Grace' (SL, 181)]. Thus, though ensconced in a rural backwater and addicted to alcohol and nicotine, Bandy skilfully adapts his oratorical power. Michon crafts these moments of dissonance and antithesis – human subjects with or without language, with or without literacy, for example. They stand as 'intrusions of the prose of the world' to borrow from Rancière's account of how words, forms, and rhythms – encompassed within human perception (aisthesis) – are 'ressentis et pensés comme de l'art' ['felt and thought as art'].[22] As the Panecastic movement insisted, the human capacity to use and participate in language serves as a marker of the egalitarian: 'le petit d'homme est d'abord un être de parole' ['the human child is first of all a speaking being'].[23]

The focalization on the language use of individual protagonists in Michon finds acute, physiological expression in the section of the Bandy narrative that focusses on the plight of an epileptic. Years earlier, the priest had helped a young girl experiencing a seizure, Lucette Scudéry (now, like the narrator, a patient in the psychiatric hospital). The look on her face provides the young priest with an arresting spectacle: 'ce visage que convulsait une nécessité plus forte que la parole, ce balbutiement d'écume aux coins des lèvres, cet œil blanc sous le plein soleil' (VM, 190) ['that face convulsed by a need stronger than speech, that stammering through foam at the corners of the mouth, the whites of those eyes in the bright sun' (SL, 164)]. Ironically, the arresting usurpation of the mouth, the organ of verbal articulation, is witnessed by Bandy, whose hallmark is his consummate verbal poise. He who masters a liturgical lexis now attends to

---

22 *Aisthesis*, pp. 10–11; *Aisthesis: Scenes from the Aesthetic Regime of Art*, p. x. The French original reads: 'ces intrusions de la prose du monde'.
23 *Le Maître ignorant*, p. 22; *The Ignorant Schoolmaster*, p. 11.

another 'tongue': 'il essuya les lèvres frémissantes: il semblait dérouler un phylactère couleur de ciel devant la bouche bavarde d'un saint' (VM, 190) ['he wiped the trembling lips; he seemed to unroll a sky-blue phylactery over the chattering mouth of a saint' (SL, 164)]. Articulation, language, and utterance, then, are central to the drama in 'Vie de Georges Bandy', as is the disruptive interplay of cultural level and linguistic and theological register. In the psychiatric hospital, the narrator steers clear of educated, city-dwelling patients, preferring, in his blunt formulation, 'le commerce des crétins de l'arrière-pays, dont l'extravagance était maladroitement sentimentale, et que ne déparaient d'autres mots appris que ceux des romances de bal-musette, de juke-box' (VM, 178) ['the company of the backwoods cretins, whose eccentricities were awkwardly sentimental, and who were only disfigured by words learned from popular dance tunes, a juke-box' (SL, 153–54]. In the figure of the eloquent Bandy gone native, a shift in style sees sentimentalism and localism now absorbing the once urbane bourgeois whose earlier, polished celebration of the liturgy had dramatically foregrounded language for Michon the boy.

Art and 'Small Lives'

If the philosopher Foucault's idea of the 'bombastic theatre of the everyday' is amply illustrated in the Georges Bandy life, another of Michon's sources for his *Vies minuscules* is André Suarès, whose collection of lives, *Sur la vie*, appeared early in the twentieth century.[24] Michon headlines the link back to Suarès in his choice of epigraph for *Vies minuscules*: 'Par malheur, il croit que les petites gens sont plus réels que les autres' (VM, 11) ['Unfortunately, he believes ordinary folk to be more real than others']. Suarès sketched a number of literary lives (among them Pascal, Stendhal, Baudelaire, and Verlaine), as does Michon.[25] Similarly, he included peripheral lives whose marginalization prompted him to reflect on how power sustains itself. In a short piece entitled 'Simplesse des barbares' ['Simplicity of the Barbarians'], he

24   Foucault, 'La Vie des hommes infâmes', p. 245.
25   See Dominique Viart, *Pierre Michon 'Vies minuscules'* (Paris: Gallimard, 2004), pp. 56–58. Viart demonstrates the striking similarity between Michon's style and the language used by Suarès to describe the death of Verlaine. For Suarès's life of Verlaine, see André Suarès, *Sur la vie*, 3 vols (Paris: Collection de la Grande Revue, 1909–1912), II, 61–70.

considers the case of a starving woman imprisoned for having damaged a canvas in the Louvre. For Suarès, the destitute rising up is a new Barbarian invasion and he reflects on the status of bourgeois art as witness to social order ['le témoin de l'ordre']:[26]

> Il est clair que le nombre immense, qui ne vit que pour manger et pour mourir, n'entend rien à notre art [...]. Esclaves sans loisir, comment auraient-ils l'amour de notre luxe dans sa rose la plus rare? Ils la croient teinte de leur sang. Ils crèvent la toile, mais c'est le palais qu'ils visent; ils abîment l'œuvre morte, en songeant aux vivants qui en jouissent. C'est la Ville tout entière qu'ils rêvent de détruire.[27]

> [It is clear that the great majority of folk, who only live to eat and to die, understand nothing of our art (...). Slaves with no leisure time, how can they be expected to love the rarest flower of our luxury? They believe it is tainted with their blood. They slash a canvas but their real target is the palace; when they destroy a dead object, they're thinking of the living who enjoy it. Their dream is to destroy the whole City.]

Suarès adds that the woman who slashes a canvas depicting a pope is aiming beyond a papal tiara and that, now facing prison, she will at least be fed: 'A quoi servent vos musées, lorsque tant de malheureux n'ont pas de pain?' ['When so many unfortunate people are without bread, what's the purpose of your museums?'].[28] Suarès concludes 'Simplesse des Barbares' by constructing an entropic vision that includes the inexorable destruction of Ancient Rome and Athens at the hands of 'l'énorme masse sans yeux' ['the great faceless mass']. He casts as mutually uncomprehending antagonists the artist and those who utter the 'cry of the stomach' ['le mot du ventre'].[29] In the confrontation between primitive bodily needs lived at a communitarian level and art destined for bourgeois consumption, Suarès disabuses his reader of the idea that art might embody universal value.[30]

---

26   Suarès, *Sur la vie*, I, 90.
27   Suarès, *Sur la vie*, I, 90–91.
28   Suarès, *Sur la vie*, I, 91.
29   Suarès, *Sur la vie*, I, 91.
30   How many, Suarès asks, will be appalled by the act of iconoclasm in the Louvre? Aggressively rejecting any assumption of widespread outrage, he estimates a thousand (discounting journalists), adding that in the earlier part of the nineteenth century, a tramp causing damage to an Ingres might well have amused Delacroix's friends, while Ingres's friends might have conspired to have a Delacroix damaged (Suarès, *Sur la vie*, I, 89).

A variant on Suarès's schematic presentation of lives from below and the commodification of art is present in Michon's *Vie de Joseph Roulin* (1988), which focusses on the relationship between Van Gogh and the eponymous provincial post office employee, members of whose family the artist regularly painted when they were neighbours in Arles in 1888. Michon stresses that, however much the artist may be motivated by a communitarian desire, the practice of writing or painting is intrinsically isolating. He cites, slightly freely, Mallarmé's dictum that to write is to withdraw ['Qui écrit ... se retranche'] and includes the poet's even more radical assertion made in a letter to a friend: 'Dieu merci, je suis complètement mort' ['Thank God, I'm completely dead'].[31] Michon describes the relish he experienced when working into *Vie de Joseph Roulin* the tension between the solipsism of the artist and the outlook of Roulin, 'ce facteur révolutionnaire, communard, habité d'un rêve de communauté mondiale' ['this revolutionary postal worker, supporter of the Paris Commune and inspired by a dream of worldwide community'].[32] Van Gogh's correspondence with his brother Theo corroborates Michon's evocation of Roulin as the embodiment of a proud proletarian tradition. Describing Roulin nursing his daughter on his lap and singing to her, Van Gogh writes:

> Sa voix avait un timbre étrangement pur et ému où il y avait à la fois pour mon oreille un doux et navré chant de nourrice et comme un lointain résonnement du clairon de la France de la révolution. Il n'était pourtant pas triste, au contraire, il avait mis son uniforme tout neuf qu'il avait reçu le jour même et tout le monde lui faisait fête.[33]

> [There was a strange purity and emotion in the timbre of his voice and I could hear a sweet and sad lullaby and also a distant echo of the clarion of the France of revolution. Yet he was not sad. On the contrary, he had put on his brand new uniform which he had just received that day and everyone was celebrating with him.]

Roulin's proud self-display as noted by Van Gogh complements Michon's reference to the strain of princely self-worth which the postal worker inwardly cultivates.

Reflecting on his choice of a modest state employee as a point of access

---

31   Michon, *Le Roi vient quand il veut*, p. 28.
32   Michon, *Le Roi vient quand il veut*, p. 33.
33   Vincent Van Gogh, *Lettres à son frère Théo*, trans. Louis Roëdlandt, ed. Pascal Bonafoux (Paris: Gallimard, 1988), p. 458.

to Van Gogh, Michon contrasts Roulin's untutored response with that of
the acquisitive connoisseurs of Van Gogh's day who were to establish the
painter's reputation through the articulation of 'un discours légitimant' ['a
legitimizing discourse'].[34] As a counterpoint to the ideology underpinning
the bourgeois consumption of art, Michon proposes an alternative
community within which a loving encounter between an artist as social
misfit and a proletarian might unfold. The encompassing, communitarian vision contrasts markedly with the alienated order represented
melodramatically by Suarès in 'Simplesse des barbares'.

In Michon's *Roulin* narrative, the contestation of value goes hand
in hand with an assertive reflection on cultural decentring. Michon
showcases the issue of the construction of value and uses this to destabilize
the terrain of art. In an epigraph drawn from Claudel's *L'Echange* ['The
Exchange'], he cites Marthe's question, 'Est-ce que chaque chose vaut
exactement son prix?' ['Is everything worth its price?'], and Thomas
Pollock Nageoire's categorical reply: 'Jamais' ['Never'].[35] Symmetrically,
Michon's narrative ends with a return to the question of value: 'Qui dira
ce qui est beau et en raison de cela parmi les hommes vaut cher ou ne
vaut rien?' (VJR, 65) ['Who can say what is beautiful and as a result,
amongst men, is deemed worthless or valuable?' (MS, 50; translation
modified)]. The relativization of worth thus frames the Roulin narrative
in which Michon offsets anonymity and visibility, the culturally iconic
and an obscure provincial encounter, late nineteenth-century Arles and
the metropolitan spaces in which the conspicuous consumption of art is
practised:

> Donc c'est là que Roulin devint tableau, matière un peu moins mortelle
> que l'autre, dans cette bicoque aujourd'hui invisible et aussi connue que
> les tours de Manhattan. (VJR, 28)

> [So it's there that Roulin became a painting, matter a little less mortal
> than flesh, all in this shack that today is invisible and as well known as
> the Manhattan skyline. (MS, 20; translation modified)]

Roulin's home (destroyed, as Michon points out, in American air raids
in 1944) is melodramatically juxtaposed both with New York and,

---

34 Michon, *Le Roi vient quand il veut*, p. 50.
35 Pierre Michon, *Vie de Joseph Roulin* (Lagrasse: Verdier, 1988), p. 9
(subsequently cited as VJR); *Masters and Servants*, trans. Wyatt Alexander Mason
(San Francisco: Mercury House, 1997), p. 5 (*The Life of Joseph Roulin* forms part
of this volume). Hereinafter cited as MS.

elsewhere in the text, Paris – metropolitan spaces in which the commodification of art entails both a disowning, and a commercially driven
promotion, of the conditions in which it is produced.

In a speculative reconstruction of Roulin's relationship with Van
Gogh, Michon recreates the postal employee's puzzled contemplation of
the enigmatic artist at work:

> Roulin regarde maintenant cet homme de médiocre volume, debout et
> occupé, incompréhensible, qui ne connaît pas les noms de ces endroits
> et qui à la place de ces lieux cadastraux met sur une toile de dimension
> médiocre des jaunes épais, des bleus sommaires, un tissu de runes
> illisibles [...]. (VJR, 35)

> [Roulin now watches this man of meagre volume, standing and
> preoccupied, incomprehensible, who doesn't even know the names of
> these places and in lieu of the cadastral marks applies thick yellows
> and perfunctory blues to a canvas of meagre dimensions, a fabric of
> unreadable runes (...). (MS, 26)]

Oblivious to the surveying and measurement that signal land ownership,
Van Gogh is presented as working beyond the human mapping of
territory and into artistic practice. Value is relocated, no longer registered
in a land survey but articulated, in Michon's characterization, as part of
a practice of pictorial creativity. As Élisabeth Arnould observes: 'Roulin
voit la peinture nue, son apparaître brut'[36] ['Roulin sees the paint in
its pure, naked visibility']. He thus stands as participant in primitive
art and exemplifies 'ce mythe du naïf redécouvrant le naïf: l'art à son
origine' ['the myth of the naif rediscovering the naif: art in its origins'].[37]

Working seductively with opposites, Michon voices the sentimentalized aspiration that the postman and painter might love one another
across the two great strands of the nineteenth century, the myths of
Art and Revolution: 'J'ai aimé frotter l'une contre l'autre ces deux
mythologies' ['I enjoyed rubbing these two mythologies against each

---

36 Élisabeth Arnould, 'Portrait de l'artiste en facteur', in Ivan Farron and Karl
Kürtös (eds), *Pierre Michon entre pinacothèque et bibliothèque* (Bern: Peter Lang,
2003), p. 112.

37 Arnould, 'Portrait de l'artiste en facteur', p. 113. Analysing Georges Bataille's
focus on sacrifice in his 'La mutilation sacrificielle et l'oreille coupée de Vincent
Van Gogh' (in Bataille, *Œuvres complètes* (Paris: Gallimard, 1970), I, 258–71),
Arnould notes an absence of reference to the plasticity of art which, she argues,
is corrected in Michon's reconstruction of Roulin's naive contemplation of the art
object (pp. 101–02).

other'].[38] In Michon's quasi-amorous projection, Van Gogh's art is cast as Roulin's boon, a more powerful mirage than the Great Revolutionary Evening (VJR, 36–37; MS, 27). In the process, an ecstatic, delusional fusion of Republican and aesthetic deliverance is signalled.

Michon transparently acknowledges, then, the element of mystification in his reconstruction of the Arles encounter. He seeks a convergence of the everyday and the aesthetic in an interpellation addressed to an eponymous hero shaped by Republican socialism and initially convinced of art's gratuitousness. The optative mode of writing favoured by Michon in his romancing of obscure lives facilitates the convergence: 'Je veux croire que [...], je veux que ce qui l'étonne' (VJR, 35) ['I would like to believe that (...), I hope what surprises him' (MS, 26)]. In a form of desire-laden analepsis, Michon wills his protagonist to reflect beyond the visionary politics of communitarian socialism that enthuse this disciple of Blanqui and to encompass imaginatively the endeavours of his painter neighbour:

> [Roulin] se demandait [...] par quelle bizarrerie ce qu'il croyait être, et qui était, la peinture, c'est-à-dire *une occupation humaine comme une autre*, qui a charge de représenter ce qu'on voit comme d'autres ont charge de faire lever le blé ou de multiplier l'argent, une occupation donc qui s'apprend et se transmet, produit des choses visibles qui sont destinées à faire joli dans les maisons des riches ou à mettre dans les églises pour exalter les petites âmes des enfants de Marie, dans les préfectures pour appeler les jeunots vers la carrière, les armes, les Colonies, comment et pourquoi ce métier utile et clair était devenu cette phénoménale anomalie, despotique, vouée à rien, vide, cette besogne catastrophique [...]. (VJR, 35–36; emphasis added)

> [Roulin asked himself (...) by what outlandishness what he believed to be and indeed was painting, that's to say *a human occupation like any other* – carrying as its burden the need to represent what is seen, as others are burdened with raising wheat or making money beget money, an occupation that is learned and passed on, producing tangible things destined to make the houses of the rich look nice, or to be placed in churches to exalt the devoted little souls of the children of Mary, or in the prefectures to call young men to a career, the army, the Colonies – how and why this occupation, useful and clear, had become this phenomenal anomaly, despotic, dedicated to nothing, empty, this catastrophic labor (...). (MS, 26–27; translation modified)]

38 Michon, *Le Roi vient quand il veut*, p. 51.

The narrator's projection sees Michon steering Roulin towards seeing artistic activity as poiesis, having him grasp art's purchase on the real and its tangible connection with the world through the ideological underpinning it delivers (taste, belief systems, and other spurs to action).[39] But while the postal employee may accept the delineation of a common burden that makes possible the homology of art, food production, and the workings of capital, he remains conflicted, unable to eradicate the perception that what the practice of art represents in the case of Van Gogh is something deeply 'anomalous'. In Michon's account, what haunts Roulin is Van Gogh's 'catastrophic labor'.

The notion of art as otherness is also present in the sacred aura with which Michon at times endows it. Specifically in relation to writing, Jefferson sees Michon working anachronistically with often nineteenth-century views on literature's sacred character.[40] This extends to the visual arts as Michon's casting of Roulin illustrates: the postal worker may know nothing about Art and yet, as depicted by Van Gogh, he wears 'sa sainte casquette' (VJR, 11) ['his sacred cap' (MS, 6)]. Likewise, in Van Gogh's series of portraits of Roulin family members, Michon sees the collection commemorating 'cette sainte famille prolétaire comme l'Autre, généreuse et souffrante' (VJR, 29) ['this holy, proletariat family just like the Other, generous and long suffering' (MS, 21)].

In the encounter with Van Gogh, Roulin is thus drawn onto the unfamiliar terrain of art and depicted as rethinking 'l'énigme des beaux-arts' (VJR, 36) ['the enigma of the beaux arts' (MS, 27)]. In doing so, he brings to his encounter with art 'un regard profondément a-théorique' ['a profoundly a-theoretical look'].[41] Arnould sees in Roulin's 'naive revalorization' of the image a swinging away from theory to focus on the work and painterly technique.[42] The materiality that so defines his daily life now opens up to, and encompasses, Van Gogh and his work.[43] As with Rancière on the subject of nineteenth-century workers' exposure to intellectual life, so Roulin represents for

---

39   See Chapter 5, pp. 122–23, for discussion of Agamben's reflections on poiesis and the figure of *homo faber*.

40   Jefferson, *Biography and the Question of Literature in France*, p. 340.

41   Arnould, 'Portrait de l'artiste en facteur', p. 99.

42   Arnould, 'Portrait de l'artiste en facteur', p. 114.

43   The admission of art to Roulin's world view now inclines him to see the merit of the young Parisian dealer who is keen to acquire the Van Gogh that hangs in the Roulin home and who thereby attunes Roulin to the worth of the painter's endeavour (VJR, 61).

Michon a figure who throws into perspective the discursive practices associated with the appreciation and theorization of art.

We have seen Michon's metaphor of a rubbing together of the paradigmatic nineteenth-century myths of Art and Revolution. At one level, the pairing squares with the insistent exploitation of binary differences in *Vies minuscules*. There, the inarticulate and the eloquent, the written word and illiteracy, the manual and the intellectual, are the subject of broad-brush juxtaposition and conflation. Yet, importantly, the specific choice of Van Gogh sees Michon align the artistic and the everyday in a manner consistent with the painter's own social formation and vision. As with Michon, the depiction of 'small lives' was integral to Van Gogh's art. After living in Paris and other cities, he reflected to his mother that this had not changed his appearance: 'I keep looking more or less like a peasant [...], and sometimes I imagine I also feel and think like them, only peasants are of more use in the world [...]. Well, I am plowing on my canvases as they do on their fields'.[44] The desire for incorporation into the world of manual labour was no flight of fancy for Van Gogh. For him, as for Simone Weil, connection with the worker had something divine about it and for both figures, as Yourgrau argues, 'the opposition of mental to physical work is one of the great lies of the modern world'.[45] Van Gogh wrote approvingly of Tolstoy that he had acquired the skills of a manual worker and embraced the march of humanity.[46] The painter was profoundly exercised by the question of the social place and use of art. As Debora Silverman explains, working as a lay preacher both in England and then with miners in the Borinage district of Belgium, the young Van Gogh was attempting to enact Thomas à Kempis's model of Christly imitation which he had learnt from his father.[47] This inheritance shaped his response to art. Silverman reflects that 'Van Gogh's consistent attempt to treat painting as woven cloth carried his long-term religious and social project of identification

---

44   Quoted in Debora Silverman, 'Weaving Paintings: Religious and Social Origins of Vincent Van Gogh's Pictorial Labor', in Michael S. Roth (ed.), *Rediscovering History: Culture, Politics, and the Psyche* (Stanford: Stanford University Press, 1994), pp. 137–68 (p. 164).

45   For reflection on important points of connection between Van Gogh and Weil, see Yourgrau, *Simone Weil*, p. 38.

46   Van Gogh, *Lettres à son frère Théo*, p. 422.

47   We saw in Chapter 4 how Gauny advised fellow worker Louis Ponty to read Thomas à Kempis's *The Imitation of Christ*; letter of May 1842 quoted by Rancière in *La Nuit des prolétaires*, p. 31; *Proletarian Nights*, p. 19.

with labor into pictorial practice'.[48] The sanctification of manual occupations connects with the communitarian instinct that Michon draws out in *Vie de Joseph Roulin* and is consistent with Van Gogh's leaning towards what Silverman terms 'the larger totalities of corporate community and redemptive labor'.[49]

* * *

Just as Van Gogh's work conveys an enduring connection with the world of labour, in a parallel way Michon argues that the writer is at one level one of the 'minuscules'. Thus Bossuet the man, he asserts, lived his life as a seventeenth-century snob, yet in the pulpit, 'il donnait les grandes orgues de son style pour s'adresser à ce qui le dépassait infiniment' ['he used the great organ of his style to address what was infinitely greater than him'].[50] The quest for transcendence through writing, whereby the writer dedicates his text 'à un plus haut qui soit Autre' ['to a higher one who is Other'], connects with the conclusion of *Vies minuscules*, which opens out to the deceased whose lives the work commemorates: 'Que dans le conclave ailé qui se tient aux Cards sur les ruines de ce qui aurait pu être, ils soient' (VM, 249) ['That in Les Cards, in the winged conclave that stands over the ruins of what could have been, they may be' (SL, 215; translation modified)].[51] Ancestors and textual antecedents are central to Michon's project. Just as the cataloguing of 'infamous lives' triggers verbal splendour (as explored by Michel Foucault), and the death of Verlaine (as told by André Suarès) becomes an occasion for baroque linguistic celebration, so in Michon the demise of figures such as the retired miller Foucault is drawn into literature.[52] The former manual worker who, in his terminal illness, conveys a celestial music embodies a redemptive fusing of labour and transcendental beauty. Michon's story conflates pathology, illiteracy, and linguistic articulation which are 'ressentis et pensés comme de l'art' ['felt and thought as art'], to draw again on Rancière's argument in *Aisthesis*.

48   Silverman, 'Weaving Paintings', p. 149.
49   Silverman, 'Weaving Paintings', p.168.
50   Michon, *Le Roi vient quand il veut*, p. 29.
51   Michon, *Le Roi vient quand il veut*, p. 30.
52   Michel Foucault observes that the language used in the telling of 'infamous lives' displays 'éclat', 'splendeur', and 'violence'; see 'La Vie des hommes infâmes', p. 244.

In the opening line of *Vies minuscules*, Michon confesses to 'mes prétentions' (VM, 13) ['my pretensions' (SL, 11)] and the text goes on to enact an undisguised working through of drive and appetite that brings risk as well as the lure of a delirious communion linking writer and subject. His textual compositions are suffused with desire and affectivity. In *Vie de Joseph Roulin*, this manifests itself in the wish to see artist, model, and writer converge: 'Est-ce que ce sont nos yeux, qui sont les mêmes, ceux de Vincent, du facteur et les miens?' (VJR, 65) ['Is it our eyes, which are the same, Vincent's, the postman's, and my own?' (MS, 50)].[53]

The transcendence of individual boundaries links to Michon's definition of a portrait as 'la représentation d'un homme par son semblable' ['the representation of one human by a fellow human'].[54] Levelling sees him valorize oral testimony and relativize the institution of literature and the prestige accorded to the written word. It also sees Michon underscoring the precariousness of writing and art, as in the conclusion of the story of the dying miller where writing becomes 'derisory' (VM, 159; SL, 138). Yet there is also, simultaneously, a will to magnify their potential: 'Oui, la peinture ou la littérature sont cette interminable, cette épuisante relance du monde, qui sans cesse retombe' ['Yes, painting and literature are that unending, that exhausting relaunching of the world which is forever falling back down'].[55]

---

53 With reference to *Rimbaud le fils*, Rancière notes Michon's relish for the fusion of life and writing in the work of *bio-graphie*. Rancière cautions that the specificity of textual practice needs to be protected from any reduction to biographical fact. See Jacques Rancière, *La Chair des mots. Politiques de l'écriture* (Paris: Galilée, 1998), p. 63; *The Flesh of Words: The Politics of Writing*, trans. Charlotte Mandell (Stanford: Stanford University Press, 2004), p. 48.

54 Michon, *Le Roi vient quand il veut*, p. 64.

55 Michon, *Le Roi vient quand il veut*, p. 63.

PART III

Audible Voices

CHAPTER EIGHT

Tales of Distribution
in À *la recherche du temps perdu*

> [Gilberte] me passait une balle; et comme le philosophe idéaliste dont le corps tient compte du monde extérieur à la réalité duquel son intelligence ne croit pas, le même moi qui m'avait fait la saluer avant que je l'eusse identifiée, s'empressait de me faire saisir la balle qu'elle me tendait.

> [(Gilberte) would pass me a ball; and, like the idealist philosopher whose body makes allowances for the external world in the reality of which his intellect does not believe, the same I who had made me greet her before I identified her, hastened to make me take the ball she was holding out to me.]

Proust[1]

Reading Proust, one is struck by the ambivalent perspectives on class proposed by a narrator whose own class provenance is wholly unambiguous. Granted, the codes of Combray rest on a rule of social segregation. Likewise, the scene in Jupien's brothel in First World War Paris in *Le Temps retrouvé* where aristocrats and working-class Parisian men are drawn together would seem to be a moment of exception that confirms the otherwise stable, partitioned character of social hierarchy.[2] The present chapter, however, explores ways in which such partitioning is disrupted specifically when the bourgeois narrator draws the expressive

---

1 Proust, RTP, I, 394; ISLT, I, 405.
2 For a detailed and wide-ranging exploration of class relations in Proust's novel, see Jacques Dubois's *Le Roman de Gilberte Swann: Proust sociologue paradoxal* (Paris: Seuil, 2018).

capacities and interventions of individuals from different classes into relations, variously, of concurrence, rivalry, and synergy. The language uses that are part of that expressivity often trigger moments of instability, exposing hierarchy as a social construct that requires regular bolstering. On the subject of the distribution of the sensible, Alison Ross observes that word-use partitions space, 'dividing and apportioning capacities'.[3] The passion for inequality diagnosed by Jacotot applies to many of the interactions between characters in the *Recherche*. Yet, as in *Le Maître ignorant*, Proust opens up a countercurrent to a logic of relegation and privilege. Indeed, the novel often gestures towards a principle of levelling in relation to uses of language as performed by characters with different class affiliations.

The Imprint of the Real

Random intrusions of the everyday frequently trigger this levelling, as illustrated in Part III of *Du côté de chez Swann*. With the young Marcel's attachment to Gilberte expressing itself in anxious speculation about her response to messages he sends her, he initially overlooks the fact that in the material transmission of the message, the autonomous actions of unknown others intervene. Thus, the stamp of the external world is literally applied when he sends Gilberte a telegram, the result being that, when she later shows him the telegram, he struggles to recognize his own handwriting:

> J'eus peine à reconnaître les lignes vaines et solitaires de mon écriture sous les cercles imprimés qu'y avait apposés la poste, sous les inscriptions qu'y avait ajoutées au crayon un des facteurs, *signes de réalisation effective, cachets du monde extérieur, violettes ceintures symboliques de la vie*, qui pour la première fois venaient épouser, maintenir, relever, réjouir mon rêve. (RTP, I, 396; emphasis added)

> [it was hard for me to recognise the insignificant, solitary lines of my handwriting under the printed circles apposed to it by the post office, under the inscriptions added in pencil by one of the telegraph messengers, *signs of actual realization, stamps from the outside world, violet bands*

3   Alison Ross, 'Expressivity, Literarity, Mute Speech', in Jean-Philippe Deranty (ed.), *Jacques Rancière: Key Concepts* (Durham: Acumen, 2010), pp. 133–50 (p. 150).

symbolizing life, which for the first time came to espouse, sustain, uplift, delight my dream. (ISLT, I, 406)]

Marcel's written word has to pass through an external agency. His communication is thus drawn democratically into a zone of social transaction and convention in that it bears the post office frank and is overwritten by the postal employee whose markings in pencil are visible. These additional marks ensure that in a form of espousal, his dream is overlaid with life ['la vie']. From a syndrome of isolation and ineffectualness (the young Marcel cannot see beyond his solitary lines of writing), he sees the dream sustained by virtue of its being channelled through material culture. For this second phase to materialize, the sign of further writing in the form of the superscription by the post office is sufficient. With Marcel's inscription joining other inscriptions, the bourgeois sender of the message and its proletarian handler are drawn into connection, albeit tangentially.

Rancière draws attention to an observation in Proust's *Le Carnet de 1908* where the hesitant aspiring novelist notes what had been a feature, he argues, of the previous forty years of modern French literature, the gap between 'la gravité de l'expression et la frivolité de la chose dite' ['the gravity of the expression and the frivolity of the subject'].[4] Flaubert's indifference to the referent and his promotion of language's poetic function forms part of the context, as Proust indicates. In the scene in the *Recherche* involving the telegram, referent and rhetoric are interwoven: the narrator uses a baroque language, hailing these markings (the postal stamp and the additional inscription in pencil) as hieroglyphs that signify the world and space of the 'réalisation effective' ['actual realization']. The idea of literal endorsement, of a superimposition effected by an external agency, is present in a variant form in the same section of the novel when the young protagonist spots Mme Swann's carriage in the Bois de Boulogne: 'je voyais – ou plutôt je sentais imprimer sa forme dans mon cœur par une nette et épuisante blessure – une incomparable victoria' (RTP, I, 411) ['I saw – or rather I felt imprint its form on my heart with a neat and exhausting wound – a matchless victoria' (ISLT, I, 422)]. The experience of outsiderness within a social order is again foregrounded at the level of the sensory.

Marcel's initial failure to recognize his own writing once it has passed into a social forum derives partly from anxiety about the transfer of the

---

4   *La Parole muette*, p. 141; *Mute Speech*, p. 145.

word into a public space. His failure is not confined to this early episode. Much later, in *Albertine disparue*, the adult Marcel is slow to recognize the breakthrough moment when his work appears in *Le Figaro*. Here, too, the process whereby the protagonist's words find their way into the world sees him anxiously anticipating their reception, this time in the society formed by thousands of newspaper readers.

Dramatizing the triangulation formed by the writer, the journalistic text, and the reader-receiver, the narrator conceives of a collective Venus, of which one possesses, he suggests, only a mutilated limb if one focusses solely on the input of the author:

> car elle ne se réalise complète que dans l'esprit de ses lecteurs. En eux elle s'achève. Et comme une foule, fût-elle une élite, n'est pas artiste, *ce cachet dernier* qu'elle lui donne garde toujours quelque chose d'un peu commun. (RTP, IV, 150; emphasis added)

> [for this (a collective Venus) is completely realized only in the minds of its readers. That is where all is accomplished. And as a crowd, however select, is not an artist, *its ultimate seal of approval* always retains something of the common touch. (ISLT, V, 534)]

In a formulation that recalls what Rancière refers to as the aristocratic temptation associated with the practice of literature, the reference to that which is common suggests that the bourgeois reader completes and at the same time degrades the endeavours of the writer.[5] Jacques Dubois identifies in the *Recherche* a process of disillusionment that sees its author move from a naive idealism to something approaching materialism, the novel becoming tied in with 'the great register of the social'.[6] Just as the telegram to Gilberte in 'Noms de pays: le nom' receives external validation, so too with Marcel's article in *Le Figaro*, the outside world provides its own authentication or seal. Jean-Luc Nancy's reflection on the 'singular plural being' has relevance to Marcel's discovery of his social insertion, Nancy writing specifically of a 'between us' ['entre

---

5   See Rancière, *La Parole muette*, text synopsis on back cover. Malcolm Bowie reflects on the tension in Proust between the narrator's carefully laid theoretical framing and the capacity of 'life' to contest such framing. 'High art, in Proust's formula, must always begin low, be prepared to plunge from its summits back into the trivial and the everyday'; see Bowie, *Proust Among the Stars* (London: HarperCollins, 1998), p. 105.

6   'le grand registre du social'; see Dubois, *Le Roman de Gilberte Swann*, p. 221.

nous'], a contiguity without continuity working between one singular and another.[7]

With the appearance of Marcel's article in the press also drawing him into the broader world of material culture, the phenomenology of distribution and consumption of the printed word is carefully acknowledged. The narrator evokes the busy, early-morning world in which newspapers are moved around the city:

> Puis je considérai le pain spirituel qu'est un journal, encore chaud et humide de la presse récente et du brouillard du matin où on le distribue dès l'aurore aux bonnes qui l'apportent à leur maître avec le café au lait, pain miraculeux, multipliable, qui est à la fois un et dix mille, et reste le même pour chacun tout en pénétrant à la fois, innombrable, dans toutes les maisons. (RTP, IV, 148)

> [Then I considered the spiritual bread that a newspaper constitutes, still warm and moist as it emerges from the press and the morning mist in which it has been delivered at crack of dawn to the housemaids who take it to their masters with a bowl of coffee, this miraculous loaf, multiplied ten-thousandfold and yet unique, which stays unchanged for everyone while proliferating across every threshold. (ISLT, V, 532–33; translation slightly modified)]

In what is presented as a felicitous, multidimensional production and dissemination of the printed word, the narrator reflects on what it is to be read by many. The text is both singular and plural, a common text (common, that is, to its many readers) and one open to dispersal and multiplication. Proust's 'un et dix mille' ['one and ten thousand'] again links in with the singular/plural dynamic in Nancy who, in stressing existence as coexistence, writes of the importance of 'the being-with of everything that is' ['l'être-avec de tout ce qui est'] and by extension the co-presence of some and others.[8] In Proust's image of the daily bread that is the newspaper, moreover, the miraculous note evoked (there are echoes of the biblical story of the eucharist and also of the multiplication of the loaves and fishes) gives material production and exchange a mystical character. The social stratification governing the circulation of the newspaper, however, underscores the apportionment of roles in material culture.

If Proust views the act of reception of the newspaper by the many as entailing a diffuse, quasi-amorous encounter, as captured by the image of

---

7 J.-L. Nancy, *Être singulier pluriel* (Paris: Galilée, 2013 [1996]), p. 23.
8 Nancy, *Être singulier pluriel*, p. 22.

the collective Venus, Rancière sees in the journey of the printed word 'le corps incorporel de la lettre errante qui s'en va parler à la multitude sans visage des lecteurs de livres' ['the incorporeal body of the wandering letter which goes off to speak to the faceless multitude of the readers of books'].[9] For Rancière, encounter via the medium of the word takes place in a common world where, as one commentator explains, 'membership [...] is expressed in adversarial terms and coalition only occurs in conflict'.[10] This has an immediate bearing on the *Recherche*, where Marcel strains to imagine the mindsets of his multiple readers. Some will be absent-minded in their reading, some will hate the article, some will not notice it. The dissensus (to use Rancière's term) present in the nexus formed by publication and reader reception comes to be understood by Marcel: 'au moment où je lis, (...) [je crois] que la pensée de l'auteur est directement perçue par le lecteur, tandis que c'est une autre pensée qui se fabrique dans son esprit' (RTP, IV, 149) ['As I read the article, (...) I assume (...) that the author's thoughts are directly perceived by the reader, whereas it is other thoughts which are constructed in his mind' (ISLT, V, 533–34)].

An intense affectivity marks the protagonist's attempts to gain a readership and he gratefully conceives of those who counter his isolation by allowing him to 'appuy[er] ma propre défiance de moi-même sur ces dix mille approbations qui me soutenaient' (RTP, IV, 150) ['counter my own self-doubt with the ten thousand voices of approval that supported me' (ISLT, V, 535)]. This multitude of supportive readers then narrows to individual responses reflecting varying social-class outlooks. Marcel receives a letter from Mme Goupil (from Combray days – not, he notes, that he had much to do with her back then). It is written in a formulaic, emotionally cramped language consistent with 'le conventionalisme bourgeois' (RTP, IV, 170) ['bourgeois convention' (ISLT, V, 555)]. The class provenance of the author of a second letter (someone by the name of Sautton) is likewise referenced: 'C'était une écriture populaire, un langage charmant. Je fus navré de ne pouvoir découvrir qui m'avait écrit' (RTP, IV, 170) ['The writing was simple, the tone charming. I was very disappointed not to be able to discover who had written it' (ISLT, V, 555)]. (Later, Marcel will realize that it is from Théodore, the former grocer's boy in Combray who had gone on to be the pharmacist in Méséglise and whose surname the protagonist had not previously

---

9   See *La Parole muette*, text on back cover.
10   The quotation is taken from Rockhill's incisive gloss on what Rancière understands by democracy; *The Politics of Aesthetics*, p. 87.

known (RTP, IV, 279; ISLT, VI, 7).) Meanwhile Bloch, always uneasy about his own class affiliation, had indeed read Marcel's *Le Figaro* article but does not contact him until years later and only once he too has been published in the same paper. By then, the jealous Bloch can only commiserate with Marcel for having his work appear in 'le journal du sabre et du goupillon, des *five o'clock*, sans oublier le bénitier' (RTP, IV, 170) ['the newspaper of the sword and the cross, of "five o'clock" tea parties, and other kinds of holy water' (ISLT, V, 555)]. Bloch declares contentiously that the newspaper's ideological alignment can only spell the humiliation of those whose work it publishes. His adversarial stance confirms how the common world that receives the printed word works dissensually.

The question of who might have read Marcel's piece in *Le Figaro* also has ludic and oneiric dimensions, as Antoine Compagnon has pointed out. The Duc de Guermantes denies all knowledge of the article while insisting that both he and his wife have read the paper (RTP, IV, 163; ISLT, V, 548); and in a moment of wish fulfilment, the aspiring writer in Marcel delights in knowing that he has finally secured Bergotte's admiration for his work, only to realize that the writer's endorsement has been a creation of Marcel's dream (RTP, IV, 171; ISLT, V, 555).[11]

If insertion in the world comes via the remote encounter with a newspaper readership or the use of the postal service, Part III of *Du côté de chez Swann* describes how, for the young protagonist, sociality is a source of disruptive volatility. His anxious attachment to Gilberte Swann is indirectly signalled in the evocation of her father, whose prestige goes unrecognized, a fretful Marcel laments, in the democratic world of after-school leisure in the Gardens of the Champs-Elysées. Having been met at three o'clock at the school gates by Françoise, she and Marcel head off to the Gardens in the sunlight. The streets are 'encombrées par la foule' (RTP, I, 397) ['choked with crowds' (ISLT, 408)] and Swann passes largely incognito against 'le fond vulgaire des promeneurs de différentes classes' (RTP, I, 399) ['the vulgar background of people of different classes' (ISLT, I, 410)] who are enjoying the Champs-Elysées and remain ignorant of Swann's distinction. The interplay between the singular and the plural is overlaid, then, with an adversarial, social-class difference. Likewise, while Gilberte plays in the park, Swann waits

11 Antoine Compagnon, 'The Day Proust Realized He Had Written a Masterpiece', public lecture given at 'Symposium Marcel Proust', Moderna Museet, Stockholm, 6–7 December 2013.

for her, taking his place 'comme tout le monde sur une chaise de fer[,] paya[n]t son ticket de cette main que Philippe VII avait si souvent retenue dans la sienne' (RTP, I, 400) ['like anyone else on an iron chair, pa[ying] for his ticket with the same hand which Philippe VII had so often held in his own' (ISLT, I, 411)]. Social elites are thus presented as contending with the materiality of daily living in a common, contingent world. Like the delivery of the telegram to Gilberte and the urban circulation of the newspaper, childhood play at the Champs-Elysées occurs in a space which, to the extent that it is democratized, is both accessible and potentially conflicted. And just as the prestige of literature is subject to society's dissensus, so class prestige is prey to the incursion of levelling.[12]

Returning to the question of publication and the social negotiation this generates, we find Pierre Barbéris arguing, though not specifically in relation to Proust, that it is through a process of reception involving multiple readers that a work comes into being, 'en tant que réalité spécifique et comme mise sur orbite, libérée de son créateur. L'œuvre, finalement, n'existe que par ses lecteurs' ['as a specific reality and one launched into orbit, freed from its creator. Ultimately, the work only exists through its readers'].[13] How might Proust have viewed the prospect of a work freed from its creator and given over to its many readers? As he worked to send *Du côté de chez Swann* into orbit, to use Barbéris's image, we see him exercised by questions to do with the book's likely reception, which indeed he tries to anticipate and manage. Writing to René Blum in February 1913, he speaks of having composed a kind of novel ['une espèce de roman'], a work that needs a resting place or, to be more faithful to Proust's metaphor, a tomb, this to be arranged before he, the author, is laid in his.[14] While the macabre language may be a tactical move in his attempt to secure publication, Proust's 1913 correspondence shows that he was keen to reach a wide readership. Hence his insistence in another letter that the novel be sold cheaply in order to ensure 'la pénétration de ma pensée dans le plus grand nombre

12   Rancière argues that the anarchic introduction of the elements of life in the *Recherche* gives the lie to the illusion of '[le] livre "architectural et prémédité"' ['the "architectural and pre-meditated" book']; *La Parole muette*, p. 164; *Mute Speech*, p. 164.

13   Pierre Barbéris, *Lectures du réel* (Paris: Editions Sociales, 1973), p. 251.

14   In the letter to René Blum which Philip Kolb dates to around 20 February 1913, Proust asks him to act as intermediary with the Grasset publishing house. See Marcel Proust, *Correspondance de Marcel Proust*, ed. Philip Kolb, 21 vols (Paris: Plon, 1970–1993), XII, 79–80.

possible de cerveaux susceptibles de la recevoir' ['the penetration of my thought into the minds of as many people as possible likely to be receptive to it'].[15] He reflects in the same letter to the publisher Bernard Grasset, written soon after 24 February 1913, that the price of his *Les Plaisirs et les Jours* when it was published (with illustrations) years earlier by Calmann-Lévy had been high, with the result that the volume 'est allé embellir seulement les bibliothèques de gens qui ne lisent pas' ['ended up embellishing the libraries of people who don't read'].[16] He wonders how many might have read the book had its price been more accessible, thereby allowing their minds and his to be in contact. The experience with *Les Plaisirs et les Jours* thus alerts him to the need for an easily available volume: 'Je voudrais quelque chose de normal, d'accessible' ['I would like something normal, accessible'].[17]

Proust intervened in other ways, too. He comments on the page layout for the *Swann* volume and the kind of paper to be used in its printing – the paper used in the specimen pages sent to him by the Grasset publishing house was, he remarked, 'trop "glacé", trop brillant' ['too "glazed", too shiny'].[18] He asks Grasset in the same letter (18 March 1913) if the margins might be reduced slightly, not in order to squeeze in more text but to make the font size less cramped.[19] Proust leaves the final decision to the printers but the correspondence points to a reluctant delegation on his part.

The contact between writers and readers as evoked in the image of a collective Venus takes a comic turn in *Du côté de chez Swann* when the impatient boy protagonist imagines a letter arriving from Gilberte. In doing so, he comes to understand that any letter she might write would necessarily have to be different from the one he imagines her composing – 'c'était moi qui venais de la composer' (RTP, I, 402) ['I was the one who had just written it' (ISLT, I, 412)]. Thus, the protagonist's fear is that he risks excluding 'justement ceux-là [les mots], – les plus chers, les plus désirés – *du champ des réalisations possibles*' (RTP, I, 402; emphasis added) ['precisely those (words) – the dearest, the most desired – *from the field of all possible compositions*' (ISLT, I, 412)]. If by some coincidence Gilberte's letter were to turn out to be the one the protagonist had invented (Borges's story of Pierre Menard's verbatim composition of *Don Quixote*

---

15 *Correspondance de Marcel Proust*, XII, 98.
16 *Correspondance de Marcel Proust*, XII, 99.
17 *Correspondance de Marcel Proust*, XII, 100.
18 *Correspondance de Marcel Proust*, XII, 112.
19 *Correspondance de Marcel Proust*, XII, 113.

comes to mind), its materialization would not deliver the wholly other externality he craves, 'quelque chose de réel, de nouveau [...], indépendant de ma volonté' (RTP, I, 402) ['something real, new (...) independent of my will' (ISLT, I, 412)].[20] The young protagonist's anxiety is predicated on an assumption of necessary difference coming from the encounter with alterity. Applying Rancière's argument in his definition of democracy, 'the space of shared meaning [...] is not a space of consensus'.[21]

In waiting for the letter from Gilberte, the protagonist makes do with another text she has managed to procure for him, a page by Bergotte on Racine's use of ancient myths. With one text standing in, as it were, for another, we are reminded of the linkage in Proust between textuality and affectivity. The consumption of literature is integral to Marcel's experience of love in the *Recherche*, from the mother's reading George Sand to her needy son in *Combray* through to the cohabitation with Albertine in *La Prisonnière* ['The Prisoner'], where the couple converse about Dostoevsky, Hardy, Tolstoy, and others (RTP, III, 878–83; ISLT, V, 347–52) and where a Racinian intertext frames their claustrophobic relationship.[22] Gilberte's gift of the Bergotte text again channels affect through literature, with Bergotte's reflection on Racine acting as antidote to Marcel's own sense of 'cette mienne vie trop connue, dédaignée' (RTP, I, 402) ['this life of mine, too well known, disdained' (ISLT, I, 413)]. The material medium for Bergotte's message itself intrigues Marcel, for as he explains, he spent as much time admiring Gilberte's elaborate wrapping of the reading matter (the wax seals and mauve ribbons) as he did the text itself.[23] If the peritext, to use the term loosely, formed by the gift-wrapping

---

20   Jorge Luis Borges, 'Pierre Menard, Author of the *Quixote*', in Borges, *Labyrinths: Selected Stories and Other Writings* (London: Penguin, 2000).

21   Rancière, *On the Shores of Politics*, p. 49. The French original reads: 'l'espace de sens commun [...] n'est pas un espace de consensus'; *Aux bords du politique*, p. 92. As Barbéris observes: 'Si le réel était ce que, naïfs ou déformés, nous voudrions qu'il soit, il ne serait plus le réel' ['Were the real to be what, in our naive or deformed way, we would wish it to be, it would no longer be the real']; *Lectures du réel*, p. 10.

22   In the Albertine cycle, the topos of literature as template for living is prevalent, Marcel and Albertine engaging in a ludic playing of roles from Racine's drama. Ironically, it is this theatrical framing which allows Albertine to abscond in the period before Marcel rings for Françoise to come through into his bedroom at the start of the day. Casting himself in the role of Ahasuerus in Racine's *Esther*, Marcel had ordered that no one interrupt his rest (RTP, III, 528; ISLT, V, 11).

23   The reference here to 'grands cachets de cire blancs' (RTP, I, 403) ['great seals

entrances Marcel, the scene corroborates Dubois's observation that 'a whole social logic governs the most individualized psychic phenomena'.[24]

Whose Letter?

Textual missives have the capacity both to disrupt and confirm social segregation in the *Recherche*. In *La Prisonnière*, the Baron de Charlus receives a mysterious letter which reads: 'Mon cher Palamède, quand te reverrai-je? Je m'ennuie beaucoup après toi et pense bien souvent à toi, *etc.* PIERRE' (RTP, III, 554) ['Dear Palamède, when am I going to see you? I'm missing you ever so much and thinking about you all the time (etc.) Your loving PIERRE' (ISLT, V, 37]. Which family member could have written to him with such familiarity, he wonders for days on end, unable to work out whose handwriting it is. Which prince from the pages of the *Almanach de Gotha* could be the author of the note? Charlus's speculation is thus predicated on an intra-class solidarity, so that, in his supposing that the *Almanach* holds the key, certain lives are invariably excluded from his hypothesizing. The restricted range of likely correspondents maps well onto the wider question of who is deemed worthy of incorporation in fiction in its classical form.

We saw at the outset how Rancière draws on Aristotle's *Poetics* in *Les Bords de la fiction* and reflects that the rationality obtaining in poetic narrative was historically predicated on an assumption of prominence for the socially influential, the so-called 'hommes actifs' ['active men'].[25] Charlus's expectation concerning the authorship of the mysterious letter implicitly rests on that assumption. Rancière dwells on Aristotle's argument that in fiction, events do not happen randomly but are shaped by a logic of cause and effect. In the *Poetics*, the devices that most sway emotion in tragedy are 'reversals and recognitions'.[26] They constitute

---

of white wax' (ISLT, I, 413)] provides the third example of a seal in the current discussion, the term serving to crystallize the power of external agency.

24 'toute une logique sociale régit les phénomènes psychiques les plus individualisés': Jacques Dubois, *Pour Albertine. Proust et le sens du social* (Paris: Seuil, 1997), p. 22.

25 *Les Bords de la fiction*, pp. 9–10; *The Edges of Fiction*, p. 4. See Introduction, p. 16 and also Chapter 6, p. 136.

26 Aristotle, *Poetics*, trans. and ed. Malcolm Heath (London: Penguin, 1996), p. 12.

fiction's paradoxical causality, as Rancière terms it, whereby the truth emerges as the opposite of what appearances suggest.[27]

Paradoxical causality is pertinent to the scene we are considering in the *Recherche*. After intense speculation, Charlus emerges from his ignorance, but with knowledge comes social disturbance. Looking at the sender's address on the envelope, he realizes that it is from a club doorman he knows. Proust's narrator reconstructs the mindset of the author of the note:

> Ce chasseur n'avait pas cru être impoli en écrivant sur ce ton à M. de Charlus qui avait au contraire un grand prestige à ses yeux. Mais il pensait que ce ne serait pas gentil de ne pas tutoyer quelqu'un qui vous avait plusieurs fois embrassé, et vous avait par là – s'imaginait-il dans sa naïveté – donné son affection. (RTP, III, 555)

> [The doorman had not thought he was being rude in writing in this style to M. de Charlus, whom in fact he greatly admired. No, he thought it would not be nice not to call someone '*tu*' who had kissed you several times, and thereby – as he naively imagined – given you a sign of his affection. (ISLT, V, 37; translation modified)]

Uninhibited by the custom of social segregation, the doorman's good faith – his use of an informal tone and his understanding of the requirements of civility and reciprocity – nevertheless has a dissensual impact. Judging, naively by the expectations of the socially dominant as posited by the narrator, that Charlus's physical contact with him signals emotional attachment, the doorman is motivated by a search for linguistic appropriateness. His intervention illustrates Auerbach's thesis, which Rancière also considers in *Les Bords de la fiction*, that the revolution in the modern novel saw 'ordinary' lives deemed worthy subjects of fiction.[28]

---

27 *Les Bords de la fiction*, p. 9; *The Edges of Fiction*, p. 3.

28 Rancière reflects on how Auerbach identifies the revolution in fiction whereby the separation between those inhabiting the time of causality and 'ceux qui vivent dans le temps de la chronique' ['those living in the time of the chronicle'] is collapsed. Rancière expresses the reservation however that, in the penultimate chapter of *Mimesis*, Auerbach appears to work back from the integration of the ordinary into the social totality by privileging scenes that involve 'les univers clos et désespérément immobiles' ['the closed and desperately motionless worlds'] such as the Maison Vauquer in Balzac's *Le Père Goriot* and the dining room in *Madame Bovary*. See *Les Bords de la fiction*, pp. 12–13, *The Edges of Fiction*, pp. 6–7; translation modified.

Charlus's response is one of amazement when confronted with the familiarity of an inferior. He finds the doorman's untutored ways wholly exotic. Elsewhere in the novel, he aggressively defends his privacy when faced with bourgeois incursions into the social and cultural spaces that are his. Thus, the scene in *Sodome et Gomorrhe* where he deliriously recites his titles of nobility shows how the theatricality at work in energetic linguistic performance may serve to bolster hierarchy (RTP, III, 333; ISLT, IV, 338–39). Proletarian intrusion, by contrast, intrigues Charlus. The ancillary figure's word composition – the letter from below – sees emotion directed across a class boundary. The reapportioning of verbal capacities, to use Alison Ross's formulation, becomes a conduit for both humour and drama, while also holding the potential to mark an emancipation at the level of expressivity. Yet part of Charlus's enjoyment of the note sent by the doorman is that the latter is unknowingly transgressive and so does not shed his social compliance. Charlus can thus fantasize erotically about a social inferior overstepping the mark, the effect being to preserve the aristocrat's self-possession. In a related sense, the assumptions in Charlus's reconstruction of cause and effect conform to the classical conception of fiction in the *Poetics* as reconstructed by Rancière:

> La rationalité de la fiction est que les apparences – ou les expectations, puisque le même mot en grec dit les deux choses – se renversent. Elle est qu'un état mène à l'état inverse et que, du même coup, ce qui était ignoré soit connu.
>
> [The rationality of fiction is that appearances – or expectations, for in Greek the same word expresses both things – are inverted. It is that one state leads to the inverse state and that, by the same token, something one was unaware of comes to be known.][29]

The reversal of appearances and the switch from ignorance to knowledge are thus integral to the fictional moment and they consolidate Charlus's would-be superior comprehension of the doorman's faux pas.

The sequel to this brief scene in *La Prisonnière* sets up a chain of homoerotic fantasies:

> M. de Charlus fut au fond ravi de cette familiarité. Il reconduisit même d'une matinée M. de Vaugoubert afin de pouvoir lui montrer la lettre. Et pourtant Dieu sait que M. de Charlus n'aimait pas à sortir avec M. de Vaugoubert. Car celui-ci, le monocle à l'œil, regardait de tous les côtés les

---

29   *Les Bords de la fiction*, p. 8; *The Edges of Fiction*, p. 2.

jeunes gens qui passaient. Bien plus, s'émancipant quand il était avec M. de Charlus, il employait un langage que détestait le baron. Il mettait tous les noms d'hommes au féminin et, comme il était très bête, il s'imaginait cette plaisanterie très spirituelle et ne cessait de rire aux éclats. (RTP, III, 555)

[M. de Charlus was in fact delighted by his familiarity. He even walked back from an afternoon party with M. de Vaugoubert so as to show him the letter. And yet heaven knows M. de Charlus did not like to be seen with M. de Vaugoubert. For the diplomat, with his monocle stuck in his eye, stared in all directions at the lads passing by. What was more, when he was with M. de Charlus, he grew more daring, and began to use a language which the Baron hated. He put all men's names in the feminine and, as he was very stupid, thought this was the height of wit and was constantly bursting out laughing. (ISLT, V, 37)]

The busy narrative concatenation – the exceptional letter from a subordinate prompts the recipient to show it to a fellow aristocrat, who in turn so flaunts his erotic curiosity in the street as to unsettle the letter's recipient – captures a hybrid moment. It contains elements of what Rancière, applying the argument of the *Poetics*, calls fiction's 'surcroît de rationalité' ['surfeit of rationality'].[30] The cameo of the doorman's letter to Charlus thus sees the conjoining of what Rancière terms 'les vies sans histoire' ['lives without hi/story'] and 'vies susceptibles de rencontrer les vicissitudes de la fortune et les incertitudes du savoir' ['lives apt to encounter the vicissitudes of fortune and the uncertainties of knowledge'].[31] Charlus's chequered life amply 'qualifies' him for the second of these categories, while also exposing him to the random chronicle of social encounters spawned by his desire.

The practice of language is, then, an important conduit for both social trespass and sexual transgression in *La Prisonnière*. Infringement at the level of register, subverting linguistic conventions on gender, orality as an experience of pleasure – the narrator orchestrates these various language moves within the overarching verbal construct that is the novel. The scene also constructs a matrix of sexual desire tightly framed around social class: the club doorman Pierre gives expression to his longing, as do Charlus and, inappropriately in Charlus's view, Vaugoubert.

Whereas Vaugoubert's acting out provides Charlus with an unwelcome display of male femininity, the later scene in Jupien's brothel allows

---

30   *Les Bords de la fiction*, p. 7; *The Edges of Fiction*, p. 1.
31   *Les Bords de la fiction*, p. 13; *The Edges of Fiction*, p. 7.

him to fantasize that the working-class men employed there possess a masculinity more authentic than that of their social superiors. Jupien hypes this up for the willingly gullible Charlus by casting the men from the working-class east side of Paris as being involved in criminality and as embodying an often violent physicality. One of them, a hotel employee, is improbably presented by Jupien as 'le tueur de bœufs, l'homme des abattoirs' (RTP, IV, 396) ['the ox-killer (...) the slaughterhouse man' (ISLT, VI, 125–26)]. The class/body nexus here becomes the stuff of pure caricature.[32]

Across a number of the authors considered in the present study, the imaginary built around the human body that toils becomes the focus for a range of projections. Péguy both romanticizes and sanctifies productive, manual labour in *L'Argent*, linking the embodied subjectivity of the artisan to notions of duty and sacrifice. Simon's portrayal of the peasant sisters in *L'Acacia* likewise stresses a dimension of sacrifice (they show a Calvinist-style moral probity, we saw, while their devotion to a younger sibling who is set to rise socially is presented as an 'incestueuse et austère passion' (A, 303) ['incestuous and austere passion' (AA, 223)]). That the sisters' physical frames are described as being masculinized is presented as embodied evidence of that austerity. In *La Condition ouvrière*, Weil urgently documents the particular sense of embodiedness experienced by the factory worker who must eat in order to be able to go on working, and work in order to eat (CO, 420). This range of earnest, morally charged portraits of labouring bodies and the varying forms of social containment they signal contrast with the scene in Jupien's hotel in *À la recherche*. There, Charlus's sado-masochistic fantasy, worked around proletarian bodies, is comically thwarted when he hears one of the young men, Maurice, speaking sentimentally about the duty to look after one's family: 'Ces sentiments touchants désappointèrent presque autant M. de Charlus que l'agaça leur expression, d'une paysannerie un peu conventionnelle' (RTP, IV, 405) ['These touching sentiments disappointed M. de Charlus almost as much as their rather conventional peasant expression irritated him' (ISLT, VI, 135)]. Maurice's language suggests a working-class self-possession and conveys a sentimentalism that frustrates the aristocrat's erotic fantasy.

---

32   For some additional material on the scene in Jupien's hotel, see Edward J. Hughes, *Writing Marginality in Modern French Literature: from Loti to Genet* (Cambridge: Cambridge University Press, 2001), pp. 52–55.

The Hugo Hub

A character such as the club doorman, in his handling of the written word, provides a vantage point from which to analyse social apportionment. A dynamic of distribution is similarly present in *Le Côté de Guermantes*. While the choice of volume title points to aristocratic allure, a conspicuous example of an inferior's claim to intellectual emancipation also features in that section of the novel. In letters that Joseph Périgot, a young footman working for Françoise in Marcel's home, sends back to friends in his native village, he draws on books of poetry belonging to his employer. On one occasion, Oriane de Guermantes quotes from the early work of Hugo, giving Marcel the urge to reread the poet. Frustratingly for him, the footman has taken Marcel's copy of *Les Feuilles d'automne* and given it to friends back home. The diegesis thus quickly establishes a chain of readers, with subordinates and superiors drawn into what hierarchical thinking would deem to be respectively unexpected and appropriate encounters with the book. Seen through an egalitarian lens, however, these plot details point to parallel longings for literature. Oriane enthuses about the early Hugo; Marcel follows her lead; and independently of both, the young footman pursues his exploration of verse, free from what Jacotot dubs 'l'abrutissement explicateur' ['explicative stultification'], the process whereby a master views knowledge proprietorially and dispenses explication.[33] Hugo's *Les Feuilles d'automne* thus becomes the common ground where readers meet. As Rancière remarks, 'Le livre *est* l'égalité des intelligences' ['The book *is* the equality of intelligence'].[34]

As with the doorman's note to Charlus, it is again written composition by a social inferior which foregrounds class relations. The narrator transcribes in full a letter, laced with florid literary allusions that often work in hit-and-miss ways, which Joseph Périgot sends home (RTP, II, 854–55; ISLT, III, 566). The autonomy of the composition is accommodated textually through the act of transcription. The *Recherche* has a limited number of letter transcriptions, the use of italicization giving them salience – the letters exchanged between Albertine and Marcel provide notable, often dramatic, examples. The footman's letter to his cousin is no less conspicuous typographically, although significantly it is less the focus of Marcel's critical scrutiny. It constitutes a

---

33   *Le Maître ignorant*, p. 25; *The Ignorant Schoolmaster*, p. 13.
34   *Le Maître ignorant*, p. 66; *The Ignorant Schoolmaster*, p. 38.

scene in the sense given to the term by Rancière when he defines it as
'une petite machine où peuvent se condenser le maximum de significations autour de la question centrale qui est celle du partage du sensible'
['a small machine in which the maximum number of meanings can be
condensed around the central issue, which is the issue of the distribution
of the sensible world'].[35]

Périgot's letters connect tightly with the issue of cultural apportionment
across the *dramatis personae* of Proust's novel. The performative
dimension of the servant's writing is striking. Composing with brio, he
includes a string of quotations from French Romantic poetry, establishing
a quirky fusion of literature and life. In the effect of randomness created,
he disturbs the norms established elsewhere in the *Recherche* in relation
to the uses of literary allusion – the example of Marcel's mother and
grandmother communicating through a recycling of elements drawn
from Mme de Sévigné's letters stands as a benchmark of practice in
that area. Far from occupying a servile position, Périgot appropriates
the business of Marcel's family life, the transcribed letter showing how
he vaunts the merits of those attending Marcel's grandmother's funeral
as well as the benefits of life in the metropolis and the allure of modern
technology. He announces that he will be sending home works by
Racine, Victor Hugo, Chênedollé, and Musset, 'car je voudrais guérir le
pays qui ma donner le jour de l'ignorance qui mène fatalement jusquau
crime' (RTP, II, 855) ['for I want to cure the land which give me birth of
ignorance which leads inevitably to crime' (ISLT, III, 566)]. The broader
cultural link in the Third Republic between education and progress
is illustrated by Jules Ferry extolling the benefits of secular education
for 'these countless young reserves of republican democracy'.[36] In a
similar vein, the footman hails exposure to poetry as a vehicle of social
amelioration. As an advocate of literature, he seeks to communicate and
persuade, no less than do Marcel's mother and grandmother in their
bubble of literary allusion-making, and indeed Marcel himself.

For the scene in question, Proust may have been drawing on a letter
which Robert Ulrich, the nephew of Félicie Fitau (a cook employed by
the Proust family), received from a mistress. In a letter to Reynaldo

35   *La Méthode de l'égalité*, p. 125; *The Method of Equality*, p. 68.
36   Ferry writing in *La Revue pédagogique*, 1882; cited in Jean-Marie Mayeur
and Madeleine Rebérioux, *The Third Republic from its Origins to the Great War,
1871–1914*, trans. J. R. Foster (Cambridge: Cambridge University Press, 1984),
p. 85.

Hahn estimated to have been written in 1907, Proust draws Hahn's attention to what appears to be a four-line extract from a poem contained in the letter and which Ulrich was quick to attribute: 'Ça c'est certainement de Victor Hugo, m'a dit Ulrich d'un ton péremptoire' ['That's definitely by Victor Hugo, Ulrich told me in a peremptory tone'], notes Proust. In fact, the four lines of verse transcribed by Ulrich's mistress do not appear to be the work of a published poet. Moreover, Proust's letter shows he is unimpressed by Ulrich's claim that his mistress is 'extraordinairement intelligente' ['extraordinarily intelligent'].[37] But that a categorical note on a literary topic should be sounded 'from below' intrigues Proust, who draws this ripple of cultural disturbance to the attention of Hahn, his bourgeois addressee. The connections the footman's letter makes to Romantic literature in Proust's novel, while appearing heteroclite and disconnected, likewise unsettle the pattern of provenance governing literary reference-making and the class apportionment underpinning it.[38]

In research undertaken for *La Nuit des prolétaires*, Rancière highlights how acquiring a poetic language was the means whereby nineteenth-century workers came to experience differently: 'C'est un régime de parole qui est un régime de désidentification' ['It's a speech regime that is a regime of dis-identification'].[39] Proust's poet-footman, in his engagement with the Romantics, enters a cultural space that is similarly disidentificatory, although the manner of its framing in the *Recherche* in no way endows the scene with an emancipatory sense.

Unlike Proust's letter to Hahn just discussed, the narrator in the *Recherche* provides no gloss on Joseph Périgot's performance in the letter. The tale of Marcel's apprenticeship as a writer is central to the diegesis of the *Recherche*, and yet the inferior's letter, while no less insistent in its advocacy of the value of literature, is reproduced without further comment. We need to allow, of course, for the compositional intricacies of a novel that was always expanding and hence intensely

---

37 My argument draws on the invaluable editorial work of Thierry Laget and Brian Rogers on RTP, II, 1820. Proust's letter to Hahn in which he mentions Robert Ulrich's response to his mistress's letter is reproduced in *Correspondance de Marcel Proust*, VII, 284–85.

38 Seen against the template constructed by Rancière in *Les Bords de la fiction*, the would-be incongruous intrusion of the servant's letter may be read as exemplifying 'la puissance du "moment quelconque"' ['the power of the "random occurrence"']: *Les Bords de la fiction*, p. 13; *The Edges of Fiction*, p. 7.

39 *La Méthode de l'égalité*, pp. 133–34; *The Method of Equality*, p. 73.

complex to manage. That said, the narrator's non-response, save for his apologetic explanation as to how he came to be looking at another person's correspondence, leaves the letter hanging, disconnected from any notion of overall design.[40]

While allowing for the novel's multiple narrative threads, the reader may be forgiven for thinking that the lines immediately following the letter's transcription are to do with the impression formed by Marcel on reading it: 'Nous sommes attirés par toute vie qui nous représente quelque chose d'inconnu, par une dernière illusion à détruire' (RTP, II, 855) ['Any life which represents something mysterious, like some last illusion to be shattered, exerts a pull on us' (ISLT, III, 566)]. In fact, the ambiguously positioned sentence frames what follows, namely Marcel's surprise on receiving an invitation to the home of the Princesse de Guermantes. The causation at work (Marcel's enduring feeling of exclusion from society's elite is now set to be reversed) connects with the overall design of the *Recherche*. As such, it can be linked to the notion of necessity and probability which Aristotle builds into his theory of what makes good literature (specifically tragedy in the argument of the *Poetics*). The servant's letter, by contrast, belongs to the *episodic* as defined by Aristotle, the category covering episodes the sequence of which is 'neither necessary nor probable'.[41] Nevertheless, the letter may be seen both as a variant on, and distraction from, Marcel's quest for social advancement. As Rancière writes in his account of Aristotle, 'le bon enchaînement des causes et des effets s'atteste par le renversement – la péripétie – qu'il produit dans l'univers des attentes' ['the proper chain of causes and effects is attested by the reversal – the peripeteia – it produces in the universe of expectations'].[42] Moreover, on either side, in terms of textual arrangement, of Proust's aphoristic 'Any life which represents something mysterious', the bourgeois narrator is negotiating a social barrier: the proletarian's letter, the aristocrat's invitation. Périgot's experience of rhetorical confidence and self-awareness is for him emancipatory. Yet we can note in passing that, in its impact

40 Périgot's letter forms a manuscript addition which is literally glued on to the first set of Gallimard galleys for *Le Côté de Guermantes*. See Alison Winton (Finch), *Proust's Additions: The Making of 'À la recherche du temps perdu'*, 2 vols (Cambridge: Cambridge University Press, 1977), II, 94. Fig. 6 below (pp. 204–205) reproduces the handwritten page in question.
41 Aristotle, *Poetics*, p. 17.
42 *Les Bords de la fiction*, p. 8; *The Edges of Fiction*, p. 2.

En rentrant je vis sur mon bureau une lettre que le
jeune valet de pied de François avait côté 5 h...
amis et q... il y avait oublié. Depuis que...
... il ne se...ait devant aucun sans de
... plus confus... d'avoir cliré de lire la lettre...
et son enveloppe largement étalée, ...
..., c'était ma seule q... lise, avait l'air de s'offrir
moi.

"Cher ami et cousin
J'espère que la santé va toujours bien et que...
de même pour toute la petite famille particulière...
mon jeune filleul Joseph dont je n'ai pas encore...
plaisir de connaître mais tout je préfère à...
vous comme... étant mon filleul, les reliques du...
on aura leur poussière, sur leurs restes sa...
portons pas les mains. D'ailleurs cher ami et
cousin que te dit que demain toi et la chère petite
ma cousine Marie, vous ne serez pas par ici les...
deux jusqu'au fond de la mer comme le mate...
... un autre du grand mât, car cette vie n'est qu'une
vallée obscure. Cher ami il faut te dire que ma

44²

principale occupation, à ton étonnement je m'en
suis certain, en... la poésie que j'aime, avec
délices, car il faut bien passer le temps. Ainsi
cher ami ne sois pas trop surpris de je ne...
encore répondu à ta dernière lettre, à défaut...
du pardon... te vouloir l'oubli. Comme tu...
... bonheur de ... à ...
... ... inoppin... avec ...
fatigance car elle a ... jusqu'à trois ma déc...
de joie et des obsèques fut un beau jour car toutes

les relations de Monsieur étaient venues en
foule ainsi que plusieurs ministres. On a mis plus
de deux heures pour aller au cimetière ce qui
vous fera tous ouvrir de grands yeux dans votre
village car on n'en fera certainement pas autant
pour la mère Michu. Aussi ma vie ne sera plus
qu'un long sanglot. Je m'amuse énormément
à la motocyclette dont j'ai appris dernière-
ment. Que diriez-vous mes chers amis si
j'arrivais ainsi à toute vitesse aux Écorres.

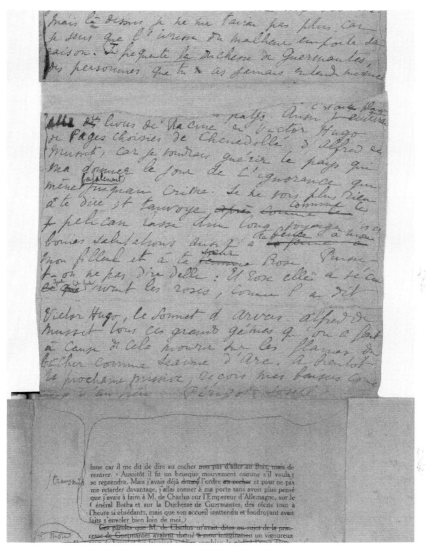

Fig. 6: Photographic reproduction of a handwritten addendum by Proust to the first set of Gallimard galley proofs for *Le Côté de Guermantes*.
© BnF.

The manuscript layer shows the footman Joseph Périgot's letter. Proust's minor adjustments to the handwritten draft include the following: 'je nai pas encore répondu' becomes 'je ne suis pas encore répondu' (p. 204, 4–5 lines below 44 [3]), marking a switch in the use of auxiliary verb; 'tu n'as jamais entendu' changes to 'tu as jamais entendu' (p. 205, l. 4), the contraction of the negative form again being consistent with popular usage; and the misspelling 'on nan feras' (p. 204, 6 lines from bottom) replaces the standard orthography in 'on n'en fera'.

on Marcel, it contrasts markedly with the case of another son of the people, Jupien, whose command of language attracts an 'emphatic encomium' from the narrator.[43] Jupien's capacities show Proust refusing to confine verbal brilliance to a particular social class.

The effect created by the letter transcription in *Le Côté de Guermantes* is one of both redistribution and confiscation. It shows its proletarian author waxing lyrical, having crossed a frontier that sees him declare to his addressee back home: 'ma principale occupation de ton étonnement j'en suis certain, est maintenant la poésie' (RTP, II, 854) ['my principal occupation to your astonishment I feel sure, is now poetry' (ISLT, III, 566)]. An effect of estrangement is generated to the extent that the presence of errors of spelling, phrasing, and punctuation in the letter contrasts with the order signalled by the orthography and syntax of the surrounding text. But just as the footman crafts his letter, so we see Proust, in his original handwritten version of the text, carefully working back through the lines of his composition, tailoring them by making orthographic amendments or 'corrections'.[44] Proust's aim seems to have been to accentuate the modest social origins of the footman and reinforce the gap between his literary aspirations and his non-standard orthography and grammar. Yet in his assertiveness, Joseph Périgot has joined the ranks of 'tous ceux qui ont décidé de se penser comme des hommes semblables à tout autre' ['all those who have decided to think of themselves as people just like everyone else'].[45] At another level, the visual work trace that Proust's manuscript constitutes shows the craft and adjustment that are intrinsic to its production. As Figure 6 demonstrates, this is Proust *at work*. Or, to draw again on Rancière/Jacotot, the artist handles words as the manual worker handles his tools.[46]

---

43   For a detailed and nuanced analysis of those who wear the 'mantle of taste' in Proust's novel, see Alison Finch, 'Aesthetic Form and Social "Form" in *À la recherche du temps perdu*: Proust on Taste', in Patrick Crowley and Shirley Jordan (eds), *What Forms Can Do: The Work of Form in 20th- and 21st-century French Literature and Thought* (Liverpool: Liverpool University Press, 2020), pp. 207–17 (pp. 210–11).

44   See Fig. 6.

45   *Le Maître ignorant*, p. 71; *The Ignorant Schoolmaster*, p. 41.

46   See *Le Maître ignorant*, p. 121; *The Ignorant Schoolmaster*, p. 71. The 'Rancière/Jacotot' formulation is taken from Hallward, 'Staging Equality', p. 156.

*   *   *

The footman's letter is one of a number of features in *À la recherche* that are referenced in the contemporary novel *Les Récidivistes* ['The Recidivists'] (2008), a work by Laurent Nunez which in part involves a pastiche of several French writers, principally Proust. Nunez's autobiographical narrator describes laughing out loud as he reads the footman's 'lettre ridicule' which is, he continues, so full of clichés that he feels compelled to reread it.[47] Yet, just as the servant in *À la recherche* is seeking to find his voice, so Nunez's novel tracks the experience of coming-to-writing, a process in which reading and living overlap. Pastiche is central to this and has an autodidactic function for a narrator who 'avais eu si peu mon mot à dire devant les autres' ['had been so unable to find my words when with others'].[48] Proust himself worked extensively on pastiche early in his career, generating what Jean Milly identifies as a dynamic of 'fidelity-autonomy' in relation to the literary predecessors he mimics.[49] As a practice, pastiche points to a particular form of participation in the democracy of literature.

While providing a structural template for much of Nunez's novel, *À la recherche* is also a source of themes, with love and betrayal, class, sexuality, literature, introspection, and the social self all featuring in the later work. With these thematic echoes come significant variations. A eureka moment in *Les Récidivistes* sees the hero's inadequacy as a writer dispelled in what is a reworking of the celebrated 'Bouleversement de toute ma personne' ['A convulsion of my entire being'] episode in Proust's *Sodome et Gomorrhe* when the boy protagonist experiences intensely the loss of his deceased grandmother. In Nunez's version, the autobiographical narrator hears a waiter use the expression 'on dirait un nœud d'Orgien' ['it was like an Orgian knot'], the same formulation as the one used by the narrator's grandmother.[50] From the garbled version of 'a Gordian knot' shared by a revered, untutored grandmother

---

47   Laurent Nunez, *Les Récidivistes* (Paris: Rivages, 2014 [2008]), p. 229.

48   Nunez, *Les Récidivistes*, p. 446.

49   Jean Milly, 'Pastiche', in Annick Bouillaguet and Brian Rogers (eds), *Dictionnaire Marcel Proust* (Paris: Honoré Champion, 2004), pp. 729–31 (p. 731).

50   The 'Bouleversement de toute ma personne' formulation is replicated in *Les Récidivistes*, p. 445. The scene involving upheaval of memory in *Sodome et Gomorrhe* (RTP, III, 152; ISLT, IV, 158) similarly contains reference to malapropisms, specifically those of the director of the Grand Hotel in Balbec.

and an unethical waiter, literary composition thus springs. The class inflection in the scene in Nunez introduces an unschooled dimension into the comparative link with *À la recherche*, with the different tonality reinforced in the impropriety associated with the waiter.

Whereas involuntary memory in Proust sees Marcel reconnect with an earlier self, the two occurrences of the same malapropism in Nunez usher in an embryonic community, for in the pregnant moment of coincidence, the waiter is both the grandmother and himself: 'il était à la fois elle et lui'.[51] Proust's stress on two moments of one individual's experience being jointly experienced in involuntary memory thus mutates into a self/other conjoining in Nunez. Using an aerial view of the earth as a metaphor for the novelist's vision, the autobiographical narrator in *Les Récidivistes* sees such a perspective as eclipsing the distinctions between women and men, customers and servers, masters and servants: 'tout s'égalait [...] un homme vaut tous les hommes [...] et moi, j'étais donc comme les autres' ['everything was equal (...) one person is as good as the next (...) and so I was like everyone else'].[52] Other images reinforce this sense of levelling. Nunez reflects on a confusion in which 'tout s'equivaut, comme le bruit et le silence aux oreilles des sourds' ['everything is equivalent, like sound and silence to the ears of the deaf']; and he evokes a state of myopia that causes forms to merge and introduces 'le règne de l'entre-deux' ['the reign of the in-between'].[53]

The frequent homing in on scenes of class animosity in Proust is mirrored in Nunez's account of a meeting with Jacques Borel. Nunez marvels at how the ageing writer manages to open *À la recherche* more or less at the page where the upwardly mobile Mme Verdurin, looking to recruit a concierge, asks Charlus if he might be able to recommend some down-at-heel aristocrat. Charlus mischievously advises against this, fearing that any such recruit might mean that elegant guests never get further than the concierge's lodge. Borel's delight in reading the scene derives not from the social snub delivered by the aristocrat but rather from the practice of language in the episode. In his delivery of the line

51   Nunez, *Les Récidivistes*, p. 445.

52   Nunez, *Les Récidivistes*, p. 225. The idea of the aerial view is also exploited by Proust in *Le Temps retrouvé*, where an assembly of disparate elements feeds into the narrator's social overview. For discussion of that overview, see the section 'A vol d'oiseau' in Hughes, *Proust, Class, and Nation*, pp. 231–34.

53   Nunez, *Les Récidivistes*, pp. 166, 226.

'que les visiteurs élégants n'allassent pas plus loin que la loge' ['that the elegant visitors might not go further than the lodge'], he dwells on the imperfect subjunctive *allassent*, a move which Nunez likens to a ball gown that Borel has himself stitched together.[54] Performances in language – Borel's, Proust's, Charlus's, Nunez's – are intrinsic to the narrative of class rivalry, then, but are also worked through the 'wandering letter' on the page and the reader's egalitarian encounter with it.

✳   ✳   ✳

A few pages before the transcription of the servant's letter in *Le Côté de Guermantes*, the Hugo hub also draws in Charlus. Feeling snubbed by Marcel (who is both younger than him and a social inferior), he grandly declares himself to be abandoned like the biblical figure Boaz in Hugo's 'Booz endormi'. He appeals deliriously to cultural hierarchies. Vaunting the beautiful objects in his home, the baron condescendingly asks Marcel if he had not noticed these when waiting to be ushered in to see him. He engages in aristocratic name-dropping and mentions the paintings by Rembrandt and Turner in his home, and all this to the sound of Beethoven's *Pastoral Symphony* being played by a group of musicians in another room. Charlus's kitschy staging of high culture and the tie-in to notions of social superiority culminates in his chiding Marcel for his lack of interest: 'Vous voulez rentrer, quitte à manquer de respect à Beethoven et à moi' (RTP, II, 850) ['You want to go home, even if it means showing disrespect for Beethoven and for me' (ISLT, III, 562)].

Charlus's arrogant, needy performance exposes the brittle hold of high culture when it is instrumentalized in such transparent fashion. His ineffectual power play is devoid of disinterested aesthetic appreciation. Schiller's assertion that it is 'by way of beauty that one approaches liberty' contrasts starkly with the scene in the *Recherche* depicting the aristocrat's bravado and emotional entrapment.[55]

The volatile encounter between an enamoured Charlus and an unsuspecting Marcel lends itself to being read precisely as a distribution

---

54 Nunez, *Les Récidivistes*, p. 324. In his essay on Proust, Borel explores the pivotal use of the imperfect tense in *À la recherche*; see Jacques Borel, *Commentaires* (Paris: Gallimard, 1974), pp. 89–169.

55 Schiller, *On the Aesthetic Education of Man*, p. 6.

of the sensible. As if to parody the line from the Internationale that we considered earlier, in Chapter 6, Charlus recalls his first meeting with the young Marcel in absolutist terms: 'j'étais tout et vous n'étiez rien' (RTP, II, 844) ['I was everything and you were nothing' (ISLT, III, 555)].[56] He luxuriates in displays of narcissism, as when he casts himself as the magnanimous victor in Velázquez's *The Surrender of Breda*. But he also claims to be egalitarian, as when he chides Marcel with the reflection that 'je crois que toutes les places sont égales, et j'ai plus de sympathie pour un intelligent ouvrier que pour des ducs' (RTP, II, 846) ['I believe all our positions are equal, and I am more sympathetically disposed towards an intelligent labourer than I am towards a great many dukes' (ISLT, III, 557)]. Yet his egalitarianism is often erotically motivated and is quickly eclipsed by the consolation he draws from rank.

Governed by his unrequited (and undeclared) desire for Marcel, Charlus's behaviour functions as a deranged parade of status in these pages of *Le Côté de Guermantes*.[57] A vocabulary of gradation, illustriousness, and prestige dominates his idiolect.[58] Berating his interlocutor in an altissimo voice, he then slowly reduces its pitch, the narrator describing him as though 's'enchantant, au passage, des bizarreries de cette gamme descendante' (RTP, II, 845) ['seeming to revel as he went in the oddities of this descending scale' (ISLT, III, 556)]. The narcissistic intensity accompanies a delirious upholding of inequality, demonstrating how what Rancière refers to as the hierarchies of knowledge and *jouissance* run counter to 'l'état sensible libéré des intérêts' ['the state of perception freed from such interests'].[59]

56   See Chapter 6, p. 146.

57   On Charlus's performance in *Le Côté de Guermantes* and the commentaries on it by both Deleuze (in *Proust et les signes*) and Barthes in his analysis of the 'Charlus-Discourse' in seminars at the Collège de France in 1977, see Thomas Baldwin, *Roland Barthes: The Proust Variations* (Liverpool: Liverpool University Press, 2019), pp. 59–61, 103–13.

58   References to superiority, usurpation, crowning, and dethroning all feature in Charlus's diatribe (RTP, II, 852–53; ISLT, III, 564–65). The scene provides a baroque enactment of what in Rancière/Jacotot is referred to as 'the society of contempt' in which 'la passion inégalitaire' ['inegalitarian passion'] is pervasive. See chapter 4 of *Le Maître ignorant*, 'La société du mépris', pp. 125–66 (p. 134); *The Ignorant Schoolmaster*, pp. 75–99 (p. 80).

59   *Aisthesis*, p. 69; *Aisthesis: Scenes from the Aesthetic Regime of Art*, p. 46; translation adapted. In his work on Jacotot, Rancière characterizes the promotion of inequality as a form of madness or *déraison* which is itself an expression of 'un

Rancière's analytical method in his exploration of workers' texts of the 1830s and 1840s has a bearing on Proust's juxtaposition of Charlus's tirade and Joseph Périgot's letter home in *Le Côté de Guermantes*. By stressing that he treats his working-class corpus like any other body of writing, Rancière sees himself drawing out 'un univers sensible instable' ['a sensible world that's unstable'].[60] A similar volatility marks this corner of *Le Côté de Guermantes*, no more so than at a diegetic level. For the encounter with Charlus triggers the most intensely physical performance by the ingenuous Marcel in the entire novel, his dancing on the Baron's top hat when the latter accuses him of having wronged him. While the protagonist's frenzy is a response to what he believes to be Charlus's overweening pride, the narrator acknowledges the workings of a sexual motive in the aristocrat which will only become clear to him later.

Asked about his method of working, Rancière has observed that in the 1970s it involved the throwing together of seemingly contrasting contexts (a nineteenth-century workers' archive and the experience of Emma Bovary, for example, or Rilke's encounter with the working-class woman Marthe Hennebert). It is in this practice of 'transversality', he observes, that cognitive gains can be made. 'Là où les territoires se perdent' ['where the different jurisdictions disappear'] is how he refers to real-life crossing points.[61] The scenes from *Le Côté de Guermantes* being considered exemplify precisely a loss of stable terrain, with the exuberant performances of Françoise's young footman and an aristocrat pointing respectively to a claim to equality and an overdetermined defence of hierarchy.

A Run of Languages

With Françoise not a participant in the literary allusion-making engaged in by other characters in Proust's novel, images of her confronted by the printed word are significant for a narrator intrigued to understand the sentimental educations of those around him, irrespective of their class.

---

travail de deuil' ['a work of grief']; see *Le Maître ignorant*, p. 137; *The Ignorant Schoolmaster*, p. 82. On the idea of inequality as a form of social mourning, see the discussion of *Antoine Bloyé* in Chapter 5.

60   *La Méthode de l'égalité*, p. 59; *The Method of Equality*, p. 29.
61   *La Méthode de l'égalité*, p. 64; *The Method of Equality*, p. 32.

She sheds tears when reading in the newspaper about tragedy befalling people she does not know; similarly, her empathy flows freely when she reads in a medical compendium about the effect of post-natal symptoms (RTP, I, 121; ISLT, I, 123–24). Yet when not looking at a hypothetical case but rather face-to-face with the kitchen maid, whose complications in childbirth had been the reason for carefully keeping open the relevant page of the medical book, Françoise lacks consideration. The written word and its evocation of human suffering in the abstract hold prestige for her and awaken her charity, whereas the embodied presence of the pregnant kitchen maid disgusts her. The location of emotion is significant in that it is the printed text which awakens more elevated emotions in Françoise.

We have seen the narrator judging the doorman Pierre to be naive for believing that Charlus's physical contact amounted to emotional attachment. Likewise, in *Combray*, Françoise, keen to identify the emotion that has led to the kitchen maid becoming pregnant, proposes naivety as the explanation for behaviour, in this case the behaviour of the one who fathers the child. Drawing on the folk wisdom that comes with her mother's vernacular, Françoise recites: 'Qui du cul d'un chien s'amourose / Il lui paraît une rose' (RTP, I, 122) ['He who falls in love with a dog's bottom / Will think it's a rose' (ISLT, I, 435)]. The trenchant formulation suggests a world-weary conviction about the folly and misrecognition generated by blind love. Significantly, it is through patois that Proust's narrator here reinforces the message that delusion is integral to the workings of erotic attachment.

Françoise's role as a commentator on relations of desire extends to Marcel's relationship with Albertine. Having first appeared at Balbec in *À l'ombre des jeunes filles en fleurs*, Albertine re-emerges in *Le Côté de Guermantes*, visiting Marcel in his family apartment in Paris. He notices an alluring change in her vocabulary: she now uses terms that are not part of the sociolect she acquired growing up in the provincial middle-class Simonet family. Expressing her admiration for the golf course at Fontainebleau, she declares: 'C'est tout à fait une sélection' ['It's quite a selection, in fact']; likewise she uses the formulation 'un laps de temps' ['a lapse of time'] to indicate that it has been a while since she has been in touch with Gisèle (RTP, II, 650; ISLT, III, 353). Albertine's new verbal formulations reflecting a language of social aspiration excite the protagonist erotically.

In the sequel to the extract, language use continues to carry an amorous charge:

C'était si nouveau, si visiblement une alluvion laissant soupçonner de si capricieux détours à travers des terrains jadis inconnus d'elle que, dès les mots 'à mon sens', j'attirai Albertine, et à 'j'estime' je l'assis sur mon lit. (II, 651)

[This was so novel, so clearly an alluvial deposit hinting at such capricious explorations on territory hitherto unknown to her, that no sooner were the words 'to my mind' out of her mouth than I drew Albertine towards me, and at 'I see it as' sat her down on my bed. (ISLT, III, 354)]

The narrator attributes many of the more predictable formulations used by Albertine at Balbec to her provincial milieu. In the same way, he judges her anti-Semitism and dress sense to be the routine baggage that comes with her family and class upbringing. To explain this process of cultural dictation, the narrator uses the unfussy analogy of communication among birds: the young in the nest learn the sounds made by their parents and that's how the goldfinch becomes a goldfinch, he observes matter-of-factly (RTP, II, 652; ISLT, III, 355).

By contrast, Albertine's new formulations are distinctly other: 'Malgré tout, "sélection" me parut allogène et "j'estime" encourageant. Albertine n'était plus la même' (RTP, II, 652) ['Despite all this, "selection" struck me as foreign and "I see it as" seemed inviting. Albertine was no longer the same' (ISLT, III, 355)]. The geological term allogenic, denoting the move away from what is indigenous, appears, not coincidentally, alongside a glancing reference to Darwin and natural selection. But all the while, the narrator is signalling the tight connection between speech acts (those of Françoise and Albertine, for example) and social distribution and stratification. Marcel's own speech and bearing leave him no less situated, both socially and linguistically.

*   *   *

Reflecting on domestic service in twentieth-century France, Geneviève Fraisse refers to the 'duo-duel féminin' that marks the relationship between bourgeois woman employer and female domestic servant.[62] In the *Recherche*, roles that are inflected by subordination associated with gender and/or social class feed into the politics of linguistic constraint. In *Combray*, Marcel's mother, keen to inquire after Swann's young

---

62   Geneviève Fraisse, *Service ou servitude. Essai sur les femmes toutes mains* (Paris: Le Bord de l'eau, 2009 [1979]), p. 65.

daughter, wrestles with the twin restrictions of patriarchy and bourgeois respectability. The presence of her husband, who disapproves of Swann's choice of Odette de Crécy as a wife, obliges her to cut short her enquiry:

> Ma mère fut obligée de s'interrompre, mais elle tira de cette contrainte même une pensée délicate de plus, comme les bons poètes que la tyrannie de la rime force à trouver leurs plus grandes beautés: 'Nous reparlerons d'elle quand nous serons tous les deux, dit-elle à mi-voix à Swann. Il n'y a qu'une maman qui soit digne de vous comprendre. Je suis sûre que la sienne serait de mon avis'. (RTP, I, 24)

> [My mother was obliged to stop, but she derived from this very constraint one more delicate thought, like good poets forced by the tyranny of rhyme to find their most beautiful lines: 'We can talk about her again when we're by ourselves, she said softly to Swann. Only a mother is capable of understanding you. I'm sure her own mother would agree with me.' (ISLT, I, 27)]

In her appeal to a maternal psychology, Marcel's mother deftly constructs a bridge across to the unnamed Mme Swann. Her delicacy and ethical stance are commended by the narrator, who likens them to the successful manoeuvre of a poet restricted by the rules of prosody.

The narrator returns to the figure of the woman contending with societal constraint when he analyses Françoise's response to the emerging relationship between Albertine and Marcel. There, too, linguistic indirectness is the response to exclusion from a space of legitimation. More particularly, the narrator reflects on how, as someone who is subordinate, Françoise is unable to comment directly on the new arrangement that sees Albertine living in Marcel's family home. The servant's restriction is likened to that facing writers in a range of repressive contexts:

> Mais surtout, comme les écrivains arrivent souvent à une puissance de concentration dont les eût dispensés le régime de la liberté politique ou de l'anarchie littéraire, quand ils sont ligotés par la tyrannie d'un monarque ou d'une poétique, par les sévérités des règles prosodiques ou d'une religion d'État, ainsi Françoise, *ne pouvant nous répondre d'une façon explicite*, parlait comme Tirésias et eût écrit comme Tacite. Elle savait faire tenir tout ce qu'elle ne pouvait exprimer directement, dans une phrase que nous ne pouvions incriminer sans nous accuser, dans moins qu'une phrase même, dans un silence, dans la manière dont elle plaçait un objet. (RTP, II, 655; emphasis added)

> [But above all, just as writers, when their hands are tied by the tyranny of a monarch or of poetic convention, by the strict rules of prosody or state

religion, often achieve a power of concentration they would not have done under a system of political freedom or literary anarchy, so Françoise, *by not being free to respond to us in an explicit manner*, spoke like Tiresias and would have written like Tacitus. She knew how to contain everything she could not express directly in a sentence we could not denounce without casting aspersions on ourselves, in less than a sentence in fact, in a silence, in the way she placed an object. (ISLT, III, 358)]

The conjoining of artistic hierarchies and political regimes recalls Rancière's reflection on what he terms the representative regime of art stretching back to Aristotle, with its 'hierarchy of the represented' ['hiérarchie des représentés'] and accompanying normativity.[63] Proust's extended analogy moves from totalitarian states to domestic infighting, from the ancient city of Thebes to the Paris of the Third Republic, and from the rigid codifications concerning prosody to what he terms literary anarchy. He situates Françoise's intervention within contexts where the capacity to express oneself in the face of repressiveness persists. The historian Tacitus is renowned for the concision of his style, while Tiresias, having lived both as man and woman, is called upon in ancient Thebes to act as arbiter in a dispute between Zeus and the goddess Hera regarding who experiences the greater pleasure in love, a woman or a man.[64] Françoise is presented as a skilled performer working within the straitjacket of social-class affiliation. If Marcel's mother circumvents patriarchy through the use of deft circumlocution, Françoise – a doubly subordinate figure by virtue of her gender and class – has to make even greater use of obliquity in her attempt to influence Marcel. Denied access to the direct spoken word, she finds her 'voice' by showcasing a letter in which Marcel criticizes her:

Ainsi, quand il m'arrivait de laisser, par mégarde, sur ma table, au milieu d'autres lettres, une certaine qu'il n'eût pas fallu qu'elle vît, par exemple parce qu'il y était parlé d'elle avec une malveillance qui en supposait une aussi grande à son égard chez le destinataire que chez l'expéditeur, le soir, si je rentrais inquiet et allais droit à ma chambre, sur mes lettres rangées bien en ordre en une pile parfaite, le document compromettant frappait tout d'abord mes yeux comme il n'avait pu ne pas frapper ceux de Françoise, placé par elle tout en dessus, presque à part, *en une évidence qui était un langage, avait son éloquence, et dès la porte me faisait tressaillir comme un cri*. Elle excellait à régler ces mises en scène destinées à instruire si bien le spectateur, Françoise absente, qu'il savait

---

63   See *La Chair des mots*, pp. 180–81; *The Flesh of Words*, p. 147.
64   See RTP, II, 1716, editorial gloss provided by Laget and Rogers.

déjà qu'elle savait tout quand ensuite elle faisait son entrée. (RTP, II, 655; emphasis added)

[For instance, whenever I inadvertently left on my table, among other letters, one which should have been kept from her eyes, because, say, it spoke about her in a malevolent way which suggested that the malevolence was shared by the recipient as well as the writer, the same evening, if I returned home with a feeling of uneasiness and went straight to my room, there on top of my letters, arranged in the right order in a neat pile, the compromising document would be the first thing to catch my eye as it could not have failed to catch the eye of Françoise, placed by her right on the top, almost separately, *with an obviousness that was a form of speech with an eloquence all of its own which, as soon as I came into the room, startled me like a sudden shout.* She excelled in setting up these stage effects, intended to provide the spectator, in her absence, with sufficient information to realize that she knew everything by the time she made her entry. (ISLT, III, 358)]

Rancière's division of the sensible which presupposes both social participation and exclusion has a direct bearing on the antagonistic relations that Proust's narrator is evoking. In the case of the otherwise silenced Françoise, the material arrangement of objects is her art of communication, as the mute becomes piercingly audible. Indeed, the silent scene functions like a violent interpellation. Ensuring visibility is Françoise's mode of contestation as she studiously positions the incriminating letter.

Françoise's communicational manoeuvre, her switch from mouth and ear to hand and eye, awakens panic in the protagonist but is admiringly related by a narrator who sees the emancipatory power of her gesture. The interconnectedness of the verbal and the manual recalls Jacotot's narrative of emancipation involving Savoyard glove makers in *Le Maître ignorant*. There, scrutiny of their skilled manual labour allows the artisans to appreciate an endeavour that is analogous to a practice of language:

Depuis qu'elles sont émancipées, elles s'appliquent à regarder, à étudier, à comprendre un gant bien confectionné. Elles devineront le sens de toutes les *phrases*, de tous les *mots* de ce gant.

[Since they became emancipated, they work hard at looking at, studying, and understanding a well-made glove. They will understand the meaning of all the *sentences*, all the *words* of the glove.][65]

65   Rancière is quoting from Jacotot's *Enseignement universel. Musique* (Paris: Boulland, 1830), p. 349; *Le Maître ignorant*, p. 65; *The Ignorant Schoolmaster*, p. 37 (emphasis in the original).

The text from *Enseignement universel. Musique* goes on:

> Il ne s'agit que d'apprendre une langue que l'on parle avec des ciseaux, une aiguille et du fil. Il n'est jamais question (dans les sociétés humaines) que de comprendre et de parler une langue.

> [One has only to learn a language spoken with scissors, needle, and thread. It is merely a question (in human societies) of understanding and speaking a language.][66]

To digress for a moment, and indeed switching continents and centuries, we find glove making featuring in another narrative of class division and hierarchy, Philip Roth's *American Pastoral*. In its depiction of mid-twentieth-century America, the novel tells of how, across several generations, an immigrant Jewish family emerges from poverty, acquiring a bourgeois lifestyle and aspiring to the kind of cultural integration signalled by the novel's title. Glove production is the route to enrichment for the Levovs and both father and son in the family business provide detailed explanations of the visual acuity, finger dexterity, and spatial awareness that are required in cutting and stitching gloves. 'The cutter was the prima donna', the founder of the family's factory reflects nostalgically.[67] The dwelling on manual expertise and the displays both of respect and social disdain for such work feed into the plot of Roth's novel and become emblems of a history of social fracture worked around religious, class, and ethnic divisions. Crucially, in an age of bourgeois consumption, the glove in *American Pastoral* serves as a symbol of prestige for its wearer while marking the social containment of the factory worker who makes it.

Just as Rancière sees as analogous the handling of words and of objects, and in Roth's novel an immigrant worker doesn't have 'to know English [...] to cut a perfect pair of gloves', so Proust's narrator likens Françoise's eloquence as a placer of objects to the work of prominent figures in nineteenth-century theatre:[68]

> [Françoise] avait, pour faire parler ainsi un objet inanimé, l'art à la fois génial et patient d'Irving et de Frédérick Lemaître. En ce moment, [elle

---

66   *Le Maître ignorant*, p. 65; *The Ignorant Schoolmaster*, p. 37.

67   Philip Roth, *American Pastoral* (London: Vintage, 1998 [1997]), p. 348. As I was completing the present book, I was encouraged by a reader of my manuscript at Liverpool University Press to consider this comparative link to Roth's novel. I am very grateful for this wise advice.

68   Roth, *American Pastoral*, pp. 128–29.

tenait] au-dessus d'Albertine et de moi la lampe allumée qui ne laissait dans l'ombre aucune des dépressions encore visibles que le corps de la jeune fille avait creusées dans le couvre-pieds. (RTP, II, 655)

[Her art of making inanimate objects speak in this way had all the inspired diligence of Irving and Frédérick Lemaître. In the present instance, (Françoise held) over Albertine and myself the lighted lamp which missed none of the still visible dents in the quilt left by the girl's body. (ISLT, III, 358)]

Henry Irving (1838–1905) was an actor renowned for his performances of Shakespeare in Victorian England, while Frédérick Lemaître (1800–1876) collaborated with Balzac on theatre projects and interpreted French Romantic drama.[69] In Françoise's improvised theatre, the material trace of erotic contact left by the leisured couple – the indentation on the bedcover – and the embodied mobility of the ancillary as she walks into the room carrying a light, both reconstruct and undermine the hierarchical social model. In the manner of its alignment of person-alities and their bodies and words, Proust's scene is both ludic and dissensual. It exemplifies what Rancière terms a literariness that 'undoes the relationships between the order of words and the order of bodies that determine the place of each'.[70]

In the literal illumination of Marcel's emotional life in the bedroom scene, Francoise's stagecraft is celebrated.[71] As she brings the evening lamp into Marcel's bedroom where he has been trying to seduce Albertine, the encounter between intelligent beings placed on an equal footing, to use Rancière's formulation, is unequivocally comic:[72]

---

69 See RTP, II, 1717, editorial notes 2 and 3.

70 Rancière, *Disagreement*, p. 37. The lines are discussed in Ross, 'Expressivity, Literarity, Mute Speech', pp. 136–37. See Chapter 1, p. 46, for discussion of these two orders in relation to Simon's *L'Acacia*.

71 Well-known examples of the conscious staging of the pursuit of desire in *À la recherche* include the family's use of a magic lantern in an attempt to distract a fretful Marcel (RTP, I, 9; ISLT, I, 13) and the description of his bedroom and the approaches to it as providing 'le décor strictement nécessaire [...] au drame de mon déshabillage' (RTP, 43) ['the bare minimum scenery (...) needed for the drama of my undressing' (ISLT, I, 46)]. Rancière links the bed on which the boy Marcel suffers in Combray and the bed 'de plaisir et de douleur' ['of pleasure and pain'] in Jupien's brothel. See *La Chair des mots*, p. 152; *The Flesh of Words*, p. 125.

72 See *Le Maître ignorant*, p. 66; *The Ignorant Schoolmaster*, p. 38.

Surpris pourtant par l'entrée inattendue de Françoise, je m'écriai:
– Comment, déjà la lampe? Mon Dieu que cette lumière est vive!
Mon but était sans doute par la seconde de ces phrases de dissimuler mon trouble, par la première d'excuser mon retard. Françoise répondit avec une ambiguïté cruelle:
– Faut-il que j'éteinde?
– Teigne? glissa à mon oreille Albertine, me laissant charmé par la vivacité familière avec laquelle, me prenant à la fois pour maître et pour complice, elle insinua cette affirmation psychologique dans le ton interrogatif d'une question grammaticale. (RTP, II, 656)

[But Françoise's unexpected entry had startled me, and I cried out:
   'What, the lamp already? Goodness, it's very bright!'
My intention might well have been in the second of these remarks to cover my confusion, and in the first to excuse the fact that I was late. Françoise replied with barbed ambiguity:
   'Am I to snuff it "orf" then, sir?'
   – '"Orf?"' "Off" surely? She's the one who's "off" if you ask me ...'
Albertine whispered in my ear, leaving me charmed by the familiar quickness of mind with which, taking me at once for master and accomplice, she insinuated this psychological affirmation in the interrogative mood of a grammatical question. (ISLT, III, 359)]

Although metaphorically inaudible as the social inferior, Françoise succeeds in conveying her emotion, whereas Marcel reflects on how his words are an attempt to conceal his. As for her sullen enquiry about turning off the lamp, her grammatical error (deftly rendered in Mark Treharne's ingenious translation) provides the cue for Albertine to demonstrate her linguistic competence and, apparently, to bolster Marcel's status as a figure of authority both linguistic and social. But given the punning around *teigne* in the original French (the word here has the sense of 'a spiteful woman' but also serves to eclipse Françoise's misconjugated subjunctive), grammatical correction doubles as class put-down.[73] The verbal exchange heightens both the erotic and the comedic charge of the encounter. In describing the orbits of desire in which each of the actors moves, the narrator shows a disapproving Françoise who enquires ironically about extinguishing the lamp and who longs to snuff out the lust being experienced by the bourgeois couple.

73 I am grateful to Antoine Compagnon for advice about the various strands in play in this scene. Mark Treharne works across from the stress on 'teigne' to word-play around 'off' in his translation of the scene.

The prestige associated with the making of literary allusion feeds into the scenes of would-be mastery and subversion. Thus, some time after the end of their relationship, Albertine writes to Marcel, replicating a style designed to appease him and secure his complicity:

> dans ses dernières lettres enfin, quand elle avait écrit probablement en se disant 'Je fais du chiqué': *Je vous laisse le meilleur de moi-même* [...] et: *Cet instant, deux fois crépusculaire puisque le jour tombait et que nous allions nous quitter, ne s'effacera de mon esprit que quand il sera envahi par la nuit complète.* (RTP, IV, 89)

> [in her last letters, finally, when, as she wrote, she probably thought to herself, 'I am faking it': *I leave you the best of myself* (...) and: *That moment, with its twofold twilight (since night was falling and since we were destined to part), will never be erased from my mind until utter darkness finally invades it.* (ISLT, V, 474)]

As she plays back to him the florid language he uses in letters to her, the ventriloquizing of his idiolect reveals her attempt to manipulate the apportionment of the sensible and to influence the dynamic of distribution and exclusion which it operates.

The Diplomat's Craft

The extent to which citation and recitation represent the feigning or the expression of emotion applies likewise to what in the *Recherche* is the male world of diplomacy to which Monsieur de Norpois belongs. A skilled ambassador, he deploys a range of stock phrases to judge international affairs. Indeed, wordcraft defines the diplomat's mission in Proust's novel, echoing Jacotot's assertion, noted above, that '[l'homme] communique en *artisan*: en manieur de mots comme d'outils' ['(man) communicates as an *artisan*: as a person who handles words like tools'].[74] Observing the wordsmith at work, the narrator relates:

> 'Comme dit un beau proverbe arabe: "Les chiens aboient, la caravane passe."' Après avoir jeté cette citation M. de Norpois s'arrêta pour nous regarder et juger de l'effet qu'elle avait produit sur nous. Il fut grand; le proverbe nous était connu: il avait remplacé cette année-là chez les hommes de haute valeur cet autre: 'Qui sème le vent récolte la tempête',

74   *Le Maître ignorant*, p. 110; *The Ignorant Schoolmaster*, p. 65. See above, Introduction, p. 6.

lequel avait besoin de repos, n'étant pas infatigable et vivace comme: 'Travailler pour le roi de Prusse'. Car la culture de ces gens éminents était une culture alternée, et généralement triennale. Certes les citations de ce genre, et desquelles M. de Norpois excellait à émailler ses articles de la *Revue*, n'étaient point nécessaires pour que ceux-ci parussent solides et bien informés. (RTP, I, 453)[75]

['As a fine old Arabian proverb puts it: "The dogs bark, the caravan moves on."' M. de Norpois paused, watching us to see what effect this quotation would have on us. It had a great effect: his proverb was well known to us. All worthy men had been using it that year instead of 'Sow the wind and reap the whirlwind', which was in need of a rest, not being a hardy annual like 'Doing the King of Prussia's work for him'. The culture of these eminent men was of the alternating variety, usually triennial in its cycle. Not that the articles M. de Norpois wrote for the *Revue des Deux Mondes* would have appeared less than sound and well informed had he not deftly sprinkled these sayings throughout them. (ISLT, II, 33–34; translation modified)]

With the diplomat's lexicon topped up by a recycling of proverbial wisdom and predictable utterance, the reader can work back from the metaphorical sense of the verb 'émailler' and from word productions that are 'solid' to literal enamelling.

Elsewhere, Proust's narrator proposes the homology of language use and manual craft. In *Combray*, the lady in pink converts the cold greeting of Marcel's father at the home of Uncle Adolphe into a thing of beauty. An approving narrator attributes to women like Odette de Crécy a skilled artisanship as they remodel male aggression and disapproval:

c'était un des côtés touchants du rôle de ces femmes oisives et studieuses qu'elles consacrent leur générosité, leur talent, un rêve disponible de beauté sentimentale [...] et un or qui leur coûte peu, à enrichir d'un sertissage précieux et fin la vie fruste et mal dégrossie des hommes. [...] elle avait pris quelque propos insignifiant de mon père, elle l'avait travaillé avec délicatesse, lui avait donné un tour, une appellation précieuse [...] elle le rendait changé en un bijou artiste, en quelque chose de 'tout à fait exquis'. (RTP, I, 77)

[it was one of the touching aspects of the role of these idle and studious women that they devote their generosity, their talent, a free-floating

<hr/>

75 In *Le Temps retrouvé*, Charlus reminds Marcel of how they are both aware of Norpois's stock of commonplaces or *lieux communs* and of the periodic renewal of these in political discourse (RTP, IV, 361; ISLT, VI, 90).

dream of beauty in love (...) and a gold that costs them little, to enrich
with a precious and refined setting the rough and ill-polished lives of
men. (...) she had taken some insignificant remark of my father's, had
worked it delicately, turned it, given it a precious appellation, and (...)
given it back changed into an artistic jewel, into something 'completely
exquisite'. (ISLT, I, 80)]

The characterization of Odette's inventive oral performance tightens the
coupling of communication and artisanship.

The tension between a language that is formulaic and the claims of
felt emotion is signalled in the response of Marcel's mother to Norpois.
She finds the career diplomat's language dull, while the narrator refers
to his 'répertoire si complet des formes surannées du langage particu-
lières à une carrière, à une classe et à un temps' (RTP, I, 429) ['such a
complete catalogue of outmoded speech forms belonging to the style
of a particular career, class, and period' (ISLT, II, 9)]. In the triad of
language, Zeitgeist, and social position, Norpois is likened, in a return
to the metaphor of theatre, to a seasoned performer at the Palais-Royal.
But for Marcel's mother, society's apportionment of roles dictates that
she find her husband's guest attractive:

> Seulement, elle sentait que c'était flatter délicatement son mari que de lui
> parler avec admiration du diplomate qui lui marquait une prédilection
> si rare. [...] Et comme elle était incapable de mentir à mon père, *elle*
> *s'entraînait elle-même à admirer l'ambassadeur pour pouvoir le louer*
> *avec sincérité.* (RTP, I, 429; emphasis added)

> [However, she felt that she was subtly pleasing her husband by expressing
> admiration of the diplomat who had so singled him out. (...) Being
> incapable of lying to my father, *she did her best to admire the ambassador,*
> *so as to be able to praise him in all sincerity.* (ISLT, II, 9)]

A schooling of the emotions, then, might foster authentic admiration in
the mother, while also underpinning gendered roles within bourgeois
marriage. Such a move by this figure of moral integrity provides a variant
on the play-acting that is a frequent dimension of social interaction in the
novel. Yet as the mother works to cultivate within herself genuine feeling
for Norpois, the narrator moves in the reverse direction, switching from
the view that Norpois was singling out Marcel's father for preferment
to arguing that, for the skilled diplomat, going to dinner was a routine
requiring little in the way of emotional investment, being 'un des
actes innombrables de sa vie sociale' (RTP, I, 430) ['one act among the
countless acts making up his social life' (ISLT, II, 10)].

Repetitiveness in language use is a phenomenon analysed by the narrator in *La Prisonnière*: 'une grande partie de ce que nous disons n'[est] qu'une récitation (RTP, III, 614) ['a large part of what we say is merely recitation' (ISLT, V, 94)], he asserts. He examines the formation of public opinion, querying the judgement of those who assume that it is in the reactions of kings that we find explanations for the affairs of nations. What is needed, he reflects, is an understanding of the psychology of the individual and in particular the psychology of the 'individu médiocre' (RTP, II, 700) ['humblest individual' (ISLT, III, 404)]. The café owner who discusses the Dreyfus Affair embodies that mindset:

> En politique, le patron du café où je venais d'arriver n'appliquait depuis quelque temps sa mentalité de professeur de récitation qu'à un certain nombre de morceaux sur l'affaire Dreyfus. S'il ne retrouvait pas les termes connus dans les propos d'un client ou les colonnes d'un journal, il déclarait l'article assommant, ou le client pas franc. Le prince de Foix l'émerveilla au contraire au point qu'il laissa à peine à son interlocuteur le temps de finir sa phrase. 'Bien dit, mon prince, bien dit (ce qui voulait dire, en somme, récité sans faute), c'est ça, c'est ça', s'écria-t-il. (RTP, II, 700)

> [In the matter of politics, the proprietor of the café into which I had just walked had for some time been applying his learning-by-rote mentality exclusively to a number of set-pieces on the Dreyfus case. If the terms he had committed to memory did not figure in the remarks of a customer or the columns of a newspaper, then he would declare that the article bored him to tears or that the customer was not giving a true picture. But the Prince de Foix's words aroused such admiration in him that he barely gave the Prince time to finish his sentence. 'Well said, Prince, well said,' (which effectively meant 'faultlessly recited') 'how true, how very true,' he exclaimed. (ISLT, III, 404–05)]

Alert to the power of cliché, the narrator asserts that these instantiations of recitation and mimicry shape the history of peoples. The café owner is a *professeur de récitation*, a role elsewhere assumed by Norpois, but also by Albertine in her interaction with Marcel. His mother and grandmother too interact citationally in their exchanges of letters where Mme de Sévigné serves as intertext.

Linguistic performances in the *Recherche*, then, are inseparable from hierarchies of gender and class. Indeed, it is in the minutiae of daily verbal exchange that Proust shows dissensus in the social distribution of emotion, prestige, and power: a naive use of *tutoiement*; a miscon-jugated verb; an acquired linguistic mimicry of the kind shown by

Albertine; women who deftly handle words and objects in moves to circumvent patriarchy; the garrulousness of career diplomat and café owner as they peddle the commonplaces of the day.

The democratization of words that Proust facilitates in his novel connects with what Rancière terms 'la parole muette' or mute speech which, as one critic writes, is 'used to articulate a critical perspective on pretensions to mastery', to counter 'the posture of authority of the supposed masters of language'.[76] The corners of the *Recherche* explored in this chapter reflect a narrator who both probes and plays with disturbances of consensual forms of hierarchy.

---

76   Ross, 'Expressivity, Literariy, Mute Speech', pp. 134–35.

CHAPTER NINE

Convocation, or On Ways of Being Together

François Bon

[H]onorer [...] cette si vieille tension des choses qui se taisent et des mots qui les cherchent.

[to honour that very old tension between things not expressed and the words that seek them]

Bon[1]

[L]e peuple, qui est une manière d'occuper à beaucoup un petit espace

[the people, which is a way for many to occupy a little space]

Rancière[2]

In François Bon's *Autobiographie des objets* ['Autobiography of Objects'], published in 2012, a seemingly desultory review of heteroclite objects effectively doubles as social and family history. Bon's inventory captures generational change and class migration in France in the twentieth century: the spinning tops which his grandparents, both maternal and paternal, looked after and which are today discarded, the advent of nylon and the washing machine, brand names such as Telefunken and Popeye, classroom photographs, a new range of cars

---

1 François Bon, *Daewoo* (Paris: Fayard, 2004), p. 10; subsequent citations abbreviated to D.

2 *Courts voyages au pays du peuple*, p. 147; *Short Voyages to the Land of the People*, p. 114.

encapsulating 'le concept de *classe moyenne*' ['the concept of *middle class*'].[3] Bon's snapshot tallies with the strong sense of periodization which Kristin Ross explores in France's modernization drive in the 1950s and '60s.[4] The gamut of subjects which Bon selects is consistent with the democratized understanding of cultural life which he promotes. He regrets the modern trend to escape complex reality by erecting 'des cloisons autour d'un soi-disant domaine littéraire qui en serait coupé' (AO, 202) ['partitions around a so-called literary domain that would be cut off from it']. The soldering iron and pliers which he keeps long after he has stopped regularly using them are inseparable from his encounter with text (price lists and item specifications) in the monthly *Le Haut-Parleur* magazine when he was at secondary school. Reflecting somewhat whimsically on 'tout ce continent de littérature populaire' (AO, 187) ['that whole continent of popular literature'] that was central to his cultural formation, Bon references the encyclopaedic claims made in the *Reader's Digest*, for example, to have its readers learn to write, to draw, or to speak thirty-five languages. Both open-mindedness and ironic detachment mark his interrogation of these memories of emancipatory promises. With the *Tout l'Univers* magazines capturing the diversity of interests of the day (archaeology, history, war, chemistry, physics, space travel), Bon is comfortable with the cultural levelling signalled by these memories. Thus, *Anna Karenina* is for him inseparable from the old 2CV car seat he occupied when reading it in a family loft littered with pieces of car body work (AO, 36). He chooses the metaphor of the pact between life and words (AO, 93) to capture his endeavour as a student of the relationship between things and language.

Bon explains how, in his life experience, books quickly acquired prestige. Thus, the user's manual for a microscope holds allure: 'la magie du livre, même d'un simple manuel, toujours plus forte pour moi que celle de l'objet lui-meme' (AO, 59) ['the magic of the book, even of a simple manual, was always more powerful for me than the object itself']. He notes soberly how, as a child, he retreated into the book, explaining that he recoiled from the school playground's culture of muted violence ['violence sourde'] (AO, 52). Likewise, reading was preferable to the experience of being taken with other children on an annual school visit

---

3   See François Bon, *Autobiographie des objets* (Paris: Seuil, 2012), p. 122. Hereinafter cited as AO.

4   See Kristin Ross, *Fast Cars, Clean Bodies: Decolonization and the Reordering of French Culture* (Cambridge, MA: MIT Press, 1994).

to a nearby farm where animal suffering could be heard. A book cabinet belonging to his grandfather (a bibliophile and primary school teacher) is similarly given privileged status. Its owner had served in the First World War as a *vaguemestre*, a soldier-postman delivering to troops on the front line, the role (given to a teacher) reflecting 'le privilège des intellectuels' (AO, 235) ['the privilege of intellectuals'], in Bon's ironic formulation. An arresting apportionment of roles caters for the transmission of messages on paper to those applying lethal military force and again juxtaposes written word and world.

In his first novel, *Sortie d'usine* ['Factory Exit'] (1982), Bon foregrounds the experience of manual work in a factory and self-consciously reflects on how this comes to be articulated through words. Late in the novel, having described the circumstances in which the protagonist decides to quit the factory, the narrator argues that it is the protagonist's earlier experience of having read Kafka's *The Castle* which equips him to leave the space of alienation that is the workplace. In a see-saw movement between book and life, the narrator senses 'l'écriture de l'usine' ['the writing of the factory'] becoming 'l'usine comme écriture' ['the factory as writing'], the action of flipping creating a transitional zone in which 'l'inconnu du vrai' ['the unknown of the real'] might resonate.[5]

As with Ernaux, Bon's account of his coming to writing in *Autobiographie des objets* is embedded in a family history that predates access to literature. He recalls his blind great-grandmother tapping her stick as she negotiates the cement path outside her home, all the while composing what Bon calls her soliloquy. This reminds him of the occasion of his own performance in a school play, where a walking stick and top hat were his props as he delivered memorized lines: 'Je trouve dans ces dialogues à la canne le premier vague soubassement du chemin pris plus tard avec l'écriture' (AO, 75) ['in these dialogues delivered with stick in hand, I find the first, vague beginnings of the path later taken when I started writing']. By association, the blind ancestor's act of probing and her solitary oral compositions performed in her native tongue of La Vendée (a language derived from Poitevin, which in the fourteenth century, Bon insists, was as widely spoken as French) are gathered in with his own compositional efforts. The lineage that stretches from blind relative's stick to writer's pen conveys a levelling reminiscent of Jacotot's assertions in *Le Maître ignorant*.

If, putting it loosely, ancestral portraits take Bon back before the book as it were, he also scopes an age after it. In *Après le livre* ['After the Book'] (2011), he reflects on the impact of the internet, although in the same work, he marvels at the image of Flaubert at his desk, on which sits a tray full of goose feathers which the novelist has himself prepared. A precursor of the industrially produced metallic pen, the quill becomes much more than an instrument for Flaubert. As he writes to Louise Colet: 'Je suis un *homme-plume*. Je sens par elle, à cause d'elle, par rapport à elle et beaucoup plus avec elle' ['I am a *man-quill*. I feel through it, because of it, in relation to it and much more with it'].[6] Bon delights in the artisanal stress on the tool used in handwriting, while being no less impressed by the search engine which today gives electronic access to Flaubert's entire correspondence.

A section on dictionaries in *Autobiographie des objets* sees Bon review the reference works he grew up with, from the postal service calendar to his later acquisition of the *Petit Larousse* and, beyond that, the *Petit Robert*. Reflecting on changes triggered by the internet, he writes nostalgically about 'le mouvement du doigt sur l'épaisseur des pages' (AO, 92) ['the movement of the finger on the thickness of the pages']. Like his blind ancestor feeling with her stick, Bon's dictionary work has a tactile, indeed attritional character as evidenced by a succession of thumb-marked reference books accumulated over time. Elsewhere, tactile manual knowledge is privileged over visual perception, as when factory workers in *Sortie d'usine* demonstrate a muscle memory that allows them to gauge fine distinctions of measurement more accurately than any visual scrutiny might provide: 'un palper, le métier oui sur le bout des doigts' (SU, 38) ['a manual feel, yes, their trade at the tips of their fingers']. Bon thus widens out notions of judgement, assessment, and, by extension, composition. By foregrounding the tactile, he unsettles visual privilege.

Manual memory thus signals a belonging marked by generational specificity, given the move into a post-industrial age in France which Bon documents. Not unlike Péguy's praise of a disappearing artisanship, Bon's instinct is to connect back: 'J'appartiens à un monde disparu – et je vis et me conduis au-delà de cette appartenance' (AO, 37) ['I belong to a world that has disappeared – and I live and behave beyond that belonging']. Cherished random objects from his past, such as an

6   Letter of 1 February 1852; quoted in François Bon, *Après le livre* (Paris: Seuil, 2011), pp. 39–42 (p. 42). Bon's source for the description of Flaubert at work is Maupassant.

aeroplane propeller made of wood, are recalled not through the mind's eye but rather via his hand which imagines the object's helicoidal form. The stress on manual connection as experienced by the factory worker in *Sortie d'usine* is thus reprised:

> combien d'objets qui [...] passent au lointain, on les tient un instant en mémoire comme on les aurait dans la main, poids, taille, consistance, mémoire tactile qui est aussi le biais d'écriture. (AO, 201)

> [there are so many objects that pass in the distance, you hold them momentarily in your memory as you would hold them in your hand, their weight, size, consistency, the tactile memory which is also the angle of writing.]

*   *   *

With the theme of class everywhere in his work, Bon can be read as a 'partisan of social art', to use Bourdieu's formulation.[7] He begins his hybrid work *Daewoo* (2004) on a note of resistance: 'Refuser. Faire face à l'effacement même' (D, 9) ['To refuse. To stand up to obliteration']. Threatened with erasure are the lived experience and collective memories of redundant workers in the deindustrialized peripheries of eastern French towns where the many factory closures include three owned by the Korean corporation Daewoo. These fringe spaces become sites of workers' contestation, throwing up for Bon the writer 'cette diffraction des langages, des visages, des signes' (D, 12) ['this diffraction of languages, faces, and signs'].

As if to illustrate what Howard Caygill refers to as 'the hospitality of art to the experience of resistance', Bon presents *Daewoo* as a novel, while also seeing his work variously as a project and an investigation, as *récit* and as theatre (D, 291).[8] The range of genres marks his resourceful attempt to grasp the historical process behind social fracture and to garner collective energies and consciousness. Indeed, the work's generic openness stands as an act of generosity and hospitality, as entailing a mode of levelling consistent with its author's aspiration to be socially available to the human subjects whose situation he is examining. Adapting Rancière, one might argue that the morality of

---

7   Pierre Bourdieu, *The Field of Cultural Production: Essays on Art and Literature*, ed. Randal Johnson (Cambridge: Polity Press, 1993), p. 182.

8   Caygill, *On Resistance*, p. 174.

the story (which involves an ethical practice of equality) is mirrored in an aesthetic practice of equality visible in the work's generic hybridity.[9] As one reviewer comments, *Daewoo*, with both its tense engagement with proletarian actuality and its intermedial character, shows the novel *at work* ['le roman au travail'].[10] The phenomenon of hybridity is articulated in somewhat different terms by Sam DiIorio, who argues convincingly that *Daewoo* does not merely 'recapitulate the real world' but 'reworks its source material to make it permeable to literature'.[11] DiIorio identifies in Bon's model of representation 'the interaction between conscious invention, literary borrowings, circulating representations, and a genuine, difficult-to-frame real'.[12]

The technique of absorption into fiction does not lessen the hold of actuality. Juxtaposed with the fear of dispersal and atomization in *Daewoo* is the verbal composure of the economically dominant: 'Les mots à voix posée et propres des puissants, mots civilisés du *geste qui écarte de l'égalité ses semblables* et ne l'est pas, le geste, civilisé' (D, 12; emphasis added) ['The poised, correctly delivered words of the powerful, civilized words in *the gesture that excludes fellow humans from equality*, the gesture that is not civilized']. As if to corroborate Rancière/Jacotot's identification of a will to reject the egalitarian, Bon's carefully crafted formulation with its use of chiasmus and alliteration undermines power by exposing its discursive seductiveness. Bon points to both the polish and violence in management speak, a subversive rendition of which is provided by one of his collaborators, Géraldine Roux, who assiduously tracks the verbal performances of government ministers and factory owners: 'Fiche les gens dehors c'est de la technique, de l'*ingénierie*' (D, 113) ['Getting rid of people, that's the technique, that's your *engineering*'], runs the factory worker's caustic gloss on the perspective of those who govern. The careful gathering in of such voices of dissent is central to *Daewoo*'s act of cultural resistance.

9   See Introduction, pp. 12–13, on the linkage between the ethical and the aesthetic proposed by Rancière in his analysis of Rossellini's *Europa 51* (*Courts voyages au pays du peuple*, p. 158; *Short Voyages to the Land of the People*, p. 123).

10   See Philippe-Jean Catinchi, 'Le Roman au travail', *Le Monde des livres*, 10 September 2004, p. 1. I am grateful to Shirley Jordan for bringing this review to my attention.

11   Sam DiIorio, 'Chaîne et Chaîne: Representation as Corrosion in François Bon's *Daewoo*', *SubStance*, 35.3 (2006), special issue, *The French Novel Now*, 5–22 (p. 13).

12   DiIorio, 'Chaîne et Chaîne', p. 17.

The book's inaugural statement of defiance entails a retrieval of perspectives both individual and collective. After initial hesitation about the nature of the text he might produce, Bon affirms that his writing will indeed have the character of a novel in that it will give voice and visibility to the women who had previously populated the deserted factories which are now reduced to a 'géométrie pure' (D, 13) ['pure geometry']. Setting out a project of cultural empowerment, Bon draws on extensive experience of directing writing workshops dating back to the 1990s and often involving people conventionally seen as falling outside the practice of textual composition (pupils in the *banlieue* and people living on the streets, for example). The volume in which he describes this collaborative work draws its title from Maurice Blanchot: *Tous les mots sont adultes* ['All Words are Adult Words'].[13] An egalitarian recognition of the value of individual lives similarly informs *Daewoo*. Bon explains how a theatre project taken forward with Charles Tordjman, director of the Centre dramatique national de Nancy, had been the initial plan of action designed to contest culturally what had happened at Daewoo. Working with Tordjman and a team of four actresses in the space of one of the disused factories, Bon's aim was to 'dire ou crier ce que cela signifiait de colère, les usines vides, ce que cela évoquait pour notre idée d'humanité en partage' (D, 95) ['say or cry out what the empty factories meant in terms of anger, what that conjured up for our idea of a shared humanity']. An ethics of engagement underpins the collaborative dimension of the project and the play was staged at the Avignon Festival in July 2004.[14]

Daewoo the novel appeared in the same year. Bon reports that the precise trigger for his turning to writing was seeing workmen at the front of the factory dismantling the giant letters of the name 'Daewoo'. In a state of malaise and with the image etched on his imagination, he stops at a motorway rest area and begins to write. A poet, he reflects, might have settled for the image of individual letters dangling in the

13   François Bon, *Tous les mots sont adultes* (Paris: Arthème Fayard, 2009). Oliver Davis has explored the connection between Bon and Rancière specifically in relation to their approaches to pedagogy; see 'The Radical Pedagogies of François Bon and Jacques Rancière', *French Studies*, 64.2 (April 2010), 178–91.

14   See Alix Mary, 'Daewoo, le choix du roman chez François Bon', *Mémoire(s), identité(s), marginalité(s) dans le monde occidental contemporain*, 9 (2013), http://journals.openedition.org/mimmoc/1009;   DOI: https://doi.org/10.4000/mimmoc.1009 [accessed 28 February 2020].

air, a playwright for projecting them on a stage, whereas the persisting, visual-memory stimulus provided by letters energizes the engaged writer in Bon. The W in DAEWOO – 'ce W à la fin promené sous la grue' (D, 95) ['that W that ended up hanging under the crane'] – serves as indirect tribute to Perec's narrative of loss, W *ou la disparition* (the title meaning literally 'W or The Disappearance').[15] As DiIorio explains, recalling Perec's dedication of W ('Pour e(ux)') ['To them']), both texts propose 'to remember individuals absent from discourse'.[16] He also points out how, when *Daewoo* was published, Bon admitted to fabricating the detail surrounding the dangling letter W on the factory facade. With the W setting up the link to Perec, this allows Bon to rework the source material gathered in Lorraine.[17] Yet the element of fabrication does not undermine his engagement, which is here drawing on the resources of fiction in the service of a project of empowerment.

The textual echoing illustrates what Bourdieu calls the 'internal logic of cultural objects, their structure as *languages'* in the field of cultural production.[18] *Daewoo* strains to capture the externality of discarded voices condemned to evanescence: 'tandis que m'assaillaient toutes ces voix, me revenaient ces regards, et qu'il me fallait traverser tous ces silences' (D, 95–96) ['whilst all those voices assailed me and the looks on those faces came back to me and I had to make my way through all those silences']. The 'difficult-to-frame real', to use DiIorio's formulation, sees Bon confessing to a feeling of engulfment with the project, to being haunted by what his mind's eye retains of empty factories and roads under street lights. In prolonged bouts of insomnia, his thoughts run to the disturbing paintings of Hieronymus Bosch in which faces acquire a distorting prominence (D, 97). Indeed, Bon sees in his own compositional method the aspiration to work as the Dutch painter-in-words.

The image of the fire that engulfed the Daewoo factory at Mont-Saint-Martin reinforces the apocalyptic tone. A Daewoo employee at Villers whose husband worked at Mont-Saint-Martin describes living with her own traumatic memory of having witnessed the blaze: 'Moi, toute seule, dans la chambre, j'appelle ça la photo' (D, 30) ['Me, all alone in

---

15   The published English translation of W *ou la disparition* is entitled *A Void*, trans. Gilbert Adair (London: Penguin, 2008).
16   DiIorio, 'Chaîne et Chaîne', p. 9.
17   DiIorio, 'Chaîne et Chaîne', p. 13.
18   Bourdieu, *The Field of Cultural Production*, p. 181.

my room, I call it the photo'], she confides. Bon taps into the concision with which she channels the effect of flashback and obsession. 'Trouver pour Fameck', he reveals, *'cette force franche, une présence, sans réflexion ni rien qui hésite*, c'est cela que je voulais pour mon livre' (D, 97; emphasis added) ['To find for Fameck *that plain strength, a presence, without reflection or any kind of hesitation*, that's what I wanted for my book']. His aim, then, is to counter any sense of the servile by conveying the energies and testimonies of the socially discarded. (In his book on writing workshops, Bon cites Bataille's reflection that, were our language to be wholly servile, we would have lost all that is human.)[19] At the same time, an ethics of listening informs his project. Thus, when his questions elicit often weary replies from redundant employees and he learns of what he believes to be the disproportionately high incidence of physical illness, suicide, and divorce, Bon wonders if he should persist in raking up 'cette poussière sale, ce qu'on traînait désormais de poids mort par le seul mot Daewoo' (D, 96) ['the dust and dirt, the dead weight hanging over people from the very word Daewoo'].[20] Crucially, his own experience of insomnia and disquiet links him into the collective dimension underpinning *Daewoo*. Through this circulation of affect, private grief mutates into an equalizing of emotions that encompasses Bon and his collaborators.

Some of the novelist's interlocutors are themselves sceptical about the likely impact of his project. Géraldine Roux concedes that Bon's wanting to write about workers is proof that there is, as she puts it, some good left in the world, though she adds trenchantly that the effect is nevertheless to leave everything in its place: 'on a fait ce qu'il fallait, posé le bouquet de fleurs à l'enterrement' (D, 104–05) ['we've observed the ritual, laid flowers on the grave']. Roux's disabused formulation is close to Bourdieu's view of the predisposition of art to 'fulfil a social function of legitimating social differences'.[21] Yet in welcoming her contestation

19 Bon is quoting from Bataille's *L'Expérience intérieure*; see *Tous les mots sont adultes*, p. 7.

20 For a discussion, beyond socio-economic questions, of mentalities and in particular of human diminution (*l'homme diminué*) in modern and contemporary France, see Emmanuel Todd, *Les Luttes de classes en France au XXIe siècle* (Paris: Seuil, 2020), chapter 5, 'Au-delà de l'économie, les mentalités: l'homme diminué', pp. 127–53.

21 Bourdieu, *Distinction*, p. 7; quoted by Johnson, 'Editor's Introduction', in Bourdieu, *The Field of Cultural Production*, ed. Randal Johnson (Cambridge: Polity Press, 1993), p. 25.

and implicitly acknowledging the risk of paternalism in his project, Bon draws collaboratively on the fluency and confidence with which Roux expresses herself. Foregrounding authentic voices is intrinsic to his endeavour. As he transcribes the words of another of his interlocutors, Valérie Aumont, she enquires about what he has noted down, and Bon replies that it is 'une construction de mots pour mettre en avant, oui, sa façon de dire les mots' (D, 103) ['a word construction to put forward, yes, her way of speaking'].

Bon also attends to the conscious use of metalanguage by the workers he interviews. The unnamed woman traumatized by the memory of the plant burning down in front of her asks pointedly: 'Pourquoi une ouvrière ne parlerait pas de l'angoisse d'être, appelez ça l'inquiétude? C'est beau, ce mot, inquiétude, il calme' (D, 31–32) ['Why would a woman working in a factory not talk about the anguish of being, call it anxiety? It's a nice word that, anxiety, it's soothing']. The laying claim to the world of interiority and the affirmation of language's therapeutic power stand as acts of reclamation and provide an indictment of cultural and class apportionment. The scene offers a restatement of Weil's protest, noted above, about 'la classe de ceux qui ne *comptent pas*' (CO, 170) ['the class of those who *don't count*'].[22] In a more precise sense, the scene also returns us to Rancière's account of the distribution of 'la parole' and 'le bruit', of speech and noise. Rancière argues that the complaints of the *sans-part*, of those excluded from the socio-political order, are, in Davis's words, 'in a more fundamental sense […] not heard as meaning-bearing language'.[23] And just as when Rancière underscores the aesthetic angle at work in politics, he has in mind the operation of perception and visibility, so in Bon's project, the factory worker's political protest involves a laying claim to a particular 'sensible'.[24]

Bon's interlocutor goes on: 'Peut-être que quelque part on se dit ça, que les ouvrières leur destin est d'être ouvrières' (D, 33) ['Perhaps that's what some people say, that women factory workers are meant to be just that, factory workers']. The tautology throws the reader back to the division of labour in Plato's *Republic*, which is pivotal for Rancière.[25] Bon's interviewee likewise rejects the essentialized management thinking whereby, if alternative forms of manual employment are found, 'on a

22 See Chapter 6, p. 146.
23 See Davis, *Jacques Rancière*, p. 91.
24 See Davis, *Jacques Rancière*, p. 90.
25 See above, Introduction, p. 5.

fait ce qu'il fallait pour qu'elles ne connaissent pas l'angoisse' (D, 33) ['we've done what was required to avoid them experiencing anxiety']. Or as Vicky, a long-standing employee in the glove factory in Roth's *American Pastoral*, reminds its proprietor when it risks being destroyed during the social unrest of the summer of 1967, 'This is mine too. You just own it'.[26]

As Rancière notes an assumption of equivalence in Jacotot's account of human intelligence, so Bon identifies in *Daewoo* the levelling present in the experience of inner psychological states. One of the strikers, Valérie Aumont, observes as she reviews events in the factory that 'Nous toutes, si on a fait du chemin, c'est à l'intérieur' (D, 101) ['If us women have all made some headway, it's in our inner lives']. In gathering evidence of autonomy and self-knowledge experienced at an individual level, Bon insists on a socially redistributive understanding of psychological interiority.

The presentation in *Daewoo* of post-industrial social fracture is in many senses far removed from Michelet's mid-nineteenth-century evocation of the nation and social class. In *Le Peuple*, he writes of his origins in an artisanal family. Offering a sentimentalized conception of society, he notes his own evolution (he was the son of a printer) and casts himself as one who suffered from the 'divorce déplorable que l'on tâche de produire entre les hommes, entre les classes, moi qui les ai tous en moi' ['deplorable divorce they try to bring about between men and classes, I who hold all of them within me'].[27] Michelet's belief in a narrative of cross-class synthesis ties in with his conception of France and of his standpoint as historian. He expresses nevertheless suspicion about the 'classes supérieures' ['upper classes'], arguing that the salons, the work of the most brilliant writers, and Romantic fiction with its sensationalist stress on robbery (rather than quotidian work) and penal colonies (rather than the *atelier*), fail to deliver what he holds up as the sacred poetry deriving from 'la famille, le travail, la plus humble vie du peuple' ['family, work, and the most humble life of the people'].[28]

While Bon's complaint, a century and a half later, about the cultural objects of the powerful is made within a clearly different set of social coordinates, his articulation of 'deplorable divorce', to apply Michelet's term, is no less urgent. Bon too questions the ways in which canonical

26   Roth, *American Pastoral*, p. 162.
27   Jules Michelet, *Le Peuple* (Paris: Hachette/Paulin, 1846), p. 39.
28   Michelet, *Le Peuple*, p. 16.

literature legitimizes certain venues and topoi: staircases and lofts in Kafka, salons overlooking gardens in Balzac. In the urban fringes of deindustrialized eastern France by contrast, he observes of the rusting furnaces at Uckange, the motorway, and the high-rise flats: 'Le monde ici [...] ne prête pas à poème' (D, 118) ['this part of the world doesn't lend itself to poetry']. Whereas Michelet saw the return to roots in Romantic terms as delivering a poetry that was sacred, Bon calls for a new poiesis: 'la tension poétique d'une prose est ce mouvement, par quoi on extorque au réel ce sentiment de présence' (D, 119) ['the poetic tension present in prose is the movement whereby one extorts from the real that feeling of presence']. Rivets, bolts, sheets of steel, cement, bitumen, and lives lived in and around urban wasteland form the material culture which writing is attempting to articulate. A reference in Bon's narrative to Lidl alongside high literature, far from being tokenistic, marks an appeal made against the violence of compartmentalization and signals what DiIorio terms the 'double investment in text and world'.[29] The writer must wring out of this difficult subject matter, Bon argues, the deep experience it holds. The verb *extorquer*, which denotes etymologically a movement of twisting and extraction and in its modern sense implies a dimension of force or threat or ruse, captures the tension in play. Bon gauges the challenge posed by the task of such representation: 'ce mystère qui soude un lieu à l'énigme des hommes se passe parfois de traces' (D, 119) ['this mystery which welds a place to the enigma of men sometimes leaves no trace'].

In an expression of the vulnerability attaching to marginal lives, Bon points to a void at the level of cultural evidence. Specifically, he depicts a writer confronted with an evanescent subject matter that canonical literature has failed to engage with: 'Etait-ce vain, cette profondeur, de la chercher ici encore, ici pourtant, dans l'usine vide et la ville qui l'entourait?' (D, 119) ['Was it futile to be still looking for that depth here, here all the same, in the empty factory and in the surrounding town?']. In the alliteration of *vain*, *vide*, and *ville*, and in the intensification present in the adverbial pairing *ici encore* and *ici pourtant*, Bon gives urgency to the writer's longing for connection and depth in what is paradoxically a scene of cultural erasure.

Rancière identifies how Michelet sets out the cure for the drama of class separation in his teaching of the winter of 1847–1848. In Rancière's words:

29   DiIorio, 'Chaîne et Chaîne', p. 6.

le langage qui manque pour lier les classes opposées, c'est le langage du lien en général. Ce dont on manque entre pauvres et lettrés, c'est de ce qui fait le lien en général chez les riches comme chez les pauvres: l'amour.

[the language needed in order to bind the classes together is the language of the bond in general. What is missing between poor and educated is what makes for a bond in general, among the rich as among the poor: love.][30]

Affective connection thus forms a necessary precondition for social engagement. The language of link-making across classes forms a primary axis in *Courts voyages au pays du peuple*, where essays on Wordsworth, Michelet, Rilke, Rossellini's *Europa 51*, and other subjects all point to cross-class interventions freighted with affect. Similarly, in *Daewoo*, emotional connection with the work's subject matter gives seriousness to Bon's focus on a 'poétique de l'urbain' (D, 117) ['an urban poetic']. A man shaking hands with people playing cards in a bar; a woman who wets her finger to turn the pages of an old directory showing lists of doctors; a young woman speaking through a car window to a young male driver inside, against a background of loud music: in his scanning of 'the indeterminacy of the everyday', Bon reflects on 'la complexité de nuances qu'un simple geste comporte' (D, 120) ['the complexity of nuances in a simple gesture'].[31] He goes on to extrapolate from this what he elliptically labels 'si vieille, très vieille histoire jamais finie' (D, 120) ['that never-ending story, so old, so very old']. The elegiac note conveyed by the truncated syntax matches the mood of haunting that Bon evokes elsewhere in *Daewoo*. With factory production due to be moved from eastern France to Turkey, Nadia Nasseri imagines proleptically how the younger Turkish woman replacing her will be looking in the same metallic mirror that was hers for eight years (the mirror which allows workers to be aware of what is literally coming along the production line). With the self-image thus mutating to deliver the face of the new factory recruit, a tight sense both of symbiosis and rivalry is evoked: 'Moi dans l'acier regardant en ce moment la fille, effectuant mes propres gestes' (D, 146) ['Me looking in the steel mirror that moment

30 *Courts voyages au pays du peuple*, p. 101; *Short Voyages to the Land of the People*, pp. 77–78.
31 Michael Sheringham draws on Blanchot's argument in 'La Parole quotidienne' that indeterminacy is a defining characteristic of the everyday; see Sheringham, *Everyday Life: Theories and Practices from Surrealism to the Present* (Oxford: Oxford University Press, 2006), chapter 1.

at the young woman performing my own gestures']. The transnational angle heightens the economic precarity confronting Nadia in that the motivation of employers in the relocation of the factory is to access cheaper labour.

In contrast with this tense image involving two women employees separated by both age and geographical distance, an impression of spectral sisterhood is present when Bon conceives of an urban montage showing the silhouettes of the 250 women who had worked for eight years in one of the Daewoo factories (D, 121). In *Sortie d'usine*, an older worker, suddenly taken ill and in a state of virtual collapse, loses all fear of workplace hierarchy. Before losing consciousness, he reflects on his predicament using the third person, repeating patiently to a foreman who wants to take charge and would have the sick man's fellow workers move away: 'laisse le possible à ceux qui l'aiment' (SU, 153) ['let those who love him do what they can']. Affective bonding thus maps onto class allegiance.

The attentiveness to living spaces occupied by individuals whose stories the work accommodates reinforces the elegiac strain in *Daewoo*. Reflecting on Sylvia F., a worker activist and mother who has committed suicide, Bon wonders if her now empty flat might serve as a more fitting mortuary mask than the plaster moulds of faces and hands used in earlier times (D, 175). The empty dwelling shares the mystery associated with ancient tombs. Nearby excavations for a new TGV line have uncovered Celtic remains, prompting him to observe that what may now be indecipherable will have been culturally intelligible in a distant past. The archaeologist's urge to know is analogous to Bon's puzzlement over Sylvia F.'s final hours (D, 177).

In a similar way, *Sortie d'usine* dwells on the funerary practice in the factory which sees the coffins of deceased workers drawn, by way of tribute, on a pallet truck towed by the now longest-serving employee, Thomas, who had taken on this role on first entering the factory, his own father having previously performed the same ritual: 'Dans le civil, la mort avait bien des rites tout aussi abstrus: alors pourquoi pas ici, pour le pauvre gars qui clamsait sur place?' (SU, 93) ['In civilian life, death rituals were every bit as abstruse, so why not here for the poor bloke who snuffed it at work?']. In the form taken by the funeral tribute known as 'le Passage' (a custom introduced by the founder of the factory), the levelling marked by death is replicated in the cacophony generated throughout the building. Workers on the factory floor bang their tools on metal, rev engines, and activate air compressors, while the design technicians bang their rulers and drum noisily on the wooden floor with their stools (SU, 88–89). In an intensely ritual ceremony, the factory owner formally initiates the funerary practice by emitting a high-pitched nasal sound to herald the cortege. The narrator adds that, in the tribute to the deceased founder of the factory, the furore created carries gravity, 'avec jusqu'une nuance de fraternel' (SU, 97) ['with even a trace of fraternal spirit']. 'Une règle du bruit' (SU, 80) ['a law of noise'] ensures a heightened perception of sound that signals a departure from capitalist rationality, with intense human endeavour being diverted away from utilitarian ends. With the extreme levels of sound comes a transformation of the space, 'ici où se mettaient en œuvre des puissances amplifiant la main de l'homme' (SU, 80) ['here where forces amplifying the human hand were set to work']. As in Simon's *L'Acacia*, where the mesmerizing sound, within a cavalry unit, of horses' hooves ringing on tarmac supplants war's utilitarian ends, or in Weil, where the *basso continuo* formed by a factory machine can awaken intense stimulation in its operator (CO, 329), so the foregrounding of aisthesis in the funerary tradition in *Sortie d'usine* displaces ergonomics (SU, 92).[32]

The experimentation with factory space in the theatre project in *Daewoo* marks another aesthetic attempt to supplant the logic of industrial capitalism. In addition, the stress on aisthesis sees working-class verbal directness coming to be valorized, Bon noting the elision of the article in a striker's comment that 'des jours c'est cafard' (D, 139) ['some days, you're down'], the brevity in Barbara G.'s description of her new job: 'Pontier, à Sollac' (D, 127) ['Crane operator, in Sollac'], and the nominal sentence she uses to affirm her class origins: 'Ouvrière dans les veines, père mineur' (D, 126) ['A worker through and through, father a miner']. Rendering audible these subordinate voices, Bon notes the economy with which linguistic tools are handled. 'On n'a pas demandé la vie tapis roulant ...' (D, 32) ['a conveyor belt wasn't our idea of life ...'], explains one woman who, seeing Bon eagerly noting her formulation, happily invites him to reuse it. This pooling of language as resource forms part of a wider project of co-production and points, Bon hopes, to redundant worker and writer engaging in a mutually beneficial self-affirmation. In the repudiation of social confinement and relegation, the synergy released counters the paternalism signalled in the adage: 'à petites vies, petites peines' (D, 33) ['small lives, small worries'].

---

32 See Chapters 1 and 6, above, for analysis of these heightened moments of aisthesis in Simon and Weil.

One of the most influential interlocutors in *Daewoo* is Sylvia F., described as having an imagination that refuses to be cramped by factory life. Her watchword, as reported by Maryse P., had been: 'quand tu mangeras ton pain tu sauras que la sueur de ton front est superflue. On est les superflues' (D, 28) ['when you eat your bread, you will know that the sweat of your brow is superfluous. We're the superfluous ones']. The rewriting of Genesis 3:19 (the biblical text refers to the eating of bread, with the sweat from labour on one's brow, this before returning to the earth as dust) stands as an act of self-assertion, as does the ironic internalization of society's violence, captured in the *superflues* label.[33] Importantly, Sylvia F.'s protest underscores the gendering of exclusion. Another of Bon's interlocutors anticipates the mechanism of social constraint functioning at a linguistic level when she insists in relation to her own state of mind: 'C'est ce que j'appelle l'angoisse d'être. Et si vous trouvez ça trop alambiqué pour une ouvrière, que voulez-vous que je vous dise' (D, 35–36) ['I call it the anguish of being. And if you find that convoluted and over-subtle for a working-class woman, what do you want me to say?']. The factory worker's complaint is redistributive in its impact in that it objects to the language of existential plight being apportioned asymmetrically following specific coordinates of gender and class. The allocation of spaces, identities, and forms of visibility which Rancière sees at work in 'des régimes d'émotion' ['regimes of emotion'] is thus strikingly applicable to *Daewoo*.[34]

Corporate discourse awakens in workers a suspicion about language, as Bon shows. Thus, those made redundant contest a 'knowledge' that is handed down to them. The Korean brand name itself, Daewoo, meaning 'vast universe' (D, 34), belies the constriction on a factory production line. Barbara G. reflects wryly on corporate mantras directed at workers, such as 'Défi, sacrifice, créativité' (D, 123) ['Challenge, sacrifice, creativity']. Marketing slogans – 'Daewoo, le rêve digital, Daewoo, la vie plus facile …' (D, 125) ['Daewoo the digital dream, Daewoo making life easier …'] – occlude the realities of a material production which sees an employee fitting doors on microwave ovens every working day over

33   Marx, it can be noted in passing, writes of how machinery is 'constantly on the point of making [the worker] superfluous'; see *Capital*, trans. Samuel Moore and Edward Aveling, 3 vols (Moscow: Progress Publishers, 1965), I, 435.

34   Rancière, *Aisthesis*, p. 10; *Aisthesis: Scenes from the Aesthetic Regime of Art*, p. x. The reflection on speech and noise, visibility and invisibility, in *Politique de la littérature*, p. 12, *The Politics of Literature*, p. 4 is also germane here.

a period of years. While the company's CEO calls for worker sacrifice, the accompanying grandiose promises are derided by Géraldine Roux, who likens it to narratives of otherworldly, biblical paradise. Roux is quick to expose the voice of capital: 'Chairman Kim, il résumait ça en express: – Partout où je vais, je sens l'argent' (D, 237) ['Chairman Kim summed it up in a word: – Everywhere I go, I smell money']. Weil writes in *L'Enracinement* of how, when money becomes the measure of all things, 'on a mis le poison de l'inégalité partout' ['we have laid the poison of inequality everywhere'].[35]

Alongside Roux's vibrant critique, other examples of workers' wit are celebrated: the crane driver who grandly proclaims himself to be above the fray that is the factory floor and can deftly use the crane to pick up a factory novice's lunch box and then set it back down, having removed its contents (D, 129); the banter surrounding the employee whose job is to check television sets by tapping them on the top and sides with a rubber hammer – he's likened to a bishop dispensing a baptismal blessing (D, 211); and the subversion of management English, as in 'Je *check le downsizing*' (D, 206). More soberly, when Bon reads in a letter written by Sylvia F. the affirmation 'Permanence du *non* intérieur [...], le socle même de ma personnalité' (D, 276) ['Permanence of the inner *no* (...), the very foundation of my personality'], it's as though he is reading the prose of Nathalie Sarraute. As DiIorio points out, the wording attributed to Sylvia F. and worthy of Sarraute is in fact taken from a speech by another leading novelist of the modern period, Assia Djebar, who in 2000 received the Friedenspreis. *Le Monde* published excerpts from that address which, DiIorio observes, 'frames writing as an exercise in resistance'.[36]

When factory closures are announced, they are the occasion for management explanation, which is offered as incontrovertible evidence to workers deemed incapable of understanding market forces. Jacotot's perspective as relayed in *Le Maître ignorant* is germane. In Rancière's formulation:

> il faut renverser la logique du système explicateur. L'explication n'est pas nécessaire pour remédier à une incapacité à comprendre. C'est au contraire cette *incapacité* qui est la fiction structurante de la conception explicatrice du monde.

35 Weil, *L'Enracinement*, p. 92.
36 The abridged version of Djebar's speech appeared in *Le Monde*, 26 October 2000. See DiIorio, 'Chaîne et Chaîne', pp. 13–14, 21.

[the logic of the explicative system had to be overturned. Explication is not necessary to remedy an incapacity to understand. On the contrary, that very incapacity provides the structuring fiction of the explicative conception of the world.][37]

Géraldine Roux notes management's preference for the term 'mutation' rather than 'crise' ['crisis'], while a government minister complains of workers' inflexibility: 'on garde toujours un haut fourneau dans sa tête' (D, 109) ['workers have this image of a factory furnace in their heads']. Yet for Roux, the powerful ['les gens du pouvoir'] are rewarded for manipulating language (D, 111). A more flagrant form of social control, signalled when riot police accompany a workers' delegation back to their coaches after a meeting with a government minister in Paris, prompts the reflection that 'le langage du pouvoir n'a pas trente-six finesses' (D, 165) ['the language of power isn't always a subtle thing'].

*   *   *

With social class often inscribed at a bodily level (Péguy, Weil, Simon, Ndiaye, and Beinstingel all document this), the hand frequently serves as a locus of identity. Péguy's lament for the worker's loss of manual strength has an epiphanic force in *L'Argent*.[38] One of Bon's interlocutors, Aurélie Loing, remarks that the hand acts like a shibboleth, allowing her to recognize fellow workers: 'Moi, ce que je regarde, c'est les mains' (D, 87) ['The hands are what I look at'], she insists, noting that 'les comme nous je les reconnais' (D, 86) ['I can spot the ones who are like us']. In a laconic reflection, she observes perceptively: 'Les mains ont la forme de ce qu'on leur fait faire' (D, 88) ['Hands are shaped by what we make them do']. More graphically, she spells out how distorted one woman's fingers became: 'Des gros doigts qui partaient directement du poignet et de la paume, tu vois?' (D, 88) ['huge fingers that seemed to come straight out of her wrist and palm, you see?']. Someone using a manual stapler on a production line is described by another worker as having 'elephant hands' (D, 190). While Bon's experience of insomnia caused by the human distress witnessed at Daewoo awakens in him memory of the work of Hieronymus Bosch, as we have seen, the graphic distortion

37 *Le Maître ignorant*, p. 15; *The Ignorant Schoolmaster*, p. 6.
38 See above, Chapter 2, pp. 58, 66.

of the production-line worker's hands actualizes that visual and affective disturbance. Similarly, in *Sortie d'usine*, it is as though the rough, often swollen hand of the factory worker only has the right to touch in the ritual of the morning handshake because it is 'enveloppée comme d'un gant de ce cuir impersonnel du travail' (SU, 52) ['enveloped in the glove, as it were, that forms from the impersonal leather of work'].

Reality TV reinforces a hostile normativity in *Daewoo*. Bon scrutinizes a chat show featuring rich and poor participants (D, 52–59) in which a camera focusses on the bodies of women factory workers and their jewellery. The instrumentalization in play complies with bourgeois codes of dress, speech, and bodily hexis, capturing how society apportions visibility to the economically privileged and the disadvantaged. The camera indulges what Stiegler refers to as the 'scopic drive' of voyeurism present in 'la *télévision pulsionnelle*'.[39] The panoptic monitoring of workers' movements in call centres in *Daewoo* extends the depiction of social control. Sylvia F. complains that at least at Daewoo, workers made television sets, whereas the absence of material traces of human productivity in the case of the call centre employee frustrates her: 'qu'est-ce que vous vendez, de la parole' (D, 272) ['all you sell is words'], is how she dismissively views such work. (As we saw, Beinstingel's *Retour aux mots sauvages* is given over to a detailed critique of such a world.) Sylvia F.'s remark registers a protest against sensory deprivation in a post-industrial age where enforced sedentariness, 'clic-clac sur le clavier' ['tap tap on a keyboard'], and the tight control of working space (5.8 square metres per employee) (D, 273) form the disciplinary arc of call centre life. As Rancière insists, 'politics revolves around what is seen and what can be said about it, [...] around the properties of spaces and the possibilities of time'.[40]

The tension between functionality and expressivity assumes numerous forms in *Daewoo*. Planning a holiday, factory workers consider Barcelona to be an exotic destination, contrasting it with what is familiar and local. As Sylvia F. remarks: 'Vous savez, les architectures folles: les nôtres sont un peu sages, ici, au pays des usines' (D, 289) ['It's the crazy architecture, you see. Here in the land of the factories, ours is a bit straight-laced']. Attempting to weaken the hold of the utilitarian, Bon's theatre project for the industrial wasteland is precisely a move to break a class-specific

---

39 Bernard Stiegler and *Ars industrialis*, *Réenchanter le monde. La valeur esprit contre le populisme industriel* (Paris: Flammarion, 2006), p. 9.
40 *The Politics of Aesthetics*, p. 8; cited in Davis, *Jacques Rancière*, p. 91.

and space-specific apportionment. To draw again on Rancière's research into nineteenth-century debates around equality,

> il ne s'agit pas de faire des grands peintres, il s'agit de faire des émancipés, des hommes capables de dire *et moi aussi je suis peintre*, formule où il n'entre nul orgueil mais au contraire le juste sentiment du pouvoir de tout être raisonnable.

> [it's not a matter of making great painters; it's a matter of making the emancipated: people capable of saying, 'me too, I'm a painter', a statement that contains nothing in the way of pride, only the reasonable feeling of power that belongs to any reasonable being.][41]

Reflecting on both individual and collective resourcefulness, *Daewoo* is indeed about empowerment and a levelling that is enabling. Just as factory workers may strain in their attempt to communicate, Bon views his own endeavour as a writer specifically as an essay in the etymological sense: '*essayant* que les mots redisent aussi ces silences, les yeux qui vous regardent ou se détournent' (D, 48; emphasis added) ['*trying* to have words express those silences, too, and the way people look at you or turn away']. The formulation recalls Michon's solemn, aspirational endeavour to retrieve obscure lives in *Vies minuscules*: 'Que [...] ils soient' (VM, 249) ['That (...) they may be' (SL, 215; translation modified)]. Theatre workshops, conversation-making, and writing serve precisely as antidotes to the experience of subordination. The factory, too, when it was operational, was a place of solidarity, a friend of Sylvia F.'s recalls from their conversations, even when workers were physically exhausted. Concerned by the need to engage directly with his subjects, Bon fears that his cultural project will be perceived as merely decorative and unconnected with the lives of unemployed women.

In one of the book's closing sections, 'échappée: l'usine blanche' ['vista: the white factory'], Bon attempts to stem that anxiety by spanning the world of the word and the material world as it confronts production-line workers. He makes explicit the desire to see manual labour and aesthetics drawn into a continuum. In a nostalgic, often romanticized evocation of a lime-processing factory close to the flooded banks of the Meuse, he comments on how the white dust from the lime 'recouvrait tout, transformait les véhicules mêmes en ébauches comme sculptés dans cette masse blanche uniforme' (D, 280) ['covered everything, transformed the vehicles themselves into sketches, sculpted

---

41   *Le Maître ignorant*, p. 113; *The Ignorant Schoolmaster*, pp. 66–67.

as it were in this white, uniform mass']. The picture painted is of a place deserted, the impression of stillness feeding a sense of aesthetic tranquillity. Yet the factory employs 170 shift workers, all engaged in intensely manual work to produce a material that has, Bon explains, many applications (steel production, water treatments, the cleaning of factory chimneys, and the production of paper, among others). He contrasts the Daewoo operation, tied to the movement of global capital, with the lime factory: 'ce très vieux métier de chaufournier traverse ainsi les plus hautes strates du moderne' (D, 282) ['this ancient craft of the lime kiln worker is thus linked with the highest strata of the modern']. Mesmerized by the scale of work at the site, he highlights the materiality of kiln production. Yet in inviting the reader to grasp the elemental quality of the labour involved, he also bridges the most physical of activities and text-production:

> Mais dans le gigantisme ici de tout, [...] le four à 1 200 degrés dans l'air gelé de la Meuse, et le paysage devenu monochrome, oui, s'ancrer dans l'idée élémentaire du travail: on arrache au sol, on broie et concasse, on transforme, et cette poussière qui nous recouvrait rejoindrait nos villes, nos trains, l'acier de nos voitures et même les pages de ce livre. (D, 282)

> [But on the gigantic scale of everything here (...), with the oven firing at 1,200 degrees in the frozen air of the River Meuse, and the countryside reduced to monochrome, yes, to be anchored in the elemental idea of work: material is excavated from the earth, crushed, pulverized, and transformed; and the dust that covered us would enter our cities, our trains, the steel used in our cars, and even the pages of this book.]

Bon attends to the scale of the vista he paints – a flooded riverbed, the intense heat, feverish human activity, the invasiveness of monochrome. The powerful affirmation in the use of *oui* invites the reader to comprehend physical work in its primal, unmediated form. No less pivotal is the closure given to the ekphrastic narrative, where, in the completion of the prose trajectory, it is as though Bon dares to reconcile physical toil and the labour of the book. Our earlier discussion of Michon included Van Gogh's reflection that 'peasants are of more use in the world' than he was as a painter. Removal from the terrain of productive necessity awakens a similar defensiveness in *Daewoo*. Yet, as if to counter what Bourdieu sees as art's predisposition to 'legitimat[e] social differences', Bon's implied hope is that paper and the word will be adequate to the task of representing a radically other, bodily experience, that of workers engaged in the calcination of lime, their day requiring unrelenting exposure to matter.[42] An underlying anxiety about writing's capacity to represent is thus irreducibly present. The broader spectrum of Bon's endeavour in *Daewoo* – an engagement with the victims of redundancy in ways that are aesthetic, ethical, and practical – is thus adumbrated in the capacious tribute to the white factory and the aspiration to connect word and world in the prose poem he constructs. Yet the spectre of unneeded-ness haunts the writer as much as it does the unemployed women who self-identify as 'les superflues' (D, 28).

Agamben's argument in *The Man Without Content* has a bearing on the attempted spanning of kiln and book in *Daewoo*. In a chapter entitled 'Privation Is Like a Face', he considers Marx's conclusions on the 'degrading division of labor into intellectual and manual labor' and explores their continuing relevance. Going back to Greek philosophy, Agamben rehearses for the reader how, in the original meaning of poiesis (from the verb *poiein*, 'to produce'), the term did not designate an art form among others but was rather 'the very name of man's *doing*, of that productive action of which artistic *doing* is only a privileged example'.[43] He goes on to reflect that, with the industrial revolution in the eighteenth century, 'the mode of presence of the things pro-duced by man becomes double: on the one hand there are the things that enter into presence according to the statute of aesthetics [...] and on the other hand there are those that [... are] products in the strict sense'.[44] Bon's evocation of the factory covered in lime dust reproduces this concurrence of the conventionally aesthetic (terms such as vista, sketch, sculpted) and technics, to borrow from Agamben (the vocabulary of working, excavating, crushing, pulverizing). At the level of his writing, Bon's scene seeks nevertheless a gathering together. This again connects with Agamben when he draws attention to the '*energetic* aspect, that is, the being-at-work of the work', an aspect that is lost, he argues, when the work is made available 'as mere support of aesthetic enjoyment'.[45] Bon's alignment of the endeavours of field worker and factory worker, the handler of stones and the wordsmith, thus comes under the sign of poiesis as 'the very name of man's *doing*'.[46] Indeed his engagement with

---

42   Bourdieu, *Distinction*, p. 7.
43   Agamben, *The Man Without Content*, p. 59.
44   Agamben, *The Man Without Content*, pp. 60–61.
45   Agamben, *The Man Without Content*, p. 66.
46   Agamben, *The Man Without Content*, p. 59.

communities of manual workers provides an emblem of the reconciliation Agamben advocates when he writes that

> it is [...] starting from this self-suppression of the privileged status of
> 'artistic work', which now gathers the two sides of the halved apple of
> human pro-duction in their irreconcilable opposition, that it will be
> possible to exit the swamp of aesthetics and technics and restore to the
> poetic status of man on earth its original dimension.[47]

The book-to-life, life-to-book oscillation in *Sortie d'usine* discussed
earlier is similarly consistent with Agamben's call for an ethics of human
activity beyond alienation.

Daewoo is not offered as a finished object for cultural consumption.
Its compositional method confirms this, the poetic tension in prose
being 'the movement whereby one extorts from the real that feeling of
presence' (D, 119). This is prose's *'energetic* aspect', to use Agamben's
formulation. Like the theatre project and the transcribing of voices in
their at-workness, this poiesis also encompasses what Bon sees around
him and actively records – in manual labour, in factory production and
furnaces, in redundant workers of whom Valérie Aumont observes,
as noted above, that if they have made progress, it's at the level of
inner knowledge (D, 101). *Daewoo*'s status as project and collaborative
production encapsulates the notion of at-workness.

Inimical to this culture of reflexivity and interrogation is the practice
of social *dressage*, as explored by Nizan in *Antoine Bloyé*. Towards the
end of *Daewoo*, Bon reports on coming across a dog training centre.
Dwelling on the trainer's manual, he wonders how later generations
might understand such material and attempt to reconstruct a wider
culture from it. Not unpredictably, he asks if the nature of relations
between trainer and animal might have a wider, societal bearing. He
thus provides an echo of 'le bon dressement' as explored by Foucault
in *Surveiller et punir*.[48] Bon notes the practice advocated by company
management in Daewoo whereby supervisors would stand immediately
behind employees for minutes on end. With the culture of subordination
consolidating the analogy with the dog trainer's manual, Bon's project,
by contrast, seeks to empower the governed through speech acts and
theatre.

---

47 Agamben, *The Man Without Content*, p. 67.
48 For earlier reference to the section in *Surveiller et punir* entitled 'Les Moyens
du bon dressement', see Chapter 5, p. 118.

Beauty is a further dimension in the protest of striking *Daewoo* workers, Nadia Nasseri referring enthusiastically to the two nights when she kept vigil in what has become the transformed space of the factory. The workings of perception will become the vehicle that gives reader and spectator access to the reality of the lives of the *superflues*. Bon explores how theatrical and filmic representation might capture the situation facing the unemployed. He imagines the faces of the 35,000 workers who lost their jobs in Valenciennes over a five-year period as forming a sequence in a silent, black-and-white film. And in a play staged in one of the empty Daewoo factories, he plans to give visual prominence to the material signs of its industrial use and to project in slow sequence photos of the women from the Villers and Fameck plants: 'apparaîtraient succes-sivement mais géants, les visages des cinq cents ouvrières' (D, 255) ['the faces of the 500 women factory workers would appear successively in giant enlargements']. Bon's theatre would thus recreate everyday factory life, 'à la chaîne et dans les vestiaires' (D, 256) ['on the production line and in the locker rooms']. It would include a 'Ways of being together?' question ['Façons d'être ensemble?'] floated in conversations involving a group of four actresses and eliciting a series of affirmations around group identity – being in tune with others on the production line, the shared silence and respite of the locker room after a shift, a folding of arms signalling group defiance of a management order, the fire as symbol of solidarity around which striking workers congregate, and so on (D, 256–57). In its resourceful exploration of individual lives and collective identities, Bon's project aims to counter social isolation. Yet he is forced to concede that a number of the women providing individual testimonies avoid eye contact with him, their tales of directionlessness, divorce, and illness reinforcing a reality of unwelcome social disaggregation.

*   *   *

Modern utopia, Rancière argues, has less to do with talk of a mythical island than the belief that one can show, in every situation, 'l'adéquation du texte et de la réalité' ['the adequation of text and reality'].[49] As though heeding Rancière's objection, Bon is cautious about the claims he makes for his Daewoo project, fearing in particular the inadequacy

---

49   *Courts voyages au pays du peuple*, p. 48; *Short Voyages to the Land of the People*, p. 36.

of writing to capture the lived reality of his subjects. He articulates nevertheless a stubborn will to resist: 'dire, contre l'effacement même' (D, 96) ['to speak out, against obliteration itself']. Referring enthusiastically to Perec and specifically to the conclusion in *Espèces d'espaces* ['Species of Spaces'] with its longing for places that would provide stable reference points, Bon similarly searches for images and words adequate to the immediate task of human engagement in an industrial wasteland. Perec concludes his text by calling for writing to provide such a trace or reference point.[50]

Caygill argues that 'it is perhaps in the very indeterminacy of poetry or art [...] that [...] openness to the future of affirmative resistance can be experienced'.[51] In the hybrid project that is *Daewoo*, Bon writes of the act of convoking ['convoquer' (D, 12)] in relation to the faces, languages, and signs encountered in the course of his collaboration with redundant workers. Feeding into the work's experimental character, the act of assembly counters the paradigm of the no-longer-needed. In this way, it recalls Rancière's observation on the politics of fiction seen in terms of 'the populations that it convokes' and the relations of inclusion and exclusion that it operates.[52]

---

50   Perec writes: 'Ecrire [...] laisser, quelque part, un sillon, une trace' ['To write (...) to leave, somewhere, a furrow, a trace'] in *Espèces d'espaces* (Paris: Galilée, 2000 [1974]), p. 180.
51   Caygill, *On Resistance*, p. 174.
52   See *Le Fil perdu*, p. 12; *The Lost Thread*, p. xxxiii.

CHAPTER TEN

Circuits of Reappropriation

Accessing the Real in
the Work of Didier Eribon

Par et dans le choix de cette écriture, je crois que
j'assume et dépasse la déchirure culturelle.

[Through, and in the choice of, this writing, I believe
I am accepting and getting beyond cultural fracture.]

Ernaux[1]

Another contemporary narrative that charts class identity specifically
through the prism of language is Didier Eribon's autobiographical
work *Retour à Reims* (2009). The author uses an array of terms to
convey the affective disturbance that he associates with the project:
'malaise', 'mélancolie' ['melancholy'], 'désarroi' ['disarray'], 'infériori-
sation' ['subordination'].[2] Aiming to retrieve his earlier life experience
in a working-class milieu in northern France, he makes numerous cross-
textual references, both in this text and its sequel, *La Société comme
verdict* ['Society as Verdict'], to theories concerning the figure of the
class migrant or *transfuge de classe* who experiences what Bourdieu
calls a 'split *habitus*' ['*habitus* clivé'] (RR, 14; RGR, 12).[3] These theories
are drawn from literature, politics, and ethnography, in particular from

---

1 Annie Ernaux, *L'Écriture comme un couteau. Entretien avec Frédéric-Yves
Jeannet* (Paris: Stock, 2003), p. 35.

2 Didier Eribon, *Retour à Reims* (Paris: Flammarion, 2010 [2009]), pp. 14,
15, 19, 23; subsequently cited as RR; *Returning to Reims*, trans. Michael Lucey
(London: Allen Lane, 2018), pp. 12, 16, 21; hereinafter cited as RGR.

3 Didier Eribon, *La Société comme verdict* (Paris: Flammarion, 2014 [2013]);
subsequent references are indicated using the abbreviation SV.

works by Annie Ernaux, John Edgar Wideman, James Baldwin, Raymond Williams, Michel Foucault, and Pierre Bourdieu. In the concluding pages of *Retour à Reims*, he reflects that the mediation constituted by this matrix of references provides a framework that allows him to approach the question of his social origins. The spectrum of intertextual reference notably serves to 'neutraliser la charge émotionnelle qui serait sans doute trop forte s'il fallait affronter le "réel" sans cet écran' (RR, p. 246) ['neutralize the emotional charge that might otherwise be too strong if you had to confront the "real" without the help of an intervening screen' (RGR, 237)]

The current chapter seeks to consider the ways in which this filtering of the real and of its emotional charge is a feature of Eribon's trajectory. It additionally considers those modern and contemporary authors whose 'confrontations with the real' he charts. Central to my argument is that in the representation of the obstacles confronting these authors – which are variously social, sexual, and racial – forms of textual digression and detour, be they theoretical, fictional, or bibliographical, constitute a recurring feature. Accessing the real may thus come via a process of circuitous reappropriation.

Such a process has ramifications for the question of form in that the reach to a real that is problematical in personal terms or that is socially contested often manifests itself precisely as anxiety or inhibition in respect of form. Venturing, for example, into recognizably literary spaces may be seen by the writer as an unpalatable intervention in that the form carries connotations of class exclusion. Yet, as Eribon asserts, it is the intertextual screen that allows him to approach the fraught question of psychosocial background. In the case of the prominent figures whose achievements he champions – Foucault, Bourdieu, and Wideman, for example – the historical archive, sociological enquiry, and the genre of conventional autobiography become the orbits along which the personal is ambiguously and obscurely tracked. These authors, then, lay claim to our attention precisely because of their interrogation of questions to do with form, detour, and indirection.

Rancière, too, considers the importance of the deflection or shift for the figure of the proletarian seeking a knowledge of self which is accessed 'par le détour du secret des autres' ['circuitously by way of the secret of others'].[4] The bourgeois world that emerges from his study of nineteenth-century workers' archives divides, he argues, into two:

4   *La Nuit des prolétaires*, p. 32; *Proletarian Nights*, p. 20.

those whose self-satisfied lifestyle points to a 'vegetative existence', and others who abandon domestic comforts 'pour partir à la recherche de l'inconnu: les inventeurs, les poètes, les amoureux du peuple et de la République, les organisateurs des cités de l'avenir et les apôtres des religions nouvelles' ['to set out in search of the unknown: the inventors, the poets, the lovers of the people and the Republic, the organizers of the cities of the future, and the apostles of new religions'].[5] The proletariat similarly divides, Rancière goes on, into those complicit with their oppression and those who seek independence. In the latter case, cultural otherness is a means of pursuing 'ces passions, ces désirs d'un autre monde que la contrainte du travail rabote continuellement' ['those passions and desires for another world which the constraints of labour continually blunt'].[6]

While Rancière's plane metaphor (in the verb *raboter*) captures emblematically lives shaped by material production, he nevertheless entertains possibilities of redemption, as *La Nuit des prolétaires* amply documents. In sharp contrast, Eribon's portrayal of what he refers to as social destinies is predicated on a sombre determinism, as the metaphor of unmediated branding conveys: 'les sentences sont gravées sur nos épaules, au fer rouge, au moment de notre naissance' (RR, 52–53) ['Our sentences are burned into the skin of our shoulder with a red hot iron at the moment of our birth'] (RGR, 47)]. This social marking is reinforced, Eribon argues, through established antinomies such as the utilitarian, slanted conventionally towards the working class, and the cultural, seen as a bourgeois preserve. This provides a variant on the class segregation outlined in the myth of the three metals posited by Plato in his *Republic*. Eribon weighs up the paradox whereby, as a thinker, he was opposed to political and intellectual hierarchy and yet in experiential terms he consciously distanced himself from 'the "people"' (RR, 73; RGR, 68).

As reconstructed by Eribon, the return to Reims of the book's title comes after decades during which its author, living in Paris, pursued his career as a journalist, thinker, and gay rights campaigner. The return to roots was prompted by the death of his father, a manual worker with the prejudices of many of his generation and class. The *retour* allows Eribon to reflect on what he presents as parallel forms of social marginality: the fact of having been born into a proletarian family living just outside

---

5   *La Nuit des prolétaires*, p. 32; *Proletarian Nights*, p. 20.
6   *La Nuit des prolétaires*, p. 32; *Proletarian Nights*, p. 20 (translation modified).

Reims, on the one hand, and the experience of being adrift from the heterosexual normativity present in the working-class community in which he grew up.

These twin expressions of outsiderness connect crucially, for Eribon, in a relationship of rivalry. He insists in somewhat binary fashion that the flight from working-class culture was the necessary precondition for his finding sexual liberation. It is as though the shelving of one aspect of his identity might allow for the realization and expression of another. Authoring *Réflexions sur la question gay* (published in 1999) would thus constitute one strand, the publication of *Retour à Reims* representing another, in the author's identitarian search. But by Eribon's admission, the two (social and sexual) are dialectically linked: 'je dus me façonner moi-même en jouant de l'un contre l'autre' (RR, 230) ['I was obliged to shape myself by playing one off against the other' (RGR, 219)]. As Michael Sheringham reflects in a discussion of the theme of new directions taken in individual lives, such turning points may 'answer a need for coherence, but at the risk of traducing something very valuable'.[7]

Through the workings of the 'retour', Eribon comes to reappropriate a discarded, proletarian identity, a past which he had found alienating. Here again, Sheringham's reflection on turning points is relevant: 'to think of a life as having a shape, as hanging together around some major articulations, is a way of bridging the gap between ourselves and others'.[8] Citing James Baldwin, Eribon refers to the return to one's origins as an embracing of life: 'To avoid the journey back is to avoid the Self, to avoid "life"' (RR, 34; RGR, 30).

These calls for attentiveness to discarded forms of 'life' are sounded not only in the projects of Baldwin and Eribon but also in texts by Ernaux, whose influence Eribon acknowledges in a series of references to her work. Coincidentally, Ernaux fashions her own 'return', the text *Retour à Yvetot* ['Return to Yvetot'] (2013) being a transcript of a lecture given in the autumn of 2012 in the town where she grew up. Ernaux looks back on how she had come to settle, selectively, for just one 'héritage', namely that of 'l'ecole, l'université et la littérature' ['school, university, and literature'].[9] There is a clear link to Eribon where a

---

7   Michael Sheringham, 'On Turning Points', a Sermon Preached in the Chapel of All Souls College, Oxford, 2 November 2008 (Oxford: All Souls College, no date), p. 6.

8   Sheringham, 'On Turning Points', p. 10.

9   Annie Ernaux, *Retour à Yvetot* (Paris: Mauconduit, 2013), p. 28.

comparable choice is made – Paris, writing, intellectual pursuits. In both cases, the adoption of literary form seals the social divorce. In the same lecture, Ernaux evokes 'un retour au réel' (RY, 29) ['a return to the real'] which she experienced when teaching in a *lycée technique* in the Haute Savoie. Faced with a class of forty pupils drawn predominantly from the region's urban and rural working class, she is drawn up short by the gap between the literature she is teaching and 'leur culture d'origine [...]. Je constatais aussi l'injustice d'une reproduction des inégalités sociales au travers de l'école' (RY, 29) ['their culture of origin (...). I also noted the injustice that saw social inequalities reproduced through school']. The reflections of both Ernaux and Eribon confirm what elsewhere Rancière refers to as 'l'ancestrale hiérarchie' ['the ancestral hierarchy'] that ensures the subordination of those destined to work with their hands to those 'qui ont reçu le privilège de la pensée' ['who have received the privilege of thought'].[10]

But to propose a conflation of the positions of Eribon and Rancière would be entirely mistaken. Both Eribon and Ernaux find in Bourdieu's work a convincing theorization of the forms of cultural exclusion they themselves evoke, Bourdieu arguing that academic inequalities are enshrined ineradicably in the social system.[11] Siding squarely with Bourdieu, Eribon vehemently accuses Rancière of being ignorant of the realities of working-class life and dismisses as an exercise in fantasizing the principle of radical equality set out in *Le Maître ignorant*: 'c'est refuser de voir ce qu'est l'inégalité dans la réalité' ['it's a refusal to see how inequality works in reality'].[12]

An important analysis by Jeremy Lane of the different standpoints of Rancière and Bourdieu allows us to understand better the respective positions in play. Lane explains how, for Bourdieu, any belief in the democratic potential of Kant's aesthetic universal amounts to 'the misrecognized expression of class privilege'.[13] Lane further argues

---

10   *La Nuit des prolétaires*, p. 8.

11   For Ernaux's tribute to Pierre Bourdieu in the wake of his death, see 'Bourdieu: le chagrin', *Le Monde*, 5 February 2002, https://www.lemonde.fr/archives/article/2002/02/05/bourdieu-le-chagrin-par-annie-ernaux_261466_1819218.html.

12   Didier Eribon, *Retours sur 'Retour à Reims'* (Paris: Editions Cartouche, 2014), p. 30.

13   Jeremy F. Lane, 'Rancière's Anti-Platonism: Equality, the "Orphan Letter" and the Problematic of the Social Sciences', in Oliver Davis (ed.), *Rancière Now: Current Perspectives on Jacques Rancière* (Cambridge: Polity, 2013), pp. 28–46 (p. 31).

that for Rancière, on the other hand, the position of seeing Kant's aesthetic judgement as a universal can only be accommodated outside the frame of sociology, given the claim of the social sciences to hold the objective knowledge that will lay bare the workings of social relations. (Rancière writes of how Marxism had retained a fundamental tenet of Plato's social order 'en inscrivant la vérité sur le corps même des prolétaires pour mieux réserver aux savants le privilège de l'y déchiffrer' ['by inscribing truth on the very bodies of the proletarians in order to reserve for experts the exclusive privilege of deciphering such truth'].)[14] For Bourdieu, aesthetics, like philosophy and education, requires 'the scholastic point of view', *scholē*, or leisure, being the condition that affords freedom from pressing material needs.[15] In this way, Lane concludes, improbable as it seems given his status as a radical sociologist of the Left, Bourdieu comes to share Plato's view that workers are unable to reflect objectively on their condition. A cornerstone of Rancière's argument, by contrast, is the interrogation of the three metals myth advanced by Plato.

*   *   *

The question of ancestral illiteracy which Ernaux addresses in *La Place* is again a feature in *Retour à Reims*. One of Eribon's grandmothers was illiterate, a condition which he sees as reinforcing 'cette soumission à la réalité' ['a submission to reality'] in which the social apportionment governing productive necessity and consumption ensures the perpetuation of a hierarchical order (RR, 47; RGR, 42). In a similar way, the *cité-jardin* in which Eribon's father lived before the author was born is referred to as 'un lieu de relégation sociale. Une réserve de pauvres' (RR, 48) ['a place of social ostracism [...] a reservation for the poor' (RGR, 43)]. In a manner that recalls the destiny of the children of cobblers as set out by Plato in the *Republic*, Eribon points to an inexorable determinism that denies the working class access to certain forms of cultural and economic capital. The factory is thus described as 'waiting for' Eribon's father, then a not-quite fourteen-year-old school-leaver (RR, 50; RGR, 45). Eribon argues that, in the case of working-class lives, the mental outlook is nothing other than 'le produit, gravé en nous, sédimenté de

14   *Le Philosophe et ses pauvres*, p. viii.
15   Lane, 'Rancière's Anti-Platonism', p. 33.

strate en strate, de la longue fréquentation du monde extérieur' (SV, 37) ['the product of the long encounter with the world, burnt into us, a layer-by-layer sedimentation']. In the case of Michon's illiterate miller in *Vies minuscules*, it is the social order, built, we saw, around medical knowledge, which provides the context for his relegation.[16]

Eribon's metaphor of geological stratification reinforces the characterization of his father as 'cet être-au-monde si précisément situé' ['this being-in-the-world so precisely situated' (translation modified)], the constriction explaining, in Eribon's words, 'la semi-folie de mon père' (RR, 35) ['the near-madness of my father' (RGR, 31)].[17] For the sociologist in Eribon, this accounts for the father's inability to establish relationality with others. Thus, with the accretions of social sedimentation comes emotional disturbance. Eribon's mother, he adds, asks him to look charitably on the faults of a father who had worked to support his family. Her intervention brings to mind for Eribon the case of James Baldwin, himself reminded by his mother of the conditioning undergone by his father.

The contradiction that Eribon sees in his own position is that, whereas he is opposed in principle, as a writer and intellectual, to social exploitation, in practice he had disowned the proletarian world in which he grew up (RR, 72, 88; RGR, 68, 84). Self-incrimination thus forms a base layer in the psychological self-portrait to be found in *Retour à Reims*. The hard manual work of a parent, Eribon writes with regret, is the precondition that allows him to study Marx, Trotsky, Beauvoir, Genet, Kant, and Aristotle. He recalls in this regard Ernaux's reflection in *Une femme* that her mother sold groceries all day long to allow her daughter to sit in a lecture theatre learning about Plato.[18] Access to literary composition, philosophy, and political theory is thus predicated on the manual toil of others. Pointedly in Eribon's narrative of family life, while the exhausted industrial labourer sleeps, her would-be radical son reads. Looking at the physically diminished body of his mother who for years had worked on a production line, Eribon reflects: 'je suis frappé par ce que signifie concrètement, physiquement, l'inégalité sociale' (RR, 85)

16   See Chapter 7, p. 167.

17   Translation modified. The depiction of the father carries a Foucauldian echo. I will come to Eribon's biographical work on the author of *Histoire de la folie à l'âge classique* later in the chapter.

18   Annie Ernaux, *Une femme* (Paris: Gallimard, 1988), p. 66; quoted in RR, 84–85; RGR, 80.

['I can't help but be struck by what social inequality means concretely, physically' (RGR, 80)]. The text thus draws out the corporeal manifestation of what Eribon terms the naked violence of exploitation. His understanding of Marxism was, he writes self-critically, 'une façon d'idéaliser la classe ouvrière, de la transformer en une entité mythique' (RR, 86) ['a way of idealizing the working class, of transforming it into a mythical entity' (RGR, 82)]. By contrast, the precariousness of working-class lives acquires for Eribon an urgent, somatic manifestation: 'Un corps d'ouvrière', he writes, 'quand il vieillit, montre à tous les regards ce qu'est la vérité de l'existence des classes' (RR, 85) ['A worker's body, as it ages, reveals to anyone who looks at it the truth about the existence of classes' (RGR, 80–81)]. In a continuation of this seam of social determinism, Édouard Louis, in a novel which he dedicates to Eribon, evokes the lives of male adolescents in modern-day, working-class northern France, referring to 'ces corps, déjà marqués par leur classe sociale' ['those bodies, already marked by their social class'].[19]

With the return to Reims, then, the textbook Marxist accounts of proletarian life which had served as reference points for Eribon are contradicted by evidence from real lives – the musculoskeletal damage sustained by one of his brothers, for example, a butcher who for decades had carried animal carcasses (RR, 113; RGR, 105). Indeed, Eribon takes left-wing intellectuals to task for what he presents as a class ethnocentrism that sees them make pronouncements he judges to be socially disconnected (RR, 155; RGR, 145). While not naming individual thinkers, his vehement, coded denunciation refers to those whose contact with working-class lives, he asserts, comes through a reading of nineteenth-century texts. The tone anticipates his overt, irascible dismissal of Rancière as a died-in-the-wool 'Maoist bourgeois intellectual' in the slim volume that forms a sequel to *Retour à Reims*.[20]

Eribon's own concern with revolutionary class politics had served to cover up 'le jugement social que je portais sur mes parents, ma famille, et mon désir d'échapper à leur monde' (RR, 88) ['the social judgment that I had passed on my parents and my family, (…) my desire to escape from their world' (RGR, 84)]. Micro-familial pressures collide, then, with a broader, theoretical perspective. In his willed social-class migration, Eribon has become blind to the aspiration of relatives to be part of a consumerist culture. In his own Marxist phase, his reflex had been, in

19   Édouard Louis, *En finir avec Eddy Bellegueule* (Paris: Seuil, 2014), p. 153.
20   Eribon, *Retours sur 'Retour à Reims'*, p. 32.

his damning self-assessment, to 'exalter "la classe ouvrière" pour mieux m'éloigner des ouvriers réels' (RR, 88) ['I glorified the "working class" in order to put more distance between myself and actual workers' (RGR, 84)]. Given that the tensions explored in *Retour à Reims* flow from the energies of class disengagement, we are able to contrast Rancière's approving exploration in *La Nuit des prolétaires* of social disaggregation and Eribon's dismissal of the phenomenon as channelling a deep alienation.

* * *

The going back to Reims brings, then, an urgent engagement with working-class lives in contemporary France and a correction of the author's 'désidentification sociale' (RR, 88) ['social disidentification' (RGR, 84)]. In another caustic review of intellectual pronouncements on the real, Eribon records his impatience with psychological and psychoanalytical explanations, these serving, he cautions, to de-socialize and depoliticize. Frustrated by, and rewriting, Lacan, he proposes:

> un stade du miroir social [...]; une scène d'interpellation sociale – et non psychique ou idéologique – par la découverte de la situation sociologique de classe. (RR, 97)

> [a social mirror stage (...) a scene of interpellation, but a social, not a psychic or an ideological one; it was an interpellation involving the discovery of a class-based sociological situation. (RGR, 91)]

Eribon similarly questions Deleuze's definition of the Left as entailing an outlook that functions globally (thereby encompassing the Third World, for example).[21] The Left which Eribon encounters in working-class north-eastern France is, by contrast, one tightly wedded to protest against immediate social conditions. Moreover, the return to Reims sees him confronted with the rise of the Front National, whose views his own family and community of origin now endorse, this deriving from a broader movement of heightened racism in the 1970s and 1980s. Eribon interprets this evolution as being in part, and however paradoxical, 'comme le dernier recours des milieux populaires pour défendre leur identité collective, et en tout cas une dignité qu'ils sentaient comme

---

21   Gilles Deleuze, 'Gauche', in *L'Abécédaire de Gilles Deleuze*, DVD, Editions du Montparnasse, 2004, quoted in RR, 43–44; RGR, pp. 38–39.

toujours piétinée' (RR, 134) ['the final recourse of people of the working classes attempting to defend their collective identity, or to defend, in any case, a dignity that was being trampled on' (RGR, 126)]. Uninhibited by political correctness, Eribon thus attempts to fathom the politics of reaction within the working class. In an analogous way, the suspicion which he directs against theory becomes part of an attempt, however conflicted, to rehabilitate a discarded way of life.

A Work of Social Vigilance

In both Eribon and Ernaux, the French educational system is depicted as a powerful vector in the propagation of a culture that is bourgeois, with an attendant relegation of particular forms of the real. Ernaux's recollection of the alienating experience of teaching in a *lycée technique* has been noted. Both writers refer to their earlier ignorance of the culture of educational elitism: the *classes prépas* and the *grandes écoles* (the former being the years of study in preparation for possible admission to the latter, which are France's most exclusive institutions of higher education). Eribon refers to it as a pathway of which he had been totally oblivious. Ernaux, in turn, refers to her family's ignorance of the *filières* or discipline-specific pathways in the school curriculum and the workings of educational exclusion, adding that *hypokhâgne* and *khâgne* (RY, 27–28) – stages in the *classes prépas* cycle – were unheard of within her class of social origin. For both authors, the privileging of very specific discursive forms reinforces the devalorization of post-war working-class culture. We might add that Paul Nizan, whose novel *Antoine Bloyé* Eribon references in *Retour à Reims*, offers an acerbic, interwar-years view of the École Normale Supérieure where he studied, the institution acting, in Nizan's image, as a concealer of 'l'existence charnelle de nos frères' ['the flesh-and-blood existence of our brothers'].[22]

Ernaux writes of her own trajectory as that of an immigrant from within ['immigrée de l'intérieur'] in French society, with her writing entailing a breaking and entering into 'le savoir intellectuel' ['intellectual knowledge'].[23] Confronted with class divisions that are reinforced at every point, Eribon protests about the presence of 'une étanchéité presque totale entre les mondes sociaux' (RR, 51) ['(a) barrier between

---

22   Paul Nizan, *Aden Arabie* (Paris: La Découverte, 2002 [1931]), p. 60. See RR, 26; RGR, 24.

23   Ernaux, *L'Écriture comme un couteau*, pp. 34–35.

social worlds [that] was utterly impermeable' RGR, 46)]. In a telling litany of social relegation and subordination, he assembles a lexicon of rules, frontiers, barriers, exclusions, and social inertia, and advocates the breaking of 'les catégories incorporées de la perception et les cadres institués de la signification' (RR, 52) ['incorporated categories of perception and established frameworks of meaning' (RGR, 47)].

Yet, in Eribon's account, the class that is so tightly governed in turn becomes the site of homophobic culture. He draws out the linguistic resourcefulness of that culture, the real being evoked in *Retour à Reims* through a language of incision, imposition, and branding: he confesses to having felt 'frappé, brûlé, glacé' (RR, 207) ['struck (...), burned, frozen' (RGR, 197)]; the experience of being gay releases a fear of being 'moqué, stigmatisé ou psychanalysé' (RR, 207) ['mocked, stigmatized, psychonanalyzed' (RGR, 196)]; and the term 'pédé' ['faggot'] 'venait me transpercer comme un coup de couteau' (RR, 204) ['seemed to stab me like a knife' (RGR, 194)]. The abusive synonyms used to denote someone who is gay – '"tapette", "tantouze" "tata"' (RR, 204) ['a "fairy", or a "fruit", or a "queer"' (RGR, 194)] – provide further evidence of the linguistic energies that feed conformism in Eribon's community of origin. Still, he speaks out against not just physical attacks on homosexuals but also 'un autre type d'agression [...] discursive et culturelle' (RR, 222) ['a different kind of assault (...) a cultural and discursive one' (RGR, 210–11)] which he specifically sees at work within psychiatry and psychoanalysis. The suspicion directed against theory is thus part of the identitarian quest that forms the core of the text.

The consequences of the process of disidentification which saw him abandon the milieu of his birth are gauged by Eribon in specifically Bourdieusian terms. Whereas his brother is employed in an abattoir, Eribon describes himself aged sixteen as constructing the ethos of a student at the *lycée*, his dress sense, hairstyle, and choice of music all distancing him from a brother who continued to show 'un *ethos* populaire' (RR, 110) ['a working-class ethos' (RGR, 103)]. Intrafamilial difference provides a negative definition of identity formation: 'ne pas être comme lui' (RR, 114) ['not to be like [my brother]' (RGR, 105)] is the imperative governing the younger Eribon's outlook.

The disowning of siblings is again in evidence in *La Société comme verdict*, where Eribon confesses to denying that he was related to a garage worker with the same surname who was in fact one of his brothers (SV, 35). He reflects moreover on how he literally excised from a photo of his parents the image of his father, an act which he classifies as being 'étrange et lamentable' (SV, 36) ['strange and appalling']. If shame is adduced by Eribon as an explanation for the mutilation of the photo, he sees the emotion as having a powerful collective hold, referring to 'la réalité hontologique du monde social' (SV, 36) ['the shame-driven reality of the social world']. Drawing on comments by Bourdieu on the Kabyle writer Mouloud Mammeri, Eribon presents shame as, in Bourdieu's view, 'cette forme suprême de la dépossession' (SV, 87) ['that supreme form of dispossession']. The disowning and evacuation of identity make all the more radical the reappropriation of a particular form of social real in *Retour à Reims*.

*   *   *

Eribon's search for models of understanding that are cognate with his own project also sees him explore anglophone literature. John Edgar Wideman's *Brothers and Keepers* (1984) offers him a parallel example of a gulf that separates siblings, in this case that between the author, who is a university teacher, and his younger brother convicted of an armed robbery that ends in homicide. Eribon concedes that the gulf in Wideman between the black neighbourhood in industrial Pittsburgh where he grew up and the university position he came to occupy is wider than the one confronting the son who goes back to Reims. He identifies nevertheless with Wideman's initial haste to shed his origins. Of his criminal brother's behaviour, Wideman writes: 'Your words and gestures belonged to a language I was teaching myself to unlearn'.[24] In Eribon, the process of social unlearning is no less tensely evoked:

> Il me fallait exorciser le diable en moi, le faire sortir de moi. Ou le rendre invisible, pour que personne ne puisse deviner sa présence. Ce fut pendant des années un travail de chaque instant. (RR, 115)

> [I needed to exorcise the devil in me, to get it out – or else to make it invisible, so that no one could detect its presence. For many years this was something I worked on during every moment of my life. (RGR, 107)]

Wideman's vigilance is thus echoed in Eribon's erasure of a social real which *Retour à Reims* will seek to reverse. In both cases, self-censorship serves as trailer to a writing of reconnection. Neither author, however,

---

24   John Edgar Wideman, *Brothers and Keepers* (New York: Vintage Books, 1995 [1984]), p. 26; hereinafter cited as BK.

sees his intervention as being unequivocally reparative. In Wideman's case, his book becomes a co-production with his imprisoned sibling, *Brothers and Keepers* containing substantial sections of first-person reflection narrated by the younger brother. Yet the book, which Wideman would wish to be redemptive, risks merely accentuating the divide between siblings; it would 'belong to the world beyond the prison walls. Ironically, it would validate the power of the walls' (BK, 199).

Wideman is thus alert to the tension between textual composition and the call of a lived reality that may be spurned by such writing. He asks if the collaborative writing project might not spell the traducing of something valuable in terms of interpersonal connection: 'Was the whole thing between us about a book or had something finer, truer been created?' (BK, 200), he asks. In a restatement of this anxiety, he acknowledges the distance between him and his sibling: 'Many of my worries clearly were not his. I was the writer, that was *my* kitchen, *my* heat' (BK, 200).

In *La Société comme verdict*, Eribon reflects that the world of intellectual liberty to which he had aspired 'se révèle le lieu d'une quasi-servilité généralisée et plus ou moins adoptée comme mode de vie et intériorisée' (SV, 112) ['shows itself to be a place of virtual slavery, generalized, adopted as a way of life more or less, and internalized']. To Wideman's image of writerly angst, we can thus add Eribon's view of an intellectual culture that enslaves those who aspire to be part of it. High culture's use of the adjective *populaire* stands as masked aggression for Eribon, who sees the term having 'une fonction d'euphémisation de la violence que comporte cette assignation à l'infériorité' (SV, 116) ['a euphemizing function in relation to the violence entailed by this relegation to a position of inferiority']. For the author of *La Société comme verdict*, his own avowedly frenetic quest for bourgeois culture has led to a powerful disidentification in relation to his roots (SV, 142).

Yet the violence practised by a more powerful social class also comes to be internalized by the social subordinate, as Eribon recalls when evoking the case of his pregnant, unmarried grandmother. She is banished from the family home by a father who, in placing a curse on his daughter, gives expression less to individual venom than to a socially conditioned response: 'sa dureté ne faisait que répéter des attitudes et des énoncés déjà produits avant lui; son propos revêt un caractère citationnel' (SV, 140) ['his harshness merely repeated attitudes and utterances already pronounced before him; his words had a citational character']. If the derivative nature of verbal violence reinforces the concept of social verdict in Eribon's title, the term may be read etymologically as a 'true saying', a *verum dictum* that remains nevertheless societal in origin.

While unambiguously endorsing Wideman's project, Eribon's review of anglophone literature that addresses specifically the question of social-class migration also throws up elements of trenchant critique. He sees Richard Hoggart's *The Uses of Literacy*, for example, as reinforcing gender stereotyping of the most conventional kind. While welcoming certain aspects of Hoggart's evocation of northern English popular culture, Eribon criticizes him for depicting negatively those working-class women who refused to follow the school-to-factory-to-marriage habitus that Hoggart evokes approvingly: 'les femmes libres', writes Eribon, 'représentent la menace que tout le livre cherche à conjurer' (SV, 201) ['liberated women represent the threat which the whole book attempts to ward off'].[25]

Specific details in Eribon's own family history help explain his scepticism regarding Hoggart's tacit assumptions about community formation. The knowledge that one of his grandmothers became a *femme tondue* at the end of the Second World War, publicly shamed for her association with the occupying German army, leaves him disinclined to endorse Hoggart's moral conservatism. Likewise, he writes with some frustration about Raymond Williams's novel *Second Generation*, a work which the author of *La Société comme verdict* sees as reinforcing social conservatism. In Eribon's stern assessment, the Marxist sociologist in Williams has become a preacher with a puritanical message (SV, 220).

Yet in these wary, often acerbic responses to Williams and Hoggart (he describes the latter as constructing an ideological artefact and passing it off as ethnographic work (SV, 207)), Eribon may be seen to be extending outwards the trenchant self-critique that marks the representation of his personal trajectory in *Retour à Reims*. As a sociologist, he endorses these classic accounts of mid-twentieth-century British reflection on working-class culture. He cites approvingly one of the closing lines in

---

25   In this regard, Eribon (SV, 200) cites the negative response to Hoggart to be found in Carolyn Steedman's *Landscape for a Good Woman: A Story of Two Lives* (London: Virago, 1986). Steedman rejects what she presents as the trend within cultural criticism in Britain to propose 'a psychological simplicity in the lives lived out in Hoggart's endless streets of little houses'; *Landscape for a Good Woman*, p. 7.

Williams's novel *Border Country* in which the social-class migrant, in an attempted calibration of the cultural distance travelled between South Wales and the metropolis where he now lives, comes to reflect: 'By measuring the distance, we come home'.[26]

The paradox of simultaneous distance-taking and belonging similarly features in *Brothers and Keepers*, where Wideman ponders the linkage between the exilic and the identitarian. As he reflects on the lives of his grandfathers who had moved up from the deep South, he asks: 'Were they running from something or to something? [...] Is freedom inextricably linked with both, running *from* and running *to*?' (BK, 24). *Retour à Reims* has its own conflicted dynamic of movement away from and towards, in that the narrative works on the twin trajectories of estrangement and reincorporation, of discarding and retrieval. Indeed, for Eribon, as we have seen, freedom lies along what he presents provocatively as two opposing vectors, the expression of his gayness and the reconnection to working-class origins. But whereas in Eribon's narration of his experience, the one had originally required the shedding of the other, in a restorative moment in the text, the narrator's father, his casual homophobia notwithstanding, staunchly defends his son when the latter appears on television to promote gay rights.

This desire for a loosening of points of fixity and the turning away from binarism is precisely the terrain that Rancière maps in *La Nuit des prolétaires*. He concludes the opening chapter of his archival study with an enthusiastic survey of 'the mixed scene' of cross-class and cross-cultural encounters as documented in the workers' texts he explores:

> Sur la voie supposée directe de l'exploitation à la parole de classe et de l'identité ouvrière à l'expression collective, il faut passer par ce détour, cette scène mixte où, avec la complicité des intellectuels partis à leur rencontre et désireux parfois de s'approprier leur rôle, des prolétaires s'essaient dans les mots et les théories d'en haut, rejouent et déplacent le vieux mythe définissant qui a le droit de parler pour les autres. A travers quelques passions singulières, quelques rencontres fortuites, quelques discussions sur le sexe de Dieu et l'origine du monde, peut-être verra-t-on se dessiner l'image et se poser la voix de la grande collectivité des travailleurs.

> [We must take this detour on the supposedly direct road from exploitation to class message, from worker identity to its collective expression.

---

26   Raymond Williams, *Border Country* (Cardigan: Parthian (Library of Wales), 2010 [1960]), p. 341; cited, in French translation, RR, 247 (RGR, 238).

We must examine the mixed scene in which some workers, with the complicity of intellectuals who have gone out to meet them and perhaps wish to expropriate their role, replay and shift the old myth about who has the right to speak for others by trying their hand at words and theories from on high. Perhaps it is through a few singular passions, a few chance encounters, and a few discussions of the sex of God and the origin of the world that we may see the image of the great labor community take visible shape and hear its voice sound out.][27]

In Rancière's intentionally speculative and paradoxical conclusion, it is through indirection, singularity, and the fortuitous that the social collective might come to be articulated. Or, to borrow from Jacotot, as paraphrased by Rancière, 'ce qui rassemble des *hommes*, ce qui les unit, c'est la non-agrégation' ['what brings *people* together, what unites them, is nonaggregation'].[28]

Retour/détour

The tension between 'running from' and 'running to' may be read paradigmatically and linked to the play between the *retour* and the *détour*, in relation not just to Eribon's work but also to authors whose projects he endorses. In Ernaux, the 'héritage universitaire' is presented, we saw, as a path followed and then regretted. Similarly, Eribon writes in *Retour à Reims* of a screening-off of the real. His earlier biographical work on Foucault again carries a significant exploration of the return/detour axis. For Eribon, Foucault's *Histoire de la folie à l'âge classique* stands as a form of elaborate detour: the work's choice of subject – the historical analysis of practices of exclusion on the grounds of madness – enables Foucault to give oblique expression to his own experience of outsiderness in the homophobic world of post-war France. While, by Eribon's own admission, his methodological approach in the biography risks being reductivist, he draws on Foucault's writings to weld together the personal and the historical. In a 1975 interview entitled 'Je suis un artificier' ['I am a pyrotechnician'], Foucault observed that in his personal life, the awakening of his sexuality placed him in a marginal social position: 'Très vite, ça s'est transformé en une espèce de menace

27   *La Nuit des prolétaires*, pp. 34–35; *Proletarian Nights*, pp. 22–23.
28   *Le Maître ignorant*, p. 99; *The Ignorant Schoolmaster*, p. 58.

psychiatrique' ['Very rapidly, it turned into a form of psychiatric threat'].[29] Six years later, he observed that each time he undertook theoretical work, the motivation for such endeavour was linked to his own life experience, to 'quelque fragment d'autobiographie' ['some fragment of autobiography'].[30] A speculative, theoretical perspective, then, connects to a substratum that is private and experiential. Arguing that each of Foucault's works has an autobiographical dimension to it, Eribon chides those who accuse him of crude reductivism in his approach to his biographical subject.[31]

Foucault claims nevertheless that the experiential may be shaped less within a familial order than by a wider social nexus. Eribon's biography refers to the primacy of the historical event for Foucault's generation growing up in the 1930s, Foucault writing of how the threat of war formed the backdrop to his early life:

> Puis la guerre vint. Bien plus que les scènes de la vie familiale, ce sont ces événements concernant le monde qui sont la substance de notre mémoire. Je dis 'notre' mémoire, parce que je suis presque sûr que la plupart des jeunes Français et Françaises de l'époque ont vécu la même expérience. Il pesait une vraie menace sur notre vie privée. *C'est peut-être la raison pour laquelle je suis fasciné par l'histoire et par la relation entre l'expérience personnelle et les événements dans lesquels nous nous inscrivons.* C'est là, je pense, le noyau de mes désirs théoriques.[32]

> [Then war came. Much more than scenes from family life, it is these events affecting everyone that form the substance of our memory. I say 'our' memory because I am almost certain that most young French people at the time lived the same experience. A real threat hung over our private lives. *Perhaps that's why I am fascinated by history and by the relationship between personal experience and the events in which we are involved.* Therein, I think, lies the core of my theoretical desires.]

The projects of Eribon and Ernaux are no less connected with the imbrication of private and public. Ernaux's childhood memory of Yvetot

---

29   Quoted in Eribon, *Michel Foucault* (Paris: Flammarion, 2011 [1989]), p. 53.

30   Eribon, *Michel Foucault*, pp. 53–54. Eribon insists that his intention is not to reduce Foucault's research to a writing-out of his sexuality.

31   See Eribon's preface to the 2011 edition of his *Michel Foucault*, p. 12; see also p. 54.

32   Interview with Stephen Riggins, *Ethos*, Autumn 1983, p. 5; quoted in Eribon, *Michel Foucault*, p. 25 (emphasis added).

as a place of rubble and destruction at the close of the Second World War, as evoked in *Retour à Yvetot*, provides an arresting image of the hold of historical specificity. Likewise, Eribon's account of the 1950s expansion of the village of Muizon outside Reims fuses collective and private histories (RR, 11–12; RGR, 9–10).

Eribon concludes his preface to the 2011 edition of the Foucault biography first published twenty years earlier with a reflection that reinforces the theme of rerouting and circumvention:

> lorsqu'il [Foucault] évoque *le long détour par l'érudition* et la plongée dans les archives que requiert cette 'ontologie de nous-même', on ressent immédiatement que la magnifique formule qu'il emploie le contient lui-même tout entier: 'Un labeur patient qui donne forme à l'impatience de la liberté'.[33]

> [when Foucault recalls *the long detour through erudition* and the immersion in the archives which this 'ontology of ourselves' requires, one immediately feels that the magnificent formula he uses encapsulates him: 'A patient labour which gives form to the impatience for liberty'.]

In Foucault's chiastic formulation, academic endeavour and emotional longing criss-cross in what may be read as a variant on the *détour/retour* paradigm we have been considering. The intense investment that marks the writing of *Histoire de la folie* would, then, signal parenthetically a freedom march on the part of its author, the archive becoming linked to an archaic that is private and personal. Once more, the narrativization of experience is channelled via the screen or detour that is, in Foucault's case, the archival project. Representation of the encounter with the real thus acquires, and in a way requires, this oblique character. The archive and associated historical enquiry become the conduit through which accommodation of self is realized.

The issue of the link between specifically printed form and the real is illustrated in the choice of book cover for *Retour à Reims*. Eribon discusses at some length the requirements of his publishers in respect of the cover illustration for the second edition (the first edition had carried a cover taken from abstract art). While Flammarion wanted a photograph of Eribon, he was initially reluctant to comply, fearing that using such an image would tend to 'personnaliser et [...] singulariser les

---

33   Quoted in the preface to the 2011 edition of Eribon, *Michel Foucault*, p. 12; emphasis added.

problèmes que j'avais voulu aborder' (SV, 18) ['personalize and render singular the problems I had wanted to address'] – his whole endeavour had been to address such problems in a collectivizing manner, to '"sociologiser" en quelque sorte' (SV, 18) ['"sociologize" in a sense'] and to eschew the narrowly personal. He reflects ironically on how he drew on his knowledge of contemporary art (an illustration from a work by Clyfford Still or Barnett Newman was what he had in mind for the book cover) to put forward counter-proposals to his publisher. The resources of intellectual and aesthetic capital would thus signal Eribon's will to grasp, in a depersonalized form, a concrete collective reality. Indeed, he had feared that the switch, between the first and second editions, from abstract art to a photograph conveying a precise social-class provenance would provoke ridicule. Yet the image he eventually provides for the new edition (a photograph of him as an adolescent leaning on his father's car) helps him achieve his goal:

> [la photo] signalait *sans détour* l'inscription sociale et, dans sa simplicité figée en noir et blanc, elle présentait [...] plus de vérité sociologique impersonnelle que les subtiles compositions de couleurs dans les tableaux des peintres dont je suggérais les noms. (SV, 19; emphasis added)

> [*avoiding any detour*, the photo marked social inscription and, in its black-and-white fixity and simplicity, carried more impersonal sociological truth than the subtle compositions of colour in the paintings of the artists whose names I was suggesting.]

Importantly, Eribon says of his reluctance to provide such a photo that it pointed to an unwillingness to assume his own familial history: 'je me sentais capable de l'évoquer *dans un discours travaillé et construit*, mais n'étais guère enclin à simplement la montrer' (SV, 17; emphasis added) ['I felt able to recall it *in a carefully worked discourse* but was very reluctant to reveal it so transparently']. The return in *Retour à Reims* thus entails a re-apprenticeship to the real, with an acceptance of its visual, photographic disclosure now throwing into relief the constructedness and artifice of a verbal text.

* * *

Writing in *Brothers and Keepers*, Wideman reflects on 'the series of roles and masquerades' (BK, 33) that he assumed as a social-class migrant. Eribon's project in evoking the position of the *transfuge de classe*, the class migrant, works similarly, entailing as it does both a confrontation with, and a withholding of, a socially specific form of the real. Screens, masks, masquerading, forays into the archive: these are some of the props and manoeuvres adopted by Eribon and also identified by him in the authors with whose works he closely engages. He writes of how Bourdieu, in his *Esquisse pour une autoanalyse* ['Sketch for a Self-Analysis'], frequently masks autobiographical reality, this being, in Eribon's view, the sociologist's attempt to draw attention away from the reality of his upbringing. For Eribon, this was Bourdieu offering *autoanalyse* and not *autobiographie*, the model of *autoanalyse* protecting him, Eribon argues, from 'une réduction trop directe – et animée par des passions hostiles – du contenu de son œuvre à ses origines sociales' (SV, 73) ['too direct a reduction (and one inspired by hostility) of the contents of his work to his social origins']. Screening is a device similarly adopted by Eribon and marks the paradox inherent in a reappropriation that works circuitously. For Eribon, that literature and intertextual reference should become a way of attending to the real demonstrates how such a matrix provides the space of possibility within which a return can be realized.

The production history of *Retour à Reims*, as the background to the book cover for the second edition shows, captures its author's conflicted response to representing the real. He explains in *La Société comme verdict* that he had originally included in his *Retour* manuscript a foreword in which he had highlighted an article by Bourdieu celebrating Mouloud Mammeri's return to his native Kabylia. 'L'Odyssée de la réappropriation' ['The Odyssey of Reappropriation'] is how Bourdieu labels this return and quest. Late in the production process, Eribon removed this framing text, believing that its inclusion risked denying his own narrative of return its violence and *radicalité* (SV, 82).

With the scaffolding of an avant-propos and indeed also a postface removed, Eribon thus attempts to foreground a lived experience, a real that has been historically marginalized within academic and literary discourse. But in the process, he demonstrates how the reach to the real often functions via circuitous channels, as *Retour à Reims* shows and as the contexts he proposes for an understanding of Wideman, Foucault, Ernaux, and others confirm. These channels are themselves articulations of what is permissible or accessible, as Eribon puts it, in cultural and economic terms (SV, 200). Unlike the emancipatory message inscribed on the Père Lachaise tombstone of Jacotot, where the human soul is described as being 'capable de s'instruire seule et sans maître'

['CAPABLE OF TEACHING ITSELF BY ITSELF, AND WITHOUT A MASTER'],[34] the commemoration of lives in *Retour à Reims* stresses the constraints that shape the 'apprentissage du monde' (RR, 35) ['apprenticeship of the world' (RGR, 31)]. The death of the author's father gives urgency to the book's recording of that social constriction and the eclipsing of perspectives it entails. The weight of society's 'verdict' leaves Eribon contending with 'un désarroi [...] provoqué par une interrogation indissociablement personnelle et politique' (RR, 19) ['a state of confusion and disarray (...) produced by something being called into question, something both personal and political'] (RGR, 16).

In a reflection on momentous forms of witnessing, Ross Chambers evokes 'the "alien" scene, the "other" context' that is no less a part of culture. He writes: 'witnessing [...] takes the form of seeking to cause some *disturbance* in well-established cultural regularities and routines: routines of thought (or its absence), regularities of discursive habitus'.[35] In Eribon's *autoanalyse* and in his response to writers with whose projects he identifies, we see disturbance formed by the disarray of lived experience and its ambiguous textual mediation. In cultural interventions of this kind, it is in the ambivalent play between running from and to such experience that the transaction between past exclusions – social, sexual, racial – and current self-positioning is negotiated.

34 See *Le Maître ignorant*, p. 230; *The Ignorant Schoolmaster*, p. 139. The block capitals are used in the English translation to signal the gravestone inscription. Rancière refers to the commemorative wording chosen by Jacotot's disciples as forming 'the credo of intellectual emancipation'.

35 Ross Chambers, *Untimely Interventions: AIDS Writing, Testimonial, and the Rhetoric of Haunting* (Ann Arbor: University of Michigan Press, 2004), xix–xx; emphasis original.

Conclusion

[La langue est] la propriété indivise des hommes et
non pas des écrivains; elle reste en dehors du rituel des
Lettres; c'est un objet social par définition, non par
élection.

[language is the undivided property of everyone rather
than of writers; it remains outside the ritual of Letters;
it is a social object by definition, not by choice.]

Barthes[1]

Lecturing on the subject of literature and memory in Kingston, Ontario
in October 1993, Claude Simon recalled giving an earlier talk to the
Union of Soviet Writers in the period before glasnost and being asked
about the main problems he faced as a writer. For those in the Soviet
audience expecting or perhaps hoping for a reply compatible with the
norms of Socialist Realism, Simon's answer came as a disappointment.
He listed three problems: how to start a sentence, how to continue it,
and how to conclude it, 'ce qui, comme on peut le deviner, a jeté un
froid' ['a reply which, as one can imagine, did not go down well'].[2] This
foregrounding of the question of syntax and the assembling of verbal text
might suggest an endorsement of formalism yet the tense relationship in
L'Acacia between the expressive function and the social referent leaves
the work far removed from textual abstraction. The anecdote about his

---

1   Barthes, *Le Degré zéro de l'écriture*, p. 177.
2   Simon's lecture 'Littérature et Mémoire' was delivered at Queen's University,
Kingston, Ontario. See Claude Simon, *Quatre conférences*, pp. 99–124
(p. 123).

communist audience leads Simon to provide his Canadian audience with an illustration of his working method, drawing on *L'Acacia*. Given the novel's autobiographical underlay and his lecture's focus on memory, he confesses to being unsure as to the veracity of the memories he reconstructs in the book. He refers specifically to a sentence in which he describes a cart loaded with the possessions of people fleeing the war and crossing paths in the night with members of a cavalry regiment moving into the area being evacuated (Simon, as was mentioned earlier, served in that regiment in northern France in the spring of 1940). He recreates the moment when he tried to conclude the sentence:

> il me fallait [...] finir un 'mouvement', celui de cette phrase qui décrivait un entassement, une pyramide élevée, et il m'a semblé qu'il et elle (c'est-à-dire le mouvement et la pyramide) devaient s'achever, être couronnés par quelque chose de léger, d'aérien.[3]

> [I had to complete a 'movement', the movement of this sentence describing a piling up, a raised pyramid, and it seemed to me that the one and the other (the movement and the pyramid of objects), needed to be completed, to be crowned with something light, airy.]

After a lengthy search, Simon finds both word and object: *bicyclette*. The finding, he adds, enables the completion of the movement of syntax, even if his memory of the particular scene from the Second World War retains nothing of a bicycle: 'quelque chose m'avait imposé ce mot' ['something had imposed that word on me'].

Simon is describing the space of writing as one of constraint but also of possibility and openness. By stressing language as movement, he anticipates Rancière's argument that within the 'regimes of emotion' in aisthesis, 'ces conditions rendent possible que des paroles, des formes, des mouvements, des rythmes soient ressentis et pensés comme de l'art' ['these conditions make it possible for words, shapes, movements and rhythms to be felt and thought as art'].[4] Rancière writes of a blurring of the frontiers between art and what he terms the prose of the world. In place of any insistence on the opposition between artistic creativity and the 'sensible fabric of experience', he is drawn to how

> une forme, un éclat de couleur, l'accélération d'un rythme, un silence entre des mots, un mouvement ou un scintillement sur une surface soient ressentis comme événements et associés à l'idée de création artistique.

3　Simon, *Quatre conférences*, pp. 123–24.
4　*Aisthesis*, p. 10; *Aisthesis: Scenes from the Aesthetic Regime of Art*, p. x.

[a form, a burst of colour, an acceleration of rhythm, a pause between words, a movement, or a glimmering surface (can) be experienced as events and associated with the idea of artistic creation.][5]

Simon's stress on textual movement and sentence completion aligns to a degree with Rancière's carefully delineated conception of the politics of literature, one that excludes the political stance of the writer or her/his representation of social structures. For Rancière, literature intervenes in a world where people live and name; it intervenes 'dans le découpage des objets qui forment un monde commun' ['in the carving up of objects that form a common world'].[6] Proposing that the reader access the literary text as a democratic space, he argues: 'La démocratie de la lettre est le régime de la lettre en liberté que chacun peut reprendre à son compte' ['The democracy of literature is the regime of the word at large that anyone can grab hold of'].[7] The particular distribution of the sensible that is present in literature, Rancière suggests, sees a process of connection that allows for 'un rapport nouveau entre l'acte de parole, le monde qu'il configure et les capacités de ceux qui peuplent ce monde' ['a new relationship between the act of speech, the world that it configures and the capacities of those who people that world'].[8] Commenting specifically on these lines and on the question of writing as intervention in social contexts, Davis signals nevertheless the need for further interrogation of how precisely in Rancière the letter – that's to say, writing in its mode of circulation – can take the human animal in particular directions.[9]

A variation on Simon's view of literature's capacity to position itself outside a prevailing political climate is present in Péguy. There, prose style functions as a mark of fidelity to the artisan, Péguy's attention to language being linked isomorphically to the level of application displayed by the manual worker. Yet Péguy also vaunts the capacity of

---

5 *Aisthesis*, p. 10; *Aisthesis: Scenes from the Aesthetic Regime of Art*, p. x.

6 *Politique de la littérature*, p. 15; *Politics of Literature*, p. 7.

7 *Politique de la littérature*, pp. 21–22; *Politics of Literature*, p. 13. A contrasting view is to be found in Bourdieu, who sees the focus on an individual sensibility in literature revealing, through a process of metaphor and metonymy, and more quickly than scientific investigation, the complexity of a social structure; Bourdieu, *Les Règles de l'art*, p. 48, cited in Dubois, *Le Roman de Gilberte Swann*, p. 20.

8 *Politique de la littérature*, p. 22; *Politics of Literature*, p. 13.

9 Davis, *Jacques Rancière*, p. 113.

literary practice. In *Notre jeunesse*, he writes, in a demonstration of both defensiveness and pride:

> On peut publier demain matin nos œuvres complètes. Non seulement il n'y a pas une virgule que nous ayons à désavouer, mais il n'y a pas une virgule dont nous n'ayons à nous glorifier.[10]

> [They can go ahead tomorrow and publish our complete works. Not only is there not a single comma we would have to disavow, there isn't a single comma we cannot take pride in.]

For Péguy, typography stands as refuge from a degraded political order. We noted how, in the same work, he complains about a moral decline in the life of the Third Republic and the loss of what he terms Republican mystique. His reaction is a binary one, in that he pits literature, seen as stoical endeavour, against politics. Seen in this light, his *Cahiers* project comes to be viewed as emancipatory encounter:

> Nos *Cahiers* sont devenus, non point par le hasard, mais [...] par une lente élaboration, par de puissantes, par de secrètes affinités, *par une sorte de longue évaporation de la politique*, comme une compagnie parfaitement libre d'hommes qui tous croient à quelque chose, à commencer par la typographie.[11]

> [Our *Cahiers* have become, in no way by accident, but (...) through a slow elaboration, through powerful and secret affinities, *through a kind of slow evaporation of the political*, like a perfectly free association of men, all of whom believe in something, starting with typography.]

In resisting political parties and demagoguery, Péguy extols the world of letters and what he presents as the localized democracy forming around the publication project.

Péguy's imbuing punctuation with virtue and Simon's quandary about sentence completion might suggest a literature restricted to form and without social purchase. Weil cautions against remaining within 'le cadre de la feuille de papier' ['the frame of the piece of paper'], insisting that thought must be methodically applied not to 'mere strokes of the pen' ['de simples traits de plume'] but rather to what she calls effective movements that leave a mark in the world.[12]

---

10   Péguy, *Notre jeunesse*, pp. 42–43.

11   Péguy, *Notre jeunesse*, p. 156; emphasis added.

12   The specific example Weil gives here is of a page on which are written mathematical signs (RCLOS, 89–90).

In *The Communist Manifesto*, Marx and Engels complain of forms of utopian thinking which mark a 'fantastic standing apart from the contest', of forces which oppose 'the progressive historical development of the proletariat'.[13] To what extent might the texts explored in this volume convey a 'standing apart' and constitute a denial of socially progressive writing? With the exception of Bon's *Daewoo* and to some extent Gauny's work, as when he evokes the image of a new humanity marching 'vers cet inconnu, ce bonheur [...] dont l'essence est en elle!' (PP, 65) ['towards that unknown, that happiness (...) the essence of which lies within it!'], none of the texts offers a focus on collective empowerment or on a social movement's achievement of shared goals of the kind to be found in a work such as Ousmane Sembène's *Les Bouts de bois de Dieu*. There, the striking railway workers' long march to Dakar is likened to 'ce grand fleuve qui roulait vers la mer' ['that great river which was flowing towards the sea'] and the blind Maïmouna, breast-feeding the baby named Grève ['Strike'], comments: 'J'arrose un arbre pour demain' ['I'm watering a tree for tomorrow'].[14] In marked contrast with this narrative of consequential social action, the texts under consideration frequently represent cycles of entrenched containment: the pre-1914 worlds depicted in Proust, Péguy, Nizan, and Simon; the lives of industrial workers in the 1930s as explored by Weil; twentieth-century peasant lives in La Creuse as retrieved by Michon; the recreations of working-class communities in France's Fifth Republic in Ndiaye and Eribon; the status of the workplace in a post-industrial age as charted by Bon and Beinstingel. Eribon paints a sombre picture of society as 'verdict' and confesses to a sense of disarray arising from this.

At the same time, these texts explore interventions (social, linguistic, thematic, intermedial) that often bring a mitigation or forthright rejection of inequalities. Ndiaye's la Cheffe is cast as an Everyperson figure by the narrator: 'l'archétype de tout visage humain, sans distinction de sexe ni d'âge ni de beauté' (CRC, 208) ['the archetype of all human faces, unmarked by sex, age or beauty' (TC, 206)]. *Daewoo* combines workshop, witness, and writing. *Vies minuscules* gives audibility to voices that structures of cultural and economic power discard. Undaunted by the constriction of manual labour, Gauny sees, and commends to others, liberation in the space of philosophy. Via the radical choice of religious

---

13   Marx and Engels, *The Communist Manifesto*, p. 117.
14   Ousmane Sembène, *Les Bouts de bois de Dieu* (Paris: Le Livre Contemporain, 1960), pp. 313, 339.

conviction, Weil proposes 'une lumière d'éternité' (CO, 423) ['an eternal light'] that would allow workers to bear the monotony of labour: they need their lives to be poetry, 'Besoin que leur vie soit une poésie', she asserts in *La Pesanteur et la Grâce*.[15] The strange equalities, expressions of aspiration, and implied forms of indistinction risk nevertheless being transient attenuations of the order of inequality, moments of exception and disturbance that ultimately reinforce that order. Palmusaari argues that whereas 'time generally functions as a form to order differences and directedness', Rancière's work privileges situations in space and these allow him to 'avoid such determinations and affirm egalitarian coexistence as such'.[16] Certainly, Rancière's research on Jacotot and the Panecastic movement does not yield, nor claim, the promise of an easily achievable egalitarian continuum.

The critical reception given to *Vies minuscules* provides an instructive angle on the question of social levelling. Reviewing the work, Jean-Pierre Richard draws on the biblical account of the Beatitudes and writes of lives that are 'minuscule' being blessed in that, through Michon's text, they are admitted to the kingdom of Letters. Richard adds that, through these lives, 'we' too are admitted.[17] While enthusiastic about Richard's response, Michon explains how his own intention in using the adjective 'minuscules' was not to suggest a climate of miserabilism but rather, putting it simply, to write about people whose destiny is to lack the qualities required by life's situations (not to be 'à la hauteur du projet'). In other words, Michon asserts, his aim was to write about everyone. Careful to acknowledge that Richard himself warns against reading 'minuscule' as a synonym for humble or modest, Michon concludes that the term signals a levelling of values ['une mise à plat des valeurs'] in which 'botched lives' ['des vies bousillées'] are redeemed in literature.[18]

Levelling also manifests itself in a departure from anthropocentrism, as in *L'Acacia* where, via the molecular workings of narrative, the pull of gravity, for example, governs – in a process of indistinction – a fallen soldier, a dead horse on the battlefield, and a sack of grain, as

---

15   Weil, *La Pesanteur et la Grâce*, p. 206; *Gravity and Grace*, p. 180.

16   Palmusaari, 'For Revolt'; quotation taken from the thesis abstract.

17   Jean-Pierre Richard, 'Servitude et grandeur du minuscule', in *L'Etat des choses: Etudes sur huit écrivains d'aujourd'hui* (Paris: Gallimard, 1990), pp. 87–106 (p. 106).

18   Michon, *Le Roi vient quand il veut*, p. 151.

has been noted.[19] The young Proust hails the art of still life in Chardin as laying bare 'la divine égalité de toutes choses devant l'esprit qui les considère, devant la lumière qui les embellit' ['the divine equality of all things to the mind that considers them and in the light that gives them beauty'].[20] Collapsing the traditional division between the aesthetic and the ordinary thus involves redistribution. It absorbs both the mundane and the socially prestigious. Léger's assertion, considered at the outset, that the beautiful is everywhere ['le Beau est partout'] echoes this. The equalization, Proust adds, entails a 'voyage d'initiation' ['voyage of initiation'] to a world that we disregard.[21] But whereas Proust's discovery of a 'divine equality' sits within the frame of *fin-de-siècle* aesthetic debate, Rancière's *Courts Voyages au pays du peuple* tracks different voyages of introduction. Encompassing lives excluded from social and economic power, his 'short voyages' culminate in forms of equalization, however transient. They throw up other forms of 'marriage [between] beings and things', to adapt Proust's phrase.[22]

The generic range of texts in the current volume (prose fiction, sociologically inflected autobiography, personal journal, social documentary, historico-critical works such as *Le Maître ignorant*) often involves what could be read as 'short voyages to the land of the people'. These voyages deliver a spectrum of outcomes. Eribon returns seeking reintroduction to a working-class habitus and concludes that society's 'verdict' entails irredeemable cultural and economic constriction. In an age of intense industrialization, Weil enters the factory, her plea being that a world all too often occluded be accessed: 'tous les remous de la classe ouvrière, si mystérieux aux spectateurs, [sont] en réalité si aisés à comprendre' (CO, 343) ['all the bustle within the working class which spectators find so mysterious is in reality so easy to understand']. In a post-industrial age in eastern France, Bon encounters those whose labour is rendered redundant by global capital and proposes a collaborative attempt to convert factory space into a site of cultural production.

19 As discussed above in the Introduction (see p. 20), Rancière references Deleuze and molecular narrative in *Politique de la littérature*, p. 35; *The Politics of Literature*, pp. 25–26.

20 Proust's comment comes in his 1895 essay on Chardin and Rembrandt, which is reproduced in *Contre Sainte-Beuve*, pp. 372–82 (p. 380). See also the editorial note on the essay provided by Clarac and Sandre, p. 885.

21 Proust, *Contre Sainte-Beuve*, p. 380.

22 Proust writes of a 'mariage [...] entre les êtres et les choses'; *Contre Sainte-Beuve*, p. 380.

The disturbance triggered by coexistence and situations of sporadic equalization is often inflected by the debate around hands and minds. In the opening pages of *Le Peuple*, which he dedicates to the Republican historian Edgar Quinet, Michelet claims to straddle class boundaries, reminding his reader that, before writing books, he was literally involved in book production in his father's artisanal printing business. A professional of the written word is thus paired with a professional of book production. To use Michelet's own image, he was, literally, an assembler of letters before becoming an assembler of ideas. 'Moi aussi', he protests, 'j'ai travaillé de mes mains' ['I too have worked with my hands'], as if to anticipate Péguy's sentimental eulogy for an age of artisanal craft in *L'Argent*.[23]

Michelet's socially obscure contemporary Gauny is more trenchant. While the historian of France writes of 'les mélancolies' of *atelier* life, Gauny exposes the blinding adherence to productive necessity experienced by workshop employees and looks to transcend the world of manual work in what is a significant move towards disaggregation.[24] The nineteenth-century workers' archives in *La Nuit des prolétaires* reveal a similar motivation. Nizan's *Antoine Bloyé*, by contrast, presents the protagonist's graduation from manual work to the supervision of those engaged in such work as a stepping into existential solitude. In the same interwar period, Denis de Rougemont identifies in the difference between the hands of the worker and the non-worker – *la main ouvrière* and *la main non ouvrière* – a perennial symbol of distinction between classes.[25] In an essay entitled *Penser avec les mains* ['Thinking with the Hands'], he aims to reconcile 'deux fonctions, que toute la culture d'hier s'évertuait à séparer: pensée et main' ['two functions which yesterday's culture strived endlessly to separate: thought and hand'].[26] Proposing his title as a metaphor for social engagement, de Rougemont makes clear that he is not calling for a retreat from mind into the purely material, as National Socialism was ominously advocating. Yet in commending writers dismissed by the academic establishment for their pursuit of 'le souci d'aboutir au concret' ['the concern to get to the concrete'], he

23   Michelet, *Le Peuple*, p. 6.
24   Michelet, *Le Peuple*, p. 6.
25   De Rougemont borrows the formulation from Henri de Man's *L'Idée socialiste*, cited in Denis de Rougemont, *Penser avec les mains* (Paris: Albin Michel, 1936), p. 27.
26   De Rougemont, *Penser avec les mains*, p. 143.

objects to the conception of culture as something ready-made, arguing that it should imply the idea of work 'comme une chose à faire, ou qui se fait' ['like a thing to do or which is done'].[27] Culture debases and undoes itself, he complains, through failing to 's'abaisser à hauteur d'homme, au niveau du réel' ['drop down to the human level, the level of the real'].[28] Rancière dramatizes the arbitrariness of the thought/hand divorce in *Le Maître ignorant*, where emancipation for the artisan involves, to repeat an earlier quotation, 'la conscience que son activité matérielle est de la nature du discours' ['the consciousness that one's material activity is of the nature of discourse'].[29]

As a touchstone of social hierarchy, the claimed separation of the mental and the manual can fuel both play and pathos in literature. A questionnaire that asked writers: 'Si vous étiez obligé d'exercer un métier manuel [... ?]' ['If you were obliged to exercise a manual trade (...?)'] left Proust unphased.[30] His matter-of-fact reply was that this would mean no change from his habitual role as writer: 'L'esprit guide la main' ['The mind guides the hand'], he asserts, invoking both Chardin's dictum that one paints with the heart as much as with the fingers, and Leonardo's view that painting is a *cosa mentale* ['mental thing']. But heeding the spirit in which the questionnaire is framed, Proust concedes that, were paper no longer available, he would switch to being a baker, this allowing him to fulfil the 'honourable' task of giving people their daily bread.[31]

This ludic rejection of the premise of a distinction between 'les professions manuelles et spirituelles' ['professions of the hand and the mind'] contrasts with the tone of reverential awe struck in *Vies minuscules*.[32] There, the figure of the miller whose explanation to doctors that he is illiterate forms a solemn verbal pronouncement, shows

---

27 De Rougemont, *Penser avec les mains*, pp. 161, 21.

28 De Rougemont, *Penser avec les mains*, p. 15. Noting the interest in de Rougemont shown by Jean-Luc Godard in his later cinematographic work, James S. Williams comments on how Godard cites at length from *Penser avec les mains* in episode 4A of *Histoire(s)*, *Le Contrôle de l'univers*; see Williams, *Encounters with Godard: Ethics, Aesthetics, Politics* (Albany: SUNY Press, 2016), p. 55.

29 See *Le Maître ignorant*, p. 111; *The Ignorant Schoolmaster*, p. 65.

30 The questionnaire was arranged in the summer of 1920 by Maurice Montabré, a journalist at *L'Intransigeant*. See Clarac and Sandre's editorial note in Proust, *Contre Sainte-Beuve*, p. 949.

31 Proust, *Contre Sainte-Beuve*, pp. 604–05.

32 Proust, *Contre Sainte-Beuve*, p. 604.

Michon dramatizing the fracture between high verbal register and the manual. In what can be read as an echo of Jacotot's outlook, the miller handles words as he might handle sacks of flour, while also being cast, as we saw in Chapter 7, as the unschooled choirmaster who conducts the purest of songs (VM, 156; SL, 135)]. But in the identification with the miller, which sees Michon melodramatically excluding himself from the literary greats on Mount Olympus, he risks underpinning a constricting social apportionment built around certain uses of the written word.

By savouring the homology that conjoins the handling of words and of tools, Rancière urges a practice of reclamation.[33] His idea of a 'community of equals' cuts in two directions: it fosters a rehabilitation of the manual while also restoring to writing the dimension of craft and construction, of poiesis. The writer Lerminier would thus labour no less than the nineteenth-century artisan he looks down on.

*   *   *

While antagonisms around class borders and forms of exclusion from social power are thematic threads running through the narratives explored, the question of the relationship in each of them between social representation and the expressive function is crucial. Commenting on the primacy given to *elocutio* among the exponents of literary style seen as an absolute, Rancière cautions that language is not to be understood in terms of its self-sufficiency. Rather language 'est déjà en lui-même expérience de monde' ['already contains within itself an experience of the world'] and thus predates us.[34] He dismisses as frivolous the critical commonplace that sets literature and art apart from any cultural or sociological relativization.[35] Refusing to choose between the primacy of fiction or of language, he adopts a hybrid position in which he rejects language's 'intransitive' or self-referential [*autotélique*] function.[36] He also dissents from the canonical view that the primary function of the mimetic text is to deliver social documentarism. Discarding the critical commonplaces about Naturalist reportage, he focusses on Zola's scriptural practice, stressing that as a writer, Zola practises '[le]

33 *Le Maître ignorant*, p. 121; *The Ignorant Schoolmaster*, p. 71.
34 *La Parole muette*, p. 43; *Mute Speech*, p. 62.
35 *La Parole muette*, p. 50; *Mute Speech*, p. 68.
36 *La Parole muette*, p. 43; *Mute Speech*, p. 62.

dédoublement langagier de toute chose' ['the doubling of each thing in language'].[37] In this way, Rancière advocates the 'neutralisation' of the opposition between the mimetic function and poetic mysticism, this paving the way for a continuity between 'la poétique représentative et […] la poétique expressive' ['representative poetics and expressive poetics'].[38]

The effect created by Rancière's notion of a doubling through language is to position the text in an ambiguous relationship to the referent. In some of the cases considered here, the doubling allows the author to weaken the hold exerted by the world being represented. Thus, Eribon sees textual and intertextual filters serving to screen the real. In an ambiguous form of retrieval, Simon transmutes memories of the chaotic experience of war into objects of studied textual assembly. Via competing repertoires of language, Ndiaye handles the tension around textual fluency and an inhibited orality, the latter being markedly present in la Cheffe's family 'chez qui le verbe était rare et malaisé' (CRC, 32) ['whose words came out sparsely and laboriously' (TC, 25)]. In an analogous way, within the copious narrative that is Proust's *Recherche*, Françoise as social subordinate contends with linguistic censorship and yet proves a match for Marcel. In the same work, it is as though the confident young footman employed by the protagonist's family confiscates canonical literature, laying claim to what hierarchical custom of the day deems out of place for the untutored. He crosses what Bourdieu terms 'the sacred frontier which makes legitimate culture a separate universe'.[39] These pressure points around expressivity and cultural selection are integral to Rancière's understanding of the politics of literature.[40]

It is also at the level of the expressive function that forms of liberation occur. Bon's interviewees in *Daewoo* develop a language of contestation and, through it, an enhanced sense of selfhood; while for Ndiaye's la Cheffe, expressive emancipation works through a liberating kinaesthesia. Yet what are often exuberantly formulated moments of redemptiveness may be notably divorced from any concept of emancipatory collective design. Hence the solitary forms of secular sanctification in Ndiaye and Péguy; the Diogenes-style withdrawal from material needs advocated

---

37   *La Parole muette*, p. 46; *Mute Speech*, p. 64.
38   *La Parole muette*, p. 143; *Mute Speech*, p. 147.
39   Bourdieu, *Distinction*, p. 6.
40   See *Politique de la littérature*, pp. 35–36; *The Politics of Literature*, p. 26.

by Gauny; or the appeal, seen elsewhere in the present study, to other-worldly spaces – the religious redemption of factory toil in Weil, or, in the case of 'Vie de Georges Bandy', Michon's revelling in the speculation that the protagonist may have experienced at the time of his death 'la bouleversante signifiance du Verbe universel' (VM, 213) ['the overwhelming significance of the universal Word' (SL, 183)].[41] At the level of the politics of language, the depiction of Bandy as a figure of urbane fluency who acquires the verbal reticence of the rural backwater where he later lives provides a metaphor of connectedness between would-be opposing cultural spaces and performances. Michon speculates that the literary medium might function reparatively in relation to discarded lives. Hence the closing lines of *Vies minuscules* and the aspiration that fiction might work restoratively in respect of the marginal lives evoked: 'que [la mort] d'Elise soit allégée par ces lignes. Que dans mes étés fictifs, leur hiver hésite' (VM, 249) ['that the death of Elise be eased by these lines. That in my fictive summers, their winter may hesitate' (SL, 215; translation modified)]. Yet the earnest commemoration barely masks a position of vulnerability, in that the retrieval through writing involves not just fears about the limitations of the medium but also an awareness of embedded social inequality.

In another way, the strained work of composition implied in Michon's summer/winter metaphor may be grafted on to Rancière's argument that the stress placed retrospectively on a work of art as event erases 'la généalogie des formes de perception et de pensée qui ont pu en faire des événements' ['the genealogy of forms of perception and thought that were able to make them events in the first place'].[42] In the same prelude to *Aisthesis*, Rancière restates the notion of a continuum at the level of the sensible by arguing that 'les raisons de cet art se mêlent sans cesse avec celles des autres sphères de l'expérience' ['art constantly merg(es) its own reasons with those belonging to other spheres of experience'].[43] Changes in the sensible fabric, to use Rancière's vocabulary, are conspicuous across the genres considered in this book.

If the forum of the novel is a democratic, participatory space for its reader, Beinstingel uses precisely the thematics of participation to

---

41 Ann Jefferson writes of Michon restoring 'the traffic between a supposedly secular literature and a sacred Christianity'; see *Biography and the Question of Literature in France*, p. 340.

42 *Aisthesis*, p. 13; *Aisthesis: Scenes from the Aesthetic Regime of Art*, p. xii.

43 *Aisthesis*, p. 11; *Aisthesis: Scenes from the Aesthetic Regime of Art*, p. xi.

give closure to his *Retour aux mots sauvages* narrative, as has been mentioned. With the protagonist involved in an organized run open to all comers, the intense physical effort required sees him throwing off a restrictive habitus in an endorphin-fuelled moment of catharsis: 'Les milliers de pensées s'estompent. Tout ce qu'il a subi, tout ce qu'on nous apprend, la compétition, l'identité, l'individu' (RMS, 232) ['A thousand blurred thoughts fill his head. Everything he has undergone, all that we're taught, competition, identity, the individual'].

Similar 'transformations of the sensible fabric' ['transformations du tissu sensible'] are found in the non-fictional narratives in the present corpus.[44] The critique of capital in *L'Argent* is grounded in affect, Péguy attempting through a practice of language to re-enact a labour that requires 'un respect de l'outil, et de la main, ce suprême outil' (Arg, 793) ['a respect for the tool and for the hand, that supreme tool']. Gauny describes a wide arc of the sensible. The worker tied to the oppressive regime of the workshop imagines taking refuge in the bark of a tree; the liberated, peripatetic pieceworker scanning the city acquires the visual acuity of a bird of prey (PP, 56, 63); and the worker-philosopher speculates: 'si la terre était une philadelphie, jardin de fraternité' (PP, 126–27) ['if the world were a philadelphia, a garden of fraternity']. The invitation to the reader's imagination inferred in Gauny's surmising shows writing as a site of transformative encounter.

The intensity of aspiration threading through many of the texts explored is no less present in Weil. In her factory journal, she evokes a 'temps divin' ['divine time'] spent in conversation with two metal workers – one a teenager, the other in his late fifties – in which, as we saw, she experiences, beyond barriers of class and gender, a moment of 'total camaraderie', one that is 'miraculous' (CO, 132–34). 'Toute la matinée, conversation à 3 extraordinairement libre, aisée' (CO, 133) ['the whole morning, an extraordinarily free, easy conversation among the three of us'], she records. Weil's morning of miracle, like Michon's 'fictive summer' and Nizan's account in *Antoine Bloyé* of childhood as being hierarchy-free, is far from any sustained programme of direct-edness. Yet, while each of these experiences is temporally delimited, they render thinkable alternative socialities. In one of the nineteenth-century source texts that underpin *Le Maître ignorant*, the argument runs that equality cannot exist over a long period: 'mais, même lorsqu'elle est détruite, elle reste encore la seule explication raisonnable des distinctions

44 *Aisthesis: Scenes from the Aesthetic Regime of Art*, p. xi; *Aisthesis*, p. 11.

conventionnelles' ['but even when it is destroyed, it remains the only reasonable explanation for conventional distinctions'].[45] The conclusion to an earlier chapter of *Le Maître ignorant* entitled 'La Raison des égaux' ['Reason Between Equals'] sees Rancière glossing another source and relaying, through free indirect discourse, the Panecastic concession that 'nous ne savons pas que les hommes soient égaux. Nous disons qu'ils le sont *peut-être*' ['we don't know that men are equal. We are saying that they *might* be']. The codicil that follows and that ends the chapter voices the conviction that it is in the *might* that 'a human society' ['une société d'hommes'] is possible.[46] Form – present here in Rancière's studied use of chapter framing – allows an egalitarian echo from a previous historical moment to resonate.[47]

Early in this study, we considered the relationship between form and the world, as set out in Rancière's analysis of the film *Europa 51*. He perceives there an egalitarian strangeness between the aesthetic (the camera lens) and the ethical (the socially engaged vision of Rossellini as enacted by the protagonist Irene). In a study two decades later of the work of photographer Alfred Stieglitz, Rancière celebrates the 'majesty of the moment'. (We might speculatively see in the formulation a condensation of Weil's 'morning of miracle', while accepting that different forms of the sensible are involved – the subjectivity of the photographer and the functioning of the camera, on the one hand, and the transformative activity of deeply enabling conversation on the other.) Observing that Stieglitz's choice of subject carries 'the metonymy of a world', Rancière concludes that photography's objectivity involves

---

45   Rancière is quoting from a source text entitled 'Musique', pp. 194–95; see *Le Maître ignorant*, p. 148; *The Ignorant Schoolmaster*, p. 88. Christopher Watkin, while expressing reservations about the account of equality in Rancière, as we saw above in the Introduction, points out that in *Le Maître ignorant* Rancière refutes the assertion that he is 'unverifiably assuming a universal equality of intelligence': 'Mais jamais nous ne pourrons dire: toutes les intelligences sont égales' ['But we can never say: all intelligence is equal']; *Le Maître ignorant*, p. 79; *The Ignorant Schoolmaster*, p. 46. See Watkin, 'Thinking Equality Today', p. 526.

46   *Le Maître ignorant*, p. 124; *The Ignorant Schoolmaster*, p. 73. The quotation immediately preceding Rancière's gloss is taken from the *Journal de philosophie panécastique*, 5 (1838), 265.

47   As Swenson explains regarding the use of free indirect discourse in *Le Maître ignorant*, Rancière's method is essentially to recount the nineteenth-century corpus of Jacotot's circle which he is exploring: 'There is no critique, only rewriting in order to understand'; see Swenson, '*Style indirect libre*', p. 265.

le régime de pensée, de perception et de sensation qui fait coïncider l'amour des formes pures avec l'appréhension de l'historicité inépuisable contenue dans toute intersection de rue, tout pli d'une peau et tout instant du temps.

[the regime of thought, perception and sensation that makes the love of pure forms coincide with the apprehension of the inexhaustible historicity found at every street corner, in every skin fold, and at every moment of time.][48]

In their respective ways, the writers considered in the present book likewise engage with form and historicity and provide their own metonymies of the social world.

48 See Rancière, *Aisthesis*, chapter 12, 'La Majesté du moment: New York, 1921', pp. 245–64 (p. 264); ['The Majesty of the Moment (New York, 1921)'], *Aisthesis: Scenes from the Aesthetic Regime of Art*, pp. 207–24 (p. 224).

Bibliography

Works by Jacques Rancière

Aisthesis. Scènes du régime esthétique de l'art (Paris: Galilée, 2011); *Aisthesis: Scenes from the Aesthetic Regime of Art,* trans. Zakir Paul (London: Verso, 2013).

Aux bords du politique (Paris: Gallimard, 2004); *On the Shores of Politics*, trans. Liz Heron (London: Verso, 2007).

Les Bords de la fiction (Paris: Seuil, 2017); *The Edges of Fiction*, trans. Steve Corcoran (Cambridge: Polity, 2020).

La Chair des mots. Politiques de l'écriture (Paris: Galilée, 1998); *The Flesh of Words: The Politics of Writing*, trans. Charlotte Mandell (Stanford: Stanford University Press, 2004).

Courts voyages au pays du peuple (Paris: Seuil, 1990); *Short Voyages to the Land of the People*, trans. James B. Swenson (Stanford: Stanford University Press, 2003).

En quel temps vivons-nous? Conversation avec Éric Hazan (Paris: La Fabrique, 2017).

Le Fil perdu. Essais sur la fiction moderne (Paris: La Fabrique, 2014); *The Lost Thread: The Democracy of Modern Fiction*, trans. Steven Corcoran (London: Bloomsbury, 2017).

La Haine de la démocratie (Paris: La Fabrique, 2005); *Hatred of Democracy*, trans. Steve Corcoran (London: Verso, 2014).

Interview with Julien Le Gros, 'Jacques Rancière, "Le Philosophe plébéien"', *Le Dissident*, 2 April 2018. https://the-dissident.eu/jacques-ranciere-philosophe-plebeien/ [accessed 12 December 2018].

'The Janus-Face of Politicized Art: Jacques Rancière in Interview with Gabriel Rockhill' (2003), in Rancière, *The Politics of Aesthetics: The Distribution of the Sensible*, trans. and ed. Gabriel Rockhill (London and New York: Bloomsbury, 2013 (2004)), pp. 45–61.

Le Maître ignorant. Cinq leçons sur l'émancipation intellectuelle (Paris: Arthème Fayard, 1987); *The Ignorant Schoolmaster: Five Lessons in Intellectual Emancipation*, trans. and ed. Kristin Ross (Stanford: Stanford University Press, 1991).

La Mésentente. Politique et philosophie (Paris: Galilée, 1995); *Disagreement: Politics and Philosophy*, trans. Julie Rose (Minneapolis: University of Minnesota Press, 1999).

La Méthode de l'égalité. Entretiens avec Laurent Jeanpierre et Dork Zabunyan (Paris: Bayard, 2012); *The Method of Equality: Interviews with Laurent Jeanpierre and Dork Zabunyan*, trans Julie Rose (Cambridge: Polity, 2016).

La Nuit des prolétaires. Archives du rêve ouvrier (Paris: Arthème Fayard/ Pluriel, 2012 [1981]); *Proletarian Nights: The Workers' Dream in Nineteenth-Century France*, trans. John Drury, intro. Donald Reid (London: Verso, 2012).

'On Aisthesis: An Interview, Jacques Rancière and Oliver Davis', trans. Steven Corcoran, in Oliver Davis (ed.), *Rancière Now: Current Perspectives on Jacques Rancière* (Cambridge: Polity, 2013), pp. 202–18.

La Parole muette. Essai sur les contradictions de la littérature (Paris: Arthème Fayard/Pluriel, 2010 [1998]); *Mute Speech: Literature, Critical Theory, and Politics*, trans. James Swenson, intro. Gabriel Rockhill (New York: Columbia University Press, 2011).

Le Partage du sensible. Esthétique et politique (Paris: La Fabrique, 2000); *The Politics of Aesthetics: The Distribution of the Sensible*, trans. and ed. Gabriel Rockhill (London and New York: Bloomsbury, 2013 [2004]).

Le Philosophe et ses pauvres (Paris: Flammarion, 2007 [1983]); *The Philosopher and His Poor*, trans. John Drury, Corinne Oster, and Andrew Parker, ed. Andrew Parker (Durham, NC: Duke University Press, 2003).

'Politics and Aesthetics: An Interview', with Peter Hallward, trans. Forbes Morlock, *Angelaki: Journal of the Theoretical Humanities*, 8.2 (August 2003), 191–211.

'Politics, Identification, and Subjectivization', *October*, 61 (Summer 1992), 58–64.

'The Politics of Literature', *SubStance*, 33.1 (2004), 10–24.

Politique de la littérature (Paris: Galilée, 2007); *The Politics of Literature*, trans. Julie Rose (Cambridge: Polity, 2011).

Les Temps modernes. Art, temps, politique (Paris: La Fabrique, 2018).

'Understanding Modernism, Reconfiguring Disciplinarity: Interview with Jacques Rancière on May 11, 2015', in Patrick M. Bray (ed.), *Understanding Rancière, Understanding Modernism* (New York and London: Bloomsbury Academic, 2017), pp. 263–89.

(with Jean-Luc Nancy), 'Rancière and Metaphysics (Continued) – A Dialogue', trans. Steven Corcoran, in Oliver Davis (ed.), *Rancière Now: Current Perspectives on Jacques Rancière* (Cambridge: Polity, 2013), pp. 187–201.

Other Primary Texts

Beinstingel, Thierry, *Retour aux mots sauvages* (Paris: Arthème Fayard, 2010).

Bon, François, *Après le livre* (Paris: Seuil, 2011).

——, *Autobiographie des objets* (Paris: Seuil, 2012).

——, *Daewoo* (Paris: Fayard, 2004).

——, *Proust est une fiction* (Paris: Seuil, 2013).

——, *Sortie d'usine* (Paris: Minuit, 1982).

——, *Tous les mots sont adultes* (Paris: Arthème Fayard, 2009).

Eribon, Didier, *Michel Foucault* (Paris: Flammarion, 2011 [1989]).

——, *Retour à Reims* (Paris: Flammarion, 2010 [2009]); *Returning to Reims*, trans. Michael Lucey (London: Allen Lane, 2018).

——, *Retours sur 'Retour à Reims'* (Paris: Editions Cartouche, 2014).

——, *La Société comme verdict* (Paris: Flammarion, 2014 [2013]).

Ernaux, Annie, *Les Armoires vides* (Paris: Gallimard, 1974).

——, *L'Écriture comme un couteau. Entretien avec Frédéric-Yves Jeannet* (Paris: Stock, 2003).

——, *La Place* (Paris: Gallimard, 1984).

——, *Retour à Yvetot* (Paris: Mauconduit, 2013).

——, *Une femme* (Paris: Gallimard, 1988).

Gauny, Louis Gabriel, *Le Philosophe plébéien*, ed. Jacques Rancière (Paris: La Découverte/Presses Universitaires de Vincennes, 1983; rev. ed. Paris: La Fabrique, 2017).

Michon, Pierre, *Rimbaud le fils* (Paris: Gallimard, 1991).

——, *Le Roi vient quand il veut. Propos sur la littérature*, eds Agnès Castiglione and Pierre-Marc de Biasi (Paris: Albin Michel, 2007).

——, *Vie de Joseph Roulin* (Lagrasse: Verdier, 1988); *The Life of Joseph Roulin* in *Masters and Servants*, trans. Wyatt Alexander Mason (San Francisco: Mercury House, 1997).

——, *Vies minuscules* (Paris: Gallimard, 1984); *Small Lives*, trans. Jody Gladding and Elizabeth Deshays (New York: Archipelago Books, 2008).

Ndiaye, Marie, *La Cheffe, roman d'une cuisinière* (Paris: Gallimard, 2016); *The Cheffe: A Cook's Novel*, trans. Jordan Stump (London: MacLehose Press, 2019).

——, 'Le Jour du président', in Didier Vergnaud (ed.), *La Double Entente du jeu* (L'Eté du livre en Gironde, 1997), pp. 29–46.

——, *La Sorcière* (Paris: Minuit, 1996).

Nizan, Paul, *Aden Arabie* (Paris: La Découverte, 2002 [1931]).

——, *Antoine Bloyé* (Paris: Grasset, 2013 [1933]); *Antoine Bloyé*, trans. Edmund Stevens, intro. Richard Elman (New York and London: Monthly Review Press, 1973).

Nunez, Laurent, *Les Récidivistes* (Paris: Rivages, 2014 [2008]).

Péguy, Charles, *L'Argent*, in *Œuvres en prose complètes*, vol. III (Paris: Gallimard (Bibliothèque de la Pléiade), 1992).

——, *Notre jeunesse*, in *Œuvres en prose complètes*, vol. III (Paris: Gallimard (Bibliothèque de la Pléiade), 1992).

Proust, Marcel, *À la recherche du temps perdu*, 4 vols (Paris: Gallimard (Bibliothèque de la Pléiade), 1987–1989); *In Search of Lost Time*, ed. Christopher Prendergast, 6 vols (London: Penguin, 2003); *Remembrance of Things Past*, trans. C. K. Scott Moncrieff and Terence Kilmartin, 3 vols (London: Penguin, 1983 [1981]).

——, *Le Carnet de 1908*, ed. Philip Kolb (Paris: Gallimard, 1976).

——, *Contre Sainte-Beuve* précédé de *Pastiches et mélanges* et suivi de *Essais et articles* (Paris: Gallimard (Bibliothèque de la Pléiade), 1971).

——, *Correspondance de Marcel Proust*, ed. Philip Kolb, 21 vols (Paris: Plon, 1970–1993).

——, 'Pour un ami (remarques sur le style)', *La Revue de Paris*, 15 November 1920.

Simon, Claude, *L'Acacia* (Paris: Minuit, 2003 [1989]); *The Acacia*, trans. Richard Howard (New York: Pantheon Books, 1991).

——, 'Claude Simon in conversation with Viviane Forrester': http://next.liberation.fr/livres/2013/10/11/l-album-de-l-ecrivain-claude-simon_938468 [accessed 10 March 2020].

——, *Quatre conférences*, ed. Patrick Longuet (Paris: Minuit, 2012).

——, *La Route des Flandres* (Paris: Minuit, 1960).

Weil, Simone, *Attente de Dieu*, préface de J. M. Perrin (Paris: Fayard, 1966 [1950]).

——, *La Condition ouvrière*, ed. Robert Chenavier (Paris: Gallimard, 2002 [1951]).

——, *L'Enracinement, ou Prélude à une déclaration des devoirs envers l'être humain* (Paris: Flammarion, 2014); *The Need for Roots: Prelude to a Declaration of Duties towards Mankind*, trans. Arthur Wills, intro. T. S. Eliot (London and New York: Routledge and Kegan Paul, 1952).

——, *Oppression et liberté* (Paris: Gallimard, 1955).

——, *La Pesanteur et la Grâce*, intro. Gustave Thibon (Paris: Plon, 1948); *Gravity and Grace*, rev. trans. Emma Crawford and Mario von der Ruhr (London and New York: Routledge, 2002 [1952]).

——, *Premiers écrits philosophiques*, ed. Gilbert Kahn and Rolf Kühn, in *Œuvres complètes*, vol. I (Paris: Gallimard, 1988).

——, *Réflexions sur les causes de la liberté et de l'oppression sociale* (Paris: Gallimard, 1998 [1955]).

Wideman, John Edgar, *Brothers and Keepers* (New York: Vintage Books, 1995 [1984]).

Secondary Material

Agamben, Giorgio, *Homo Sacer: Sovereign Power and Bare Life*, trans. Daniel Heller-Roazen (Stanford: Stanford University Press, 1998).
——, *Infancy and History: On the Destruction of Experience*, trans. Liz Heron (London: Verso, 2007).
——, *The Man Without Content*, trans. Georgia Albert (Stanford: Stanford University Press, 1999).
——, 'Notes on Gesture', in *Infancy and History: On the Destruction of Experience*, trans. Liz Heron (London: Verso, 2007), pp. 147–56.
Alexander, Zeynep Çelik, *Kinaesthetic Knowing: Aesthetics, Epistemology, Modern Design* (Chicago and London: Chicago University Press, 2017).
Arendt, Hannah, *The Human Condition*, intro. Margaret Canovan (Chicago and London: University of Chicago Press, 1998 [1958]).
Aristotle, *The Nicomachean Ethics*, trans. David Ross, ed. Lesley Brown (Oxford: Oxford University Press, 2009).
——, *Poetics*, trans. and ed. Malcolm Heath (London: Penguin, 1996).
——, *The Politics*, trans. T. A. Sinclair, rev. ed. Trevor J. Saunders (London: Penguin, 1992).
Arnould, Élisabeth, 'Portrait de l'artiste en facteur', in Ivan Farron and Karl Kürtös (eds), *Pierre Michon entre pinacothèque et bibliothèque* (Bern: Peter Lang, 2003), pp. 97–122.
Auerbach, Erich, *Mimesis: The Representation of Reality in Western Thought*, intro. Edward W. Said (Princeton: Princeton University Press, 2003 [1953]).
Baldwin, Thomas, *Roland Barthes: The Proust Variations* (Liverpool: Liverpool University Press, 2019).
Barbéris, Pierre, *Lectures du réel* (Paris: Editions Sociales, 1973).
Barthes, Roland, *Le Degré zéro de l'écriture*, in *Œuvres complètes*, vol. I: *Livres, textes, entretiens, 1942–1961*, ed. Éric Marty (Paris: Seuil, 2002).
Baudelaire, Charles, *Œuvres complètes* (Lausanne: La Guilde du Livre, 1967).
Bayle, Thierry, 'Pierre Michon: un auteur majuscule', *Le Magazine littéraire*, 353 (April 1997), 97–103.
Borel, Jacques, *Commentaires* (Paris: Gallimard, 1974).
Borges, Jorge Luis, *Labyrinths: Selected Stories and Other Writings* (London: Penguin, 2000).
Bourdieu, Pierre, *Distinction: A Social Critique of the Judgement of Taste*, trans. Richard Nice (London: Routledge, 1984).
——, *The Field of Cultural Production: Essays on Art and Literature*, ed. Randal Johnson (Cambridge: Polity Press, 1993).
——, *Outline of a Theory of Practice*, trans. Richard Nice (Cambridge: Cambridge University Press, 1977).
Bowie, Malcolm, *Proust Among the Stars* (London: HarperCollins, 1998).

Bray, Patrick M., (ed.), *Understanding Rancière, Understanding Modernism* (New York and London: Bloomsbury Academic, 2017).

Britton, Celia, *Claude Simon: Writing the Visible* (Cambridge: Cambridge University Press, 1987).

Calle-Gruber, Mireille, *Claude Simon. Une vie à écrire* (Paris: Seuil, 2011).

Camus, Albert, *Le Mythe de Sisyphe*, in *Œuvres complètes*, vol. I (Paris: Gallimard (Bibliothèque de la Pléiade), 2006).

Catinchi, Philippe-Jean, 'Le Roman au travail', *Le Monde des livres*, 10 September 2004.

Caygill, Howard, *On Resistance: A Philosophy of Defiance* (London: Bloomsbury, 2013).

Celan, Paul, *Le Méridien et autres proses* (Paris: Seuil, 2002).

Certeau, Michel de, *The Practice of Everyday Life*, trans. Steven Rendall (Berkeley: University of California Press, 1984).

Chambers, Ross, *Untimely Interventions: AIDS Writing, Testimonial, and the Rhetoric of Haunting* (Ann Arbor: University of Michigan Press, 2004).

Compagnon, Antoine, *Les Antimodernes: de Joseph de Maistre à Roland Barthes* (Paris: Gallimard, 2005).

——, 'The Day Proust Realized He Had Written a Masterpiece', public lecture given at 'Symposium Marcel Proust', Moderna Museet, Stockholm, 6–7 December 2013.

Craig, George, Martha Dow Fehsenfeld, Dan Gunn, and Lois More Overbeck (eds), *The Letters of Samuel Beckett*, vol. 4: *1966–1989* (Cambridge: Cambridge University Press, 2016).

Crowley, Patrick, *Pierre Michon: The Afterlife of Names* (Oxford: Peter Lang, 2007).

Cukier, Alexis, *Qu'est-ce que le travail?* (Paris: Vrin, 2018).

Davis, Oliver, *Jacques Rancière* (Cambridge: Polity, 2010).

——, 'The Radical Pedagogies of François Bon and Jacques Rancière', *French Studies*, 64.2 (April 2010), 178–91.

——, (ed.), *Rancière Now: Current Perspectives on Jacques Rancière* (Cambridge: Polity, 2013).

Deleuze, Gilles, *Critique et clinique* (Paris: Minuit, 1993); *Essays Critical and Clinical*, trans. Daniel W. Smith and Michael A. Greco (London: Verso, 1998).

Deranty, Jean-Philippe, (ed.), *Jacques Rancière: Key Concepts* (Durham: Acumen, 2010).

DiIorio, Sam, 'Chaîne et Chaîne: Representation as Corrosion in François Bon's *Daewoo*', *SubStance*, 35.3 (2006), special issue, *The French Novel Now*, 5–22.

Dubois, Jacques, *Pour Albertine. Proust et le sens du social* (Paris: Seuil, 1997).

——, *Le Roman de Gilberte Swann. Proust sociologue paradoxal* (Paris: Seuil, 2018).

Duffy, Jean H., *Reading Between the Lines: Claude Simon and the Visual Arts* (Liverpool: Liverpool University Press, 1998).

Duffy, Jean H., and Alastair Duncan (eds), *Claude Simon: A Retrospective* (Liverpool: Liverpool University Press, 2002).

Farge, Arlette, 'Pierre Michon, Arlette Farge: Entretien', *Les Cahiers de la Villa Gillet*, 3 (1995), 151–64.

ffrench, Patrick, 'Proust and the Analysis of Gesture', in Nathalie Aubert (ed.), *Proust and the Visual* (Cardiff: University of Wales Press, 2012), pp. 47–67.

Finch, Alison, 'Aesthetic Form and Social "Form" in *À la recherche du temps perdu*: Proust on Taste', in Patrick Crowley and Shirley Jordan (eds), *What Forms Can Do: The Work of Form in 20th- and 21st-century French Literature and Thought* (Liverpool: Liverpool University Press, 2020), pp. 207–17.

Foucault, Michel, *Surveiller et punir. Naissance de la prison* (Paris: Gallimard, 1975); *Discipline and Punish: The Birth of the Prison*, trans. Alan Sheridan (London: Penguin, 1991).

——, 'La Vie des hommes infâmes', in *Dits et écrits*, vol. III: *1976–1979* (Paris: Gallimard, 1994), pp. 237–53.

Fraisse, Geneviève, *Service ou servitude. Essai sur les femmes toutes mains* (Paris: Le Bord de l'eau, 2009 [1979]).

Freed-Thall, Hannah, *Spoiled Distinctions: Aesthetics and the Ordinary in French Modernism* (Oxford: Oxford University Press, 2015).

Gefen, Alexandre, 'Politiques de Pierre Michon', in Pierre-Marc de Biasi, Agnès Castiglione, and Dominique Viart (eds), *Pierre Michon, la lettre et son ombre* (Paris: Gallimard, 2013), pp. 375–90.

Genet, Jean, *Le Funambule*, in *Œuvres complètes*, vol. V (Paris: Gallimard, 1979), pp. 7–27.

Gosetti-Ferencei, Jennifer Anna, *The Life of Imagination: Revealing and Making the World* (New York: Columbia University Press, 2018).

Le Grand Robert de la langue française (Paris: Dictionnaires-Le Robert, 2001).

Hallward, Peter, 'Staging Equality: Rancière's Theatrocracy and the Limits of Anarchic Equality', in Gabriel Rockhill and Philip Watts (eds), *Jacques Rancière: History, Politics, Aesthetics* (Durham, NC and London: Duke University Press, 2009), pp. 140–57.

Harrison, Nicholas, *Postcolonial Criticism: History, Theory and the Work of Fiction* (Cambridge: Polity Press, 2003).

Hewlett, Nick, *Badiou, Balibar, Rancière: Re-thinking Emancipation* (London: Continuum, 2007).

Hollier, Denis, '1931, June – Plenty of Nothing', in Hollier (ed.), *A New History of French Literature* (Cambridge, MA: Harvard University Press, 1994), pp. 894–900.

Hughes, Edward J., 'Circuits of Reappropriation: Accessing the Real in the Work of Didier Eribon', in Patrick Crowley and Shirley Jordan (eds), *What Forms Can Do: The Work of Form in 20th- and 21st-century French Literature and Thought* (Liverpool: Liverpool University Press, 2020), pp. 179–94.

——, '"Les lignes vaines et solitaires de mon écriture": "Word" and "World" in Proust's *Recherche*', *Romanic Review*, 105.3–4 (2014), 201–13.

——, 'Pierre Michon, "Small Lives", and the Terrain of Art', *Romance Studies*, 29.2 (2011), 67–79.

——, *Proust, Class, and Nation* (Oxford: Oxford University Press, 2011).

——, *Writing Marginality in Modern French Literature: from Loti to Genet* (Cambridge: Cambridge University Press, 2001).

Hugo, Victor, *Les Misérables*, 2 vols (Paris: Garnier-Flammarion, 1967).

Jackson, Julian, *France: The Dark Years, 1940–1944* (Oxford: Oxford University Press, 2001).

——, *The Popular Front in France: Defending Democracy, 1934–38* (Cambridge: Cambridge University Press, 1988).

——, 'Rethinking May 68', in Julian Jackson, Anna-Louise Milne, and James S. Williams (eds), *May 68: Rethinking France's Last Revolution* (London: Palgrave Macmillan, 2011), pp. 3–16.

Jacotot, Joseph, *Enseignement universel. Musique* (Paris: Boulland, 1830).

Jefferson, Ann, *Biography and the Question of Literature in France* (Oxford: Oxford University Press, 2007).

Jordan, Shirley, *Marie Ndiaye: Inhospitable Fictions* (Cambridge: Legenda, 2017).

Kaprièlian, Nelly, '*La Cheffe, roman d'une cuisinière* de Marie Ndiaye: une vie mystique', *Les Inrockuptibles*, 27 September 2016.

La Boétie, Estienne de, *Slaves by Choice*, trans. Malcolm Smith (Egham: Runnymede Books, 1988).

Lajer-Burcharth, Ewa, *The Painter's Touch: Boucher, Chardin, Fragonard* (Princeton: Princeton University Press, 2018).

Lane, Jeremy F., 'Rancière's Anti-Platonism: Equality, the "Orphan Letter" and the Problematic of the Social Sciences', in Oliver Davis (ed.), *Rancière Now: Current Perspectives on Jacques Rancière* (Cambridge: Polity, 2013), pp. 28–46.

Léger, Fernand, *Fonctions de la peinture*, ed. Sylvie Forestier (Paris: Gallimard, 2009).

Linhart, Robert, *L'Établi* (Paris: Minuit, 1981 [1978]).

Louis, Édouard, *En finir avec Eddy Bellegueule* (Paris: Seuil, 2014).

Marx, Karl, *Capital*, trans. Samuel Moore and Edward Aveling, 3 vols (Moscow: Progress Publishers, 1965).

——, *The Eighteenth Brumaire of Louis Bonaparte*, trans. Terrell Carver, in Mark Cowling and James Martin (eds), *Marx's 'Eighteenth Brumaire': (Post)Modern Interpretations* (London and Sterling, VA: Pluto, 2002).

Marx, Karl, and Friedrich Engels, *The Communist Manifesto*, trans. Samuel Moore, intro. A. J. P. Taylor (London: Penguin, 1985).

——, *The German Ideology*, Part One, ed. C. J. Arthur (New York: International Publishers, 1970).

Mary, Alix, 'Daewoo, le choix du roman chez François Bon', *Mémoire(s), identité(s), marginalité(s) dans le monde occidental contemporain*, 9 (2013), http://journals.openedition.org/mimmoc/1009; DOI: https://doi.org/10.4000/mimmoc.1009 [accessed 28 February 2020].

Maton, Karl, 'Habitus', in Michael Grenfell (ed.), *Pierre Bourdieu, Key Concepts* (London: Routledge, 2014), pp. 48–64.

Mayeur, Jean-Marie, and Madeleine Rebérioux, *The Third Republic from its Origins to the Great War, 1871–1914*, trans. J. R. Foster (Cambridge: Cambridge University Press, 1984).

Memmi, Albert, *Portrait du colonisé* précédé de *Portrait du colonisateur* (Paris: Gallimard, 1985 [1957]).

Michelet, Jules, *Le Peuple* (Paris: Hachette/Paulin, 1846).

Milly, Jean, 'Pastiche', in Annick Bouillaguet and Brian Rogers (eds), *Dictionnaire Marcel Proust* (Paris: Honoré Champion, 2004), pp. 729–31.

Moretti, Franco, *The Bourgeois: Between History and Literature* (London: Verso, 2013).

Nancy, Jean-Luc, *Être singulier pluriel* (Paris: Galilée, 2013 [1996]).

Palmusaari, Jussi, 'For Revolt: Breaks from Time and Uses of Spatiality in the Work of Jacques Rancière' (unpublished PhD thesis, Kingston University, London, 2017).

Panagia, Davide, *Rancière's Sentiments* (Durham, NC and London: Duke University Press, 2018).

Pascal, Blaise, *Pensées*, ed. Michel Le Guern (Paris: Gallimard, 2004).

Perec, Georges, *Espèces d'espaces* (Paris: Galilée, 2000 [1974]).

Plato, *Republic*, trans. Robin Waterfield (Oxford: Oxford University Press, 2008).

Prendergast, Christopher, *The Classic: Sainte-Beuve and the Nineteenth-Century Culture Wars* (Oxford: Oxford University Press, 2007).

Richard, Jean-Pierre, 'Servitude et grandeur du minuscule', in *L'Etat des choses. Etudes sur huit écrivains d'aujourd'hui* (Paris: Gallimard, 1990), pp. 87–106.

Rockhill, Gabriel, and Philip Watts (eds), *Jacques Rancière: History, Politics, Aesthetics* (Durham, NC and London: Duke University Press, 2009).

Ross, Alison, 'Expressivity, Literarity, Mute Speech', in Jean-Philippe Deranty (ed.), *Jacques Rancière: Key Concepts* (Durham: Acumen, 2010), pp. 133–50.

Ross, Kristin, *Fast Cars, Clean Bodies: Decolonization and the Reordering of French Culture* (Cambridge, MA: MIT Press, 1994).

——, 'Historicizing Untimeliness', in Gabriel Rockhill and Philip Watts (eds), *Jacques Rancière: History, Politics, Aesthetics* (Durham, NC and London: Duke University Press, 2009), pp. 15–29.

——, *May '68 and Its Afterlives* (Chicago and London: University of Chicago Press, 2002).

Roth, Philip, *American Pastoral* (London: Vintage, 1998 [1997]).

Rougemont, Denis de, *Penser avec les mains* (Paris: Albin Michel, 1936).

Rousseau, Jean-Jacques, *Émile, ou de l'éducation* (Paris: Garnier, 1957).

Schiller, Friedrich, *On the Aesthetic Education of Man*, trans. Keith Tribe, ed. Alexander Schmidt (London: Penguin, 2016).

Scriven, Michael, *Paul Nizan: Communist Novelist* (Basingstoke: Macmillan, 1988).

Sembène, Ousmane, *Les Bouts de bois de Dieu* (Paris: Le Livre Contemporain, 1960).

Sheringham, Michael, *Everyday Life: Theories and Practices from Surrealism to the Present* (Oxford: Oxford University Press, 2006).

——, 'On Turning Points', a Sermon Preached in the Chapel of All Souls College, Oxford, 2 November 2008 (Oxford: All Souls College, no date).

Sherry, Patrick, 'Simone Weil on Beauty', in Richard H. Bell (ed.), *Simone Weil's Philosophy of Culture: Readings toward a Divine Humanity* (Cambridge: Cambridge University Press, 1993), pp. 260–76.

Silverman, Debora, 'Weaving Paintings: Religious and Social Origins of Vincent Van Gogh's Pictorial Labor', in Michael S. Roth (ed.), *Rediscovering History: Culture, Politics, and the Psyche* (Stanford: Stanford University Press, 1994), pp. 137–68.

Stiegler, Bernard, *De la misère symbolique* (Paris: Flammarion, 2013).

——, 'Individuation et grammatisation: quand la technique fait sens', *Documentaliste-Sciences de l'Information*, 42.6 (2005), 354–60.

——, 'Serions-nous en train de perdre la raison?', Les Nuits de France-Culture, 25 June 2016.

Stiegler, Bernard, and *Ars industrialis*, *Réenchanter le monde. La valeur esprit contre le populisme industriel* (Paris: Flammarion, 2006).

Still, Judith, 'Disorderly Eating in Marie NDiaye's "La Gourmandise", *or* The Solitary Pleasure of a *Mère de famille*', in Shirley Jordan and Judith Still (eds), *Disorderly Eating in Contemporary Women's Writing*, special issue of *Journal of Romance Studies*, 20.2 (June 2020), 365–89.

Suarès, André, *Sur la vie*, 3 vols (Paris: Collection de la Grande Revue, 1909–1912).

Supiot, Alain, 'Simone Weil', *L'Obs*, 27 July 2017, 56–59.

Swenson, James, '*Style indirect libre*', in Gabriel Rockhill and Philip Watts (eds), *Jacques Rancière: History, Politics, Aesthetics* (Durham, NC and London: Duke University Press, 2009), pp. 258–72.

Thompson, E. P., *The Making of the English Working Class* (London: Penguin, 1968 [1963]).

Todd, Emmanuel, *Les Luttes de classes en France au XXIe siècle* (Paris: Seuil, 2020).

Van Gogh, Vincent, *Lettres à son frère Théo*, trans. Louis Roëdlandt, ed. Pascal Bonafoux (Paris: Gallimard, 1988).

van Zuylen, Marina, 'Dreaming Bourdieu Away: Rancière and the Reinvented Habitus', in Patrick M. Bray (ed.), *Understanding Rancière, Understanding Modernism* (New York and London: Bloomsbury Academic, 2017), pp. 199–218.

Viart, Dominique, *Pierre Michon 'Vies minuscules'* (Paris: Gallimard, 2004).

Watkin, Christopher, 'Thinking Equality Today: Badiou, Rancière, Nancy', *French Studies*, 67.4 (October 2013), 522–34.

Watt, Adam, *Reading in Proust's 'À la recherche': 'le délire de la lecture'* (Oxford: Clarendon Press, 2009).

Williams, James S., *Encounters with Godard: Ethics, Aesthetics, Politics* (Albany: SUNY Press, 2016).

Williams, Raymond, *Border Country* (Cardigan: Parthian (Library of Wales), 2010 [1960]).

Winton (Finch), Alison, *Proust's Additions: The Making of 'À la recherche du temps perdu'*, 2 vols (Cambridge: Cambridge University Press, 1977).

Yourgrau, Palle, *Simone Weil* (London: Reaktion, 2011).

Index

and Gauny 91, 92, 108
in Michon 162, 174, 277
in Proust 196–97, 202, 219
in Suarès 172–74
see also proletarian identity
Voltaire 14

Walhausen, J. J. 118
Watkin, Christopher 11n40, 286n45
Watt, Adam 48n33
Watts, Philip 18
Weil, Simone 131–56, 234, 239, 241,
    279, 286
  advocacy of reflection in 153
  on attention as prayer 147, 150
  comradeship as miraculous 145, 285
  concept of non-servile work 142
  Creation myth 139
  embodied existence 133, 155, 199,
    242
  and equality of opportunity 134
  exercise of intelligence 157–58
  factory hierarchy 136
  the faculty of attention 138
  and figure of mathematician 133,
    134, 149, 276n12
  grace 149
  human misery and grandeur 142
  industrial production for war 147
  intellectual capacity 157
  the intellectual in a material world
    133
  labourer and intellectual linked 149
  laws of mechanics 149
  link to Rancière on *Europa 51*
    141–42
  the longing for social incorporation
    135
  as manual worker 132, 137
  on need for social efficacy 276
  post-artisanal industrial culture
    132, 155–56
  on reification of human endeavour
    148, 151
  on religious thought and manual

  labour 142, 144, 145, 147,
    149–50, 156, 277–78, 284
  rhythm in agricultural labour 138
  on science as monopoly 134
  slaves in Ancient Rome 132
  specialization as nefarious 16–17,
    134, 155, 156
  on thought and manual skill 137
  and Van Gogh 179
  'vital needs of the human soul'
    158
  workers' need of poetry 148, 278
  worker's respect for education 145
  on workplace servitude 145
  writing and social action 276
  Attente de Dieu 132, 135–36, 145
  La Condition ouvrière 16, 132, 133,
    140, 151, 199
  'Journal d'usine' 132, 136–38, 142,
    143, 148, 150, 285
  L'Enracinement 134–35, 158, 241
  La Pesanteur et la Grâce 131, 142,
    148, 149, 278
  Premiers écrits philosophiques 157
  *Réflexions sur les causes de la
    liberté et de l'oppresion sociale*
    132–34, 135, 137, 144–45, 147,
    151–52, 155, 276
Wideman, John Edgar 252, 262–63,
    264, 270
  the book accelerating sibling divide
    263
  as class migrant 269
  exile and identity link 265
  Brothers and Keepers 262–63, 265,
    269
Williams, James S. 281n28
Williams, Raymond 252, 264–65
  on class migration 265
  Eribon's critique of 264
Winckelmann, Johann 47
Winton (Finch), Alison 203n40
women
  Arendt on role of in Ancient Greece
    32